THE FESTIVALIZATION O

The Festivalization of Culture

Edited by

ANDY BENNETT, JODIE TAYLOR and IAN WOODWARD
Griffith University, Australia

Routledge
Taylor & Francis Group

LONDON AND NEW YORK

First published 2014 by Ashgate Publishing

2 Park Square, Milton Park, Abingdon, Oxfordshire OX14 4RN
52 Vanderbilt Avenue, New York, NY 10017

Routledge is an imprint of the Taylor & Francis Group, an informa business

First issued in paperback 2020

British Library Cataloguing in Publication Data
A catalogue record for this book is available from the British Library

The Library of Congress has cataloged the printed edition as follows:
The festivalization of culture / [edited] by Andy Bennett, Jodie Taylor, and Ian Woodward.
  pages cm
Includes bibliographical references and index.
 ISBN 978-1-4094-3198-5 (hardback) -- ISBN 978-1-4094-3199-2 (ebook) -- ISBN 978-1-4094-7279-7 (epub) 1. Festivals--Cross-cultural studies. 2. Festivals--Case studies. I. Bennett, Andy, 1963- II. Taylor, Jodie. III. Woodward, Ian (Sociologist)
 GT3940.F493 2014
 394.26--dc23

                                                                              2014006820

ISBN 13: 978-1-4094-3198-5 (hbk)
ISBN 13: 978-0-367-60036-5 (pbk)

Contents

List of Figures and Tables

Figures

Tables

List of Contributors

Michael Balfour is Chair of Applied Theatre, Griffith University, Australia. Michael's research expertise is in the social applications of theatre: theatre in communities, social institutions and areas of disadvantage and conflict. He is currently engaged in four Australian Research Council (ARC)-funded projects, including drama-based projects with newly arrived refugees and 'The Difficult Return', developing arts-based work with returning military personnel and their families. Resent publications include *Refugee Performance* (Intellect, 2012) and *Performance: In Place of War* (Seagull Press, 2009), co-authored with James Thompson and Jenny Hughes. Previously, Michael was a researcher on the Arts and Humanities Research Council (UK) project 'In Place of War' and worked extensively in prisons in the United Kingdom and Europe, developing a range of cultural programs.

Brydie-Leigh Bartleet is Deputy Director of the Queensland Conservatorium Research Centre, Griffith University, Australia. She was a Research Fellow on the ARC-funded project 'Sound Links' (2007–08), which examined the dynamics of community music in Australia. Her current research projects include an ARC-funded project, 'Captive Audiences' (2011–12), which explores performing arts rehabilitation programmes in prisons, and an Office for Learning and Teaching-funded project, 'Enhancing Indigenous Content in Performing Arts Curricula Through Service Learning with Indigenous Communities' (2011–13). She has produced over 100 publications on music-related topics. She is a Commissioner on the International Society for Music Education's Community Music Activities Commission, a board member of the Music Council of Australia, is actively involved in the MCA's Music in Communities Network and is on the editorial boards for the International Journal for Music Education and International Journal of Community Music. As a community music facilitator, she has conducted bands, orchestras, choirs and jazz ensembles from Australia, Thailand, Singapore and Taiwan.

Andrew Bengry-Howell is a Research Fellow in the School of Psychology at the University of Southampton, and a Visiting Research Fellow in the Department of Psychology at the University of Bath, UK. His interests are in youth, identity and youth culture, but also qualitative research methodology and research ethics. He has published in the *International Journal of Social Research Methodology*, *Sociology*, *Journal of Youth Studies*, *Sex Education* and the *International Journal of Drug Policy*, and co-authored a number of book chapters.

Andy Bennett is Professor of Cultural Sociology and Director of the Griffith Centre for Cultural Research at Griffith University, Australia. He has authored and edited numerous books, including *Popular Music and Youth Culture* (Macmillan, 2000), *Cultures of Popular Music* (Open University Press, 2001), *Remembering Woodstock* (Ashgate, 2004) and *Music Scenes* (with Richard A. Peterson, Vanderbilt University Press, 2004). Andy is currently lead Chief Investigator on a three-year, five-country project funded by the ARC, entitled 'Popular Music and Cultural Memory: Localised Popular Music Histories and Their Significance for National Music Industries'. He is Editor-in-Chief of the *Journal of Sociology*, a Faculty Fellow of the Center for Cultural Sociology, Yale University and an Associate Member of PopuLUs, the Centre for the Study of the World's Popular Musics, Leeds University.

Jasper Chalcraft is Visiting Research Fellow at the University of Sussex and Honorary Research Fellow at the University of Leicester, UK. His research interests and publications cover festivals, cultural cosmopolitanism, ethno-archaeology and heritage. He is co-editor with Camila del Mármol and Marc Morell, of *The Making of Heritage: Seduction and Disenchantment* (Routledge, 2014).

Joanne Cummings is a social researcher at the University of Western Sydney, Australia. Her research interests and publications investigate the sociological aspects of music festivals, youth cultures, neo-tribalism and environmental sustainability.

Timothy J. Dowd is Associate Professor of Sociology at Emory University in Atlanta, Georgia, USA and was the Erasmus Chair for the Humanities as Erasmus University Rotterdam, the Netherlands (2007–08). He specializes in cultural sociology, with much of his published research focusing on music. He and Susanne Janssen are currently Editors-in-Chief of *Poetics: Journal of Empirical Research on Culture, Media, and the Arts*.

Michelle Duffy is a Senior Lecturer in Sociology at the School of Applied Media and Social Science, Federation University, Australia. Her current research explores the intersections of sound, embodiment, listening and affect in processes of subjectivity and place-making.

Gerard Delanty is Professor of Sociology and Social and Political Thought at the University of Sussex, UK. He is the author of 11 books including *Inventing Europe: Idea, Identity, Reality* (with C. Rumford, Macmillan, 1995), *Rethinking Europe: Social Theory and the Implications of Europeanization* (Routledge, 2005) and *The Cosmopolitan Imagination* (Cambridge University Press 2009). He has also edited more than 11 volumes, including (both with Stephen P. Turner) *The International Handbook of Contemporary Social and Political Theory* (Routledge, 2011) and *The Handbook of Cosmopolitan Studies* (Routledge, 2012). Recent articles have appeared in the *British Journal of Sociology* and the *Sociological Review*. His most recent book, *Formations of European Modernity*, was published by Palgrave in 2013. He is currently working on cultural encounters.

Christine Griffin is Professor of Social Psychology at the University of Bath, UK. Her recent work explores the relationship between identities and consumption for young people, with a long-standing interest in young women's lives. Recent projects include a study of young people's experiences of 'branded' leisure at music festivals and free parties led by Andrew Bengry-Howell and a project on clubbing and dance cultures as forms of social and political participation led by Sarah Riley, both funded by the British Economic and Social Research Council (ESRC). She recently led a major study on the role of branding and marketing of drinks in relation to young adults' everyday drinking practices as part of the ESRC's Research Programme on 'Identities and Social Action'.

Susan Luckman is an Associate Professor of Cultural Studies in the School of Communication, International Studies and Languages at the University of South Australia. She is the author of the *Craft and the Creative Economy* (Palgrave Macmillan, 2015), *Locating Cultural Work: The Politics and Poetics of Rural, Regional and Remote Creativity* (Palgrave Macmillan, 2012), co-edited *Sonic Synergies: Music, Technology, Community and Identity* (Ashgate, 2008) and is the author of numerous book chapters, peer-reviewed journal articles and government reports on cultural work, creative industries and creative micro-entrepreneurialism.

Greg Martin is Senior Lecturer in Socio-Legal Studies at the University of Sydney, Australia. He carried out ethnographic research on New Age travellers for his doctorate, which was awarded from the University of Exeter in 1997. Subsequently, Greg was a high school teacher, temporary lecturer and research fellow. After spending a brief period travelling, he studied law at the University of Western Australia before moving to Sydney. Greg has published a number of articles in international journals, including the *British Journal of Sociology, Crime Media Culture* and *Policing & Society*. His current research interests lie in criminology and law.

Yvette Morey is a Research Fellow at the Bristol Social Marketing Centre (University of the West of England, UK). Her primary research interests are youth, identity and practices of consumption. She is particularly interested in the use of social media and Web 2.0 in digital ethnography and online research, as well as the challenges posed by problematic or risky user-generated content online. She has published in *Sociology, Young* and *Addiction, Research & Theory*.

Sarah Riley is a Senior Lecturer in the Psychology Department at Aberystwyth University UK, interested in exploring identity from a social constructionist perspective. Recent projects include looking at dance music cultures as forms of social and political participation (Economic and Social Research Council). She has co-edited *Critical Bodies: Representations, Identities and Practices of Weight and Body Management* (Palgrave Macmillan, 2008) and *Doing Your Qualitative Psychology Project* (Sage, 2012), and with Adrienne Evans is writing *Sex, Identity and Consumer Culture* (Oxford University Press, forthcoming).

Monica Sassatelli is a Lecturer in the Sociology Department at Goldsmiths, University of London, UK. She is the author of *Becoming Europeans: Cultural Identity and Cultural Policies* (Palgrave, 2009) and co-editor of *Festivals and the Cultural Public Sphere* (with L. Giorgi and G. Delanty, Routledge, 2011).

Lisa Slater is a Lecturer in Cultural Studies at the University of Wollongong, Australia. Her research seeks to understand the processes of Australian neo-colonialism, the conditions of production of contemporary indigeneity and settler-colonial belonging, with a particular focus on the role of cultural production – most recently Indigenous festivals – as sites for the expression of Indigenous sovereignty and ethical inter-cultural engagement. Her recent projects have a strong focus on remote, rural and regional Australia.

Isabelle Szmigin is Professor of Marketing at Birmingham Business School, the University of Birmingham, UK. Her interests lie primarily in the areas of consumer research, services and ethical and social marketing. She has held ESRC and British Academy research grants, and has published in the areas of psychology and marketing, sociology and consumption, and markets culture in the *European Journal of Marketing, Journal of Business Research, Journal of Business Ethics* and *Journal of Marketing Management*. She is also the author of *Understanding the Consumer* (Sage, 2003).

Graham St John is a cultural anthropologist with a research interest in electronic dance music cultures and festivals. A current Research Associate at the University of Queensland's Centre for Critical and Cultural Studies, Graham is the author of several books including *Global Tribe: Technology, Spirituality and Psytrance* (Equinox, 2012), *Technomad: Global Raving Countercultures* (Equinox, 2009) and the edited collections *The Local Scenes and Global Culture of Psytrance* (Routledge, 2010), *Victor Turner and Contemporary Cultural Performance* (Berghahn, 2008), *Rave Culture and Religion* (Routledge, 2004) and *FreeNRG: Notes From the Edge of the Dance Floor* (Commonground, 2001). He is Executive Editor of *Dancecult: Journal of Electronic Dance Music Culture*.

Jodie Taylor is a Senior Lecturer in Media and Cultural Studies at Qantm College, Brisbane. Previously, she held a postdoctoral research fellowship at the Centre for Cultural Research, Griffith University, where this work was completed. She is the author of *Playing It Queer: Popular Music, Identity and Queer World-making* (Peter Lang, 2012) and a co-author of *Redefining Mainstream Popular Music* (Routledge, 2013). She has published numerous scholarly journal articles and book chapters on popular music and identities, queer subcultures and ethnographic methods.

Ian Woodward is Associate Professor in Sociology in the School of Humanities and Deputy Director of the Centre for Cultural Research, Griffith University, Australia. His research on material culture, consumption, taste and performativity is published widely. His reconstruction of the field of consumption studies, *Understanding Material Culture*, was published by Sage in 2007. Ian also researches dimensions and practices of cultural openness, and his research on cosmopolitanism (most of which is co-authored with Zlatko Skrbiš and Gavin Kendall) has been published in journals such as *Theory, Culture and Society*, *The Sociological Review*, the *Journal of Sociology* and *The British Journal of Sociology*. Their collaborative book in this area, *The Sociology of Cosmopolitanism* which connects classical sociological theory to ideas on mobility, hospitality, technology and community, was published by Palgrave in 2009. With a group of Griffith colleagues and an international team of authors, Ian is a co-author of the book *Cultural Sociology: An Introduction* (Blackwell, 2012). Ian has served on the executive board of the Australian Sociological Association. He is a board member on the *American Journal of Cultural Sociology*. In 2010–11, he was a Fellow of the Kulturwissenschaftliches Kolleg, University of Konstanz, Germany.

Introduction

Andy Bennett, Jodie Taylor and Ian Woodward

Historically, festivals, carnivals and fairs have been important forms of social and cultural participation, used to articulate and communicate shared values, ideologies and mythologies central to the world-view of relatively localized communities. In anthropological and historical literatures, festivals traditionally are conceived as ritualistic or recurrent short-term events in which members of a community participate in order to affirm and celebrate various social, religious, ethnic, national, linguistic or historical bonds (Bakhtin 1984; Falassi 1987; Gertz 1991; Turner 1982). The festival may retain this function in the contemporary setting, but it often takes on a variety of other purposes – particularly in relation to the expression of the cultural identities and lifestyle practices of its audience (Bennett 2004; McKay 2000). In a world where notions of culture are becoming increasingly fragmented, the contemporary festival has developed in response to processes of cultural pluralization, mobility and globalization, while also communicating something meaningful about identity, community, locality and belonging. For the most part, festivals balance the dual needs of representing the local within a broader context of rapid social change (Sassatelli 2008). The contemporary festival therefore becomes a potential site for representing, encountering, incorporating and researching aspects of cultural difference.

In the last decade of the twentieth century in particular, all continents not only witnessed a surge in the number of annual festivals, but also a diversification in the types of festival that became a mainstay of cultural calendars, as well as diversification in local and global festival audiences. As an increasingly popular means through which citizens consume and experience culture, festivals have also become an economically attractive way of packaging and selling cultural performance and generating tourism (Picard and Robinson 2006; Roche 2000). As Gibson and Connell (2012) observe, these aspects of the contemporary festival rationale can be of particular significance in rural and remote communities where, in addition to the economic role of the festival in promoting tourism and other related aspects of cultural boosterism, it can also be an important means of strengthening community ties and a sense of local identity. In a variety of ways, then, festivals are a significant aspect of the socio-economic and cultural landscape of contemporary everyday life. Once seasonally located, festivals now punctuate the cultural calendar of many nations and regions at regular intervals, offering myriad opportunities for the celebration of different cultural events and also offering occasions for the shared consumption of music, literature, film, food, wine and a variety of other leisure and lifestyle pursuits.

Outline of the Book

Focusing on specific cultural identities, lifestyles, political ideologies, leisure practices, creative styles, taste cultures and audiences, the chapters in this collection provide compelling analytical accounts of various local and global festivals and modalities of festival participation. The authors take up an understanding of festivals as integral components of the contemporary cultural landscape and as key sites that inspire community, cultural critique, social mobility and change. Organized into three parts – 'Lifestyle, Identity and Cultural Politics'; 'Local and Global Communities'; and 'Spatial and Temporal Narratives' – the chapters in this book address the festival both as a physical site and as a performative construct, drawing on their own research expertise across a range of disciplines, including cultural studies, sociology, cultural geography, media studies, anthropology and popular music studies.

In Part I, the authors explore the ways in which festivals operate as politicized zones of community-building, lifestyle narration and social protest across divisions of identity. They examine how festivals give their participants access to cultural capital, an opportunity to perform identity and a way to negotiate and secure individual and collective meaning and belonging.

Andy Bennett and Ian Woodward's chapter begins the collection by offering a range of theoretical perspectives for examining the cultural significance of festivals as forms of collective life in contemporary social settings. Bennett and Woodward draw on contemporary theories of lifestyle and cosmopolitanism in their analysis of the festival space as a site for forms of encounter and exchange that often transcend those that characterize the more mundane spaces of everyday life. Conceptualizing lifestyle as the product of a process of reflexive engagement with goods and resources that produce distinctive identities framed around particular articulations of taste, Bennett and Woodward situate festivals as significant nodal points for the anchoring of what Chaney (1996) refers to as lifestyle sites and strategies. In the second part of the chapter, Bennett and Woodward go on to explore the ways in which the different cultural experiences available in the festival setting may often facilitate the acquisition and development of cosmopolitan sensibilities as individuals are given access to new ways of seeing the world around them and also enabled to be in that world.

In Chapter 2, Jodie Taylor presents a detailed overview of the history, politics, discourses and polemics of gay, lesbian, bisexual, transgender and queer (GLBTQ) pride festivities in both global and local contexts. She argues that in times and places where queer bodies are denied public visibility and performance, pride marches and festive celebrations have been and remain important modes of collective action, place-making and territorialization. This chapter also illustrates that in the context of larger Western cities, there has been an increasing shift towards consumption, tourism and the commodification of gay pride festivals as mega-events, which have in turn incited radical counter-discourses of gay shame. Taylor argues that while both discursive and counter-discursive strategies can be useful, their function is contextually relevant. Using an illustrative case example from Brisbane, Australia, Taylor posits that pride can be read as a multi-discursive platform, and that festival celebrations of sexuality remain necessary, meaningful and transformative.

In Chapter 3, Graeme St John addresses psychedelic culture through an examination of the complex performances and architectonics of the world's premiere visionary arts dance festival, Boom, held biannually in Portugal. According to St John, Boom serves as an effective site for an investigation of what he identifies as *logics of sacrifice*. Akin to the psytrance counter-culture from which it draws its heritage, St John argues that Boom manifests disparate modalities of experience: on the one hand, participants are committed to an ecstatic self-abandonment that sees dancefloor habitués transcending their routine consciousness in states of drug and music-induced self-dissolution and performances of risk; on the other, festival participants motivated by humanitarian concerns and ecological sustainability may be considered reflexive activists and disciplinarians, responding to crises of person, culture and planet. Drawing on interview data, media analysis and his own festival experiences, St John offers compelling detail of the sacrificial practices and cultural heterogeneity of contemporary arts festivals.

In a similar fashion to Taylor, in Chapter 4 Brydie-Leigh Bartleet examines discourses of pride. In Bartleet's case, however, this is done in the context of Indigenous Australian youth and their participation in hip-hop festivals. Now a common feature in the musical lives of Indigenous youth, hip-hop, Bartleet argues, allows young people to positively engage with contemporary themes of indigeneity. Illuminating key social and cultural issues, Bartleet focuses on Australia's largest Indigenous-owned hip-hop festival, Stylin' Up, which was initiated by community elders in an effort to instil in their youth the importance of 'Pride in Self, Pride in Community, Pride in Culture'. Taking an ethnographic approach, this chapter argues that hip-hop festivals offer a compelling vehicle for expressions of Indigenous pride, the negotiation and performance of contemporary Indigenous identity and, through a rigorous consultation process with local Indigenous organizations, schools and the local city council, a way of building a shared sense of community ownership of the event.

Grounded in new social movement theories, Chapter 5 sees Greg Martin examining the cultural politics of New Age travellers, ravers and anti-road protestors, with a focus on the creative, performative and festival-like aspects of their lifestyles and forms of protest. Martin presents three cases studies in order to demonstrate how New Age travellers, ravers and anti-road protestors each possessed a unique blend of politics, pleasure and performance. While each group or culture contained festive and/or performative elements, Martin argues that these functioned in different ways. Typically, for anti-road protestors, creativity and performance were integral to their politics of direct action, while for New Age travellers and ravers, festivals and performance had less political meaning. Martin's chapter considers some implications of this analysis for the study of new social movements, and explores what possible role festivals and carnival might play in contemporary societies dominated by commercialism.

In Part II, authors ask what it is that festivals reveal about the social, cultural, economic and political life of local and global communities; how festivals may allow organizations within communities to be fostered, generate opportunities to work together for a discursively constructed 'common good', negotiate shared cultural values, shape and/or remake a community, and function as the basis for community formation and amalgamation beyond the constraints of a specific locality.

Taking up recent literatures on cosmopolitanism, in Chapter 6 Jasper Chalcraft, Gerard Delanty and Monica Sassatelli use their large bank of empirical material from festivals in the European context to explore how, why and to what extent particular forms of cosmopolitan engagement and meaning are constructed across a range of festival settings. As Bennett and Woodward outline in Chapter 1, the notion of cosmopolitanism – with its theoretical logics of exchange, relationality and encounter – seems well suited to an analysis of aspects of the festival setting. Chalcraft, Delanty and Sassatelli seek to explore the opportunities for transnational identification, revealing the dynamics of cosmopolitan identification in the context of festival places that are often necessarily embedded within local settings. They seek to transcend the view of festivals that reproduces what might be seen as tired logics of academic analysis – often arising from literatures on cultural consumption and leisure – that are based on dichotomies such as authentic and standardized, commercial and alternative. Clarifying the meaning of cosmopolitanism in the festival context, they reinforce that while the visible cosmopolitan character of festivals may describe one aspect of the experience, cosmopolitanism relies on being activated through interpretation. That is, in the festival setting it derives from the interpretive work of festival participants themselves – who, when encountering the other, are in various ways critically engaged with it. Extricating the meaning of cosmopolitanism in spatial settings, they reveal the processes of recognition, relativization, evaluation and consciousness-formation that cosmopolitan meaning-making entails.

In Chapter 7, Lisa Slater draws upon her extensive participation and observation of Indigenous cultural festivals in Australia. She situates such festivals as creative endeavours designed to advance a commitment to country and to non-Western sociality and ritual life. Interweaving the historical context of Australian Indigenous and settler relations and ontologies into her discussion, Slater draws a contrast between mainstream formulations of Indigenous culture within festivals, which she argues have tended to commodify or essentialize Indigenous cultures, reifying them as a series of almost touristic traditional practices. In contrast, she sees the many hundreds of Indigenous festivals within Australia as composing a form of anti-colonial relations. Moreover, rather than reproducing the forms of governmental logic that she sees as at the core of mainstream Indigenous festivals, these local community events focus on contemporary practices and issues, fostering an intervention and negotiation of state power. She argues that festivals are crucial to reinvigorating culture, regenerating tradition and strengthening Indigenous community and capacity.

In Chapter 8, Timothy J. Dowd shows how trans-national music scenes are organized. Dowd's methodological approach is instructive for studying facets of coordinated mobilization among scene insiders. Beginning with the premise that music travels across time and space, and that this happens via the efforts of various social actors, Dowd shows how the production, circulation and exchange of progressive rock music occurs in the context of over 120 festivals within the prog rock scene. Dowd situates these festivals in the context of the ongoing definition and evolution of music genre discussions, which themselves happen online as well as in listening contexts, and occur trans-locally. These genre discussions are crucial for defining the boundaries of this particular music scene, and can influence the programming and reception of festival content. These genre discussions seem never to succeed in fixing scenes, but rather enliven and energize discussions around them. In this context, music festivals become occasions for shaping the development of genres, where aspects of heritage and memory are an important part of festival rituals. Festivals also assist in overcoming the fragmentation of this trans-local music scene. Additionally, Dowd undertakes simple but revealing network analyses to illustrate and explore the trans-local connections in this scene. In doing so, he offers a unique empirical approach for undertaking a type of archaeology of these trans-local festivals.

The role of music festivals in catering to and also promoting a sense of global responsibility is dealt with by Joanne Cummings in Chapter 9. Cummings shows that the greening of music festivals is a necessary response to the massification of some types of festival, and the realization that the scale and intensity of these festivals generate a significant amount of environmental waste and destruction within a relatively small timeframe. On the one hand, this is a development arising from festival organizers being drawn into regimes of environmental governance emerging from requirements for environmental responsibility and sustainability. Moreover, music festivals need to demonstrate to their attendees that they are acting responsibly in managing waste; otherwise, over time, the integrity of their festival brand might be called into question. Cummings explores how this requirement for greening fits with certain festival narratives and how greening strategies are instituted within the festival context. The question within the festival context is whether music festivals become sites of eco-political consciousness; furthermore, in what ways does consuming the music festival also provide an opportunity to perform certain sorts of political consciousness?

The chapters in Part III consider the experiential dimensions of festivals within a limited set of spatial and temporal parameters. In both physical and virtual contexts, authors explore the affective processes and meaning-making practices operative within festival sites.

In Chapter 10, Susan Luckman focuses on the significance of the outdoor music festival in the creation of what she refers to as a secular liminal culture. Luckman draws on the work of Victor Turner, and applies this in the context of outdoor music festivals featuring 'doof' – the local Australian terminology for contemporary dance music styles such as 'house'. Using Turner's concept of liminality, Luckman considers how the combination of the featured music, the outdoor (often rural) setting and the effort invested by festival attendees to reach these locations can give rise to a sense of having crossed a line from mundane, everyday existence into an alternative social space, with the latter facilitating a form of transcendentalism characterised by heightened levels of sensual and corporeal experience. As Luckman argues, although the kinds of experiences afforded by doof and similar outdoor music festivals are temporal in nature, they do offer participants an important means of transcending the strictures of everyday urban life and provide a platform for new forms of social identity and socio-cultural organization.

Adopting a different perspective on the spatial and temporal narratives created by and through immersion in the festival space, in Chapter 11 Michael Balfour examines how festivals can be used to strategic effect in urban and regional development through staging events that involve the community. In particular, Balfour argues, the community festival can be an important means of helping communities to come to terms with and learn to accept and tolerate patterns of rapid community change that have occurred in recent decades due to the emergence of new diasporic trends – which often have been created through forced migration due to social-political unrest in many regions. Focusing on Margate, a small coastal town in the south-east of England, Balfour uses the example of the Margate Exodus Project to consider how the local community festival can serve both the social and economic needs of peripheral spaces – that is, spaces on the margins of public and cultural life due to high levels of socio-economic dislocation. As Balfour illustrates, in such 'high-risk' spaces, festivals often play a critical role in helping to break down barriers of prejudice and indifference, and to reinstate processes of social inclusion and acceptance.

In Chapter 12, Michelle Duffy focuses on the sonic qualities of festivals, notably in relation to music, sound and silence, as important in contributing to what she refers to as the emotional ecology of the festival. Duffy's approach moves beyond the individual agent to consider how individual subjectivity is embedded through the emotional ecology as part of a collective embodied experience of the festival. According to Duffy, such qualities of the festival are important, as they underpin imagined connections between people. In this way, emotional ecologies are a significant, if intangible, aspect of what is frequently referred to as the festival community. Duffy develops this thesis with reference to two distinct examples of contemporary Australian festivals: the Swiss-Italian Festa held in the twin towns of Daylesford-Hepburn Springs in rural Victoria and the Four Winds Festival (a classical music festival) held in the New South Wales coastal town of Bermagui. Despite being quite different types of festival, and drawing discrete audiences, these two events are, according to Duffy, emblematic of the way in which emotional ecologies grounded in specific soundscapes resonate with audiences and draw them into particular circuits of encounter that produce highly particularized notions of community and belonging.

Finally, in Chapter 13, Yvette Morey, Andrew Bengry-Howell, Christine Griffin, Isabelle Szmigin and Sarah Riley examine the relationship between festivals and online technologies. Specifically, the authors consider how the emergence of different forms of online technology shape the ways in which festival-goers engage with specific festival events. As they observe, a critical shift afforded by online technologies is that they create new spaces of interaction and dialogue between festival-goers that transcend the physical space of the festival itself. Indeed, through the use of different online platforms, festival-goers are empowered to participate in broader process of consumption and identity construction through, for example, engaging with festival web forums and the creation and dissemination of festival videos via YouTube. According to Morey, Bengry-Howell, Griffin, Szmigin and Riley, through access to such online media, festival-goers both consume and produce the festival experience. As such, the online technologies that have emerged – particularly in the transition from Web 1.0 to 2.0 – have significantly enhanced the properties of the festival as an 'interactive' space, within which the creation and promotion of differentiated and highly nuanced meanings are possible.

References

Bakhtin, M. 1984 [1968]. *Rabelais and His World*, translated by H. Iswolsky. Bloomington, IN: Indiana University Press.

Bennett, A. ed. 2004. *Remembering Woodstock*. Aldershot: Ashgate.

Chaney, D. 1996. *Lifestyles*. London: Routledge.

Falassi, A. 1987. Festival definition and morphology, in *Time Out of Time: Essays on the Festival*, edited by A. Falassi. Albuquerque, NM: University of New Mexico Press, 1–10.

Gertz, D. 1991. *Festivals, Special Events, and Tourism*. New York: Van Nostrand Reinhold.

Gibson, C. and Connell, J. 2012. *Music Festivals and Regional Development in Australia*. Aldershot: Ashgate.

McKay, G. 2000. *Glastonbury: A Very English Fair*. London: Gollancz.

Picard, D. and Robinson, M. (eds) 2006. *Festivals, Tourism and Social Change: Remaking Worlds*. Clevedon: Channel View Publications.

Richards, G. 2007. The festivalization of society or the socialization of festivals? The case of Catalunya, in *Cultural Tourism: Global and Local Perspectives*, edited by G. Richards. Binghamton, NY: The Haworth Press, 257–80.

Roche, M. 2000. *Mega-Events and Modernity: Olympics and Expos in the Growth of Global Culture*. New York: Routledge.

Sassatelli, M. (ed.) 2008. *WP1 Main Report on European Public Culture and Aesthetic Cosmopolitanism*. Available at: www.euro-festival.org/docs/Euro-Festival_D1_MainReport.pdf [accessed: 20 December 2012].

Turner, V. 1982. *Celebration: Studies in Festivity and Ritual*. Washington, DC: Smithsonian Institute Press.

van Elderen, L.P. 1997. *Suddenly One Summer: A Sociological Portrait of the Joensuu Festival*. Joensuu: Joensuu University Press.

PART I
Lifestyle, Identity and Cultural Politics

Chapter 1

Festival Spaces, Identity, Experience and Belonging

Andy Bennett and Ian Woodward

In the current literature on festivals, significant emphasis is placed on the importance of the festival setting as a space for the articulation, performance and rediscovery of identity (Aitchison and Pritchard, 2007). According to some festival researchers, a pivotal quality of festivals in this respect is their liminality. As liminal spaces are removed from the more mundane process of everyday life, it is argued that festivals offer opportunities for experimentation with identity and the articulation of identity politics that may often be less feasible and acceptable – and in some cases socially circumscribed – in everyday settings. Thus, as Dowd, Liddle and Nelson (2004: 149) observe, 'Drawn together from geographically dispersed locations and away from the expectations of everyday life, fans and performers can immerse themselves in a particular culture and experiment with different identities'.

Although this facet of the festival has arguably become more prominent in recent times due to the increasing diversity of festival events on a global scale, the importance of the festival as a space within which to experiment with identity is by no means limited to the late modern experience. Indeed, according to Bakhtin (1984), types of public gatherings that predate the contemporary festival have long served as spaces for the negotiation of more regulated aspects of everyday life. Focusing on fairs, carnivals and similar events that took place during medieval times, Bakhtin argues that a key attraction was the particular types of experience that they afforded participants to engage in revelry, hedonism and other forms of anti-hegemonic behaviour not generally regarded as legitimate forms of social conduct in everyday life. An associated attraction, suggests Bakhtin, was the significance of such public gatherings as spaces for the articulation of alternative, liminal forms of identity; he maintains that such unbridled sociality was what gave these public gatherings their distinctive quality as spaces of celebration and escape from the mundane, orderly nature of everyday living. The temporal opportunities given to individuals to step outside of their more routinized identities and engage in unregulated forms of behaviour – for example, excessive drinking, loud singing, lewd behaviour and so on – was as important for the well-being of citizens as it was for ensuring the maintenance of social order through providing opportunities for ordinary individuals to 'let off steam'. Similar qualities can be identified in the contemporary festival. In addition to the relatively unregulated forms of individual and collective experience that are afforded by the liminal characteristics of the festival, it is also the case that festivals offer opportunities for encountering other types of social and cultural difference, through various forms of sensual and embodied experience based on engagements with different tastes, sounds, forms of dress and behaviour, and cultural norms.

Unsurprisingly perhaps, and as demonstrated by several of the chapters in this book, researchers of contemporary festivals often see connections between Bakhtin's interpretation of medieval carnivals and the contemporary festival setting. At the same time, though, it is important to note that there are a number of critical differences between the kinds of events now categorized as festivals and the types of public gatherings focused on in Bakhtin's work. Indeed, as the chapters in this book illustrate, the concept of the festival is increasingly complex and bespeaks a highly diverse range of themes, issues and tastes in a global context. By their very definition, festivals today are highly organized and commodified events targeted at particular – and in some cases quite niche – audiences. They are a perfect opportunity to achieve both economic and cultural economies of scale; economically, the mega-festival is able to collect and present a range of performers within a space or a site over a limited time period, offering economies of scale in terms of cultural production. Moreover, the possibilities for cultural aggregation are great within festivals, and this is part of their attraction for both producers and consumers: the opportunity to coalesce, play together, find synergies and enrol different consumers, experiences and cultural tastes. This is potentially good business for festival organizers. Similarly, the settings for festivals can be quite diverse, spanning dense areas of urban population (see Fredline, Deery and Jago 2005) through to greenfield sites (McKay 2000) and, in cases such as Nevada's Burning Man Festival, remote desert areas (Bowditch 2010). Thus the contemporary festivalscape is, in many respects, quite removed from the more spontaneous forms of public gathering that took place during pre-modern times. At the same time, however, many of the same qualities seem to connect the gatherings of historical festivals and those taking place in the present day. This is particularly evident in the way that festivals allow for the playing out – including the representation, performance and celebration – of particular expressions of socio-cultural identity.

The forms of identity politics at play in the contemporary festival scene are as diverse as the scene itself. In each case, however, a critical function of the festival is to allow a collective representation, a collective celebration and, in many cases, a collective outpouring of a commonly articulated form of socio-cultural identity. Music festivals are a clear case in point in this respect. Thus, in the context of an Indie rock festival, the physical space of the festival is predisposed to the collective articulation of an indie aesthetic (Cummings 2006). The soundscape of the festival is constructed through the live performance of well-known and upcoming indie rock bands, whose presence and the music they create are embodied by the audience through dancing and singing along to the music and through collective shows of appreciation for the bands' performances. As Cummings (2008) argues, it is through such collective involvement in and contribution towards the production of the indie festival experience that fans acquire cultural competencies instrumental to the construction of a legitimate indie identity.

In addition to taste-based and stylistic competencies, music festivals are also spaces that lend themselves to the exploration of political sensibilities – particularly when these are bound up with alternative ideological standpoints. McKay (1996) observes that there is a strong historical link between music festivals in this respect, running back at least as far as the mid-twentieth century when the free jazz festivals of the 1950s meshed musical taste with participation in social movements such as CND (see also McKay 2004). By the mid-1960s, this relationship between music, politics and anti-hegemonic identity had consolidated itself through the rise of the hippie movement (Bennett 2001, 2013a). The music festival became a nodal point for the articulation of the hippies' alternative ideology with the 1969 Woodstock Music and Arts Fair being a signature event in this respect (see Bennett 2004) – one that has since become highly mythologized and deeply romanticized, through its representation as the swansong of the hippie counter-culture (Street 2004). Held during a time of growing racial and political tension in the United States – the latter being tied largely to the US government's foreign policy, including the ongoing deployment of soldiers in Vietnam – Woodstock was advertised as three days of peace, love and music. In addition to heavy rock bands, the festival also featured a number of acoustic folk balladeers of the time, notably Joan Baez and Arlo Guthrie. This combination of the rich variety of music featured at Woodstock, the greenfield site chosen for the event (in Bethal, upper New York State) and its relatively peaceful nature (even as the audience swelled to an unprecedented 460,000 people) chimed well with the aesthetic of the hippie era. Laing (2004) accurately suggests that Woodstock became the template for the commodification of the music festival. Equally, however, the event became a critical template for the aestheticization of the music festival; much of the aesthetic understanding of the relationship between music, politics and identity that manifested itself at Woodstock has flowed through to similar music festivals – large and small – that have emerged in the ensuing years, notably the annual Glastonbury festival in Somerset in the United Kingdom.

Festivals and Lifestyle

In addition to their significance as spaces for the acquisition and articulation of identity, festivals are also linked increasingly to various forms of lifestyle. As societies in developed regions of the world become more diverse in terms of lifestyle orientation, taste and political outlook (Chaney 2004), this has been mirrored by the global festival scene. Indeed, such is the diversity of the contemporary global festival landscape that an ever-expanding range of lifestyle tastes and preferences are now accommodated into a variety of different festival settings. The concept of lifestyle has its origins in the work of Weber (1978), which challenged Marx's model of economic determinism through positing emergent practices of consumption and leisure during the early twentieth century as new modes for the demonstration of wealth and status. Weber's ideas were further developed in the work of Veblen (1994) and Simmel (cited in Frisby and Featherstone 1997). In more recent times, sociologists such as Giddens (1991) and Chaney (1996) have drawn on and significantly developed the concept of lifestyle as a means of theoretically conceptualizing the ways by which individuals reflexively appropriate and reinscribe objects, images and texts from the cultural and media industries as everyday resources. Chaney, in particular, has posited an elaborate theory of lifestyle *sites* and *strategies* as a means of mapping the way in which forms of consumption underpin the aestheticization of everyday life. Thus, according to Chaney, lifestyle sites and strategies refer to the ways in which individuals creatively rework the cultural resources at hand into their everyday lives as physical and symbolic markers of identity and taste.

As the festival genre continues to expand, many of the themes featured and focused on in festival settings draw in increasingly specific ways on patterns of lifestyle and taste that have long since become embedded in everyday culture. Obvious examples here include festivals based around music, art, literature and food. Although each of these festival types typically draws a different kind of audience, what links them is the fact that each effectively accentuates – and indeed celebrates – a particular form of lifestyle project through using a collectively shared assemblage of images, objects and texts as an occasion for sociality. The liminality of the festival space thus takes on another level of significance: as a site for the convergence of individuals whose shared lifestyle preferences generally are articulated at an individual and perhaps quite subtle, if not subliminal, level. Festivals therefore produce a temporal, yet highly visible and in some cases inherently spectacular, display of commonly shared lifestyle preferences.

An interesting example of this is seen in a rapidly expanding sub-genre commonly referred to as the nostalgia festival. Transcending the conventional blend of music, food and merchandise, the repertoire of such festivals typically extends to a range of other generationally marked icons, such as classic cars, period fashion and various retro or reproduction consumer accessories associated with the era celebrated by the festival. A pertinent instance of this is the annual Wintersun festival, held every June in New South Wales, Australia.[1] In the case of Wintersun, the focus for the collective celebration of nostalgia is the rock'n'roll era of the 1950s and early 1960s – and in particular, the music, dance and cars associated with this era. A three-day festival, Wintersun showcases an elaborate mix of live rock'n'roll music (including a highly popular Elvis impersonators competition), dancing, memorabilia stands and a vintage car procession. The festival began in the 1970s, adopting its 1950s/60s theme in 1988. Wintersun has

---

1   Originally held in the town of Coolangatta, on the border between Queensland and New South Wales, in 2011 Wintersun was relocated further south to Port Macquarie. A new festival, 'Coolie Rocks On', was subsequently established in Coolangatta to replace Wintersun.

since become an important meeting point for a trans-local scene (Peterson and Bennett 2004) of rock'n'roll fans – old and young – who share a deep investment in this musical genre. Travelling interstate from various regions of Australia, and to a lesser extent overseas, fans converge at the Wintersun festival to collectively revive the spirit of the rock'n'roll era in a space dedicated to this effort. Their attachment to rock'n'roll music and its broader cultural milieu is manifested through a variety of media, most notably the carefully reproduced fashion of the era worn by people of all ages who attend the festival. In providing a space for this collective celebration of the rock'n'roll lifestyle, Wintersun takes full advantage of its temporary appropriation of an urban space. Streets and parkland areas become settings for live music performances, dancing, street stalls and vintage car exhibitions. Local venue spaces and bars provide additional space for the festival and also allow it to carry on into the evening when noise restrictions and cooler temperatures constrain the outdoor activities enjoyed during the day. Examples of similar festivals can be seen elsewhere, both in Australia (for example, the Kurri Kurri Festival) and elsewhere in the world (for example, the UK festival Shake, Rattle and Roll).

As noted earlier, in common everyday parlance, festivals such as Wintersun are often referred to as 'nostalgia' events – a seemingly accurate descriptor, given the way in which they function to draw together distinct, generationally bonded audiences to collectively engage in taste and consumer practices acquired during their youth. Arguably, however, the term 'nostalgia festival' fails to capture in any wholly meaningful sense the nature of the festival experience for those participating. Thus, rather than merely celebrating a collective representation of the past, 'nostalgia' festivals may also play an important role in helping festival-goers to define their individual and collective identities in the present. Indeed, for many of those who attend such festivals, the critical draw would appear to revolve not around the rehearsal of a lifestyle generally confined to memory – or a chance to relive one's youth – but rather the opportunity to participate in a gathering of like-minded individuals whose collective investment in the cultural texts and artefacts on display at the festival are part of their ongoing lifestyle project.

The merging of lifestyle choice and festival destination also takes on a range of other dimensions, settings and contexts. St John's (2013) highly instructive work on eclipse festivals, for example, examines the global cult of the eclipse chaser, who seeks out opportunities to experience total solar eclipses as they occur in different parts of the world. These individuals are motivated by a range of different lifestyle orientations and ideologies that typically blend elements of green ideology, neo-paganism, astrology and earth mysteries. Taking some of their inspiration from the large greenfield-site rock festivals of the late 1960s and early 1970s, eclipse festivals continue to embody the 'hippie' spirit of the latter, updating this for a new, younger audience through the inclusion of electronic dance music and state-of-the-art special effects utilizing digital media. A rather more sedate, yet equally distinctive, set of lifestyle sensibilities and tastes is catered for by food and wine festivals (Hall and Sharples 2008). Providing opportunities to savour and consume a range of different foods and wines from around the world, such festivals are becoming increasingly popular among educated, middle-class audiences, for whom these festivals form part of a cosmopolitan lifestyle.

Again, there has been an interesting convergence between food, drink and music in more recent years, with the increasing popularity of wineries as locations for rock and pop concerts featuring classic rock and pop artists from the 1960s and 1970s, such as Leonard Cohen and Patti Smith. As the baby boomer audiences for such artists have reached middle age and achieved financial independence, their lifestyle preferences and habits have grown in ways that reflect their taste and status. As Bennett (2013b) observes, a new range of lifestyle options and marketing strategies have emerged in response to this. In this context, the winery rock gig seamlessly combines a desire on the part of the boomer generation for a more relaxed and comfortable setting in which to enjoy their favourite music artists, while invoking a memory of the outdoor, greenfield rock festival experiences of their youth.

Festival Spaces of Exchange and Encounter

Aligned with, but also extending beyond, literatures on lifestyle and the cultural turn, recent bodies of research have focused on the diversification of portfolios of cultural consumption, whereby people's preferences are becoming less bound to hierarchical and narrowly channelled consumption tracts, instead opening up to possibilities for different consumption experiences. Over the last decade or so, literatures on cosmopolitanism have proven themselves a promising tool for rethinking the transformative implications of such social engagements across cultural, geographic and social borders, and within and across scales of social interaction from the local to the global. Cosmopolitanism is defined partly by the diversity of its meanings, and in our reading there are three main skeins in the literature on cosmopolitanism, emphasizing institutional, political or cultural dimensions. At its most macro level, cosmopolitanism refers to an ambition or project of building regimes of global governance, and legal-institutional frameworks for regulating events and processes that have impacts beyond any one nation. At a political level, cosmopolitan is a democratic principle referring to a position or principle, emphasizing hybridity, multiplicity, inclusivity and acknowledgement of diverse cultural forms and expressions. Finally, as a cultural phenomenon – and there appears to be a high degree of agreement on this point in the literature – cosmopolitanism is defined by an engagement with and openness to other cultures, values and experiences. Such a cultural outlook is identified as being underpinned by new types of mobilities of capital, people and things (Beck 2006; Hannerz 1990; Szerszynski and Urry 2002); elaborated, flexible and heterogeneous outlooks and modes of corporeal engagement among citizen-publics that are grounded in cultural-symbolic competencies founded in a type of 'code-switching' capacity (Bernstein 1972; Chaney 2002; Emmison 2003; Hall 2002;

Waldron 1992), and an expanded, inclusive ethical core emphasizing worldliness and communitarianism (Hannerz 1990; Nussbaum 1994; Tomlinson 1999). In this body of the cosmopolitan literatures, cosmopolitanism can be conceived as a set of practices and outlooks that seek out and value cultural difference and openness. Cosmopolitanism is also inextricably linked to networked elements of material infrastructure and spatial organization, which both configure and enable its expression. Many of these things that enable forms of cosmopolitan mobility and openness are fixed in place and actually immobile, enlisted into an interdependent technological system that supports massive systems of mobility and movement. In addition, and to a large degree in contrast, to such global networks, cosmopolitanism is best understood when performed or identified in particular local time-space settings. For example, Mica Nava (2002, 2007) shows how cosmopolitanism existed in the department stores of the early twentieth century, promoted by commercial interests as an alternative to stultifying and insular forms of traditional British modernism. What we suggest is that festivals can in some cases open social spaces for, or at least make representations of, otherwise socially and culturally marginalized people or cultural forms.

At the core of recent and antique conceptualizations of cosmopolitanism is the idea of openness. While openness is based upon a range of elemental practices and attitudes, and can be defined in terms of these components, it is also the case that cosmopolitan openness is something that is situationally and contextually dependent. In fact, this form of openness is amenable to expression and flowering in some contexts more than others. The implication of this context dependency is that openness has a performative dimension; it must be brought into social frames by actors who mobilize particular ways of seeing, which in turn elevate openness as a relevant and operational schema or discourse. Rather than focusing on delimiting expressions of openness to fixed expressions of agreement or disagreement, because of the contingency of expressions of openness researchers must focus on the performative dimensions of cosmopolitan openness. Thus being culturally open is neither a universal concept, nor necessarily more or less ubiquitous. It is more of a strategic practice, resource or frame for managing meaning in settings infused by different types of individuals and groups, and different modes of social communication and gathering. Openness is not the same thing for every person, nor is it the same for each person across particular settings. It may rest on similar conceptual dimensions – such as curiosity, for example – though its objects can be diverse. This means that researchers must look not to absolute expressions of openness, but to its performance, effervescence and manifestation across a diversity of settings by a range of citizens. If this is the case, then the contemporary festival, with its liminal frames and the cordoning off of routinized forms of social engagement, can be one type of cosmopolitan setting.

In order to understand the power of setting, space and context for underpinning cultural effervescence and exchange associated with the festival, we can turn to the idea of a cosmoscape (Kendall, Woodward and Skrbiš 2009). The cosmoscape is a zone structured by particular spatial and social characteristics, which afford and indeed encourage cosmopolitan socialization. While it is the case that cosmopolitan encounters can occur routinely and mundanely in any social space or context, cosmoscapes are particularly conducive to promoting cosmopolitan encounters. The ethnographer of urban life in the United States, Elijah Anderson (2004), has developed the idea of a 'cosmopolitan canopy', usefully indicating the way spatial zones within cities foster of forms of cosmopolitanism civility. Anderson's ethnographic analysis gives us some important clues about why such spaces seem more conducive to cultivating other-focused forms of civility that transcend class, racial and ethnic lines. Anderson suggests that some urban locations – such as Reading Terminal Market or Rittenhouse Square in Philadelphia – facilitate contact with cultural difference, and that social interaction within these spaces occurs across the usual boundaries of class and race in ways that might be routine components of everyday life. He suggests that it is inherent within the meanings of these spaces – that is, the meaning participants collectively assign to them – that they are spaces where one expects civil association with others, where the usual rules of association are relaxed. More than this, within these spaces people feel both relatively comfortable with the mix of people in the vicinity, but they also reflexively perform, monitor and reproduce this ease with cultural difference thorough various accommodations and rituals of mixing.

We could also suggest that some contemporary cultural festivals have become an important site for representing, encountering, incorporating and understanding aspects of cultural community and cultural difference. In effect, they function as a type of prime cosmoscape, identifiably canopy-like by design. A key example here is the WOMAD Festival, a long-standing and geographically dispersed world music event that has extended into a variety of domains, encouraging audiences to 'taste the world' by sampling music, food and lifestyles from around the globe. The contemporary festival therefore becomes a potential site for representing, encountering, incorporating and researching aspects of cultural difference. More generally, in communicating something about community, locality and belonging, the contemporary cultural festival dedicated to music, food or lifestyles develops in response to processes of cultural pluralization, mobility and globalization. Yet, at the same time as festival discourses point to being open to the swirl of multiple and heterogeneous cultural differences, they also assert the importance of the local and the rooted. For the most part, festivals balance the needs of representing the local within a broader context of rapid social change (Sassatelli 2008). The question of whether such festival spaces can be planned, or whether they emerge organically and unconsciously from the pragmatic movements of their publics, cannot easily be answered – but they can be both. It is obvious that forms of consumptive engagement are potentially exploitative and based on modes of cultural appropriation, though they are also motivated by curiosity and a genuine yearning for engagements with alterity (Binnie, Millington and Young 2006). Such questions need further empirical exploration, and indeed such themes are explored in numerous chapters within this collection. The emphasis on the expression of cosmopolitanism in spatial settings is a useful reminder of where, why and under what material contingencies cosmopolitanism openness is manifested. Networks of people and things do indeed, under conducive political and cultural conditions, 'allow for the surfacing of cosmopolitical agendas and practices, and, indeed, provide the frameworks for their interpretation as evidence of "cosmopolitanization"' (Kendall, Woodward and Skrbiš 2009: 154). Importantly, it is the elaborate and variable cultural work of framing, interpreting, narrating, excluding and categorizing that turns such relations into a meaningful cultural form such as 'cosmopolitan'.

The Film Festival: Sites of Passage and Visualizing the Other

As an ethical and political project, cosmopolitanism involves the transformation of systems of governance, law and decision-making, taking into account principles of hospitality and solidarity in the light of matters transcending both transnational and local interests. Such a project requires formal, institutional interventions that enhance or redesign structures of global governance (Kurasawa 2004: 236). Yet, on their own, these institutional initiatives are not sufficient developments for the widespread acceptance, adoption and practice of a cosmopolitan form of ethics. As well as institutional innovations, this would require a widespread redefinition of normative bonds of solidarity and a robust sense of mutual belonging 'without bounds' (Kurasawa 2004). This would, as Szerszynski and Urry (2002: 465) note, require 'massive cultural work' to generate bonds of community across more extensive territories – both geographic and normative. As a middle-ground space of cultural productivity lying between the high-flown discourses of cosmopolitan ethics and the ongoing work of everyday cosmopolitan practices, the sphere of mass media and communicative institutions and experiences plays a significant role in both reflecting society and public opinion as well as structuring them and, in a broad sense, helping to create them (Alexander 2006). This suggests that to understand the possibilities for cosmopolitanism, we must examine the role of various mediating aesthetic and cultural forms in helping to create a cosmopolitan culture. In considering visual, aural and material disseminators of cosmopolitanism, we need to reflect on a number of preliminary matters. Most importantly, we must consider what is meant by the idea of mediation. This refers not to the unreflexive and suffocating intrusion of all types of media into people's lifeworlds to the extent that daily existence is thoroughly dominated by such media, but points to the ways in which various types of media – including traditional mass media such as newspapers and television, but also the power of music, photography and objects – bring people into contact with thoughts, ideas and transformative experiences through their connecting and performative capacities. This generates a series of relevant questions. For example, is it possible for television, music, art and photography to nurture a cosmopolitan culture? Can mobile objects, images and non-human entities possess, and even convey, the seeds of cosmopolitanism? Do these forms of aesthetic, mediated cosmopolitanism more richly develop cosmopolitan bonds than formalist political means, or are they merely reflective of thin, economically driven processes associated with global capitalism's cultural industries?

In recent times, film festivals have begun to capture the attention of various scholars (such as Evans 2007; Iordanova and Rhyne 2009; Ruling and Pedersen 2010), yet there is a surprising lack of connection made between film events and cosmopolitanism. Nevertheless, there are observations that can be drawn from the existing body of literature on film festivals, which indicate they might be considered sites of cosmopolitanism, both in terms of how the films they screen can generate feelings of worldly connections and how the programming and promotions are often designed to appeal to a cosmopolitan appreciation of differences. The discussion that follows briefly explores broader literature on film festivals to highlight how they are useful sites of research for studies of cosmopolitanism.

Ruling and Pedersen (2010) claim that there are over 3,500 film festivals held worldwide, and explain that while the history of film festivals began with desires to showcase national content, processes of globalization have contributed to the rise of international film festivals, a global film scene and world cinema (see Roberts 1998). As Friedberg (1993: 147) also proposes, cinema spectatorship can bring about a 'virtual mobility' comparable with shopping and tourism; she suggests that films provide a way for individuals to sample differences at a safe distance without risk, contact or an intensive immersion. Film festivals provide a conducive spatial and social setting for experiencing arresting sensual and narrative material that affords global encounters of the virtual kind. Rather than requiring physical mobility, films (and videos, a comparatively new medium to be shown in cinemas that arose with the arrival of high-definition technology) can expose and transport audiences to almost anywhere in the world with considerable ease, through the visual imagery, sounds and stories with which people can engage on the screens in their local cinemas and theatres. And, although a virtual or mediated encounter of difference, watching films can still arouse powerful memories, longings and imaginations of faraway places, foreign peoples and cross-cultural experiences.

The impact and influence of film festivals also stretch beyond the intimate interplay between screen and viewers in the darkness of local cinema and theatres, and films can become 'sites of passage' (de Valck 2007) for audiences to move to and between the local and the global. Cultural festivals, including film festivals, are also argued to be a significant source of tourism (Prentice and Andersen 2003), and can also serve the double purpose of entertaining and educating audiences about social issues such as human rights (Gamson 1996; McLagan 2008). Evans (2007: 33) investigated three major European film festivals – Cannes, Berlinale and Karlovy Vary; he adopts a post-colonial framework to argue that, 'European film festivals might have a key role to play in the evolution of world cinema in the 21st century by mounting a concerted, coherent challenge to Hollywood hegemony' (2007: 33). In other words, these festivals represent an attempt at showcasing a level of diversity not found in films made in the United States, with Hollywood used as shorthand for the country's entire film industry.

It is important to note that film festivals can differ significantly in their character, style and agendas, as they are influenced by a range of factors. These include the locations where they are held, but also the scale of expense and degrees of prestige they are accorded (de Valck 2007). At the end, characterized by glamour, celebrity and big business, there is the spectacle and grandeur of the Cannes Film Festival, which attracts a powerful mixture of celebrities, artists, promoters, distributors and journalists annually (Segal and Blumauer 2011). Nevertheless, Turan (2003) reminds us that film festivals can pop up just about anywhere and everywhere, from 'Sundance to Sarejevo', highlighting the broad expanse and popularity that film festivals have achieved.

There is also a temporal aspect and predictability that contributes to film festivals being a flexible and non-demanding vehicle for encountering differences. Whatever the genre, films usually follow set conventions in time and narrative structure, typically requiring individuals' attention for minutes if in short form, and around one to two hours (or even longer) when in feature form (Vorderer, Wulff and Friedrichsen 2009). Moreover, film festivals themselves are occasional experiences, traditionally held as annual events – usually for the duration of a week – with audiences allowed to participate in as many or as few films on the programme as they wish.

While focused on films rather than film festivals, a few observations from Roberts' (1998) discussion of world cinema can be made, which further emphasize how studies of film festivals are well suited for future research on, and furthering understandings of, cosmopolitanism. For instance, Roberts (1998: 63) highlights how, 'if film industries in many parts of the world today remain strongly national in character, the business of film making and film watching have equally long been transnational in nature, as any African who grew up on westerns, Indian musicals, and kung fu movies knows only too well'. He adds that, 'Transnational cinema, the films of diasporic subjects living in cosmopolitan First World cities, has become a proliferating film genre rivaling older national cinemas' (1998: 63).

The contact zones available for individuals to meet people who are different from them and live far away have been pushed wide open through films and screen technologies, although not everyone has the same opportunities. Roberts (1998) acknowledges that transnational films and world cinema can reproduce stereotypes, colonialism and racism in their desires to appeal to global audiences, with Westerners having the most pull economically. At the same time, Roberts explains how films do offer more people more opportunities for cosmopolitan encounters. He states that, 'In the nomadic cinema of Wenders or Jarmusch, Herzog or Kaurismaki, middle-class Euro-American audiences can experience the glamour of cosmopolitanism without leaving home, even if their budget prevents them from traveling the world' (1998: 67).

Conclusion

This chapter has considered the significance of contemporary festivals as spaces that provide resources, experiences and encounters extending beyond those that typically characterize the everyday lives of individuals in urban, regional and rural settings. Drawing on Bakhtin's (1984) conceptualization of the carnival as an unregulated space for the articulation of forms of activity and behaviour, we have considered how such traits can be identified in the contemporary festival setting, where the physical and sensory environments experienced often allow individuals to transcend the mundane happenstance of their more usual everyday existence. In addition, we have explored the way festivals may be spaces and sites of cultural exchange and transformation. In drawing on nascent literatures on cosmopolitanism, we have explored how the festival as aesthetic and community experience allows it to be a space of cosmopolitan exchange and encounter. In exploring these issues, we have drawn on two key examples of the contemporary festival genres: music and film. Each of these genres, we have argued, provides opportunities for festival-goers to acquire experiences that resonate with their established tastes, while at the same time offering avenues for the acquisition of new tastes and cultural competencies in safe and relatively risk-free environments. As such, contemporary festivals can be viewed as important nodal points within the matrix of lifestyle sites and strategies through which individuals create, manage and articulate their identities. In this sense, festivals can be seen to constitute a significant part of the cultural repertoires through which individuals engage in the critical boundary work by which commonality and collectivity, as well as distinctiveness and difference, are maintained.

References

Aitchison, C. and Pritchard, A. 2007. *Festivals and Events: Culture and Identity in Leisure, Sport and Tourism*. Eastbourne: Leisure Studies Association.

Alexander, J.C. 2006. *The Civil Sphere*. Oxford: Oxford University Press.

Anderson, E. 2004. The cosmopolitan canopy. *Annals of the American Academy of Political and Social Science*, 595(1), 14–31.

Bakhtin, M.M. 1984. *Rabelais and His World*, translated by H. Isowolsky. Cambridge, MA: MIT Press.

Beck, U. 2006. *The Cosmopolitan Vision*. Cambridge: Polity Press.

Bennett, A. 2001. *Cultures of Popular Music*. Buckingham: Open University Press.

Bennett, A. ed. 2004. *Remembering Woodstock*. Aldershot: Ashgate.

Bennett, A. 2013a. Reappraising counterculture, in *Countercultures and Popular Music*, edited by S. Whiteley and J. Sklower. Farnham: Ashgate.

Bennett, A. 2013b. *Music, Style and Aging: Growing Old Disgracefully?* Philadelphia, PA: Temple University Press.

Bernstein, B. 1972. *Class, Codes and Control*. London: Paladin.

Binnie, J., Millington, S. and Young, C. 2006. Introduction: Grounding cosmopolitan urbanism – approaches, practices and policies, in *Cosmopolitan Urbanism*, edited by J. Binnie, S. Holloway, S. Millington and C. Young. London: Routledge, 1–34.

Bowditch, R. 2010. *On the Edge of Utopia: Performance and Ritual at Burning Man*. Chicago, IL: University of Chicago Press.

Chaney, D. 1996. *Lifestyles*. London: Routledge.

Chaney, D. 2002. Cosmopolitan art and cultural citizenship. *Theory, Culture & Society*, 19(1–2), 157–74.

Chaney, D. 2004. Fragmented culture and subcultures, in *After Subculture: Critical Studies in Contemporary Youth Culture*, edited by A. Bennett and K. Kahn-Harris. Basingstoke: Palgrave.

Cummings, J. 2006. It's more than a t-shirt: Neo-tribal sociality and linking images at Australian indie music festivals. *Perfect Beat: The Pacific Journal of Research into Contemporary Music and Popular Culture*, 8(1), 69–84.

Cummings, J. 2008. Trade mark registered: Sponsorship within the Australian Indie music festival scene. *Continuum*, 22(5), 675–85.

de Valck, M. 2007. *Film Festivals: From European Geopolitics to Global Cinephilia*. Amsterdam: Amsterdam University Press.

Dowd, T.J., Liddle, K. and Nelson, J. 2004. Music festivals as scenes: Examples from serious music, womyn's music and skatepunk, in *Music Scenes: Local, Translocal and Virtual*, edited by A. Bennett and R.A. Peterson. Nashville, TN: Vanderbilt University Press, 149–67.

Emmison, M. 2003. Social class and cultural mobility: Reconfiguring the cultural omnivore thesis, *Journal of Sociology*, 39(3), 211–30.

Evans, O. 2007. Border exchanges: The role of the European film festival. *Journal of Contemporary European Studies*, 15(1), 23–33.

Fredline, E., Deery, M. and Jago, L. 2005. *Host Community Perceptions of the Impacts of Events: A Comparison of Different Event Themes in Urban and Regional Communities*. Gold Coast, Queensland: ARC Collaborative Research Centre for Sustainable Tourism.

Friedberg, A. 1993. *Window Shopping: Cinema and the Postmodern*. Berkeley, CA: University of California Press.

Frisby, D. and Featherstone, M. 1997. *Simmel on Culture: Selected Writings*. London: Sage.

Gamson, J. 1996. The organizational shaping of collective identity: The case of lesbian and gay film festivals in New York. *Sociological Forum*, 11(2), 231–61.

Giddens, A. 1991. *Modernity and Self Identity: Self and Society in the Late Modern Age*. Cambridge: Polity Press.

Hall, M.C. and Sharples, L. (eds) 2008. *Food and Wine Festivals and Events Around the World*. Amsterdam: Elsevier/Butterworth-Heinemann.

Hall, S. 2002. Political belonging in a world of multiple identities, in *Conceiving Cosmopolitanism: Theory, Context, Practice*, edited by S. Vertovec and R. Cohen. Oxford: Oxford University Press, 25–31.

Hannerz, U. 1990. Cosmopolitans and locals in world culture. *Theory, Culture and Society*, 7(2–3), 237–51.

Iordanova, D. and Rhyne, R. (eds) 2009. *Film Festival Yearbook 1: The Festival Circuit*. St Andrews: St Andrews Film School.

Kendall, G., Woodward, I. and Skrbiš, Z. 2009. *The Sociology of Cosmopolitanism*. New York: Palgrave Macmillan.

Kurasawa, F. 2004. Cosmopolitanism from below: Alternative globalization and the creation of a solidarity without bounds. *European Journal of Social Theory*, 45, 233–55.

Kurasawa, F. 2007. *The Work of Global Justice. Human Rights as Practices*. Cambridge: Cambridge University Press.

Laing, D. 2004. The three Woodstocks and the live music scene, in *Remembering Woodstock*, edited by A. Bennett. Aldershot: Ashgate.

McKay, G. 1996. *Senseless Acts of Beauty*. London: Verso.

McKay, G. 2000. *Glastonbury: A Very English Fair*. London: Victor Gollancz.

McKay, G. 2004. 'Unsafe things like youth and jazz': Beaulieu Jazz Festivals (1956–61), and the origins of pop festival culture in Britain, in *Remembering Woodstock*, edited by A. Bennett. Aldershot: Ashgate.

McLagan, M. 2008. Circuits of suffering. *PoLAR: Political and Legal Anthropology Review*, 28(2), 223–39.

Nava, M. 2002. Cosmopolitan modernity: Everyday imaginaries and the register of difference. *Theory, Culture and Society*, 19(1–2), 81–99.

Nava, M. 2007. *Visceral Cosmopolitanism: Gender, Culture and the Normalisation of Difference*, Oxford: Berg.

Nussbaum, M.C. 1994. Patriotism and cosmopolitanism. *Boston Review*, 19(5), 3–34.

Peterson, R.A. and Bennett, A. 2004. Introducing music scenes, in *Music Scenes: Local, Translocal and Virtual*, edited by A. Bennett and R.A. Peterson. Nashville, TN: Vanderbilt University Press, 1–15.

Prentice, R. and Andersen, V. 2003. Festival as creative destination. *Annals of Tourism Research*, 30(1), 7–30.

Roberts, M. 1998. 'Baraka': World cinema and the global culture industry. *Cinema Journal*, 37(3), 62–82.

Ruling, C-C. and Pedersen, J.S. 2010. Film festival research from an organizational studies perspective. *Scandinavian Journal of Management*, Special Issue on International Strategy and Cross-Cultural Management, 26(3), 318–23.

Sassatelli, M. (ed.) 2008. *European Public Culture and Aesthetic Cosmopolitanism*. Euro-festival Project, Deliverable 1.1. Available at: www.euro-festival.org [accessed: 20 November 2012].

Segal, J. and Blumauer, C. 2011. Cannes: A French International Festival, in *Festivals and the Public Sphere*, edited by L. Giori, M. Sassatelli and G. Delanty. Abingdon: Routledge, 156–72.

St John, G. 2013. Total solar eclipse festivals, cosmic spirituality and planetary culture, in *Pop Pagans*, edited by D. Weston and A. Bennett. London: Equinox.

Street, J. 2004. 'This is your Woodstock': Popular memories and political myths, in *Remembering Woodstock*, edited by A. Bennett. Aldershot: Ashgate.

Szersynski, B. and Urry, J. 2002. Cultures of cosmopolitanism. *The Sociological Review*, 50(4), 461–81.

Tomlinson, J. 1999. *Globalization and Culture*. Cambridge: Polity Press.

Turan, K. 2003. *Sundance to Sarajevo: Film Festivals and the World They Made*. Berkeley, CA: University of California Press.

Veblen, T. 1994 [1924]. *The Theory of the Leisure Class: An Economic Study of Institutions*. New York: Mentor Books.

Vorderer, B.P., Wulff, H.J. and Friedrichsen, M. (eds) 2009. *Suspense: Conceptualizations, Theoretical Analyses, and Empirical Explorations*. Mahwah, NJ: Lawrence Erlbaum.

Waldron, J. 1992. Minority cultures and the cosmopolitan alternative. *University of Michigan Journal of Law Reform*, 25(3), 751–93.

Weber, M. 1978 [1919]. The distribution of power within the political community: class, status, party, in *Economy and Society: An Outline of Interpretive Sociology*. Berkeley, CA: University of California Press.

Chapter 2

Festivalizing Sexualities: Discourses of 'Pride', Counter-discourses of 'Shame'

Jodie Taylor

Festivals have been an important part of social and cultural life for thousands of years. The morphology of festivals is not universal, as they take on different significance, form and meaning in various cultural, historical and contemporary contexts as well as within their own space-time constructions. Turner (1982), for example, argues that festivals function as liminal spaces and ritualized sites of transcendence and *communitas*. In Falassi's (1987) classic festival study, festivals are considered to be a means to reinforce the shared values, identities, histories, ideologies and mythologies that bind a community, testifying to the longevity and triumph of a community while also indulging in spectacle and celebration. In Bakhtinian (1984) terms, festivals can temporarily facilitate the playful transgression of authority and the symbolic inversion of social hierarchies through carnivalesque ritual and spectacle. In other words, festivals can function as politicized cultural practices and sanctioned forms of collective dissent, offering a limited means of defying hegemonic culture and social norms of the time. Through temporary public gatherings of ideologically aligned communities and/ or minoritarian people, festivals can at the very least expose cultural boundaries and afford some communities greater visibility. At best, they can command the attention of the majoritarian public sphere, making visible what is usually suppressed and generating a collective voice of resistance to cultural authority.

Contemporary gay pride festivals, it could be argued, perform all of these functions. A now-ritualized practice of subjugated sexually non-normative communities, pride festivals can be understood as 'a means by which the imagined gay community can be materialized in space through publicly celebrating their culture, pride, traditions, symbols, and mythologies, which for much of the time remain hidden from public view' (Waitt and Markwell 2006: 217). In times and places where lesbian, gay, bisexual, transgender, intersex and queer (LGBTIQ) bodies have been denied public visibility and performance, pride festivals have emerged as defiant outcries for public acknowledgement and as strategic modes of place-making and territorialization for sexual counter-publics. By pressuring civic and political institutions to acknowledge sexually non-normative bodies in the most public of places – streets, parks, squares and the like – pride festivals have performed important social operations, symbolizing empowerment and social change (Duncan 1996; Valentine 2002). Implicit in such practices is a challenge to the tactics of 'heteronormativity' (Corber and Valocchi 2003) that privatize non-normative sexualities. By destabilizing the public/private dichotomy that structures the compulsory heterosexuality of civic space, ritualized pride festivities mark certain public spaces and cityscapes – such as Christopher Street in New York, The Castro district in San Francisco and Oxford Street in Sydney – as places of pilgrimage that symbolize sexual minority communities' fight for public life.

However, as this chapter demonstrates, for a growing number of people the rhetoric and celebration of pride are becoming increasingly outmoded, and this is evidenced by a distinguishable shift in the culture, politics and motivations underpinning pride festivities. Radical queer activists would likely describe this as a shift towards commodification and assimilation – that is, from pride festivities as grassroots celebrations of collective mutiny through disruptive, politicized and socially transformative action, to pride festivities as orderly and corporatized displays of consumerism and 'homonormativity' (Duggan 2003). Over the last decade, the gay pride agenda has been scrutinized by a new movement towards both a politics and a festive spectacle of gay shame (Bernstein Sycamore 2004; Halperin 2009; Halperin and Traub 2009). According to the gay shame agenda, the official images of gay visibility, gay institutions and economic power further alienate and work to exclude the 'less wholesome' sexual minority communities from public life.

Drawing on current theoretical debates, international queer activist literatures, LGBTIQ press and my own participant observation of local pride festivities, this chapter will examine the meanings and functions of gay pride in the festival context. Its approach makes use of a methodological framework that offers 'nuanced comparisons of multiple particulars' (Jones 2010: 271), situating knowledge in historical, social, global and local contexts. To begin, I will give a brief historical overview of pride festivities that bespeak the illusory authenticity of current pride rhetoric. I will unpack the performative affect of pride events, collectively imagined as deconstructive spatial tactics. With reference to processes of festivalization, I will examine the trend towards consumption, tourism and the commodification of gay pride as a global event in international cities. Following this, I will discuss the increasing opposition to neoliberal sexual citizenship and the ideological impulses towards and counter-discursive strategy of gay shame as posited by some radial queer activists. Drawing on my hometown of Brisbane, Australia as an illustrative case example, I will then look at localized pride festivities as multi-discursive platforms.

Gay Pride: Bringing Sexuality into the Streets

The origins of contemporary gay pride festivals such as the Sydney Gay and Lesbian Mardi Gras or the Christopher Street Day celebrations are imbued with a history of oppression, injustice, rebellion and dissent. The origins of such events are discursively traced to the gay liberation movement and the Stonewall riots, now an enshrined and somewhat romanticized moment in the chronicles of gay history (Duberman 1993; Carter 2010). In the early hours of the morning of 28 June 1969, police raided a New York gay bar called the Stonewall Inn in Christopher Street, Greenwich Village. Given the illegal status of homosexuality at the time, such raids were quite common; however, on this particular night the patrons fought back with unprecedented vigour and the riots are reported to have continued for two nights and three days. For the majority of the twentieth century, gay social life was largely confined to bars such as the Stonewall Inn, and this particular bar is said to have been frequented by the so-called disreputable elements of gay culture – drag queens, hustlers, butch dykes, trans folk and the like. While liberation efforts were underway prior to Stonewall, this event has become collectively memorialized, marking a shift in homosexual rights agendas from the pre-Stonewall homophile movements to the post-Stonewall gay liberation fronts (Altman 1972; D'Emilio 1983).

In the late 1960s and 1970s, homophile groups such as the Mattachine Society and the Daughters of Bilitis that had been operating – in the United States at least – since the 1950s were gradually being challenged by the counter-cultural discourses of gay liberation. The homophile movements' conservative and assimilationist politics tended to proffer a notion of the homosexual as an unwilling victim of his or her psychic abnormality – someone who should not be punished on the grounds that homosexuality was an innate affliction (Altman 1972; Sullivan 2003). Contrary to this, the liberationist movement celebrated being gay, calling for an acceptance of sexual difference as an identity, culture and lifestyle. According to Altman (1972: 109), gay liberation was 'concerned with the assertion and creation of a new sense of identity, one based on pride in being gay'. Liberationists imagined universal social change centred on sexual choice and the unrepressed erotic expression of all people, aiming to liberate individuals from the normative constraints of the sex/gender system (Altman 1972; Sullivan 2003).

As an event, the Stonewall riots encapsulated the rhetoric of 'gay pride' and the provocation for others to 'come out of the closet' and take to the streets. One year after the riots, New York gay activists called for the event to be commemorated both locally and in other national cities where activist groups were present. This became known as Gay Pride Week, and included a public parade on Sunday, 28 June 1970 to mark the anniversary of the Stonewall raids and concomitant resistance efforts. As Armstrong and Crage (2006: 740) argue, 'in 1970 hosting a gay parade was indistinguishable from a gay protest or political demonstration: a public gathering of homosexuals was perceived by authorities as confrontational and by homosexuals as a courageous display of political commitment'. Stonewall quickly become emblematic of a new era of defiance, visibility and pride, and via annual festive commemorations, pride events are now seen as crucial in redefining the mainstream view of the gay citizenry and materializing gay counter-publics. Accordingly, hermeneutic performances of pride in a festival context have authenticated its place in contemporary gay politics. Employing Alexander's theory of cultural pragmatics, pride has become a symbolic cultural performance, 'a script [that] seems to ring true to the background culture precisely because it has an audience-fusing effect' (Alexander 2004: 550).

Every year since 1970, Gay Pride Week has been celebrated in New York. It now attracts hundreds of thousands of participants, and each year since it began, more cities around the globe have taken to staging their own pride events. London, for example, saw its first gay pride rally in 1972; Barcelona staged its first in 1977; Sydney in 1978; Johannesburg in 1990 (still the only pride rally on the African continent); Manila in 1994 (the first pride celebration in Asia); Amsterdam in 1996; São Paulo in 1997; and Istanbul in 2003. June is now globally recognized as the official pride month, during which festivals, rallies, parades and performing arts events are organized to celebrate a range of non-normative genders and sexual identities and lifestyles, including lesbian, gay, bisexual, transgender, intersex and queer (LGBTIQ). However, in different cities pride festivals may be staged outside of June to accommodate local circumstances such as weather or festival permit regulations.[1] According to the website of the international pride organization InterPride (www.interpride.org), in 2010 it recorded membership by 171 city-based pride organizations from 17 geographical regions around the world. From 1–9 July 2000 – the same year as the Catholic Church's Great Jubilee – InterPride organized the first WorldPride festival in Rome, Italy. This inaugural event claimed to have attracted around 250,000 participants (Johnston 2000), much to the disgust of Pope John Paul II, who is reported to have said: 'In the name of the Church of Rome, I cannot fail to express bitterness for the affront to the Great Jubilee of the year 2000 and for the offence to Christian values in a city that is so dear to the heart of Catholics around the world' (Ferrisi, cited in Waitt and Markwell 2006: 203). Since 2000, InterPride has coordinated WorldPride celebrations in Jerusalem (2006) and London (2012), with WorldPride Toronto scheduled for 2014.

While in many global cities such as New York and London, pride parades now represent roughly 40 years of public sexual dissent, in many locations such festivities are still highly controversial and impeded not only by verbal expressions of moral objection, as was the case with WorldPride Rome, but subject to discriminatory law and the very real threat of physically violent retaliations from local authorities and/or other protest groups within society. In very recent times, in parts of Central and Eastern Europe, pride events have been subject to violent attacks by right-wing movements, and have been banned by local and national authorities for fear of public disorder (Gruszczynska 2009). In 2001, a pride march organized in the

---

1   For example, the Sydney Gay and Lesbian Mardi Gras is staged in February so as to align with the Australian summer. In its original form, Mardi Gras was first held in June 1978 to commemorate the Stonewall riots and protest against police harassment and anti-homosexual laws. However, in 1981 the parade was shifted to the much warmer month of February to accommodate costume displays, scantily clad bodies and outdoor festive celebrations.

Serbian capital of Belgrade was savagely attacked by approximately a thousand anti-gay protestors. The event ended in a bloody scene when local police were unable to protect pride participants, and subsequently led to pride marches being banned in Belgrade until 2010. Again in 2010, anti-gay counter demonstrators attempted to attack pride participants who had been cordoned off by police for their protection. According to various media reports, hundreds of people – many of them police – were injured, and many of the right-wing religious extremists subsequently were arrested (Lowen 2010).

In Moscow during 2011, neo-Nazi extremists attacked a pride rally, and local police arrested many of the gay rights campaigners for attempting to stage the rally – an act of public assembly that Russian government authorities had officially banned. According to eyewitness reports by internationally renowned human rights and LGBTI freedom campaigner Peter Tatchell (2011), police used excessive force, violently bashing gay activists, and collusion between local police and extremist groups was evident. Also in 2011, the first ever pride demonstration in Split (the second largest city in Croatia) was tainted by homophobic abuse and violent unrest. It is reported that a mere 24 hours after it was announced that Croatia could join the European Union in 2013 – which involved a pledge to protect human rights – an estimated 10,000 protestors converged on a pride demonstration of approximately 300, resulting in many people sustaining injury (*UK Gay News* 2011).

While such violent clashes have obvious negative physical and perhaps psychological impacts on the lives of many LGBTIQ people who are subjected to street violence, as with Stonewall, the act of protesting remains an important one. Pride demonstrations and festivities can be politically significant events that discursively transform heterosexualized public places into temporary queer landscapes, generating material spaces for the articulation on non-normative gender and sexual identities. According to Duncan (1996: 138), 'marches, Gay Pride parades, public protests, performance art and street theatre as well as overtly homosexual behaviour such as kissing in public' are forms of 'deconstructive spatial tactics'. Space functions significantly in the making and remaking of social identities. Similarly, 'social identities, meanings and relations are recognized as produced in material and symbolic or metaphorical spaces' (Valentine 2002: 146). As work on sexualities from feminist and queer geographical perspectives has demonstrated, the assumption of heterosexuality works as a performative act to structure and normalize public space as heterosexual through repartition and regulation (e.g. see Bell and Valentine 1995; Brown, Browne and Lim 2007; Duncan 1996; Foucault 1979; Valentine 1996, 2002). These repetitious gestures, which congeal over time to give the appearance of 'naturalized' heterosexuality, pervade the public sphere in myriad forms – including, for example, the unproblematic displays of affection between heterosexual couples in public, heterosexual imagery in advertising and the expression of heterosexual desire in popular music and film narratives.

The regimes of heteronormalization that produce quotidian public spaces reinforce the invisibility, marginalization and social subjugation of queer subjects, relegating expressions of queerness to the darkened corners of public places and preferably to the privatized, subjugating, metaphorical space of the closet (Sedgwick 1990). According to Polchin (1997: 386), the phenomenon of pride parades and festivities encapsulates the (re)enactment of:

> a political expression of visibility within the public realm, and asserts a sense of self by locating the queer body within a particular social environment – namely, the street. Such visibility reacts against the confined space of the 'closet', which has been perhaps the most compelling metaphor for visibility and identity within gay and lesbian narratives in the past twenty-five years. The closet symbolizes the space of denial, darkness, confinement. To come out depends upon emerging from the spatial structures of the closet and into the public, onto the street.

The public performance of queer desires not only makes queerness visible, but can effect a temporary (re)articulation of space by twisting or 'queering' the normative spatialization of desire, undermining spatially constituted heterosexuality and threatening the social production of everyday space. For example, political strategies such as public kiss-ins, die-ins or mass gatherings of queers in typically unwelcoming places such as sports bars – tactics that commonly were employed by queer activist groups such as ACT UP (AIDS Coalition to Unleash Power), Queer Nation and Lesbian Avengers in the 1990s – challenge 'the essentialist construction of community with new spatial tactics for social change' (Davis 1995: 285). In those temporary moments when queerness invades heterosexual public space, a crack appears in the public/private partition, with each crack potentially weakening its fortification. Normative sexual geographies and concomitant spatial marginalization beget what Duncan (1996: 139) calls an 'everything in its place mentality'. Subsequently, when something such as a queer body is noticed as being 'out of place', it is not only the body, but also the sensibilities of spatial division and place-based appropriateness, that can become a public issue.

Pride for Sale

As I have argued, public sexual dissent has the potential to jeopardize the power and privilege that heterosexuality assumes though occupation of the public sphere. According to some, pride festivities can perform this function, queering space and revealing counter-public communities. However, with gay pride parades, festivals and parties in cosmopolitan Western cities now attracting considerable corporate sponsorship and featuring as major tourist attractions, there is growing concern that pride is rapidly being commodified, and pride festivals are becoming little more than displays of material consumption. The question, then, is whether pride has been reduced to festivalized spectacles of Otherness in the marketing of cities and commodities. Or is it still able to maintain its potential for political and sexual agitation?

According to Richards (2007: 270), 'the critique of festivalization is usually built on two premises: first, that the level of commodification is increasing; and second that the locus of control is shifting away from the civic and local toward the market and the global'. The question of pride festivals as a now desexualized commodity is, as Casey (2007: 126) argues, 'particularly visible in the growing move from community based sponsorship of lesbian and gay events to an intensification of corporate sponsorship by "mainstream" corporations such as Absolute Vodka, Red Bull, American Airlines, Virgin Atlantic and Qantas'. In an article on San Francisco's pride festival, Chadburn (2002) points to her outrage at what she refers to as 'queer visibility co-opted by consumerism', evidenced by 'creepy corporations like Budweiser, Smirnoff, and Clear Channel Communications literally jumping on the queer bandwagon, adding their own rolling advertisements to the parade'.

Furthermore, as Bell and Binnie (2004) remind us, pink economy[2] discourses and the globalization of pride festivals as mega-events and tourist attractions construct once undesirable sexual Others as now commercially desirable 'agents of consumer citizenship' (2004: 1809). For example, while watching the Sydney Mardi Gras parade is free, tickets are required to attend the majority of events on the month-long Sydney Gay and Lesbian Mardi Gras festival calendar, with events such as the infamous parade after-party and the harbourside dance party costing around A$130 each in 2011. As Markwell (2002: 84) has argued previously, 'full participation in the festival is an expensive undertaking, especially when coupled with the cost of outfits; body treatments such as waxing, tanning, gym training, hairstyling, and party drugs; and for tourists, accommodation and transportation costs'. Both the high costs and various norms around (predominantly male) self-presentation at the events disenfranchise many working-class, suburban and non-white and non-male-bodied people.

As pride festivals and mega-events become 'potent driver[s] for the international gay tourism industry', which 'inject[s] many millions of dollars into local economies' (Waitt and Markwell 2006: 245), a number of cities now incorporate pride celebrations into local marketing and promotion strategies. Organizations such as the International Gay and Lesbian Travel Association (www. iglta.org) or Gay and Lesbian Tourism Australia (www.galta.com.au) provide details of destinations, events and activities that may entice the gay or lesbian traveller, listing gay-specific or gay-friendly accommodation directories, tour companies and cruises, among other things. Many affiliated sites also offer special

---

2 'Pink economy' refers to the collective spending power of gays and lesbians. In 2007, gay media mogul Peter Walton stated that the conservative value of the pink dollar in Australia was $25 billion (Cincotta 2007).

accommodation package deals around the time of local pride festivities to entice the 'supposedly affluent' gay or lesbian tourist. While gentrified 'gay villages' and large-scale pride parades have, for some time now, been touted by gay media and gay travel agencies as 'must see' sites for the gay traveller (Johnston 2005; Waitt and Markwell 2006), these same sites are increasingly becoming liminal sites of interest and intrigue to the non-gay/queer traveller as well (Binnie 2004; Mason and Lo 2009; Rushbrook 2002). Moreover, as Mason and Lo suggest in their audience study of the Sydney Gay and Lesbian Mardi Gras, often for the non-gay/queer spectator, the 'ludic qualities of the parade ... mitigate against it being taken too seriously ... [It is] an encounter with the homosexual stranger in an environment that is secure because it requires little immediate comradeship, reciprocity or future obligation' (2009: 117).

According to Rushbrook, many cities now stake their claim to cosmopolitanism on promoting their more sexually risqué – but never perverse – enclaves: 'In a growing number of instances, "queer space" functions as one form of this ethnic diversity, tentatively promoted by cities both as equivalent to other ethnic neighbourhoods and as an independent indicator of cosmopolitanism' (2002: 183). With many pride festivities now featured on official national tourism calendars,[3] these events and the urban spaces they occupy often become more tightly controlled by police, and are subject to greater state intervention and planning restrictions (Binnie 2004). Pointing to an oft-cited example, in 1992 Montreal Pride's organizing committee attracted harsh criticism and a queer backlash when it set modesty rules and regulations for how people should dress and behave in the parade, warning against offensive or overtly sexual displays (Bell and Valentine 1995). In Manchester, Hughes (2006: 25) argues that the growing appeal of its 'GLBT festivals', increased awareness of Manchester as a 'gay village' and the 'influx of non-gay customers' have partly contributed to a 'de-gaying effect' (2006: 250). Therefore, while queers (usually gay men) are targeted as consumers in the grab for pink dollars, they also become commodities to be looked at and consumed by the straight exotic-seeking cosmopolitan tourist (see also Rushbrook 2002; Skeggs 2004).

The increased visibility of the sexual citizen and gay public spaces produces a commercialized, easily digestible and G-rated image of sexual differences that necessarily conforms to (hetero)normalized performances of gayness – or what Duggan (2003) calls the 'new homonormativity' of neoliberal sexual politics. Concomitantly, these new forms of generally white, middle-class gay male visibility and spatial reclamation disavow the non-commercial, indigestible and X-rated sexual dissident, forsaking what Casey (2007) might call the queer unwanted.

---

3   See for example Tourism Australia's listing of the Sydney Gay and Lesbian Mardi Gras at http://www.australia.com and the British Tourist Authority's listing of London Pride at https://www.visitengland.com.

The Shame of It All

In Probyn's study of the 1998 Gay Games[4] in Amsterdam, she is critical of the apolitical version of pride it peddles, reminding us that 'if we are to continue to mobilize the figure of Pride, we must also pay attention to its mirror image': shame (2000: 25). 'Pride is dependent on shame', says Munt, 'pride is predicated on the – sometimes conscious – denial of its own ostracized corollary, shame' (1998: 4). Moreover, argues Munt (2000: 536), 'the presence of shame has been repressed in the discourse of homosexual rights in an unhelpful way, and in order to gain greater agency, we must learn to revisit its ambivalent effects'. Shame is a volatile mechanism of exclusion and failure. However, as a counter-discursive strategy, shame can reveal the privilege afforded to some queer subjects at the expense of others. In the rush to assert gay pride, the polemic drive of shame directs critical attention to the most abject of queer proclivities: those that threaten to sully the image of the respectable white, middle-class gay male sexual citizen – he who pride has established as the (homo)norm. Shame, argues Halberstam (2005: 220), 'can be a powerful tactic in the struggle to make privilege (whiteness, masculinity, wealth) visible'.

While the assimilationist, neoliberal and self-affirming politics of 'official' post-Stonewall gay pride have successfully worked to transform and legitimize (albeit partially) same-sex desire in the West, removing the stigma of corporeal defectiveness, psychic trauma, mental illness, sinfulness and sexual perversion, these same politics work to conceal the unsettling and disreputable elements of queerness. Now that pride is increasingly a platform for civic, political and economic endorsement, those whose bodies, identities, social circumstances or desires pose a risk to the staid and marketable image of the (homo)sexual citizen – the poor, the homeless, the differently abled, people of colour, immigrants, unfeminine women, feminine men, fat bodies, ageing bodies, HIV positive people, trans people, bi/pansexuals, polyamorists, pederasts, sadomasochists, sex workers, drug users – find themselves out of place in bourgeois pride festivities. Moreover, as Halperin and Traub (2009: 9) suggest, 'in the context of gay pride celebrations, the presence of such marginal, or overtly sexual, populations can be a cause of shame'. Consequently, gay shame offers a site of refuge and solidarity for those who 'feel alienated from gay pride and who have had increasing difficulty finding a place for themselves in its civic pageants, with their contingents of gay policeman, lesbian mothers, business leaders, corporate employees, religious devotees, athletes, and politicians' (Halperin and Traub 2009: 9).

In the context of grassroots queer activism, gay shame emerged as an exhibition of hostility directed towards the commodification, sexual normalization and, one

---

4 The Gay Games (see www.gaygames.com) is an international sporting carnival similar to the Olympic Games. In addition to competitive sporting events, it also features a number of cultural events, including a band and choral festival, visual arts exhibitions and film screenings.

might argue, festivalization of gay pride events. In an antithetical response to the ethos of gay pride celebrations, in 1998 a group of direction-action queer activists, including Mattilda (aka Matt Bernstein Sycamore) launched the first Gay Shame Festival in Brooklyn, New York. According to Bernstein Sycamore (2004: 238)

> by 1998, New York's Gay Pride had become little more than a giant opportunity for multinational corporations to target marked gay consumers. The goal of Gay Shame was to create a free, all-ages space where queers could make culture and share skills and strategies for resistance, rather than just buy a bunch of crap.

The initial festival, which was held in June at the time of official pride festivities and reportedly attended by several hundred people, featured a range of free activities, music and theatrical performances, free vegan food, speeches, information and skill-building workshops. Participants were encouraged to dress in excessive or outrageous ways and to publicly perform their gender and/or sexual differences in a ludic and hyperbolized manner.

The success of the first Gay Shame Festival inspired other queer activist networks nationally and internationally – in, for example, Toronto, Stockholm, Barcelona, Atlanta and San Francisco – to stage their own spin-off festivities in following years. In 2002, members of the Gay Shame collective in San Francisco took it upon themselves to directly confront the official San Francisco Pride celebrants with what they termed a 'festival of resistance'. This took the form of the inaugural Gay Shame Awards. Angered by the San Francisco Pride committee's decision to adapt the motto of its corporate sponsor, Budweiser beer, as the official theme for the festival and parade that year,[5] the Gay Shame Awards emerged as a direct-action response to what they saw as the 'rabid assimilationist monster' of San Francisco Gay Pride (Bernstein Sycamore 2004). According the official Gay Shame Awards website:

> Held in late June near the time of the Pride Parade, the awards ceremony will be a festival of resistance, a queer takeover of the bland, whitewashed gayborhood and a chance to express our queer identities in ways other than just buying a bunch of crap ... We encourage you and your organization to nominate those institutions and individuals who should be ashamed of their disservice to the queer community, progressive politics and social justice – in other words, the CEOs, the landlords, the cops and the dot-com criminals who make 'gay' sound glum. We are particularly interested in the ways some gays and lesbians have traded their movement's radical roots for 'a place at the table'. It's a movement,

---

5   According to gay shame activists and subsequent media reports (see Bernstein Sycamore 2004; Chadburn 2002), the pride committee took Budweiser's motto, 'Be yourself – make it a Bud' and adapted it to 'be yourself – change the world', making the latter the official theme of the pride festival that year.

not a market – and we need your help to make sure the right people get the recognition they deserve. (Gay Shame San Francisco 2003)

In an approach similar to that of the Gay Shame collective, other radical queer activist organizations, such as UK-based Queer Mutiny, the US-based Bash Back! and, most prominently, the internationally renowned Queeruption, have also developed anti-capitalist festivals, staged as alternatives to mainstream pride festivals. In 2001, a local collective of Queeruption members held the first DIY 'alternative to pride' festival in London, called LaDiDah. It was an attempt to reclaim what organizers believed was a more radial, unapologetic and anti-exploitative ethos of pride, akin to the earlier efforts of the Gay Liberation Front (Queeruption 2001). According to a flyer handed out to participants that year, the organizers suggested:

> we want Mardi Gras[6] to be free and different from its current banality. Basically, Pride has been hijacked. What began as a free, community event has now become a commercial operation ('Mardi Gras') with a turnover of roughly £1,500,000. An expensive ticket system has been introduced, the political element has been dumbed down and the organisers have alienated the very people Pride was meant to exist for. Mardi Gras is now a sad reflection of the triumph of capitalism, just look at the overt sponsorship and the commodification of sexuality as an image. (cited in Brown 2007: 2691)

In addition to these local efforts, almost annually, Queeruption festivals have taken place in numerous international cities, including London (1998, 2002), New York (1999), San Francisco (2001), Berlin (2003), Amsterdam (2004), Sydney (2005), Barcelona (2005), Tel-Aviv (2006), Vancouver (2007) and Manchester (2010). In a political manoeuvre that was intended to draw critical attention to the WorldPride festival in Jerusalem in 2006, Queeruption decided to hold its event in Tel-Aviv in the same year. According to Queeruption organizers, WorldPride was being 'used as a chance for the Israeli office of foreign affairs to hide the government's war crimes behind a rainbow flag' (Queeruption 2006).

According to the numerous online discussion forums and articles about Queeruption festivities and Gay Shame events, all the celebratory elements of what one would expect at a regular pride festival – extravagant costuming, flamboyance, speeches, music, theatrics, dancing and performance, art and crafts, food and drinks – are present. However, most accounts of alternative festivities claim to be more dyke-centred, youth focused, racially inclusive, sex-radical and resolute opponents of corporate branding and capitalism (Bernstein Sycamore 2004; Brown 2007; Queeruption 2001). Symbolic of a counter-discursive challenge to what they see as the commodification of pride, hand-sewn

---

6 In 2001, London's pride festival was rebranded London Mardi Gras. The name LaDiDah was created as a playful yet political send-up of this rebranding.

banners and the consumption of communally prepared vegan food, for example, are pitted as 'ethical' alternatives to Budweiser and 'sweatshop-produced rainbow flags' (Bernstein Sycamore 2008).

Both conventional pride celebrations and their alternative forms evoke a postmodern challenge to traditional boundaries between oppositional categories, such as the marginal versus the mainstream, gay versus straight and queer versus gay. In the context of large-scale commodified pride festivals, this oppositional challenge works to subvert heteronormative culture through gay culture's ritualistic use of spectacle and celebration in its contestation of the straight heteropatriarchy and its 'naturalized' claim to public space. Thus, in a Western context, the challenge enacted through pride works primarily at the junction of identity politics and civil rights. While also employing spectacle and celebration, although in far less programmatic ways – ways that tend to be reactionary and revelatory rather than ritualized – smaller-scale alternatives to pride work to subvert both hetero- and homonormativity, not only challenging the normative discourses of straight culture and commodified sexual citizenship, but also employing shame as a tactical counter-discursive critique of the exclusionary politics operating within discourses of pride. In many ways, shame has emerged as a circular narrative that functions as a contestation of assimilationist pride rhetoric in the same way that pride originally emerged in contestation of what was then seen as the assimilationist goals of the homophile movement.

Of course, it is always problematic to assume that all 'mainstream' Western pride festivals operate in a passive bubble of consumption, and all pride celebrants seek assimilationist ends. As Kates and Belk (2001) argue in their study of Toronto Pride, consumption has ambiguous qualities and can also performatively function as resistance. While consumption may be difficult to align with radical political transgression, demonstrating market power through consumption can contribute to the social legitimization of gay communities. Moreover, political resistance can be 'conceptualized in the spectacle of the event itself, a key aspect of consumption in modernity' (Kates and Belk 2001: 404). Furthermore, is it not possible to celebrate pride in concert with tactical acknowledgements of shame? Drawing on the aforementioned discourses of pride and shame, in the final section of the chapter I will discuss the Brisbane Pride Festival in order to show how these discursive corollaries may be operative simultaneously.

Local Articulations of 'Pride'

It is currently July in Brisbane – where I live – and, like many other cities around the world, a month of pride celebrations has just come to an end for another year. This was the sixth year I had attended the Brisbane Pride Festival and the fifth year I had participated in the rally and march. Over the years, marching and attending cultural events and the fair day festivities has not only provided me with an emic understanding of how it feels to be a part of a collective pride demonstration in

Brisbane, it has also given me significant opportunity to observe and talk with other people marching and revelling. The personal communications and field observations from 2011, to which I refer in this section, were collected in situ, and more reflective notes on the actual festivities were made in a field journal the day following the 2011 Brisbane Pride march and fair day.

The Brisbane Pride festival began in 1990 and has occurred annually ever since. Initially, it was run by a collective and eventually incorporated as a non-profit organization in 2002. It is now the third largest annual LGBTIQ event in Australia (following the Sydney Gay and Lesbian Mardi Gras and Melbourne's Midsumma Festival) and the largest LGBTIQ event in Queensland. Queensland was one of the last Australian states to enact homosexual law reform, finally decriminalizing homosexual activity in 1990 (followed by Tasmania in 1997), and continues to uphold inequitable age of consent laws.[7] As is evidenced by placards carried by participants in the pride march, the festival offers a context to protest this discriminatory law as well as societal homophobia and institutional heterosexisms. Presently, and dominating the pride agenda for the last few years now, has been the right for gays and lesbians to marry.

Like most official pride celebrations, in its early years Brisbane Pride was primarily a political rally, where participants gathered in protest, then – stopping traffic – marched through the streets of Brisbane's CBD and gathered for celebrations in Musgrave Park, South Brisbane. Over the years, the march – which is famously led by the local Dykes on Bikes club – and park gathering grew into a four-week festival of creative arts, exhibitions, political and sporting events, workshops and parties at various venues around Brisbane. According to the festival website, the festival celebrations are attended by roughly 50,000 people annually, and the signature event on the pride calendar, the fair day celebrations in Musgrave Park, reports attendance of up to 25,000 people annually (Brisbane Pride 2011a).

Unlike pride mega-events in Australia, such as the Sydney Gay and Lesbian Mardi Gras – which, as stated earlier, requires significant expense if you wish to attend the celebratory dance party at the end of the parade – the Brisbane Pride Festival is relatively inexpensive. Anyone so inclined may take part in the march, and unlike the Mardi Gras parade, which is administered by New Mardi Gras Ltd, Brisbane Pride does not require marchers to register or pay a fee, nor does Brisbane Pride requires submission of creative concepts, banners and protest messages prior to the march for compliance checking against the organization's 'core values'. Brisbane Pride festival-goers can attend many free events, such as a Pride Choir sing-along, community barbecues and storytelling, queer family picnics and

---

7 As the law currently stands in Queensland, vaginal and oral sex is permissible at age 16; however, anal intercourse under the age of 18 is punishable under the Sodomy Law (§§ 208–209 of the Criminal Code of 1899) with up to 14 years' imprisonment. Queensland is the only state that still holds an unequal age of consent law, which potentially puts young people at greater risk of harassment, impedes strategies for HIV and AIDS prevention and hinders the provision of support services for Queensland's queer youth.

dance parties, as well as a range of free public forums on topics such as LGBTIQ racial and religious diversity, gender diversity, legal rights and marriage equality. Other ticketed events such as the fair day, film screenings, lawn bowls and roller skating activities, musical and theatre performances, a men's leather/bondage slave auction, women-only club nights and a selection of other dance parties, cost between A$5 and A$30 per entry, with the majority of events asking a A$10–$15 entry fee. Of course, entry fees are not the only expense that pride revellers will incur. At fair day and at ticketed pride parties, food and alcohol are sold, and prices are quite often inflated at this time. Moreover, at the fair day there is a range of market stalls touting the products of local gay and gay-friendly small businesses, such as rainbow pride flag t-shirts, bumper stickers and homewares, herbal highs, LGBTIQ books and DVDs. Seemingly of more concern to some pride revellers, is the small but increasing contingent of non-LGBTIQ-specific stalls and businesses present, such as mortgage lenders and travel agents, 'swooping in for their piece of the pink pie', as one fair day attendee remarked to me (field notes, 11 June 2011).

Unlike Sydney's Mardi Gras and Melbourne's Midsumma festival, which currently attract corporate sponsorship from the likes of Google, Foxtel and Virgin Australia in Sydney, and Telstra, Mercedes-Benz and IBM in Melbourne, Brisbane Pride has minimal mainstream corporate sponsorship. While Energex (a national utilities company) was cited as a supporter of different aspects of Brisbane Pride in 2011, sponsorship listing in programs and on websites appear largely community based, with local LGBTIQ businesses, media outlets, community health services and LGBTIQ-friendly businesses providing the majority of sponsorship and in-kind support (see www.pridebrisbane.org.au and www.brisbanecarnivale.com.au). Community discussion around the organization of the festival in 2011 demonstrate scepticism towards to level of involvement by local gay business owners, who some feel are profiteering from organizing pride events in venues that serve their financial interests and appeal to a largely middle-class gay male clientele (field notes, 7 May 2011). According to Markwell and Waitt's (2009) account of the Brisbane Pride Collective, in 1998 it was cynical about involving gay businesses in its fight for social change, and 'rejected the idea of becoming an incorporated organization to prioritize the ongoing aim of social transformation of a heteropatriarchal society through a collective structure' (2009: 160).

This would suggest that while Brisbane Pride is still far less 'branded' than Mardi Gras or Midsumma, it has been unable to resist commodification, as there is certainly some evidence of what Casey (2007) refers to as an intensification of corporate branding – an aspect Richards (2007) identifies as part of the festivalization process. Also indicative of this is the loss of self-regulation within the festival space. In both 2010 and 2011, many participants objected to 'seeing queers in cages' (field notes, 11 June 2011). By this, they meant the two caged-off designated areas for alcohol consumption and smoking that are now a legal requirement if Brisbane Pride is to be granted a festival permit. Objections to regulatory security fencing/caging are prevalent in Queeruption and Gay Shame literatures as well. Furthermore, the support/sponsorship and promotion of Brisbane Pride by the City Council and the Queensland government suggests that the arts and cultural elements of the festival potentially operate as mechanisms of urban economic and cultural policies (Knopp 1995). While assessing the degree of this incorporation is beyond the scope of this chapter, it is worth noting that as part of the pride festival in 2010, the Museum of Brisbane commemorated the 20-year anniversary of the decriminalization of homosexuality in Queensland with an LGBT local history exhibition.

In 2011, there was a significant shift in the management of the festival. While there were initial rumours in the community that the fair day would be cancelled altogether due to organizational and financial issues, eventually a caretaker committee was formed and a local gay media entrepreneur stepped in to financially back a fair day celebration. Subsequently, the fair day was rebranded Brisbane Carnivalé. The new management shifted the fair day to Perry Park on Brisbane's north side and, after some challenging negotiations with the local council and police, the route of the march was changed, beginning in Brisbane's Fortitude Valley – a renowned gentrified 'gay' inner-city suburb – and ending in Perry Park. While it is important to acknowledge that the event was modified in 2011, this does not directly impact on this discussion, as the structure and style of the festival as a whole remained largely unchanged. However, some people did remark that they felt the new march route was 'less subversive' than it normally was when conducted through the CBD (field notes, 11 June 2011). Similarly, in Johnson's study of pride parades in Australia and New Zealand, she too is of the opinion that parades in the CBD represent a queer infiltration of the 'public and "straight" mind' of a city. Conversely, the suburbs are analogous to a city's 'private gay "body"' – a space that is more appropriate for queer displays and thus less subversive (2005: 80). Apart from its early years, Brisbane's pride celebrations typically garner no mainstream media attention and even marching routes through the CBD have, in recent years, been amended to cause less of a disturbance. Unlike the nationally televised Sydney Mardi Gras parade, which is also staged in a gentrified gay suburb, this non-touristic, local affair appears to lack the shock value, scale and campish extravagance necessary to be either intriguing or repulsive enough to attract the heterosexual media's attention.

In the spirit of Stonewall commemorations, Brisbane Pride is held in June, and thus coincides with the region's winter. While the weather undoubtedly impacts on what one wears in the march and at the fair day, many people still choose to dress in elaborate clothing, drag, fetish attire and playful garish costumes, pointing to the carnivalesque tradition of celebrating the grotesque or sexual side of human nature (Bakhtin 1984). Bare skin, however, is an option only available to the bravest of celebrants, and it is one that few people choose to take up on a cold winter morning compared with the displays of flesh at other LGBTIQ festivities such as Big Gay Day that occur in Brisbane's summer months. Also representative of Bakhtin's (1984) topsy-turvy state of the carnival are those who employ satirical parody in their costume and self-presentation. By way of example, I point to one gay man who stood on the street across from this year's rally wearing a full nun's habit and waving a placard that said 'repent, rejoice, redecorate'. Nearby to him were a small group of 'genuine' Christian protestors bearing signs of the 'God hates homosexuals' and 'you will burn in hell' variety (field notes, 11 June 2011).

The rhetoric of post-Stonewall pride and the collective 'we' of a homogenized gay community with unified political goals are certainly evident in much of the references to pride celebrations in Brisbane's gay press. The official Brisbane Pride program reads:

> Want to tell *our* politicians that *we* want equality? Want to march for *gay* marriage? Want to march for GLBTI *solidarity*? Want to march demanding safer streets? Or do you just want to march in a colourful crowd and have fun? ... At the rally you can hear the *leaders of our community* speak about the issues that are *important to us*. Show your pride by creating a banner, or waving the rainbow flag and show the Brisbane public *we* can not [sic] be ignored. (Brisbane Pride 2011b: 9, emphasis added)

Community 'leaders' who spoke at the rally this year also drew on this rhetoric, championing 'our' communal force in the fight for mainstream acceptance, legislative change and marriage equality. While speakers seem careful to refer to 'our community' as the 'GLBT community' (sometimes remembering the 'I', but quite often not), I am yet to attend a pride rally where the political specificities of the 'Bs', 'Ts' and 'Ls' receive their due attention, let alone attending to the racial and class-based differences among us. Ceremonious gay pride seems to lack the robustness to attend to this diversity, and remains committed to showing 'those who have not experienced our community before ... [that] we're just like everyone else ... we are not different' (Brisbane Pride president Scott Hampson, cited in Smith 2010). However, the multiple subjectivities and degrees of difference between this supposed 'we' is clear when observing the pride celebrants themselves, and stands in stark contrast to the overwhelmingly homonormative and falsely unifying discourse of official pride orations.

Looking back on the ralliers as we proceeded to march, one could see that 'our' pride was multiple and contingent. Moreover, Brisbane's pride celebrations appear to function as a multi-discursive platform where, for example, members of the Lesbian and Gay Business Network could be seen marching alongside anti-capitalist collectives; LGBTIQ Christian groups could be seen marching alongside those demonstrating their collective pride as BDSM practitioners; and gay marriage lobbyists could be seen marching alongside people espousing polyamory. Some people marched in representative clusters, thus aligning their demonstration of pride with, for example, leather collectives, youth groups, ethnic communities, trans communities or political parties. Many people simply marched with their friends and even their pets, sometimes carrying portable music players and small amplifiers, chanting, laughing and dancing their way through the streets. Others marched in kinship-familial formation, some pushing strollers, some standing alongside their queer child.

Revellers ranged in age from the very young to the elderly, and although predominantly white, there was certainly a more visible presence of Indigenous and ethnic minorities in the pride march than there generally is at Brisbane's mainstream gay venues. Unlike the everyday gay spaces – bars, nightclubs, saunas – which some would argue are exclusive, predicated on the youthful white gay masculinity these spaces privilege, 'Pride is for everyone', said one participant. 'I see people here and it reminds you of everything beyond the scene, 'cause you don't see a lot of these people anywhere else and it's awesome', said another (field notes, 11 June 2011). Of the thousand-plus people who turn out to march, many carry balloons, rainbow flags, banners and placards that call attention to a broad range of LGBTIQ issues, some of which extend beyond those 'outsiders' might consider native to the LGBTIQ public sphere, such as anti-war, anti-racist and animal liberation slogans.

This year, however, one placard image dominated. It was an image from the Rip & Roll safe-sex advertising campaign, which only a week earlier had been removed from public display after the Australian Christian Lobby protested to the Advertising Standards Bureau. The ad, which was later reinstated, featured two fully clothed men hugging and smiling, one of whom was wearing a small crucifix on a chain around his neck. Coupled with outrageous comments by the Christian Lobby, which had previously likened gay marriage to 'legalizing child abuse', the removal of this ad sparked a huge controversy and the image quickly became a political motif for the 2011 pride rally (Blythe 2011).

I also noted a number of hand-made placards carried by small groups of people that stood in stark contrast to the collective force and the slick professional banners advertising prominent local gay businesses and homonormative organizations, such as gay marriage lobby group Equal Love. For example, one young man marched with a hand-painted cardboard sign reading 'let gays marry and be as unhappy as the rest of them' (field notes, 11 June 2011). Throughout the day, a number of conversations suggested that a minority of people who gathered to demonstrate their pride did so with a degree of hostility towards what a young genderqueer student activist referred to as the 'gaystream agenda' (field notes, 11 June 2011). In further conversation, while their anti-capitalist politics were ideologically at odds with all forms of marriage, they also acknowledged that, as a political platform, Pride needs to be available to everyone in the community. The political conflicts that separate the more radical queers from the so-called 'gaystream' did not appear to wholly prevent the former from participating in a celebration of pride and rallying around its discourse. In fact, many of those who clearly stood in opposition to homonormative politics (me included) used the pride march to express their counter-discourses and queerer proclivities. By carrying placards, wearing badges and slogans on their clothing, declaring their HIV status, dressing in sexually risqué fashion or marching as supporters of Indigenous reconciliation, many people demonstrated their refusal to be incorporated into the ostensibly unifying 'rainbow flag-waving brigade' (field notes, 11 June 2011). As one person remarked, 'while there's so much that makes you want to puke, I think of it as the real colours of queer on the streets: black, young, old, genderqueers, leathers, families, everyone, if only for a day' (field notes, 11 June 2011).

While shame was not a rubric under which people officially organized in opposition to Brisbane's Pride Festival, there is certainly evidence to suggest that shame-like discourse was not critically absent. But in Brisbane at least, it would seem that the rampant commodification and corporate branding of pride that are escalating in larger Australian capitals and global cities represent less of a threat to pride's relevance. More urgent, I would suggest, is the need to resituate more radical queer agendas that attend to race and gender inequalities, and work to counter exclusionary identity politics that impede the transformative potential of pride for *all* queers. Incorporating these forms of counter-discursive narratives into pride may be a way of dually exposing the cultural boundaries that marginalize LGBTIQ communities within the heteropatriarchal public sphere while also looking inwards, attending to the cultural boundaries that operate within LGBTIQ communities where cultural authority still appears to be the province of white gay men.

Conclusion

This chapter has examined the often contentious and paradoxical meanings and functions of pride festivals across a range of social, geographical and political contexts. Although all have their genesis in the post-Stonewall politics of pride, conflicting discourses of societal change, political transgression, spatial reclamation and commodification reconfigure pride protests and celebrations in accordance with local circumstances. Internal tensions arising from the increased festivalization of pride in global Western cities have provoked many to question its contemporary relevance, generating antidotal spectacles of shame predicated on pride's homonormalizing rhetoric and its 'uneven geometries of power and difference' (Markwell and Waitt 2009: 160). When comparing, for example, pride mega-events in London with bloody street scenes in Belgrade, the need for ongoing conscious-raising, transnational solidarity and transgressive tactics of special reclamation is indisputable. Thus the collective unity that pride engenders is certainly not redundant, but perhaps thinking through shame in order to deconstruct social processes that whitewash difference and unevenly distribute power might offer a way to reconfigure the ethics and effects of pride in the most rampant neoliberal contexts.

References

Alexander, J.C. 2004. Cultural pragmatics: Social performance between ritual and strategy. *Sociological Theory*, 22(4), 527–73.

Altman, D. 1972. *Homosexual Oppression and Liberation.* Sydney: Angus & Robertson.

Armstrong, E. and Crage, S. 2006. Movements and memory: The making of the Stonewall myth. *American Sociological Review,* 71, 724–51.

Bakhtin, M. 1984 [1968]. *Rabelais and His World,* translated by H. Iswolsky. Bloomington, IN: Indiana University Press.

Bell, D. and Binnie, J. 2004. Authenticating queer space: Citizenship, urbanism and governance. *Urban Studies,* 41(9), 1807–20.

Bell, D. and Valentine, G. 1995. Introduction: Orientations, in *Mapping Desire: Geographies of Sexualities,* edited by D. Bell and G. Valentine. London: Routledge, 1–27.

Bernstein Sycamore, M. 2004. Gay shame: From queer autonomous space to direct action extravaganza, in *That's Revolting: Queer Strategies for Resisting Assimilation,* edited by M. Bernstein Sycamore. Brooklyn, NY: Soft Skull Press, 237–62.

Bernstein Sycamore, M. 2008. There's more to life than platinum: Challenging the tyranny of sweatshop-produced rainbow flags and participatory patriarchy, in *That's Revolting: Queer Strategies for Resisting Assimilation,* 2nd edition, edited by M. Bernstein Sycamore. Brooklyn, NY: Soft Skull Press, 1–7.

Binnie, J. 2004. Quartering sexualities: Gay villages and sexual citizenship, in *City of Quarters: Urban Villages in the Contemporary City,* edited by D. Bell and M. Jayne. Aldershot: Ashgate, 163–72.

Blythe, A. 2011. Adshel caves to homophobic pressure. *Queensland Pride,* 1 June. Available at: queenslandpride.gaynewsnetwork.com.au/news/adshel-caves-to-homophobic-pressure-003597.html [accessed: 5 August 2011].

Brisbane Pride 2011a. Festival history. Available at: www.pridebrisbane.org.au/history [accessed: 19 July 2011].

Brisbane Pride 2011b. 2011 event guide. Available at: qnews.com.au/article/brisbane-pride-festival-guide-out-now [accessed: 20 July 2011].

Brown, G. 2007. Mutinous eruptions: Autonomous spaces of radical queer activism. *Environment and Planning A,* 39(11), 2685–91.

Brown, G., Browne, K. and Lim, J. 2007. Introduction, or why have a book on geographies of sexualities?, in *Geographies of Sexualities: Theory, Practice and Politics,* edited by K. Browne, J. Lim and G. Brown. Aldershot: Ashgate, 1–18.

Carter, D. 2010. *Stonewall: The Riots That Sparked the Gay Revolution.* New York: St Martins Press.

Casey, M. 2007. The queer unwanted and their undesirable 'otherness', in *Geographies of Sexualities: Theory, Practice and Politics,* edited by K. Browne, J. Lim and G. Brown. Aldershot: Ashgate, 125–36.

Chadburn, A. 2002. The problem with pride. *San Francisco Bay Guardian,* 26 June. Available at: www.sfbg.com/36/39/cover_shame.html [accessed: 19 July 2011].

Cincotta, K. 2007. Queer eye for the pink buy. *B&T,* 20 November. Available at: www.bandt.com.au/news/bb/0c051dbb.asp [accessed: 5 August 2011].

Corber, R. and Valocchi, S. 2003. Introduction, in *Queer Studies: An Interdisciplinary Reader*, edited by R. Corber and S. Valocchi. Oxford: Blackwell, 1–17.

Davis, T. 1995. The diversity of queer politics and the redefinition of sexual identity and community in urban spaces, in *Mapping Desire: Geographies of Sexualities*, edited by D. Bell and G. Valentine. London: Routledge, 284–303.

D'Emilio, J. 1983. *Sexual Politics, Sexual Communities: The Making of the Homosexual Minority in the United States, 1940–1970*. Chicago, IL: University of Chicago Press.

Duberman, M. 1993. *Stonewall*. New York: Dutton.

Duggan, L. 2003. *The Twilight of Equality?: Neoliberalism, Cultural Politics, and the Attack on Democracy*. Boston, MA: Beacon Press.

Duncan, N. 1996. Renegotiating gender and sexuality in public and private spaces, in *BodySpace: Destabilising Geographies of Gender and Sexuality*, edited by N. Duncan. London: Routledge, 127–45.

Falassi, A. 1987. Festival definition and morphology, in *Time Out of Time: Essays on the Festival*, edited by A. Falassi. Albuquerque, NM: University of New Mexico Press, 1–10.

Foucault, M. 1979. *The History of Sexuality: Vol. 1. An Introduction*, translated by R. Hurley. London: Allen Lane.

Gay Shame San Francisco. 2003. Gay shame seeks nominations for annual shame awards. Gay Shame San Francisco, 18 April. Available at: www.gayshamesf.org/awards2003.html [accessed: 19 July 2011].

Gruszczynska, A. 2009. Sowing the seeds of solidarity in public space: Case study of the Poznan March of Equality. *Sexualities*, 12(3), 312–33.

Halberstam, J. 2005. Shame and white gay masculinity. *Social Text*, 23(3–4), 219–33.

Halperin, D. 2009. Why gay shame now?, in *Gay Shame*, edited by D. Halperin and V. Traub. Chicago, IL: University of Chicago Press, 41–46.

Halperin, D. and Traub, V. 2009. Beyond gay pride, in *Gay Shame*, edited by D. Halperin and V. Traub. Chicago, IL: University of Chicago Press, 3–40.

Hughes, H. 2006. Gay and lesbian festivals: Tourism in the change from politics to party, in *Festivals, Tourism and Social Change: Remaking Worlds*, edited by D. Picard and M. Robinson. Clevedon, OH: Channel View Publications.

Johnston, B. 2000. Rome defies Vatican to go gay for a day. *The Telegraph*, 9 July. Available at: www.telegraph.co.uk/news/worldnews/europe/italy/1347643/Rome-defies-Vatican-to-go-gay-for-a-day.html [accessed: 22 July 2011].

Johnston, L. 2005. *Queering Tourism: Paradoxical Performances at Gay Pride Parades*. New York: Routledge.

Jones, C.C. 2010. Playing at the queer edges. *Leisure Studies*, 29(3), 269–87.

Kates, S. and Belk, R. 2001. The meanings of lesbian and gay pride day: Resistance through consumption ad resistance to consumption. *Journal of Contemporary Ethnography*, 30(4), 392–429.

Knopp, L. 1995. Sexuality and urban space: A framework for analysis, in *Mapping Desire: Geographies of Sexualities*, edited by D. Bell and G. Valentine. London: Routledge, 149–61.

Markwell, K. 2002. Mardi Gras tourism and the construction of Sydney as an international gay and lesbian city. *GLQ: A Journal of Lesbian and Gay Studies*, 8(1–2), 81–91.

Markwell, K. and Waitt, G. 2009. Festivals, space and sexuality: Gay pride in Australia. *Tourism Geographies*, 11(2), 143–68.

Mason, G. and Lo, G. 2009. Sexual tourism and the excitement of the strange: Heterosexuality and the Sydney Mardi Gras Parade. *Sexualities*, 12(1), 97–121.

Munt, S.R. 1998. Introduction, in *Butch/Femme: Inside Lesbian Gender*, edited by S.R. Munt. London: Cassell, 1–11.

Munt, S.R. 2000. Shame/pride dichotomies in *Queer as Folk. Textual Practice*, 14(3), 531–46.

Lowen, M. 2010. Scores arrested in Belgrade after anti-gay riot. *BBC News Europe* 10 October. Available at: www.bbc.co.uk/news/world-europe-11507253 [accessed: 24 July 2011].

Polchin, J. 1997. Having something to wear: The landscape of identity on Christopher Street, in *Queers in Space: Communities, Public Places, Sites of Resistance*, edited by G.B. Ingram, A. Bouthillette and Y. Retter. Seattle: Bay Press, 381–90.

Probyn, E. 2000. Sporting bodies: Dynamics of shame and pride. *Body and Society*, 6(1), 13–28.

Queeruption. 2001. Can't really afford Mardi Gras 2001? Then come along to LaDiDah. Available at: www.queeruption.org/queeruption4/background.htm [accessed: 19 July 2011].

Queeruption. 2006. *Queeruption 9: August 3rd–13th Tel-Aviv*. Available at: queeruption.org/q2006/index.html#Invitation [accessed: 19 July 2011].

Richards, G. 2007. The festivalization of society or the socialization of festivals? The case of Catalunya, in *Cultural Tourism: Global and Local Perspectives*, edited by G. Richards. Binghamton: Haworth Press, 257–80.

Rushbrook, D. 2002. Cities, queer space, and the cosmopolitan tourist. *GLQ: A Journal of Lesbian and Gay Studies*, 8(1–2), 183–206.

Sedgwick, E.K. 1990. *Epistemology of the Closet*. New York: Harvester Wheatsheaf.

Skeggs, B. 2004. *Class, Self, Culture*. London: Routledge.

Smith, A. 2010. Brisbane Pride 2010. *SameSame*, 1 June. Available at: www.samesame. com.au/features/5422/Brisbane-Pride-2010.htm [accessed: 24 July 2011].

Sullivan, N. 2003. *A Critical Introduction to Queer Theory*. Armadale, Vic: Circa.

Tatchell, P. 2011. Moscow police collude with neo-Nazis. *Peter Tatchell: Human Rights, Democracy, Global Justice, LGBTI Freedom*, 29 May. Available at: www. petertatchell.net/international/russia/moscow-pride-police-collude-with-neo-nazis.htm [accessed: 24 July 2011].

Turner, V. 1982. *Celebration: Studies in Festivity and Ritual*. Washington, DC: Smithsonian Institute Press.

UK Gay News 2011. Split Gay Pride abandoned amid riots by 10,000 anti-gay protestors. *UK Gay News*, 11 June. Available at: www.ukgaynews.org.uk/Archive/11/Jun/1104.htm [accessed: 24 July 2011].

Valentine, G. 1996. (Re)negotiating the 'heterosexual street': Lesbian productions of space, in *BodySpace: Destabilising Geographies of Gender and Sexuality*, edited by N. Duncan. London: Routledge, 146–55.

Valentine, G. 2002. Queer bodies and the production of space, in *Handbook of Lesbian and Gay Studies*, edited by D. Richardson and S. Seidman. London: Sage, 145–60.

Waitt, G. and Markwell, K. 2006. *Gay Tourism: Culture and Context*. Binghamton, NY: Haworth Press.

Chapter 3

The Logics of Sacrifice at Visionary Arts Festivals

Graham St John

If a new paradigm based on principles of sustainability, compassion and integral wisdom finds the space to flourish, then the conditions may be set to begin remedying and reprogramming humanity's more savage and lethal tendencies. (*Boom Book* 2007: 77)

Space started bending and this wind came to spiral the entire party off into another dimension. A time/space portal opened up to put me into this futuristic dream, where we were all part of this PERFECT world. (Omananda 2004)

Amid concerns of rapacious change and rampant consumption, the first statement in the epigraph is about the purpose of the Liminal Village (subsequently the Liminal Zone) at the 2006 Boom Festival in Portugal, while the second was inspired by an experience at Boom's Dance Temple in 2002, with its mind-altered author having ingested '2 grams of Hawaiian mushrooms'. Described as a 'temple for a planetary culture', the Liminal Zone is a centre for an 'interactive curriculum spotlighting emergent mythologies, integrative philosophies, and techniques for sustainable and holistic living',[1] instrumentalized via a range of media, including workshops, panels, presentations, art galleries, cinema and theatre. In 2002, the Dance Temple was a gigantic geodesic dome, an arena evolving in the subsequent decade to become one of the world's largest outdoor dancefloors, host to multiple genres of psychedelic trance music. The Liminal Zone and the Dance Temple stand in relation to each other like the head to the body of the world's premiere visionary arts dance festival, which in 2010 attracted nearly 25,000 people holding passports from some 75 countries.[2] From the contemplative audiences of the Liminal Zone to the ecstatic massive of the Dance Temple, these event-hubs at this biennial festival represent diverse and yet integral aspects of *visionary arts culture* and the psychedelic movement in which it is rooted. Boom and other events like the Burning Man in Nevada harbour experiments in intentional ritualization, as the active embrace of the concept of the 'liminal' conveys. Featuring sometimes contested and other times complementary ritualizations, these and related festivals

---

1 'Transmissions from the Edge'. Available at: boomfestival.org [accessed: 9 February 2007].

2 Official Boom figures.

are dynamic expressions of their diverse counter-cultural roots and the integral dimensions of the visionary experience to which its participants aspire. This chapter examines the liminal noise (hyperliminality) of such events by way of an investigation of what I identify as *logics of sacrifice* motivating participants. The elucidation of these logics will assist clarification of the cultural heterogeneity of contemporary arts festivals.

The chapter was produced as part of longitudinal and multi-sited research I have conducted on global psytrance culture since the mid-1990s (see St John 2012a).[3] It is designed to contribute to an understanding of the interfacing of pleasure/politics and spirituality/technology within the visionary arts movement, as expressed in its paramount cultural achievements (that is, its festivals). It offers an introduction to the congruity of transgressive and progressive pursuits of participants and event management within these events, figured as the iterated result of decades of optimization. The study belongs to a body of ethnographic and documentary literature on alternative cultural festivals and gatherings that has flourished largely since the 1960s and 1970s. Much of this research recognizes heterogeneity and complexity, and does not subsume events under singular narratives and one-dimensional frameworks typically adopted by commentators who are often far removed from events, and by advocates who may indeed be too close to the events in question. A classic entry on the mosaic of freedoms sought and enacted at the United Kingdom's early 'free' and 'pop' festivals was Michael Clarke's *The Politics of Pop Festivals* (1982). The complex of 'ultimate concerns' recognized as being performed by participants within alternative cultural festivals – such as the Maleny Folk Festival's (now Woodford Folk Festival's) 'Fire Event' (Lewis and Dowsey-Magog 1993) and Australia's alternative lifestyle festival ConFest (St John 1997, 2001) – offer background to this study. Also pertinent is research I have conducted on the 'vibe' as the core festal moment across electronic dance music cultures (EDMC) (St John 2009a). In the case of ConFest, the recognition of the event as an 'alternative cultural heterotopia' advanced upon the study of traveller festivals in the United Kingdom (see Hetherington 2000) and in the case of EDMC, 'the vibe' was considered to possess a 'hyper-responsive' character shaped by the multiple intentions of participants.

While there has been little research conducted on visionary arts – or psychedelic – festivals to date, related extant research includes ethnographies and cultural histories of alternative music and arts festivals that have addressed politics internal to events as well as tensions with non-festival communities – for example, the Rainbow Gathering (Niman 1997), Glastonbury Festival (McKay 2000), Beaulieu Jazz Festival (McKay 2004), Stonehenge Summer Solstice Festival

---

3   The material in this chapter draws on a mixed-methods approach that incorporates fieldwork at the Boom Festival in 2006, 2008 and 2010, along with various other festivals, interviews conducted in situ at events and conversations conducted electronically with event organizers and festival participants, as well as the analysis of movement niche media and micro-media.

(Worthington 2004), and Burning Man Festival (Jones 2011) – and there is a sub-body of work addressing the radical, spiritual and ritual multiplicity of Burning Man (see Gilmore and Van Proyen 2005; Bowditch 2010; Gilmore 2010).[4] While these are important studies, the current project makes a specific entry on visionary arts festival culture. This culture is recognized as a *culture of experience*, which itself carries an ecstatic/reflexive dynamic rooted in occultic traditions, romanticism, bohemianism, the trad jazz festival scene of the 1950s and the psychedelic counter-culture of the 1960s/1970s, with its turn to the East. From this latter period, *visionary arts* had its most effusive expression within alternative gatherings and festivals accommodating interactive media, performance and dance, where an assemblage of modified sensory technologies – digital, chemical and cyber – have been optimized and deployed in the interests of consciousness dissolution and expansion. Such events have evolved rapidly since the mid- to late 1990s. Erik Davis, who is a past presenter at Boom's Liminal Village, pointed to the significance of these festivals, exemplified by Boom and Burning Man. As he stated in a zine distributed at Boom 2008, the visionary festival is recognized as

> an incubator of novelty. A petri dish of possibility where the future forms of community and consciousness are explored. We often think that our social pleasures are separate from the serious work of envisioning and implementing a more healthy, harmonious and sustainable world. But the festival suggests that maybe our future lies in both directions at once and that maybe you can have your cake and eat it too. (Davis 2008: 50)

In an effort to uncover the internal logics of these events and their roots, this chapter investigates both of the 'directions' to which Davis refers.[5]

Goa Trance and Visionary Arts Festivals

The visionary arts festival has its immediate roots in the seasonal party scene that evolved in Goa in India from the late 1960s through to the early 1990s. Over that period, a 'trance dance' culture emerged that was shaped first by cosmic rock fusion through the 1970s and then electronic music in the 1980s. Through the 1980s, Goa became a DJ-led scene with influences from a host of electronic

---

4   Indeed, Burning Man may be considered to be the exemplary visionary arts event, given its commitment to the 'ten principles', as outlined on the Burning Man website. Available at: www.burningman.com/whatisburningman/about_burningman/principles.html [accessed: 9 October 2011].

5   Thereby complementing a body of work I have produced on psytrance and its festivals. The disparate liminal logics of alternative culture were first observed to be in practice at the 2007 Sonica Festival in Italy (St John 2010a), and core tensions in the global psytrance movement are addressed in St John (2012).

music styles imported by traveller DJs and mixed at parties in this seasonal haven for self-exiled 'freaks' from around the world. By the mid-1990s, 'Goa trance' had become a genre and marketed commodity, developing into 'psytrance' and numerous sub-genres thereafter. In this period, mass tourism, and criminal and regulatory forces conspired in the demise of the scene in Goa (D'Andrea 2007; Saldanha 2007; Elliott 2010), and by the late 1990s Goa/psytrance festivals had appeared in many national locations, as scene brokers, DJ-producer 'ambassadors', label heads and party promoters translated the Goa 'state of mind'. As Goa/psytrance was transposed from Goa to local scenes (see St John 2010b), events – from smaller parties to major international festivals – mushroomed all over Europe (beginning in the United Kingdom, Germany and France), Israel, North America, Australia, Japan, South Africa, Mexico, Brazil and elsewhere in South America, typically accommodating a diversity of sub-scenes and styles. Lasting overnight or perhaps over week-long campouts, events would be held in open-air locations with dancefloors positioned in bushland, forest, beach or desert settings, with participants often celebrating celestial events (e.g. the full moon or a total solar eclipse) or holding parties to mark seasonal transitions. Indeed, the full moon was an occasion for parties in Goa from the late 1960s, and the passage from the night into sunrise was especially marked at these events.

Emerging during a period of optimism (from the late 1980s to the late 1990s), which saw the collapse of the Soviet Union and the end of the Cold War, the dismantling of apartheid in South Africa, the popularization of the drug ecstasy (MDMA) and the internet, a unique and yet diverse transnational movement evolved, the chief expressions of which were ephemeral open-air communities in which ecstatic dancing to electronic music mixed by DJs remained the central activity. This development was achieved as individuals travelled physically from 'home' locations and mentally from normative subjectivity – freedoms of movement enabled by relative disposable wealth and assisted by transpersonalizing digital, chemical and virtual media. The simultaneous 'horizontal' and 'vertical' mobility typical of 'neo-nomads' frequenting sites like Ibiza and Goa occasioned rather diverse pursuits and outcomes, including 'self-cultivation' and 'self-derailment' (D'Andrea 2007: 6). Given the multiplicity of sites, expectations and aesthetics, the psycho-geographic mobility – transnational and transpersonal – experienced within this movement is characteristically heterogeneous.

Goa trance became a worldwide festival traveller phenomenon, heir to this heterogeneity. Initially, these festivals were havens for expatriate travellers, and with such traveller festivals mounted in locations the world over at different times throughout the calendar, a festival traveller culture developed, contiguous with earlier festival traveller scenes – notably that of the UK free festival tradition (see Partridge 2006). Festivals became chief contexts for 'travellers of the world' to party and partygoers to become 'worldly' travellers. Even cursory glances at scene publications like *Mushroom Magazine*, *Psychedelic Traveller* and Chaishop.com reveal that events manifesting in far-flung locations into the 2000s would become contexts within which those who had never set foot in Goa – or indeed anywhere else in India – or perhaps had never travelled far from home or taken LSD, could access the Goa exile sensibility. Travel and entrance to festivals would constitute an initiatory experience once associated with backpacking to Goa and other sites. Goa festivals like Germany's Voov and Antaris Project, and France's Gaia Festival, along with many others that emerged in their wake, developed into outlandish worlds apart, where one could experience transportation from the ordinary into the extraordinary. In these psychedelic festivals, one could meet in chai tents, shop in bazaars and head shops, do yoga and meditation workshops, relax in chill zones, experience a fusion of world and electronic musics, and converge on exotic dancefloors. Technologies of transcendence were assembled and integrated to facilitate the experience of being-in-transit, with such events becoming the norm for a variety of participants, including those John Robert Howard identified as the 'plastic hippies' – that is, those who simply wear the paraphernalia of the outsider and adopt the requisite codes of rebellion, where the 'symbols which might at one time have powerfully expressed outrage at society's oppression and absurdity become merely fashionable and decadent' (Howard 1969: 50) – and those he identified as 'visionaries'.

These evolving visionary arts events – where the *arts* include all media of art and thus all sensory medium, not simply the 'visual' – weren't simply occasions for the consumption of art produced by the few for the many, but rather catered for a collective participation in mystical experiences involving multi-mediated and synesthetic expression of altered states and alternative styles of living. For DJ, *sadhu* and raconteur Goa Gil, psytrance events are indeed staged as an initiation ritual in which the ego is ostensibly shattered in an 'apocalypse' of the self, assisted by the DJed performance of dark trance or 'darkpsy' (see St John 2011a). In other cases, events are campaign stages for drug reform and cognitive liberty, and sustainable energy use, as well as for practitioners in the integral well-being movement. Events, then, are 'cultural dramas' (Turner 1984) for the performance of a host of agendas, but notably occasions in which *transition* is itself an ultimate concern, operationalized and dramatized according to variable intent, and in response to various lifeworld conditions actors seek to alter in temporary or more enduring commitments. The Boom Festival's Liminal Zone exemplifies this conscious effort to adopt a language, architecture and vision of initiation using anthropological discourse forged in the study of ritual, and specifically ritual-initiation thresholds.[6]

---

6   It was reported in the *Boom Book* (2007: 88) that 'liminal' comes from the Latin word for 'threshold' (*limen*) and identifies Victor Turner (1982, 1984), whose theories are reported to 'use liminality to describe the quality of the second stage of a rite of passage where the participant undergoes a transformation of some kind. The liminal, in this respect is a realm where one's sense of identity dissolves, suspending one's normal limits of thought, self-understanding and behavior'.

Sustainable Entertainment and the Logics of Sacrifice

In these festival contexts, designed to maximize the trance dance experience, the assembled technologies of the senses – including psychoactive compounds,[7] music and audio systems, lighting and visual projections, décor and so on – facilitate the temporary liquidation of *differences* and the enduring expression of *difference* via optimized and prolonged alteration of spatio-temporal conditions. The circumstance is that of a profusion of 'tribal' styles in the Maffesolian dynamic (Maffesoli 1996). The proliferation of electronic music styles impacting on and influencing populations who themselves continuously cut'n'mix from this profusion speaks of the 'compositional sensibilities' of the last few decades (Bennett 1999: 610), and of the 'cosmopolitan emotion' (Rietveld 2010) felt by citizens of global cities who seek attachments outside ethno-nationalism, circumstances oiled by post-1960s psychedelia, amplified by post-1980s electronic arts scenes and virtualized by post-1990s and 2000s net culture. But while the *tribus* offers a useful lens on fleeting engagements, multiple sites of belonging and re-enchantment – especially in observations on a scene that itself frequently adopts the 'tribe' moniker – Maffesoli's perspective falls short of recognizing the variable and competing movements of intent – or indeed consciousness – within event culture. Events within the visionary trance dance movement are designed to facilitate the dissipation and/or expansion of consciousness, attracting participants partial to these variable and sometimes competing pursuits, who may form camps dedicated to getting wasted by obliterating rational consciousness and evading responsibility, or to raising consciousness in the quest to evolve a responsible 'planetary culture'.[8] These extremes in event behaviour illustrate that the 'freedoms' sought by participants are not singular, and that the 'trance' experience is not homogeneous.

This diversity has deep historical roots. The 'vibe' is the term most commonly adopted by insiders to characterize the trance party experience. It holds currency across EDMCs, as reported by researchers who have often explained this by way of 'communitas' (see St John 2009a: 94–5) – a circumstance where individuals, often strangers to one another, may obtain in gatherings of extraordinary 'energy', a spontaneous 'flash of mutual understanding on the existential level, and a 'gut' understanding of synchronicity' (Turner 1982: 48). Yet commentators often miss the drama native to the 'vibe' and its diverse actors, just as the Turners may have stressed unity in pilgrimage and other social liminal occasions at the expense of cultural discord and power contestation. As 'realms of competing discourses',

---

7   Ordinarily a diversity of substances, including marijuana and *charas*, MDMA (ecstasy), LSD, *psilocybin*-containing mushrooms, DMT, methamphetamines, ketamine, cocaine and mescaline.

8   Spatial constraints have prevented further discussion on this division in 'consciousness' and its interfacing within the precincts of visionary arts festivals, but for further detail see St John and Baldini (2012).

pilgrimage centres are thought to accentuate as much as they dissolve distinctions between pilgrims and travellers (Eade and Sallnow 1991). Similarly, traveller festivals and other EDM events may facilitate the performance of difference at the same time as they annihilate distinctions. As the ultimate liminal zone – or, perhaps more accurately, 'interzone' (Burroughs 1992) – Goa was an enduring context not only for the obliteration of memories and national identity in apocalyptic party paroxysms, but for the construction of meaningful alternatives, a perplexing circumstance inherited by festivals arising in the gulf stream of Goa. Such events are host to discrepant liminal figures who have long populated experimental centres, notably the bohemian district that acted as an explosive mid-1960s progenitor site for the cultural logics to come.

San Francisco's Haight-Ashbury district had been recognized as a 'crucible of dynamic interchange' in a period when 'left wing activists cross-fertilized with turned-on poets, drifters, artists and dropouts that were refashioning themselves into living articulations of the struggle against bureaucracy' (Lee and Shlain 1985: 168). At the close of this scene, sociologists recognized that the 'indigenous typifications' of 'head' and 'freak' reflected 'ongoing value tensions in the subculture ... a millenial vision of society versus an apocalyptic one' (Davis and Munoz 1968: 161). In John Robert Howard's classic analysis of the 'internal contradictions of the hippie ethic', 'freaks' and 'heads' are contrasted with 'visionaries' like those who underwent 'voluntary poverty' in their repudiation of property, prejudice, and preconceptions of im/morality (Howard 1969: 46, 47). The counter-cultural dynamic of political activism and playful creativity that Frank Musgrove regarded as 'the dialectics of utopia' (1974: 16) came to shape liminalities, lifestyles and festivals thereafter. As a convergence of disparate counter-cultural elements, the Gathering of the Tribes in Golden Gate Park on 14 January 1967 is often celebrated as the scene's high-water mark. Twenty years hence, the ecstatic/activist crucible of San Francisco sired the 'hypercommunity' (Kozinets 2002) that is Burning Man, held annually in Nevada's Black Rock Desert. More recently, California's Symbiosis Gathering, promoted as an 'eco-music festival', and various other visionary music and cultural events, have grown from the region, including San Francisco's annual How Weird Street Faire, which evolved from the Consortium of Collective Consciousness traveller parties held in a warehouse in Howard St from 1995, initiated by returned Goa 'ambassadors'.

But the most important descendent of the Goa 'state of mind', and heir to its schizoid condition, is Portugal's Boom Festival. From the outset, Boom was designed as an extension of Goa seasons, while at the same time providing an alternative to the 'open air *underground discotheque*' reputedly characterizing most festivals at the time (*Boom Book* 2007: 27). Initiated in 1997 by Diogo Ruivo and Pedro Carvalho (who met as children in Goa), Boom is held by a lake near the village of Idanha-a-Nova in the mountainous Beira Baixa province. Promoted as a 'harmonic convergence of people, energy, information and philosophies from around planet earth and beyond', and commanding 'a balance of the organic and the cyber-technologic',[9] Boom has become a pilgrimage centre for participants in the global visionary arts community.[10] As a stage for freaks and visionaries (not to mention 'plastic hippies') to communicate and exchange, a model for transgressive and proactive lifestyle practices rooted in the earlier counter-culture, and a vehicle for amnesia and conscientiousness, Boom is a producer of what it calls 'sustainable entertainment'. Boom and other events in the Goa tradition facilitate the expression of differential logics of practice. On the one hand, there is the social orgiasm of the dance party whose intoxicated habitués hold concern for what is *happening now* – indeed deploying an assemblage of technologies of the senses to invest in making *now* last longer. Here, participants are physically im/ mobilized by bass, to which they may be said to willingly surrender. On the other, they become mobilized in the service of causes other than self-indulgence. Here, movement concerns are dramatized within events by those who raise awareness of crises, such that the festival becomes a staging ground, a recruitment centre, for the personal, social, cultural and political transitions desired. When motivated by the former attitude, habitués are preoccupied with today or tonight, where nothing matters more than *nothing*. In the latter, they are responsive to risks to themselves and the world, with festal occupants (in possession of humanitarian, ecological and well-being concerns) anxious about life 'after the orgy'. While the former prolong the eternal present, the latter are bent on reclaiming the future.

These festal aptitudes or 'works' possess logics of sacrifice pursuant to varying ideas of the sacred. The former can be recognized with the assistance of Georges Bataille (1989), since the expenditure of that which he recognized as society's 'accursed share' constitutes a path towards obtaining a sacred otherness in which those formerly separate may share intimately as they 'consume *profitlessly*':

> If I thus consume immoderately, I reveal to my fellow beings that which I am *intimately*: Consumption is the way in which *separate* beings communicate. Everything shows through, everything is open and infinite between those who consume intensely. (Bataille 1989: 58–9, italics in original)

While psytrance festivals are remote from the violence of human sacrifice inspiring Bataille at this juncture, these comments nevertheless evoke the subterranean and orgiastic communication transpiring within their precincts. As dancefloor occupants experience the diminution of their status as separate 'things', a shared chemical and sonorous romance softens the boundaries between unique individuals. But while such festivals facilitate the means by which enthusiasts 'spend' their personal resources in the pursuit of transcendence, they also enable practices (personal and environmental) of resource conservation, most often expressed as 'sustainable' or 'self-sustainable' practice. Articulated in the

---

9 According to promotions for the 2008 edition. Available at: www.boomfestival.org [accessed: 9 June 2008].

10 For further relevant analyses of Boom, see St John (2009b, 2012).

'carbon neutral', 'low footprint' and self avowedly 'green' lifestyles of the ethical consumer, for whom resource conservation and renewable energy are paramount, sustainability practices and incentives adopted within alternative festival culture draw attention to an underlying tension played out between commitments to spend and to conserve/recycle energy. Within the context of dance events, this *intracultural energy crisis* sees a sometimes tense dialogue between those whose practices, passions and causes are diametrically opposed, their commitments and causes determining how events are interpreted and evaluated. At other times, events facilitate compromise between disparate parties expressing variant logics, and indeed internal resolutions within individual event entrants.

Edgework: Rites of Risk

The visionary/psychedelic festival is first and foremost a dance festival whose participants may spend dozens of hours on dancefloors experiencing altered states of consciousness over the course of week-long events that participants have often travelled great distances to attend. The physical 'trip' to remote and exotic regions at the risk of one's health and person, and the psychological 'trip' resulting from the use of psychoactive substances (risking one's rational consciousness, and also one's mental health), combine in the psychedelic festival to potentiate liberation and fulfilment in ways paralleling risk-taking within extreme sports like skydiving and motorcycle riding, and other forms of wild recreation in which one voluntarily abandons 'home', sobriety and certainty. As such, psychedelic festivals exist among extreme and experimental leisure industries, facilitating the performance of psycho-somatic risk-taking in the tradition of voluntary 'edgework' that, according to Stephen Lyng (2005: 9), includes recreational pursuits as a 'means of freeing oneself from social conditions that deaden or deform the human spirit through overwhelming social regulation and control'. It is no coincidence that publications like *Psychedelic Traveller* magazine promote psytrance scenes in nations like New Zealand alongside other adventurous and risk-laden leisure pursuits such as white-water kayaking and bungee jumping.

Arguing provocatively that 'the physical limit has come to replace the moral limit that present-day society no longer provides', David Le Breton (2000: 1) initiated discussion on states of ecstasy and spirituality deriving from ordeals associated with elective challenges to one's own physical limits. Le Breton's observations shed light on the significance for travellers of dance pushing physical and emotional limits (in conjunction with moral limits) in remote outdoor locations:

> Through extreme exhaustion, the ecstasy that fuses an individual with the cosmos, gives only a temporary feeling of royalty but the memories will last and will be there to remind him or her of the pre-eminence of their own personal value; the privilege of having merited such a moment of bliss is acquired.

While trance dancing hardly possesses the perils of bungee jumping or skydiving, the following passage is compelling:

> Playing on the razor's edge is an elegant way of putting one's life on a par with Death for an instant in order to steal some of its power. In exchange for exposing oneself to the loss of life, the player intends to hunt on Death's territory and bring back a trophy that will not be an object, but a moment; a moment impregnated with the intensity of self because it bears within it the insistent memory that, through courage or initiative, he or she succeeded for a moment in extracting from Death or physical exhaustion, the guarantee of a life fully lived. (Le Breton 2000: 7)

Psytrance is clearly not the near-death experience spectacularized, for instance, in the film *127 Hours* (2010, directed by Danny Boyle). Yet this passage likely draws nods from those who have met with unexpected transpersonal states, having experienced an apocalypse of subjectivity such as that which is orchestrated by DJs facilitating the passage of participants into extreme physical exhaustion towards the end of a long festival where they obtain the 'little death' of entrancement. Sjoerd Los from Holland recalled such a moment on the fifth day of Boom 2008:

> Time has become liquid, temporarily meaningless, flexible … Days and days of dancing, sweaty tanned bodies, exhilaration and neurochemical stimulation made arriving at this night possible. Closing in on the illuminated Groovy Beach the big thumping bass starts resonating inside my mind, sparking new energy where one rationally wouldn't expect it. My step quickens, and soon I arrive to indulge in this madness. Dancing for hours, I lose all sense of time – even all sense of 'me' – my mind and body take flight. My bare feet jumping and shuffling across the sandy dancefloor seem to move effortlessly, my whole body seems in a state of pure affect. I have stopped rationalizing. Having eliminated thought for the most part I enter a transcendental state. I *am* music at that moment, and standing in front of the speakers I enter into a vacuum. A solitary space on a crowded dancefloor where a direct conversation between me and the music is possible. Closing my eyes in that state of mind and body makes the experience complete – worlds unfold as beautiful visuals appear.[11]

Sjoerd had apparently transited to a duration beyond time, the experience of eternity that is sought after, cherished and spoken about long afterwards by psytrance enthusiasts. Not unlike other realms of extreme recreation, and other EDM scenes, with the assistance of an assemblage of psycho-actives and high-performance sound and visual design techniques, psychedelic dance parties are optimized contexts manifesting transcendent states of mind. As such, they facilitate 'experiential anarchy' (Ferrell 2005: 76). A further passage from Le Breton, this

---

11   Sjoerd Los, communication with the author on Facebook, 24 September 2011.

time of the shared experience, is reminiscent of the commitments of the hardcore enthusiast whose experience of the psychedelic vibe compels their return, not to the sky (to skydive), to the road (to run a marathon) or the ocean (to sail across the Atlantic), but to the dancefloor, in psycho-geographically removed spaces:

> Never before had they reached such legitimacy, such a fullness of being that instantly seems to justify all their efforts, the future and the past being swept away in a culminating moment. This moment of illumination, of trance, is not rooted in religious fervour though it is related to the sacred, in other words to a personal generation of meaning. The search is for personal transfiguration caused by exhaustion or disorientation of the senses, a sudden and incredibly strong feeling of being at one with the world, an ecstasy that then forms such a strong memory that the player does everything possible to relive it (Le Breton 2000: 10)

There are direct parallels with psytrance participants, who pass from exhaustion into transfiguring moments when 'it all makes sense' – even wearing their exultation and belonging 'on their sleeves' (that is, retaining event wristbands for days, weeks and, in some cases, years afterwards). Commenting on her experience during the final set by Man With No Name on the final day of the 2009 OZORA Festival – a week-long 'psychedelic tribal gathering' – Turkish/German co-owner of Blue Hour Sounds records, Jasmine Gelenbe, stated:

> People were freaking out! It had been a great party, nobody wanted it to end, everybody gave the last power reserves! We danced and danced, and after a while the whole dancefloor seemed to be a twister. I got into this bunch of people, jumping one around the other, always moving, never standing – we hardly touched the ground, smiling at each other, holding hands, turning, turning … wow! I saw the funniest expressions, the most touching interactions between people, everybody was full of love, hugging, kissing and sharing this moment of trance … When the music stopped it was like an explosion of joy, we were screaming, clapping our hands, everybody was begging just for another track! And we got it! Another roundabout, this time even more powerful, and it was over … pure satisfaction! I will never forget that.[12]

Such exhilarating climaxes are not uncommon, and have been observed in other EDM cultures. Figuring modern expressions of the 'quest for excitement' that Elias and Dunning (1986) argue has been dialectically necessitated by restraints on overt emotionality since the Renaissance, Jackson (2004: 123) acknowledges that metropolitan (queer, trance, techno, drum'n'bass and sex) clubs, with their immediate 'chemical intimacy', bizarre conversations and sensual intensity between strangers fuelled by a range of psycho-actives, challenges the 'logic' of

---

12   Jasmine Gelenbe, communication with the author on Facebook, 21 September 2011.

the *habitus* and enable fresh and open forms of sociality where participants 'derive a sense of satisfaction and meaning from people, rather then things' (2004: 163).

As a dance cultural movement, psytrance similarly makes possible the transcendence of normative embodiment, subjectivity and citizenship, and the concomitant reinhabitation of the world, through the outlandish contexts of chemically assisted sensual intimacies. Tales of radical edgework are repeated the world over. Journeying to and inhabiting exotic events, the use of illicit compounds enabling alternative states of consciousness and unusual modes of public intimacy are common to the experienced. Becoming a player is dependent on maintaining an ambiguous relationship with regard to the law: workplaying the edges of morality, gender and sexual norms, aesthetic conventions and criminal codes. Variously ritualized, the entire psytrance assemblage facilitates the refashioning of identity, most powerfully marked at those limits where rules, codes and laws, of propriety, morality and the state, are freely transgressed. Taking risks holds numinous results achieved within states of transgression/transcendence – especially that achieved on the dancefloor, where risk is experienced not in conditions of absolute extremes where individuals are pitted against wild nature or are tempted by gravity, but in a context where habitués confront their fears and anxieties of the Other – that is, the strangers in their midst, those who are witness to one's most intimate expressions, short of orgasm. Thus it is not death but other people who constitute the limit worked and negotiated on the dancefloor – especially that of a multi-day psychedelic festival. This limit, the edge that distinguishes and separates individuals, is softened by shared exposure to bass frequencies and soaring melodies, and also through gifting practices, the sharing of mind-altering substances. Acts of shared sonicity and intoxication reduce the gulf between event-goers from manifold backgrounds. It is such experiences of intimacy that trigger dedication within the world of psytrance. The experience returns me to Lyng:

> When people separated by divisions of age, gender, class, race, occupation, and intellectual temperament come together and discover deep-seated commonalities of personal experience, they often feel a sense of connection rooted in something basic to their souls. Such is the case with edgeworkers. Whatever else may distance them from one another, risk takers almost always recognize one another as brothers and sisters genetically linked by their desire to experience the uncertainties of the edge. (Lyng 2005: 4)

Shared transgression, then, becomes a source of community, where participants form identifications amid extremes of travel and exposure to extreme weather events, becoming 'trashed' from long periods of dancing, a shared alternative state of consciousness and exposure to high-volume sound systems for consecutive days and nights, during which sleeping routines are disrupted and circadian rhythms broken. Sometimes abusive excesses lead partygoers to haunt the festival grounds like citizens of a post-apocalypse; at other times, entrancement and personal epiphanies involving deep and lasting connections with others and nature are inaugurated.

Ethical Lifestyles

The depletion of personal resources on the dancefloor is an exercise in ecstatic expenditure, sharing a sometimes tense and other times amicable relationship with the ethical consumer lifestyle native to the Goa/psytrance tradition. Boom is a benchmark event in sustainable consumer practice, as showcased within the Liminal Zone, which – as described in a zine distributed during the 2006 event – beseeches participants to 'take the important steps towards implementing the evolutionary changes required if humanity and our biosphere are to survive' (Eve, *Pathways*, 2006: 9). At that event, Lucia Legan from the Ecocentro IPEC (Instituto de Permacultura e Ecovilas do Cerrado) in Brazil – where Boom organizers had completed courses on sustainability – had been contracted to construct 'eco-toilets' and promote sustainable living in the festival's Biovillage. In their commitment to provide solutions to challenges posed by the over-consumption of energy, food and water on site, in 2008 and 2010 Boom organizers undertook new projects in composting and refertilizing as they reused organic waste to initiate a reforestation process on the land of the festival. Following those events, Boom distributed electronic newsletters providing statistics and thanking participants for 'depositing your minerals' and 'reducing your footprint'.[13] In 2008, the 'Your Oil is Music' initiative collected 45,000 litres of waste vegetable oil from the local region and Boom restaurants for use in generators to power the festival, thus avoiding the use of non-renewable fossil fuels and the emission of 117,000 kg of carbon dioxide into the atmosphere. In 2008, 90 per cent of all festival structures were made from organic and compostable materials, and materials from other events (Rock in Rio Lisbon and the Amadora International Comic Strip Festival) were collected and reused. This practice was continued in 2010, with Boom reusing 86,475 kg of materials (thus claiming to avoid the emission of 254,000 kg of carbon dioxide). By initiating the use of composting toilets in 2008, Boom avoided dumping 106.5 cubic metres of excrement into the public sewage-treatment system. In 2010, 98 per cent of Boom toilets (159 toilets) were composting toilets, with 70,000 litres of high-quality organic liquid fertilizer generated for agricultural production. With 'water' becoming the theme of Boom 2010, festival management claimed that all 'grey water' from restaurants and showers was treated onsite and recycled for irrigation, with 100 per cent of all waste water treated using a bio-remediation and evapo-transpiration system, part of an integrated system designed to restore the area's natural hydrology cycle. Additionally, in 2010 Boom built several mobile photovoltaic stations, and 20,000 portable 'ashtray' tubes were distributed. As these figures demonstrate, with Boom

---

13   The following data are taken from these newsletters.

the party is a stage for enacting ecological principles implemented according to commitments towards ethical consumption – a commitment attracting a Greener Festivals 'outstanding' award in 2008.

Sustainable event management is a means by which organizers and participants perform redressive behaviours within festival contexts in response to recognized crises and risks. While attention to redress is illustrated in a variety of ways within visionary arts festivals, this chapter will now discuss how such events became vehicles for the planetary consciousness movement, as inscribed in the Planetary Art Network (PAN) – principally its Dreamspell Calendar. Also called the '13 Moon Calendar', the Dreamspell is a tool for consciousness change developed by José and Lloydine Argüelles (founders of PAN), and is based in part on their translation of the Mayan Calendar. PAN activists understand calendar change to be an eight-year process (2004–12). For the Argüelles and members of 90 PAN groups worldwide, since the artificial time frequency of the 12-month Gregorian calendar and the 60-minute hour is arbitrarily imposed, the avoidance of an environmental catastrophe and the survival of humanity depend upon the use of a 'harmonic' calendar adopted as a means to redress global ecological crises, and responsive to irresponsible consumer lifestyles. Many dance and festival groups have aligned their gatherings with the new calendar, with PAN nodes holding a presence at large international and smaller local gatherings over the past 20 years. These events and music productions (see St John 2011b) have been common sites for the pedagogical transmission of 'the New Time'.

In 2006, Boom hosted a 'Galactic Temple', an open geodesic dome adjacent the Liminal Village with hanging banners of Dreamspell glyphs. Workshops and discussions were held daily inside the temple dome, at the centre of which was an impressive 'Telektonon board' with crystals, resembling a game board with tokens. Workshop participants learned that the 13 Moon Calendar consists of an annual cycle of 13 moons, each 28 days long, and is held to demonstrate harmony with the earth and natural cycles – coded, for instance, in the human female biological cycle. Kwali, a 'Red Magnetic Skywalker' who had 'upgraded' 1,500 people to their Dreamspell sign or 'galactic signatures' (of which there are 260), stated: 'Why do I feel like I'm running out of time? Why am I not in the right place at the right time?'[14] According to Kwali and her fellow PAN activists, the questions haunt those of us who are removed from our natural cycles, and the Dreamspell evidences the logic of sacrificial commitment to the ultimate cause: the future. The commitment of Dreamspell practitioners appears to lie in dramatic contrast to that which reveals no concern for the morrow. Both, in a sense, are antagonists of 'time'. The former are dissenters from Gregorian time and the calendar imposed by the Roman Catholic Church. As Kwali stated: 'People want to be free from the clock that ticks and this is an opportunity for people to have their freedom within a society that does not want them to be free'. For the latter, the dissention from routine 'time' and rational consciousness is expressed

---

14   Kwali, interviewed at Boom Festival, Portugal, 2 August 2006.

in the commitment to the eternity that is *now* into which one passes on the dancefloor. Apparently, by contrast with the headlong charge towards an orgiastic suspension of time characterizing one's approach to dance, the 13 Moon Calendar movement offers a profound teleological expression of the concern for life 'after the orgy' – including the 'orgy' of history or, more accurately, the history of ecological despoliation characterizing modernization. Such is a commitment to the future, a possible future downstream from the actions of the present, a future that relies upon one's choices now. This is the message of much PAN activism: a discourse and practice of responsibility towards the natural environment and one's self evolving post-1960s.

But are these diverse experiences of altered time incompatible? Why would advocates of the PAN elect to have a regular presence at events where frivolities and getting 'wasted' in a 'time out of time' are rife? These are questions addressed by self-identified 'Chrononaught' and PAN devotee Even Dawn (2008), who observed that in these luxurious episodes in energy use and wildlife disturbance, 'we've discovered how to amp up just about all the parameters that our sensory input organs can sustain'. But having attended the 2008 Winter Solstice Gathering in Far North Queensland, Australia, operated by PsyTek Productions, where she experienced the operations of the company Natural Event, whose composting toilets convert human waste into usable compost or 'humanure', Dawn became convinced that festival culture was 'maturing into a more responsive and responsible party animal'. An adept of the 13 Moon Synchronometer, Dawn acknowledges the importance of the role played by dance, and the 'apparent frivolity of cultural festivals', in the coming 'synchronization'. She considers those who attend these planetary gatherings to be representatives of 'the emergence of the coming culture of life on planet Earth'. Articulating eco-centric and Earthen religious views common to PAN enthusiasts, these sites are viewed as the most recent in a 'heritage of nomadic corroborees, gypsy caravans, celebrated feasts and fairs' inhabited by those who celebrate 'the human species' rightful, artistic role in relation to the whole'. But offering a perspective that conveys Arguelles' co-evolutionary thesis and the ideas of Russian scholar and 'noosphere' theorist Vladmir Vernadsky, the view is that 'these humans are returning to a style of living which aims to exist in accordance with the well-being of the planetary life-support system, the Biosphere' (Dawn 2008). Furthermore, these festivals are reckoned to be

> the meeting grounds of the AltarNation, the pro-Native movement towards collective recognition of the Sanctity of Nature. On the dancefloors, throughout the day and night there can be found devout dance pilgrims from a diverse spectrum of cultures, some having trekked land, sea and sky to make their offerings of movement on that particular place on earth. The language which unites them all is expressed through the art and the music. (Dawn 2008)

Conclusion

In consideration of its ambition to creatively and responsibly design human life on earth, Eric Davis states in regard to the visionary arts festival that

> part of the excitement of the festival, which you can feel even before you cross the threshold, is the sense that the normal rules that govern our behavior have begun to mutate and change, that a possible world is emerging and that a new self is rising to greet it (2008: 50, 53).

The artifice in this endeavour is not one-dimensional. While transformation is the zeitgeist for festivals in the transnational visionary arts and dance milieu downstream from Goa and the counter-culture of the 1960s/1970s, as a legacy of the latter they occasion spectacular departures from 'rational consciousness', yet are harnessed to paradigms of consciousness evolution. This hyperliminal noise is characteristic of Portugal's Boom Festival, the world's premiere visionary arts dance festival, where works of ecstasy and conscientiousness are built into festival architectonics, as embodied by the Dance Temple and the Liminal Village, along with other event areas not discussed here. It is one of the chief objectives of Boom and other events to find balances and compromises between these practices in optimized events. It is the case that, in these events, efforts to promote renewable energy practices consistent with an ecological sensibility, and the consumption of resources in delirious expenditures, cause tensions and rifts – especially as they are motivations possessing logics of practice associated on the one hand with risk-avoidance and on the other with the performance of risk.[15] Attracting participants with differential expectations and causes, visionary arts festivals operationalize disparate sacrificial practices, exposing an acute ecstatic/activist paradox.

Contradictory practice and management hypocrisy may fuel discord between camps committed exclusively to transcendent or conscientious causes – and, perhaps more to the point, anxieties within individual entrants themselves, who participate in luxurious abandonment and ethical consumerism for the duration of events. As experimental sites for 'sustainable entertainment', and as interactive, participation-oriented events, visionary arts festivals encourage participants to oscillate between 'edgework' and ethical commitments. That is, by exposing participants to disparate modes of self-dissolution and reflexivity, festivals facilitate experiments and alliances across the sacred divide. Indeed, this is implicit to the design of events that are optimized stages, and in some cases global summits, for negotiating the tensions between the idealistic and ecstatic dimensions of a transnational movement whose participants seek the eternal

---

15   The full implications of these logics have not been addressed in this chapter. See St John (2012) for a discussion of prestige that is converted from both the lifestyle risks that are negotiated and the ecological risks triggering personal and campaign efforts within the context of these events.

present *and* the sustainable future. Host to rites of transgression and unparalleled states of transfiguration, the psychedelic festival is a primary means to, as Even Dawn (2008) observes, 'get out of it'. And yet, as paragons of disciplinary and conscious ritualizing, they are also contexts, as Dawn further avers, to 'get into it' – that is, these events are means to access a mystical experience in which an integral or ecological relationship to the whole is potentiated. Indeed, the artifice of the festival facilitates the latter through ecstatic self-abandonment in the context of others. While there are similarities with the revitalizing function of seasonal festivals since antiquity, the objective of the visionary arts festival that has grown in popularity internationally over the last decade is to actively transform culture through the stimulation of mutant forms of innovative and responsible living.

References

Bataille, G. 1989 [1967]. *The Accursed Share, Vol. 1*, translated by Robert Hurley. New York: Zone Books.

Bennett, A. 1999. Subcultures or neo-tribes? Rethinking the relationship between youth, style and musical taste. *Sociology*, 33(3), 599–617.

Boom Book 2007. Portugal: Good Mood/Boom Festival.

Bowditch, R. 2010. *On the Edge of Utopia: Performance and Ritual at Burning Man*. Chicago, IL: University of Chicago Press.

Burroughs, W. 1992 [1959]. *Naked Lunch*. New York: Grove Press.

Clarke, M. 1982. *The Politics of Pop Festivals*. London: Junction.

Davis, E. 2008. The festival is a seed. *Pathways: Liminal Zine* 02, 50–54.

Davis, F. and Munoz, L. 1968. Heads and freaks: Patterns and meanings of drug use among hippies. *Journal of Health and Social Behavior*, 9(2), 156–64.

Dawn, E. 2008. Planetary gatherings of galactic garden culture. *Undergrowth* Available at: undergrowth.org/planetary_gatherings_of_galactic_garden_culture_by_even_dawn [accessed: 14 September 2011].

D'Andrea, A. 2007. *Global Nomads: Techno and New Age as Transnational Countercultures in Ibiza and Goa*. New York: Routledge.

Eade, J. and Sallnow, M. 1991. Introduction, in *Contesting the Sacred: The Anthropology of Christian Pilgrimage*, edited by J. Eade and M. Sallnow. London: Routledge, 1–29.

Elias, N. and Dunning, E. 1986. *Quest for Excitement: Sport and Leisure in the Civilizing Process*. Oxford: Blackwell.

Elliott, L. 2010. Goa is a state of mind: On the ephemerality of psychedelic social emplacements, in *The Local Scenes and Global Culture of Psytrance*, edited by G. St John. New York: Routledge, 21–39.

Eve 2006. Between experience and imagination: A liminal invocation. *Pathways: Liminal Zine* 01, 5.

Ferrell, J. 2005. The only possible adventure: Edgework and anarchy, in *Edgework: The Sociology of Risk-Taking*, edited by S. Lyng. New York: Routledge.

Gilmore, L. 2010. *Theater in a Crowded Fire: Ritual and Spirituality at the Burning Man Festival.* Berkeley, CA: University of California Press.

Gilmore, L. and Van Proyen, M. (eds) 2005. *Afterburn: Reflections on Burning Man.* Albuquerque, NM: University of New Mexico Press.

Hetherington, K. 2000. *New Age Travellers: Vanloads of Uproarious Humanity.* London: Cassell.

Howard, J.R. 1969. The flowering of the hippie movement. *The Annals of the American Academy of Political and Social Science*, 382(1), 43–55.

Jackson, P. 2004. *Inside Clubbing: Sensual Experiments in the Art of Being Human.* Oxford: Berg.

Jones, S.T. 2011. *The Tribes of Burning Man.* San Francisco: CCC Publishing.

Kozinets, R.V. 2002. Can consumers escape the market? Emancipatory illuminations from Burning Man. *Journal of Consumer Research*, 29, 20–38.

Le Breton, D. 2000. Playing symbolically with death in extreme sports. *Body & Society*, 6(1), 1–11.

Lee, M.A. and Shlain, B. 1985. *Acid Dreams: The Complete Social History of LSD: The CIA, the Sixties and Beyond.* New York: Grove Press.

Lewis, J.L. and Dowsey-Magog, P. 1993. The Maleny Fire Event: Rehearsals toward neo-liminality. *The Australian Journal of Anthropology*, 4(3), 198–219.

Lyng, S. 2005. Edgework and the risk-taking experience, in *Edgework: The Sociology of Risk-Taking*, edited by S. Lyng. London: Routledge, 3–16.

McKay, G. 2000. *Glastonbury: A Very English Fair.* London: Victor Gollancz.

McKay, G. 2004. 'Unsafe things like youth and jazz': Beaulieu Jazz Festivals (1956–61) and the origins of pop festival culture in Britain', in *Remembering Woodstock*, edited by A. Bennett. Aldershot: Ashgate, 90–110.

Maffesoli, M. 1996 [1988]. *The Time of the Tribes: The Decline of Individualism in Mass Society.* London: Sage.

Musgrove, F. 1974. *Ecstasy and Holiness: Counter Culture and the Open Society.* London: Methuen.

Niman, M. 1997. *People of the Rainbow: A Nomadic Utopia.* Knoxville, TN: University of Tennessee Press.

Omananda 2004. 'For all the Boomers … here is a story about faith, magic, and universal love vibrations'. Available at: www.chaishop.com/static?url=www.chaishop.com/text1/r/sam07.htm [accessed: 18 November 2010].

Partridge, C. 2006. The spiritual and the revolutionary: Alternative spirituality, British free festivals and the emergence of rave culture. *Culture and Religion*, 7(1), 41–60.

Rietveld, H. 2010. Infinite noise spirals: Psytrance as cosmopolitan emotion, in *The Local Scenes and Global Culture of Psytrance*, edited by G. St John. New York: Routledge, 69–88.

Saldanha, A. 2007. *Psychedelic White: Trance and the Viscosity of Race.* Minneapolis, MN: University of Minnesota Press.

St John, G. 1997. Going feral: Authentica on the edge of Australian culture. *The Australian Journal of Anthropology*, 8(2), 167–89.

St John, G. 2001. Alternative cultural heterotopia and the liminoid body: Beyond Turner at ConFest. *The Australian Journal of Anthropology,* 12(1), 47–66.

St John, G. 2009a. *Technomad: Global Raving Countercultures.* London: Equinox.

St John, G. 2009b. Neotrance and the psychedelic festival. *Dancecult: Journal of Electronic Dance Music Culture,* 1(1), 35–64.

St John, G. 2010a. Liminal culture and global movement: The transitional world of psytrance, in *The Local Scenes and Global Culture of Psytrance,* edited by G. St John. New York: Routledge, pp. 220–46.

St John, G. (ed.) 2010b. *The Local Scenes and Global Culture of Psytrance.* London: Routledge.

St John, G. 2011a. DJ Goa Gil: Kalifornian exile, dark yogi and dreaded anomaly. *Dancecult: Journal of Electronic Dance Music Culture,* 3(1), 97–128.

St John, G. 2011b. The 2012 movement, visionary arts and psytrance culture, in *2012: Decoding the Countercultural Apocalypse,* edited by J. Gelfer. Sheffield: Equinox.

St John, G. 2012. *Global Tribe: Technology, Spirituality and Psytrance.* Sheffield: Equinox.

St John, G. and Baldini, C. 2012. Dancing at the crossroads of consciousness: Techno-mysticism, visionary arts and Portugal's Boom Festival, in *Handbook of New Religions and Cultural Production,* edited by C.M. Cusack and A. Norman. Leiden: Brill, pp. 521–52.

Turner, V. 1982. *From Ritual to Theatre: The Human Seriousness of Play.* New York: PAJP.

Turner, V. 1984. Liminality and the performative genres, in *Rite, Drama, Festival, Spectacle: Rehearsals Towards a Theory of Cultural Performance,* edited by J.J. MacAloon. Philadelphia, PA: Institute for Study of Human Issues, pp. 19–41.

Worthington, A. 2004. *Stonehenge: Celebration & Subversion.* Albion: Alternative Books.

Chapter 4

'Pride in Self, Pride in Community, Pride in Culture': The Role of Stylin' Up in Fostering Indigenous Community and Identity

Brydie-Leigh Bartleet

As I leave the familiar sights of Brisbane's inner city and head south-west towards the suburb of Inala, I notice the landscape begin to change. The cityscape gives way to long stretches of industrial blocks and modest housing. This urban context, known for its high Indigenous Australian population,[1] is one of the case studies in a large nationwide project called Sound Links, on which I am working (for further details, see Bartleet et al. 2009). In particular, we are focusing on Stylin' Up, an Indigenous-owned hip-hop and R&B festival and skills-development program, which is hosted in the suburb of Inala. This afternoon I am undertaking fieldwork at a local community centre involved in the program. Soon after arriving at Elorac Place, I notice the loud vibrations of hip-hop beats coming from an adjoining room. After a few minutes, Craig Cranston from Inala Youth Service walks in and warmly greets me. Craig is supervising the afternoon's hip-hop workshops. 'Do you want to come take a look at what the guys are doing?' he asks.

As we walk out the back door, a small group of Indigenous children congregates around us. I smile at them and they smile back, not saying a word. The hip-hop beats stop for a moment and Craig turns towards me, deciding to make the most of the silent reprieve. He explains that since its inception in 2000, Stylin' Up has been guided by three key themes – 'pride in self, pride in community, and pride in culture' – and tells me that organizers are expecting an audience of over 10,000 this year. The hip-hop beats suddenly start up again. Craig smiles. 'The guys are practising for the festival in a few weeks. All these workshops culminate in a big festival day in May every year'. As we wait outside for an appropriate moment to enter, I notice the brightly coloured Stylin' Up poster on the door. Seeing my interest, Craig explains these workshops do not only focus on music, but other creative arts such as graphic design, dance, events management and video

---

1   I use the term 'Indigenous' to refer to Aboriginal and Torres Strait Islander peoples. Members of both cultural groups are involved with Stylin' Up.

production. 'Local schools and community centres, like Elorac Place, provide the facilities for all these workshops to happen', he adds.

When there is a brief moment of silence, we enter the room. Four teenage boys are standing in the centre with microphones, discussing what they've just finished. A few young Indigenous children are sitting at the side of the room, silently watching. A community music facilitator, Luke O'Sullivan, is working from a laptop, manipulating the beats. The group decides to start a new song and suddenly the room is filled with loud beats and rapping again. This song is called 'Straight Up Murri'. I notice the ways in which the young men assist one another – with lyrics, music production ideas and stagecraft – and essentially support one another's development. Their nodding heads, moving bodies, grunts and verbal assurances offer critical peer feedback and encouragement. I can see that they want their music to be good: it has to tell the story of their experiences and they want to be proud of it.

After a while, Kelvin Lui, one of the Indigenous elders who oversee these workshops, comes to greet me. He suggests we step outside so we can chat. We find a wooden bench in front of a bright wall mural depicting two Indigenous travellers. It seems the perfect backdrop for our conversation. As we sit down, Kelvin tells me that some locals originally questioned whether hip-hop was the most appropriate genre for this program, particularly because of its heavy American influences and associations with violence, machismo and misogyny (see Mitchell 2006). However, as he goes on to explain, many have come to acknowledge that this genre gives the young Indigenous people of this area a voice to express their life experiences:

> It's about self-respect; it's about moving away from all the negative things that are happening around the place – the drugs, the alcohol and everything else that happens in the urban environment … So these young people are trying to get that message out there and in some ways they're trying to set themselves up as role models for young people to say that even though we've come from this sort of background you can do something with your life and take positive steps towards making it better, making a better quality of life, you know … It builds your self-confidence and it empowers you to move forward. (Kelvin Lui, personal interview, 22 May 2008)

Kelvin's observations echo those of Dunbar-Hall and Gibson (2004: 126), who suggest that hip-hop provides Indigenous youth with 'a means for developing confidence and pride'. As I discovered in the two months that preceded and followed this interview with Kelvin, these activities are indeed empowering young people in Inala to engage with contemporary themes of indigeneity (see Dunbar-Hall and Gibson 2000: 43–4), and inspiring them to explore their sense of cultural identity in positive ways (see Stylin' Up 2011). It's worth noting that such outcomes seem to be indicative of a wider movement across the country, with other Indigenous hip-hop and R&B programs and artists achieving similar aims at various festivals and events – for example, the Dreaming Festival (Woodford), the Vibe Alive Festival (Weipa, Kalgoorlie, Mildura, Coonamble and Port Augusta), the Barunga

Festival (Katherine), the Garma Festival (Gulkula), the Alice Desert Festival (Alice Springs) and the Big Fella Festival (Falls Creek), to mention just a few (see also Neuenfeldt 2001). Likewise, due to the popularity and success of Stylin' Up in Inala, the concept has been taken out to regional and rural communities. The Stylin' Up and Out program has established itself in Goondiwindi, Cherbourg, Woorabinda, Logan City and Ipswich.

In this chapter, I draw on observations and interviews with Inala community members and Stylin' Up participants to explore the ways in which Stylin' Up achieves such aims and provides a strong vehicle for community-building and collective identification. In particular, I focus on the ways in which the festival and skills development program engender a strong sense of Indigenous ownership, and encourage positive processes of place-making, social engagement, dynamic music-making and learning.

Outlining the Research Approach

The research that informs this chapter was conducted under the umbrella of a much larger project called Sound Links, which sought to learn more about the dynamics of community music in Australia and its potential synergy with music in schools. To accommodate the aims of the research project, a combination of qualitative methodologies – including ethnographic case studies – and quantitative methodologies – including a nationwide survey – were used. This chapter focuses specifically on the ethnographic case study findings, including insights from field visits, semi-structured interviews, focus groups, participant and non-participant observations, and analyses of relevant documentation. This particular methodological approach lent itself well to uncovering the individual stories of the community musicians, the dynamics of their practice, and the broader socio-cultural issues and structural frameworks that arose from these settings. As Higgins (2006: 265) points out, 'ethnographic strategy and method unmask the traits of Community Music *in action*' (emphasis added).

Because an ethnographic approach focuses on openness and reciprocal exchange, with its point of departure being the *lived* experiences of the researched, it was necessary for us to come face to face with the participants themselves. This entailed us entering into a close interaction with the Stylin' Up participants and Inala community members in their everyday musical lives to better understand their beliefs, motivations and behaviours (see Tedlock 2000: 455). Over a period of two months, we undertook interviews and focus groups with more than 16 key facilitators and participants in the event, and Sarah Patrick (the project's Indigenous research assistant) undertook four focus group interviews with over 26 young people involved in the Stylin' Up workshops. Participants in both sets of interviews and focus groups included school students, school music teachers, Stylin' Up facilitators, participants, event organizers, youth workers and local council workers. We also visited a number of the workshop sites, including

Elorac Place (mentioned in the opening narrative), Glenala High School, the Murri School and the youth-based organizations Inala Wangarra, CONTACT Inc. and Speakout, as well as attending the festival itself.[2]

The analysis phase involved identifying a number of key themes, coding and then thematically sorting the data from the ethnographic case studies and the online survey into categories. Given that each of the case studies in the broader project represented a very different set of circumstances and environment, many of the characteristics of the community music activities explored were unique to their specific participants, facilitators, sites, contexts, aims and infrastructure. However, there were also strongly shared underlying characteristics among the activities. During the analysis phase, it also became clear that nine major themes (which we called domains) were present (in varying degrees) in all the community music activities observed – and indeed in the research team's recollections of similar projects across the world. These domains included: infrastructure; organization; visibility and public relations; relationship to place; social engagement; support and networking; dynamic music-making; engaging pedagogy and facilitation; and links to school (see Bartleet et al. 2009 for further details). Elements of these domains are all touched on in this chapter, and highlight the ways in which Stylin' Up fosters a strong sense of community and pride in Indigenous culture.

At this point, I should acknowledge my subject position as a non-Indigenous researcher. My positioning obviously impacted upon the ways in which I engaged with the community, and was something about which I had to be continually mindful as I conducted my fieldwork. This is also why we followed the advice of the Stylin' Up community crew – comprising local elders, school representatives, businesses and Indigenous community-controlled organizations such as the Aboriginal and Islanders' Sport, Health and Recreation Association (AISHRA), One Tribe, Inala Wangarra, Wandarrah Preschool and the Murri School – and employed Sarah Patrick to undertake focus group interviews with the young people involved in the Stylin' Up workshops. Sarah is a local Indigenous musician who has also been involved in Stylin' Up as a participant and a facilitator, and is well known within the Inala community. As the community crew explained to us, having Sarah undertake the interviews with our young participants made the research process more accessible and less intimidating for them. My subject position also influenced the ways in which I then wrote about my experiences and observations. Because of my position, I could not write from the perspective of an insider in this community or attempt to speak on its behalf. I could only write from the perspective of an interested observer, openly acknowledging the cultural politics of my non-Indigenous position, and asking readers to view my work from this perspective. As other scholars working within the field of Indigenous studies have pointed out, the only way to appropriately negotiate such issues is through the building and maintenance of relationships with

---

2   Full ethical clearance was given by Griffith University to undertake this research, and participants gave 'informed consent' for their identities and words to be used in resulting publications.

those in our fields of inquiry (see Barney and Solomon 2009; Haig-Brown 2001; Mackinlay 2008; Selby 2004; Somerville and Perkins 2003). To this end, I would like to thank those in the community who have remained in contact with me and been kind enough to provide their feedback on this work. Such responses have enriched the stories and ideas that follow, and assisted me to negotiate the cultural politics of my own subject position in relation to this particular field.

Developing Local Community Ownership and Engagement

As I explained in my opening description, Stylin' Up is a partnership between the Indigenous community of Inala and the Brisbane City Council. It was originally developed in 2000 in response to the local Inala community and Brisbane City Council coming together to address young Indigenous people's engagement in the arts and their culture. When speaking about the local community's original motivations for developing the event, Athol Young (Developer of Stylin' Up, Brisbane City Council) explained: 'They acknowledged the change in their own community. They acknowledged all the social indicators ... It was about: how do you identify a sense of place and space and connection? And how do you build cohesion?' (Athol Young, personal interview, 12 June 2008). Local elders initially gravitated towards a country music festival, reflecting the predominant musical preferences of their generation. Country music has been recognized by various writers as one of the stylistic mainstays of contemporary Aboriginal popular music, and it is hugely popular with many elders (see Breen 1994; Castles 1992; Mudrooroo 1997; Dunbar-Hall and Gibson 2000: 48). However, in time they became convinced that hip-hop and R&B were more appropriate genres for engaging Indigenous youth.

Since those early beginnings, Stylin' Up has grown to become Australia's largest Indigenous hip-hop and R&B festival, and is recognized nationally as a significant contemporary Indigenous creative arts development program (see www.stylinup.com.au). In the 12 years since its inception, it has expanded from a humble audience of 500 to more than 15,000 people. The audience base of Stylin' Up is now geographically wide, and many people travel thousands of kilometres to participate, from places as far away as Cairns and Newcastle, as well as many regional areas. People from a wide range of cultural and ethnic groups also participate. This is also aided by the Brisbane City Council's access to corporate sponsorship and wide range of networks, which have assisted in increasing the profile of the event.

Despite its continual growth, Stylin' Up has retained its grassroots nature and deep connection to the Inala community. This is largely because of the 12-month community consultation process, which occurs via a community crew (as mentioned earlier). A number of local generations are also involved in the organization of the workshops and festival, from the elders organization that auspices the event[3] to the community crew and coordinators who are primarily in their thirties, to the facilitators who are mainly in their early twenties, and the participants who are primarily in their teens. Despite the festival being a youth event, as is customary in Indigenous culture, the local elders organization also plays a key role in the decision-making processes attached to Stylin' Up. In Inala, the elders organization has considerable influence in the community, and liaises with government, non-government agencies and charitable organizations. Many see the Inala elders organization as the representative body for Indigenous people in Inala (Greenop 2008: 18), and as a matter of cultural protocol the Brisbane City Council defers to the group in all aspects of the festival's organization. Many suggested that this event would not function as well as it does without its community consultation processes and resulting support from the local Indigenous community. As Kelvin Lui explained:

> The main factor I find is the community support and it's through the community support that this program has worked. This Stylin' Up event has worked in Inala because of the support Brisbane City Council gets from the Inala community. We had to get behind this and drive this. (Kevin Lui, personal interview, 22 May 2008)

In addition to the strong sense of local engagement and support shown by the Indigenous community of Inala, a number of the participants also spoke about the sound collaboration with Brisbane City Council as a key part of the festival's organizational structure. This collaboration has been built on an enduring sense of trust between the Brisbane City Council team that founded the event and the local community. They suggested that this collaboration has made the event more coordinated, and allowed for a successful interface with major sponsors and stakeholders. However, this collaboration has not been without its own complexities. Some participants spoke about the challenges of trying to map professional frameworks from governing bodies, such as the council, on to community programs such as Stylin' Up. They spoke of the difficult balancing act between it being a community event owned by the community and the fact that the community does not necessarily possess the relevant know-how when it comes to organizing such a big event. Many participants also spoke about the notion of the Brisbane City Council handing the program over to the community, given that this was one of the strategic goals when Stylin' Up was originally set up. While most agreed that this was still a desirable concept, they also acknowledged that at present there is no single organization that could provide the required infrastructure, and the Brisbane City Council is not keen to hand it over and then let it 'fall flat'. The Brisbane City Council has suggested that it would be happy to hand particular organizational

---

3   The Inala Elders Aboriginal and Torres Strait Islander Corporation is a self-declared and officially incorporated institution. While this organization plays a key role in the local community, it does not necessarily represent or include all community elders who have traditional owner status in Inala.

components over, resulting in a scenario whereby compartmentalized sections of the community work together in a collaborative effort. This is something towards which the council and festival organizers will continue to work in the coming years.

Creating a Collective Sense of Identity and Place

Many of the participants we interviewed were emphatic that Stylin' Up is unique to Inala. They suggested that this is because Inala is a significant Indigenous place. Prior to European settlement, Inala was part of the territory of the Jagara people, and there are a number of acknowledged traditional owner families that currently live in Inala, and have the right to 'speak for' the community with traditional owner status (Greenop 2009a: 7). In the pre-colonial and colonial eras, many gathering events for Aboriginal people occurred in places such as Inala, where people from distinct groups and disparate regions would gather to feast together in times of abundance, to help initiate each other's youth, and to share songs, stories and settle disputes. There was a tradition of hospitality, and the reciprocation of hosting events (see Greenop 2008: 6). The establishment of Inala as a suburb occurred in 1946, in an effort to develop affordable accommodation during the post-war housing shortage. The name Inala was coined in 1953 and is said to mean 'a peaceful place' in an unknown Aboriginal language (Greenop 2009a: 4–6). Indigenous people were among the first people to settle into the state government housing in Inala in the mid-1950s, alongside post-war refugee families from Italy, Greece, Poland and Russia. Many people had a shared history of difficult life in the missions, and Inala became their first stable home since that era (Greenop 2009a: 4–6). In the 1970s, there was an influx of people from Vietnam, and in recent times from other Asian countries, leading to significant cultural diversity in the area.

At present, Inala is home to the largest Aboriginal and Torres Strait Islander population in Brisbane (approximately 7.2 per cent, compared with Brisbane's overall Indigenous population of approximately 1.4 per cent). The suburb is now seen as 'a centre for cultural activities, not only Indigenous residence' (Greenop 2008: 12), and as a result Inala hosts a number of formalized gatherings, including Indigenous cultural festivals such as NAIDOC (National Aboriginal and Islander Day Observance Committee) Week, the Urban Dreaming Art Exhibition and, of course, the Stylin' Up festival.

Given its history, there is no one 'Indigenous Inala'. Likewise, there is no single, coherent hip-hop 'community' in Inala (see Maxwell 2003: 129). Having said this, the suburb has become a place of belonging for the Indigenous community (see Greenop 2008: 12), and hip-hop has been an 'unambiguous presence' that has played a key role in the articulation of that sense of belonging (see Maxwell 2003: 131). Outsiders and the popular media have at times characterized Inala in terms of high levels of violence, crime and poverty; in contrast, local residents feel a very positive identification with place and community pride (see Peel 2003; Bond 2007). Participants explained that events such as the Stylin' Up festival provide community members with the opportunity to enact this sense of belonging, and the chance to engage with ideas about place and where they fit within Inala's Indigenous history (see Duffy 2003: 104). This was a theme that appeared consistently across the interviews that Sarah conducted with the young participants, and can also be seen in the lyrics of some of the songs written in the Stylin' Up workshops. As Chelsea Bond (community crew member) explains:

> For Indigenous people Inala is like a new tribe and it's no less real than the remote communities. There are lots of people here that don't traditionally come from here but you say, 'Where do you come from?' and they say, 'Inala', like Inala is home. There were songs that showed that – revealed that. How people spoke about 4077 and about coming from Inala and about it being their homeland … those lyrics show how new attachments to a place have been formed that aren't just grounded in old traditional notions of attachment to land and stuff. (Chelsea Bond, personal interview, 16 June 2008)

As Chelsea's comment indicates, Indigenous relationships to place in Inala are individually constructed and vary greatly based on personal experiences, family affiliations and history within the suburb (see also Brough, Bond and Hunt 2004, 2006). Among the youth, there are common place-identity terms used, such as the common tag 'Inala Boy' or 'Inala Girl', which have specific meanings of attachment to the suburb from birth or early childhood. A further distinction is now being made, whereby 'Original Inala Boys' – also expressed as OIB – distinguish themselves by their family's long history in the suburb, and hence claim a stronger relationship to place (see Greenop 2009b: 10). These terms are used in social networks, and expressed on t-shirts, in graffiti and via tattooing, and often manifest themselves during the Stylin' Up workshops and festival event day in clothing, music lyrics and performances. An example of this can be seen in the lyrics of the hip-hop song 'Straight Up Murri' by Stylin' Up participant Jeffry D:

> We got the Woodridge, Inala, Acacia Ridge connection. Us together we're a new generation. White people think they control the nation, that's why we're a minority population. 1788 they came over on their boats … Us Murris have been waiting for too long. We're still fighting what was originally wrong. I'm not hating, I'm talking about the land. Us black fellas travelled on the coast and the sand. The women used to depend on the man, to go out hunting and gather food for the clan.

Stylin' Up has provided an important vehicle for the articulation of these connections to place, and allowed the young participants to imagine their sense of cultural identity in a positive way:

> The one thing I love about Stylin' Up is that is recognizes the diversity of our identity … It is an example of where we can feel really proud of our community,

of our young people. They're not just criminals. They're not just a group with immense social problems. They're actually resourceful, resilient, inspiring people that we can all learn from. So it puts young people up in front, which I think is really good. But it recognizes that our identity as Indigenous people is not just grounded in this idea of the exotic Other and that we all have to be in lap-laps and traditional dance. We've still retained our culture but we're articulating it in different ways and that is the main reason why I invest in Stylin' Up in my own time over the years as a community crew member, is that it engages with an imagining of me and my community that is grounded in the reality of how we see ourselves and I think that's much of its success is that now people think about Aboriginality in very different ways. Stylin' Up is our corroboree for today and that's what I think has pulled people in over the years and attracted people to it, is that it's imagined us very differently to how we're frequently talked about. (Chelsea Bond, personal interview, 16 June 2008)

As Chelsea's comment suggests, the festival allows people – both Indigenous and non-Indigenous – to engage in a musical dialogue with the Stylin' Up performers as 'real rather than imagined subjects' (see Mackinlay 2008: 259), and to reconsider their impressions of the Inala community and contemporary Indigenous culture in light of this.

Fostering Social and Cultural Engagement

As the aforementioned comments demonstrate, there are many challenging social issues facing young Indigenous people in Inala. Given the suburb's distance from Brisbane's CBD, youth in Inala also do not have easy access to entertainment, or much money for movies, skating, swimming pools, BMX tracks and the shopping mall experiences that many of Brisbane's teenagers have. A number of participants mentioned that substance abuse is now prevalent among youth in this urban context, and that there have been a handful of youth suicides in recent years. Such issues – alongside experiences with drinking, breaking into houses and getting chased by the police – appear to be surfacing in the lyrics that the young men of this community are writing for the Stylin' Up program. Despite such issues, participants spoke about the importance of giving young people an opportunity to speak about these experiences in order to combat these negative influences and create a greater sense of self-respect, personal empowerment and pride in themselves and their community. Such sentiments echo those of Dunbar-Hall and Gibson (2004: 132), who suggest: 'In Aboriginal contexts [hip-hop] has special importance as a source of black transnational solidarity and as a means of expression rather than mere absorption of American culture, or loss of Aboriginality'. Many participants acknowledged the significant role that Stylin' Up has played in providing such a means of expression and socially engaging Indigenous youth in this process. As Fred Leone (a Stylin' Up facilitator) explained:

**Figure 4.1   Naomi Wenitong from The Last Kinection
                performing at Stylin' Up in 2009**

Source: Photographer Adam Nicholas (used with permission from Brisbane City Council).

Before Stylin' Up there were a lot of angry people, with no outlet. Now Stylin Up's been here ... you see all these guys expressing themselves and all, in different ways, through dance, music or production, and it's crazy man. There's a lot of, heaps and heaps of, really good talent ... It's also like a platform to start off and come back next year, and it gets bigger and bigger ... Trying to get young people to voice themselves. Before I started getting into rap I was doing a lot of the stuff that Aboriginal and Torres Trait Islander kids get into because they don't have that ability to express themselves ... you know ... the ability to articulate what they're going through. Like I went from one extreme, thinking this sucks man, I go to school and get treated like shit, go here get treated like shit, I get served last at stores, and then turn it all around to talking about it with people in a way that's, like I'm not having a go off my head, saying 'Why is this happening?' I'm just stating the facts and articulating it and people come up and say, like 'We didn't know that happened', and I go 'Yeah, that happens all the time'. So it's cool to be able to do that, yeah, to tell our story and have people listen. (Fred Leone, personal interview, 13 May 2008)

Echoing Fred's comments, Dunbar-Hall and Gibson (2004: 130) suggest that: 'Regardless of the political stances (or not) adopted in rap lyrics, hip-hop enables cultural expressions that can reverse patterns of domination and invert meanings of place that revolve around alienation and marginalization'. As Maxwell (2003: 129) further explains, hip-hop achieves this sense of social engagement through an 'ongoing process of integrating practices of performance, embodiment, and the production of various forms of discourse'. Central to this process, he argues, 'is the articulation of those practices to place'.

Creating this sense of social engagement and positive place association also extends to the non-Indigenous community of Inala. As I mentioned earlier, Inala is not only known as a significant place for Indigenous people in Brisbane, it is also known for its cultural diversity, given the large number of refugees and migrants who have moved there since the 1950s. This cultural diversity is strongly reflected on the day of the festival. Although it is seen as an Indigenous event, a number of young Pacific Islanders are part of the hip-hop and R&B acts featured, and many local food stalls represent a wide range of cultures. Having said this, such a cultural mix is not without its social challenges. Some participants spoke about the complex issues that arise for the Inala community, given that Stylin' Up is a specifically Indigenous project. Christine Hayward (HOD Music and Art, Glenala High School) spoke frankly about the ways in which the school has worked very hard to create a sense of harmony between the different cultural groups, particularly the large Pacific Islander and Indigenous populations. She said singling out the Indigenous students somewhat counteracts the school's efforts to create a sense of harmony among the different groups:

Here our philosophy is integration, you know. We've got a lot of cultures and I don't like separating kids off for that reason when we've tried to work for so many years in harmony, particularly since the school merged with Richlands. Back in the early days there was a lot of disharmony with the Polynesian students and the Indigenous students. And we worked really hard to try and get them together. So it goes against our grain in some respects, you know, segregating kids off. (Christine Hayward, personal interview, 23 May 2008)

In response to such criticisms, organizers from the Brisbane City Council have been quick to point out that while Stylin' Up is an Indigenous-specific event, the workshops are not restricted to Indigenous young people. Indeed, in recent years a number of Pacific Islanders have become involved, and I certainly observed this on the festival day and in the workshops.

Facilitating a Space for Dynamic Music-making and Learning

Many identified the music workshops as one of the most important aspects of the Stylin' Up program. One of the reasons for this is the access provided by these workshops to young people wanting to learn a new set of skills, which can then be shared with younger generations, and also the impressive music equipment, to which they wouldn't otherwise have access. Another reason is the pedagogical approach of facilitators such as Luke O'Sullivan, who view the young people as active participants and collaborators, and allow them to be very hands-on. Luke also involves members from a highly successful local Indigenous band – Indigenous Intrudaz – throughout the process, in order to lend the workshops a sense of 'street cred' and an affirmation of the styles and aesthetics that young people appreciate. The members of the Indigenous Intrudaz also act as significant role models for the young Indigenous artists participating in the workshops and on festival day.

In the Laydeez Biz workshops, which are run specifically for young women and girls, a slightly less structured approach is used. Facilitators work to balance the social side of meeting together with the performance side of creating dances. In this context, giving young women an opportunity to develop a greater sense of self-respect, personal empowerment and pride in themselves and their community is of the utmost importance. The benefits of this are shown in the following comment from Jackie Saunders (a participant in the Laydeez Biz workshops and a traditional Aboriginal dance group):

I like the dancing and the singing and the different Aboriginal dancers that come and do dancing, and the different hip-hop dancers you see dancing, and it helps me to not feel shame and make me get up there and have a go. (Jackie Saunders, personal interview, 13 May 2008)

The cultural concept of 'shame' is something that came up repeatedly in the young participants' interviews, particularly in relation to getting up in front of

Figure 4.2   Damien Bani and Douglas Patrick from Indigenous Intrudaz
performing at Stylin' Up in 2009

Source: Photographer Adam Nicholas (used with permission from Brisbane City Council).

an audience to perform. The concept of shame is very important within many Indigenous communities, and shows a strong sensitivity to the opinion of a wider group. As Vallance and Tchacos (2001) explain, 'Shame has resonances of being singled out so that the individual is unduly the focus of attention' and 'a sense of being powerless and ineffectual'. The fact that many young people identified that this festival helps them combat this shame, and feel a sense of pride in their Indigenous identity, shows the important role that Stylin' Up plays in creating a sense of social engagement.

During Sarah's interviews with the young participants, a few also mentioned that by engaging in the Stylin' Up music workshops, they were inspired to engage more at school. This is something community members have also noticed. As Chelsea Bond explains:

> There have been some really significant outcomes in terms of effecting positive social change, but that wasn't on the agenda. These are just sort of flow on effects that have happened because that's what happens when you engage people in things that they're good at. Good things happen. So for instance, a few years ago the principal at the high school said that school attendance improved during the period of Stylin' Up because the workshops were happening in school and kids were wanting to come to school to participate in that process. So the intent wasn't to do something to improve attendance at the high school, but it happened to come about because the process was so successful and young people wanted to get on board with the event. (Chelsea Bond, personal interview, 16 June 2008)

Similarly, within the field of arts education, Dreeszen, Aprill and Deasy (1999: 3–4) observe that when communities and schools come together for projects such as Stylin' Up, they can help 'mitigate social problems including drug abuse, violence, teenage pregnancy, poverty, and lack of community pride. Arts and education partnerships enable young learners to reflect upon and represent themselves in their own communities, to become active citizens in their own neighbourhoods'. The Stylin' Up program has not only offered young people an avenue to communicate about their life experiences, but also provided inspiration for them to re-engage with their education (for further details, see Bartleet 2012). Mitchell (2006: 136) echoes such observations when he suggests:

> As an educational format, a vehicle to express anger at discrimination and marginalization and pride in one's heritage, a way of binding communities together through dance and performance, a declamatory form of storytelling set to music, and above all a means of expressing oral history, hip-hop's affinities with Aboriginal cultural forms make it an ideal means for youth to get in touch with their tribal identity, history and cultural background.

Conclusions

As I walk around the C.J. Greenfield Sports Field on the Stylin' Up festival day, I am struck by the scale of the event. I stop for a moment at one stage and watch the Nunukul Yugerra Aboriginal Dance Troupe perform a welcome dance of the Gabi-Gabi and Wakka Wakka peoples. On the adjoining stage, a hip-hop dance battle is taking place, and three young men are showcasing an impressive array of manoeuvres. The audience is cheering them along. I walk to another part of the sportsfield where there is a local hip-hop stage, and two Indigenous women are performing to an enthusiastic crowd of onlookers. As I walk between the stages, tantalizing smells from the Vietnamese, Chinese and Malaysian food stalls waft past me.

After I finish filming the performances on all the stages, I decide to sit quietly under a tree and soak in the atmosphere. There are thousands of people here (later I find out that around 15,000 attended that year) from every generation. All seem to be enjoying the music and cultural experience. I am taken by the strong sense of community, culture and support for these young Indigenous people. As I have seen during the time I have spent in Inala, Stylin' Up really does show how a community-driven festival and skills-development program – strongly supported by a local council – can be used to engage young Indigenous people in an urban context, and allow them to feel a sense of pride about their cultural identity. As I look over to the elders' tent – placed in a prime position presiding over the whole event, I am reminded of the rigorous community consultation process that takes place in order to engender this strong sense of community engagement and collective identification. Likewise, as I have observed, positive processes of place-making, social engagement, dynamic music-making and learning are all crucial elements of this community-driven process. Watching the young people perform also reminds me of the importance of choosing a musical genre that engages its target group – in this case, hip-hop and R&B music provides a powerful means for creating a sense of cultural identity, community and empowerment among Indigenous and disadvantaged youth at a local level.

This brief glimpse into Stylin' Up has shown how such festivals can provide ways for Indigenous artists to gain control of cultural spaces, challenge dominant non-Indigenous ideologies, and move Indigenous-specific issues such as identity-making and culture maintenance to the forefront (see Sharpe 2008: 219). In particular, it has shown how festival spaces such as this can provide Indigenous musicians with the opportunity to not only build cultural networks, but also celebrate a sense of cultural solidarity, thus making them powerful 'cultural zones' for the negotiation and performance of contemporary Indigenous community and identity.

Acknowledgements

My thanks go to the community members who were kind enough to provide feedback on this work, as part of the Sound Links project. I would also like to thank Chelsea Bond and Kelly Greenop for reading this chapter and providing thoughtful comments on the draft. This research was made possible by a research grant under the Linkage scheme of the Australian Research Council (2007–08), and my thanks go to the other research team members involved: Huib Schippers, Peter Dunbar-Hall and Richard Letts.

References

Barney, K. and Solomon, L. 2009. Looking into the trochus shell: Autoethnographic reflections on a cross-cultural collaborative music research project, in *Music Autoethnographies: Making Autoethnography Sing/Making Music Personal*, edited by B.L. Bartleet and C. Ellis. Brisbane: Australian Academic Press, 208–24.

Bartleet, B.L. 2012. Building vibrant school–community music collaborations: Three case studies from Australia. *British Journal of Music Education*, (29)1, 45–63.

Bartleet, B.L., Dunbar-Hall, P., Letts, R. and Schippers, H. 2009. *Sound Links: Community Music in Australia*. Brisbane: Queensland Conservatorium Research Centre.

Bond, C. 2007. When You're Black, They Look at You Harder: Narrating Aboriginality Within Public Health. PhD thesis, School of Population Health, University of Queensland.

Breen, M. 1994. I have a Dreamtime: Aboriginal music and black rights in Australia, in *World Music: The Rough Guide*, edited by S. Broughton et al. London: Rough Guides, 655–62.

Brough, M., Bond, C. and Hunt, J. 2004. Strong in the city: Toward a strength based approach in Indigenous health promotion. *Health Promotion Journal of Australia*, (15)3, 215–20.

Castles, J. 1992. Tjungaringanyi: Aboriginal rock, in *From Pop to Punk to Postmodernism: Popular Music and Australian Culture from the 1960s to 1990s*, edited by P. Hayward. Sydney: Allen & Unwin, 25–39.

Dreeszen, C., Aprill, A. and Deasy, R. 1999. *Learning Partnerships: Improving Learning in Schools with Arts Partners in the Community*. Washington, DC: Arts Education Partnership.

Duffy, M. 2002. We find ourselves again? Recreating identity through performance in the community music festival. *Australasian Music Research*, 7, 103–12, 135.

Duffy, M. 2005. Performing identity within a multicultural framework. *Social and Cultural Geography*, 6(5), 677–92.

Dunbar-Hall, P., and Gibson, C. 2000. Nitmiluk: Place and empowerment in Australian Aboriginal popular music. *Ethnomusicology*, 44(1), 39–64.

Dunbar-Hall, P. and Gibson, C. 2004. *Deadly Sounds, Deadly Places: Contemporary Aboriginal Music in Australia*. Sydney: UNSW Press.

Greenop, K. 2008. *Uncanny Brisbane: New Ways of Looking at Urban Indigenous Place*, Proceedings of the SAHANZ25: History in Practice Conference, Geelong: Deakin University.

Greenop, K. 2009a. *Inala Traditions: People, Places and History in Urban Indigenous Communities*. Brisbane: International Association for the Study of Traditional Environments.

Greenop, K. 2009b. Place meaning, attachment and identity in Indigenous Inala, Queensland, paper presented to Australian Institute of Aboriginal and Torres Strait Islander Studies Conference, Canberra, 28 September–2 October 2009. Available at: kellygreenop.weebly.com/publications.html [accessed: 18 December 2011].

Haig-Brown, C. 2001. Continuing collaborative knowledge production: Knowing when, where, how and why. *Journal of Intercultural Studies*, 22(1), 19–32.

Higgins, L. 2006. Boundary-walkers: Contexts and Concepts of Community Music. PhD thesis, University of Limerick.

Mackinlay, E. 2008. Making space as white music educators for Indigenous Australian holders of song, dance and performance knowledge: The centrality of relationship as pedagogy. *Australian Journal of Music Education*, 1, 2–6.

Maxwell, I. 2003. *Phat Beats, Dope Rhymes: Hip-hop Down Under Comin' Upper*. Middletown, CT: Wesleyan University Press.

Mitchell, T. 2006. Blackfellas rapping, breaking and writing: A short history of Aboriginal hip-hop. *Aboriginal History*, 30, 124–37.

Mudrooroo 1997. *The Indigenous Literature of Australia: Milli Milli Wangka*. Melbourne: Hyland House.

Neuenfeldt, K. 2001. From silence to celebration: Indigenous Australian performers at the Woodford Folk Festival. *World of Music*, 43(2–3), 65–91.

Peel, M. 2003. *The Lowest Rung Voices of Australian Poverty*. Melbourne: Cambridge University Press.

Selby, J. 2004. Working divides between indigenous and non-indigenous: Disruptions of identity. *International Journal of Qualitative Studies in Education*, 17(1), 143–56.

Sharpe, E.K. 2008. Festivals and social change: Intersections of pleasure and politics at a community music festival. *Leisure Sciences*, 30(3), 217–34.

Somerville, M. and Perkins, T. 2003. Border work in the contact zone: Thinking Indigenous/non-Indigenous collaboration spatially. *Journal of Intercultural Studies*, 24(3), 253–66.

Stylin' Up 2011. Fact sheet. Available at: www.atsis.uq.edu.au/birranews/docs/stylinup_factsheet.pdf [accessed: 22 December 2011].

Tedlock, B. 2000. Ethnography and ethnographic representation, in *Handbook of Qualitative Research*, edited by N.K. Denzin and Y.S. Lincoln. Thousand Oaks, CA: Sage.

Vallance, R. and Tchacos, E. 2001. Research: A cultural bridge, paper presented to Australian Association for Research in Education (AARE) Conference, Fremantle, Australia, 2–6 December 2001. Available at: www.aare.edu.au/01pap/val01102.htm [accessed: 2 January 2012].

Chapter 5

The Politics, Pleasure and Performance of New Age Travellers, Ravers and Anti-road Protestors: Connecting Festivals, Carnival and New Social Movements

Greg Martin

> In times past, people often complained about the excessive drinking, fighting and fornication as they do today, yet these things posed no grave threat to the established order. And even though many towns celebrated feasts of fools, when figures of authority such as the local bishop made way for mocking caricatures (a 'boy bishop', for example), these were safety values, in effect allowing people to let off steam without meaningfully challenging the way things were. (Sandbrook 2011: 41)

On this reading, festivals of the past were not radically counter-cultural, and did not possess subversive elements, but were an accepted and familiar part of the annual calendar – usually with a religious emphasis. In fact, Sandbrook (2011: 41) argues that, while traditional fairs and festivals were a form of escapism, they were also 'gigantic exercises in making money'. Although this remains largely true today, many festivals nowadays also contain some radical and/or political element. At one extreme, there are festivals like the Hillside Festival in Ontario, Canada, that *enact* (rather than *embed*) their politics by prefiguring a desired society and way of life, as opposed to merely critiquing existing social and political relations and institutions (Sharpe 2008). At the other more commercial extreme, there is a recent example at the 2011 Glastonbury festival where Art Uncut organized a peaceful direct action – using the slogan 'Bono Pay Up' – to highlight the hypocritical decision of mega-band U2 to switch its publishing base to the Netherlands after the Irish government imposed a cap of €250,000 a year on tax exemptions for artists' royalties (Trilling 2011).

This chapter contributes to analyses of the politics and cultural politics of festivals and processes of 'festivalization' by looking at three relatively intertwined cultures – New Age travellers, ravers and anti-road protestors – that existed more or less contemporaneously in Britain during the 1990s until they became 'unpopular cultures' (Redhead 1995) and were effectively outlawed under provisions of the *Criminal Justice and Public Order Act 1994* (UK) (the *Criminal Justice Act*). As will be shown, these three groups each had a lifestyle and culture that contained to varying degrees festive, carnival or festival-like performative elements, although this was by no means always their sole focus. Accordingly, the chapter shows how each culture comprised a distinctive mix of politics, pleasure and performance. Broadly speaking, road protestors are seen as more politically engaged than New Age travellers, who are viewed as more 'political' but less interested in pleasure than ravers, who were the most hedonistic and least politically oriented of the three groups.

Before looking at the cultural, or 'lifestyle', politics of these groups – including their creative, performative and festival-like qualities – the first section of the chapter considers how festivals and carnivals have been theorized, showing specifically how this relates to theories of contemporary 'new' social movements. That section is followed by a brief examination of some forms of social protest that have incorporated performance into their repertoire of collective action. After discussing the three case studies, the chapter concludes by considering some ways in which (new) social movement theory might help make sense of the cultural politics of New Age travellers, ravers and anti-road protestors, and explores what possible role festivals and carnival may perform in societies dominated by commercialism.

Theories of Carnival and Collective Action

It is now something of a cliché for commentators to refer to Mikhail Bakhtin's (1968) characterization of the medieval carnival or *carnivalesque* to discuss modern-day festivals (see also Stallybrass and White 1986), as Chris Anderton (2008: 41) implies when he says that 'many academic authors have drawn on the carnivalesque to help explain the role and meaning of modern music festivals, especially those events that have their roots in the imagery of the 1960s counterculture'. Bakhtin's argument was that the carnival represented a topsy-turvy world – a world turned upside down. It was a time and place where the dominant authority structures could be challenged, reversed or overturned. Importantly, acts of transgression were allowed to occur. Accordingly, Anderton (2008: 41) argues, 'the medieval carnival can be regarded as a kind of societal "safety valve": the peasantry were permitted to let loose for a limited period of time, allowing tensions and contradictions in society to be raised and released, while the status quo remained protected'.

Echoing Sandbrook (2011), Anderton's argument is that Bakhtin's carnivalesque concept only really relates to festivals with an alternative, radical or counter-cultural base, and has limited application when considering the full range of contemporary outdoor music festivals. He talks in terms of 'commercializing the carnivalesque' to capture the 'underlying tension between commercialism and the countercultural carnivalesque' (Anderton 2008: 45). Moreover, since balancing the sanitized and commercialized aspects of festivals with the counter-cultural or carnivalesque dimensions is key to securing their future success, some of the more commercial festivals now deliberately incorporate counter-cultural features, such as showing a concern for environmental sustainability by establishing on-site recycling bins to reduce the festival's carbon footprint (Anderton 2008: 49). These issues of alternative versus mainstream, authentic versus commercial and so on are recurring themes for festival-goers and academic researchers alike.

Cultural criminologists, for instance, note 'a commercial exploitation of the pursuit of pleasure and a commodification of transgression across a spectrum of illicit and exceptional activities in Western performative culture' (Measham 2004: 212; see also Rojek 2000). Mike Presdee argues that these processes of commodification and commercialization are now so virulent that it is hard to talk of 'authentic' carnival or carnivalesque in the original Bakhtinian sense. Presdee (2000: 44) says that '[s]o potent are the excitements of carnival that the pleasure and leisure industries have utilized carnival as a form and as a metaphor, providing commodified carnival experiences and excitements in a variety of contexts, some mainstream, others far more marginal'. Thus acts of body modification, sadomasochism, rave, recreational drug use, joyriding, gang ritual, festivals and extreme sports all represent only 'the marginal performance of carnival fragments in the late twentieth century' (Presdee 2000: 47). Undoubtedly, they all exhibit carnival laughter or carnival resistance, 'but in these cases the carnival has been appropriated and redelivered; it is, for want of a better phrase, secondary carnival' (Presdee 2000: 47). In other words, as Presdee (2000: 47) argues, 'these events are not carnival in their entirety, nor are they carnival exclusively, but they all contain elements of the performance of pleasure at the margins in opposition to the dominant values of sobriety and restraint'.

Given that many festivals have fallen prey to commercializing forces and experienced, at one time or other, cynical exploitation of counter-cultural values and lifestyles, it would seem important not to over-estimate – or indeed romanticize – the counter-cultural function of festivals. Indeed, while some festivals and festival-like events undoubtedly provide genuinely oppositional, radical or counter-cultural experiences, many do not. Any analysis should therefore consider how resistance, protest and political action – incorporating performance, festivals and festival-like forms – might play out in a context that is now so dominated by the cultural industries and processes of commercialization and consumerism. And it is essential here to always keep in mind that tension between alternative/mainstream and authentic/commercial (highlighted earlier) that is an underlying, albeit often implicit, theme of the data presented in this chapter, and is examined more explicitly in the concluding discussion. However, before moving on to explore the empirical case material, we must consider Victor Turner's (1969) influence on the field of study, not least because his ideas have been applied to social movement activity as well as to New Age travellers.

Turner's (1969) ideas about 'liminality' and 'communitas' are similar to Bakhtin's concept of the carnivalesque. Drawing on anthropological studies, Turner notes that certain rituals attached to rites of passage involve a three-stage process whereby participants leave a structured world with one status, enter a liminal phase then re-emerge into the structured society with a new status. During the liminal or 'anti-structure' stage, participants inhabit a place that is 'betwixt and between' the structure of the surrounding society, and in that phase they experience *communitas* – a sort of camaraderie, sense of togetherness, social solidarity and equality. In their study of festivals, Purdue et al. (1997: 660) draw on Turner's work, saying that '[a] festival is a liminal opportunity to experiment with pleasure and meaning'. They consider festivals part of 'do-it-yourself' (DIY) culture, which they define as the self-organizing networks with overlapping memberships and values that challenge the symbolic codes of mainstream society (Purdue et al. 1997: 647). For them, festivals are about *pleasure*. Thus the 'life politics' (Giddens 1991) of festivals is expressive rather than instrumental. Moreover, festivals depend upon social networks and embody a social movement milieu. Accordingly, Purdue et al. (1997) connect their analysis of festivals to Alberto Melucci's (1989, 1996) theory of contemporary 'new' social movements, which stresses the 'latent' processes involved in social protest and mobilization, and depicts movements as networks submerged in everyday life or as 'cultural laboratories' involved in the formation of new collective identities. Erin Sharpe (2008) has also shown how festivals can inspire attendees to adopt alternative practices that lead to personal transformation.

It was Melucci's view that we live in an increasingly 'complex society', where material production is being replaced by the production of information, signs, symbols and social relations. Contemporary social movements are correspondingly heterogeneous, fragile and complex (Bartholomew and Mayer 1992: 142). For Melucci, social movements act as 'symbolic challenges' to the homogenizing logic of the system. Contemporary collective actors pose symbolic challenges by overturning dominant cultural codes, by living out alternative lifestyles that ask us to recognize and accept their right to be different.[1] As power tends now to be masked by operational codes, formal rules and bureaucratic/technocratic procedures, contemporary movements 'act as "revealers" by exposing that which is hidden or excluded by the decision-making processes' (Melucci 1989: 175). Moreover, since social movements are complex and comprise a plurality of meanings and orientations (Melucci 1985: 794), a premium is placed on resolving conflicts and tensions to develop a collective identity. It is vital that movement actors construct a collective identity in order to present a clear and coherent message of difference to the rest of society. From this perspective, festivals might act as places (or spaces) where heterogeneous groups and lifestyles come together to form a collective identity.

New social movement theory has been subject to extensive criticism. Some doubt the real challenge of cultural politics or struggles waged exclusively at the level of lifestyle, while others question the efficacy of collective actors that seek autonomy and eschew the wider political system (Martin 2002a, 2002b, 2004; Maddison and Martin 2010). Looking at historical movements, other scholars

---

1   While it may be tempting to draw parallels between Melucci's work and that of Bakhtin and Turner, any similarities that do exist are essentially superficial. Whereas Melucci regards overturning dominant codes as a challenge to the system limits, Bakhtin and Turner see carnival and liminality as sanctioned by the system.

have questioned the novelty of 'new' movements, such as the women's movement, which they argue have roots in the early nineteenth century (Calhoun 1994: 22). Others argue that, like new movements, 'old' movements were also concerned with autonomy and identity (Tucker 1991), and that the early twentieth century working-class movement, for example, was more multi-dimensional than new social movement theorists care to admit, as that movement was concerned with 'women and children working, community life, the status of immigrants, education, access to public services, and so forth' (Calhoun 1995: 179).

Finally, some critics have argued that new social movement theory applies only to a 'privileged' section of the contemporary movement scene. It ignores movements that are not interested in 'post-materialism' (Inglehart 1977), quality of life and recognition, but are concerned instead with social welfare, material well-being and redistribution (Martin 2001). Among other things, these movements and collective actors have been affected adversely by global neoliberalism and post-Fordist restructuring processes; accordingly, they reflect and develop their identity around newly relevant 'survival issues' such as precarious employment, migrant rights and decent housing (Bartholomew and Mayer 1992: 150). Examples here include New Age travellers (Martin 1998, 2001), the *sans-papièrs* or undocumented immigrants ('without papers') in France (Freedman and Tarr 2000; McNevin 2006) and, more recently, campaigns against 'precarity', which encompass the *sans-papièrs* and other non-citizen migrants employed in precarious jobs (Neilson and Rossiter 2008; Doerr 2010). This chapter shows how some of these movements and groups have incorporated performance, carnival and festival-like features into their protest repertoire.

Lastly, it is worth mentioning that Purdue et al. (1997) also note a convergence of new social movement theory and Michel Maffesoli's (1996) ideas about the increasing relevance of nomadic 'neo-tribal' identities. In Australia, Joanne Cummings (2006) has used Maffesoli's work to show how indie music festivals are neo-tribal forms of sociality, whereby group identities are not formed around fixed structural determinants like gender or class but are fluid forms generated via individual consumption practices. Like new social movement theory, however, the concept of the neo-tribe has been critiqued. Especially in the context of subculture studies, scholars have argued that the idea of all young people being freely able to make lifestyle choices denies the reality that is faced by many working-class youth today of being simultaneously excluded economically yet included culturally and commercially (Martin 2009).

Social Protest as Performance

Before showing how the ideas discussed so far apply to New Age travellers, ravers and anti-road protestors, we turn to look briefly at how some contemporary social movements have utilized festive, theatrical and creative repertoires of collective action. Some festival organizers are confronted by the dilemma of attempting to appeal to a mainstream audience in a way that does not compromise the underlying (political) message/s. Essentially, that entails striking a balance between keeping the message real while at the same time drawing in a diverse range of people. In such circumstances, festival organizers can seek external sponsorship, which might lead to the festival becoming commercialized and the message diluted (Anderton 2008; Cummings 2008). On the other hand, there is a growing tendency for political events to incorporate music, dance, theatre, play, puppetry and other festive, creative and expressive elements into their repertoire of collective activism (Sharpe 2008: 228) – although this is not an entirely novel phenomenon, having been recognized by Benford and Hunt (1992: 41–2), for example, as an aspect of the 'dramaturgy of social movements'.

Chesters and Welsh (2004) show how 'Rebel Colours' were used to differentiate the three marches that took place in Prague on 26 September (S26) 2000 at the beginning of the World Bank/IMF Conference. Of most relevance to the subject-matter of this chapter is the pink colour or pink frame, which derived from protest repertoires developed in the United Kingdom by the groups Reclaim the Streets and Earth First!, both of which have been involved in anti-roads protests, impromptu street parties and numerous ecological and 'anti-capitalist' campaigns. Chesters and Welsh (2004: 328–9) show how:

> This frame privileges playful, ludic and carnivalesque forms of protest, valorises the creative and expressive over the instrumental and rational, and utilises a variety of performative repertoires that are dependent upon sophisticated and nuanced understandings of protest dynamics.

As a signifier, the colour pink derived from two distinct sources. First, pink was chosen because of its lack of political connotations,[2] and to provoke socialists who would have to self-classify as pink rather than the standard colour of red. Second, pink (as well as silver) was chosen by a group called 'Tactical Frivolity', whose name 'evokes playful, performative and carnivalesque repertoires' (Chesters and Welsh 2004: 329). Tactical Frivolity was a group comprising mainly women and 'individuals who were marginal to the decision-making processes and organizational networks through which the Prague protests evolved' (Chesters and Welsh 2004: 329), although their influence was significant for emphasizing non-violence:

> Tactical Frivolity, in both name and practice managed to distil some of the symbolic resources and affective currents that have helped construct successful roads protests and large scale carnivalesque collective actions in the UK since the early 1990s. Theirs was a deliberate intervention provoked by a desire to move set-piece confrontations in a particular direction, a standpoint that is

---

2   Chesters and Welsh (2004: 334) recognize that pink is a colour long associated with the gay and lesbian movement, but say that association was absent from the argumentation of their interviewees.

implicitly critical of a perceived slide towards routinized conflict leading to violence. (Chesters and Welsh 2004: 329)

Tactical Frivolity's use of pink as a frame inferring 'active non-violence' derives from a larger social movement milieu that prioritizes the affective, emotional and intuitive dimensions of collective action, which facilitates the conscious and active opening of a *performative space* where provocation and contestation (such as that between police and protestors) may take place in a non-violent, playful way (Chesters and Welsh 2004: 329–30). Notwithstanding the specific achievements and broader significance of Tactical Frivolity, Chesters and Welsh (2004: 324) argue that the pink march generally was the most successful in getting close to the conference centre, and thereby disrupting the World Bank/International Monetary Fund meeting. Protestors in that march nearly breached the police cordon when they got to within 50 metres of the conference centre, although two marchers did manage to enter the conference security zone, where one of them 'had a great chat with a man from the Royal Canadian Mint' (2004: 324). Another measure of the success of this particular march was that, because it was 'highly mobile, fluid and infectious', it drew 'people away from the other two routes to join it as the day progressed' (2004: 324).

Graham St John (2008: 168) has talked of similar events in terms of 'protestival', which is a polyvalent tactic involving the festal, mobilized by the alter-globalization movement, 'a creative response to the traditional political rituals of the left', building upon the meta-political tactic of new social movements by rendering power visible and posing symbolic challenges. St John argues that while new social movement theory has recognized the significance of movement cultural politics, new approaches are needed to understand the festal and carnivalesque character of contemporary activism, and especially transnational activism associated with the alter-globalization movement. Although St John proposes no way to fill the lacuna he identifies, it may be that one fruitful line of inquiry would be to look at the European precarity movement, which has used some tactics associated with 'carnivalesque forms of protest' (Chesters and Welsh 2004: 328).

Initially feeding off the wider anti-globalization movement and campaigns against the Iraq war (Bodnar 2006: 685; De Sario 2007: 25, 26; Neilson and Rossiter 2008: 57), since 2001 the precarity movement has become synonymous with the EuroMayDay protest events held on 1 May each year across European cities. The movement consists largely of workers in precarious forms of work ('the precariat'), who demonstrate against temporary, casualized and 'flexible' employment (lack of job security) under neoliberal post-Fordist conditions, as well as the dismantling of the welfare (social security) state and a decline in trade unionism, which combine to makes their conditions of existence doubly precarious. As such, it is an example of a contemporary movement that does not fit the new social movement model – which, as discussed above, is predicated on a theory of post-materialism and relative affluence. Tactics used by precarity protestors include the use of performance, street parades and festivals, visual images and counter-images on posters – and, seemingly at odds with Chesters and Welsh's (2004: 334) participants mentioned earlier (see note 2), the adoption of the colour pink to express affinity with queer politics and global justice protests (De Sario 2007; Mattoni and Doerr 2007).

Having presented some key ideas and theories about festivals, carnival and the carnivalesque, and considered briefly how those relate to social protest and collection action, the chapter now moves on to examine the cultural politics of New Age travellers, ravers and anti-road protestors, with a particular focus – where relevant – on how each group variously incorporated festive and performative elements into its lifestyle, culture and politics. As stated in the introduction, the cultural politics of each group differed both in terms of its quality and orientation. Thus anti-road protestors were generally seen as more politically engaged than travellers, whose 'politics' largely consisted of adopting a culture or way of life that was oppositional to the wider sedentary society. Ravers tend to be regarded as the least politically motivated of all three groups – indeed, rave can be read as quite a conservative cultural form, which not only accommodated but was, at times, in cahoots with mainstream consumer culture. Although the three groups examined here no longer exist, as was shown above, festivals, performances or festival-like action continue to figure in the repertoire of certain social movements and collective actors today. However, whether the use of such tactics is genuinely carnivalesque, in the original Bakhtinian (1968) sense, or is restricted to 'secondary carnival', to use Presdee's (2000) term, is an empirical question to be explored – although, as the conclusion to this chapter contends, when considering the role of festivals in contemporary social and political life, it must be remembered that festivals and carnivals (in the traditional sense, anyway) only ever performed a 'safety valve' function – operating within permitted system limits – and were not supposed to break the system limits in the way social movements are meant to.

New Age Travellers

In his book, *Senseless Acts of Beauty*, George McKay (1996) implies that anti-road protestors, New Age travellers and ravers are located at different points on a continuum: from politics to pleasure respectively. McKay aims to reclaim the power of the notion of counter-culture. He wants to uncover 'cultures of resistance' in Britain that have their roots in the 1960s counter-culture. However, he is selective about the cultures and subcultures he studies, only choosing those that are oppositional and politically radical (McKay 1996: 6). Also, very much in line with studies of contemporary 'new' social movements discussed above, McKay wants to understand cultures of resistance that diverge from the old politics of class and material/economic concerns. His focus is on campaigns around single issues, the politics of direct action and DIY lifestyles.

McKay (1996: 42) begins his analysis by looking at the Fairs of Albion that took place in East Anglia during the 1970s and early 1980s. He likens these fairs to Bakhtin's (1968) notion of carnival, as they represent 'a subversive moment in which fixed social roles and mores are overturned'. However, the fairs eventually died out. According to the elders of the (hippie) counter-culture who organized them, the fairs began to decline when the Peace Convoy (so called because of its association with peace camps at Royal Air Force bases such as Greenham Common and Molesworth) started to show up and intimidate punters out of money and rip off other festival-goers, and leave burnt-out cars and piles of rubbish behind when they left. At this time, Green Fairs, which focused on forestry and consciousness-raising to combat desertification (McKay 1996: 40), also moved from being small in scale and with local ties to become festivals or large-scale national events. However, McKay argues that the Peace Convoy was less a cause of the death of the fairs than it was a symptom of broader transformations occurring in Thatcher's Britain from the late 1970s. Moreover, he says, the free festivals that came to be associated with the Peace Convoy and New Age travellers did in fact continue the ideals and ideas of the Fairs of Albion – namely, 'land, alternative society, travelling, impermanence, even the initial connection with gypsies' (McKay 1996: 43).

Some of these arguments are echoed in the work of Kevin Hetherington and Greg Martin. For Hetherington, the travellers' scene consisted of tribes or 'neo-tribes' (Maffesoli 1996), since people chose to adopt an alternative lifestyle that valued expressive and affectual social bonds. Hetherington (1994) compares the concept of neo-tribe to Schmalenbach's concept of the *Bund*, which he applies to travellers. Meaning 'communion', the concept of the *Bund* was meant to be the intermediary of Tönnies' twin concepts, *Gemeinschaft* ('community') and *Gesellschaft* ('society'), whereby *Bünde* are 'small-scale, achieved rather than ascribed, unstable and affectual forms of sociation' (Hetherington 1992: 93). Because of this emphasis on affectivity and social solidarity, Hetherington (1994: 19) argues that *Bünde* are also pre-conditions for new social and religious movements.

Despite their non-commercial spirit, free festivals were marketplaces where people bought and sold their wares (Martin 1998: 741). The festival season reached its peak during the annual summer solstice celebrations at Stonehenge, although this event ceased in 1985 after police clashed violently with travellers during the infamous Battle of the Beanfield. Hetherington (2000: 16) invokes the work of Turner (discussed above) to describe Stonehenge as a liminal space where 'the rules of society are overturned, mocked and transgressed, often through festival and carnival forms where the social world is momentarily turned upside-down in some kind of drama ritual of disordering'. Moreover, for Hetherington (1996), Stonehenge was a place of 'social centrality' for travellers, where the various *Bünde*-like tribes gathered to consolidate the traveller identity. From a new social movement perspective, festivals might be seen as places where different groups or traveller 'tribes' could gather to develop a collective identity and transmit a message of difference. However, it may be argued that festivals, as the visible face of the traveller way of life, were only made possible by what Verta Taylor (1989) calls 'abeyance structures', or the hidden cultural spaces, networks and communities that sustain movements (and other forms of collective action) over time, and especially during dormant periods. In this way, festivals represented the tip of an iceberg, supported and maintained by a multitude of quotidian structures, people and groups of people who practised or lived out alternative lifestyles. This helps give meaning, in one sense at least, to the notion of the 'festivalization of everyday life', because for travellers, festivals were integral to their way of life.

Research conducted by Greg Martin (1998, 2002a, 2002b) confirms the idea that Stonehenge and other festival sites acted as places where different groups of travellers could congregate to consolidate a collective identity. However, Martin shows how, beyond festivals – and even sometimes at festivals – the travellers' scene was far from harmonious and came to be dominated by inter-generational conflict; although communitas, in Victor Turner's sense of the term, could be experienced when travelling in convoy either to and from festivals, or between sites, following eviction (Martin 2002b: 731). The older generation of travellers, who were members of the Peace Convoy, made a conscious decision to move on to the road and adopt a lifestyle that was connected to themes in new social and new religious movements, such as New Age spirituality, ecological and green politics, and peace/anti-nuclear campaigning. Here, '[s]pirituality meets politics meets new age travellers' (McKay 1996: 58). However, Martin argues, there was another less engaged and less politically active section of the traveller population that emerged during the late 1980s and early 1990s. These generally younger travellers were 'economic refugees', who moved on to the road to escape the ravages of Thatcherism – namely unemployment and homelessness. This is how one traveller put it:

> New Age travellers of the seventies and early eighties were driven by visions, ideals, inspiration. The influx of what I would called economic refugees has changed it completely. They're driven by desperation basically and they haven't got the ideals that drove us on the road looking for something better. What they're doing now is driving on to travellers' sites all the shit of the city. (Lowe and Shaw 1993: 138)

During this time, and somewhat ironically, the older generation of travellers blamed the younger generation of 'crusty' travellers (and ravers) for the demise of the free festivals, just as the organizers of the Fairs of Albion once blamed the Peace Convoy for the demise of the Green Fairs. For McKay (1996), however, the differences between travellers are more political than generational. He traces the emergence of New Age travellers to the 1980s housing crisis, which led to a squatting movement. Thus it would seem that the older generation of travellers took to the road not out of choice, as Hetherington and Martin have argued, but as a solution to homelessness (as did their younger counterparts some years later).

Like Martin, McKay (1996: 53) states that many young travellers of the 1990s identified as 'economic refugees' who had been living on the margins of society and were 'pushed rather than dropped out'. Accordingly, they may be likened to those less privileged social movements (discussed above) that, unlike the more privileged 'new' social movements, reflect and develop a collective identity around issues of survival and material well-being. Moreover, while the older generation were politically engaged in such things as anti-nuclear campaigning and alternative/green lifestyles, and thus tied to the politics of new social movements, the younger generation of travellers tended not to be, as Jeremy from traveller band the Levellers explains: 'We weren't a movement, just a bunch of pissed up people, some so nasty not even I would talk to them' (McKay 1996: 52).

Ravers and Rave Culture

During the mid-1990s, the traveller lifestyle itself became politicized when nomadic lifestyles, including the traditional gypsy way of life, were effectively criminalized under the *Criminal Justice Act*. The introduction of this piece of legislation was partly a response by the British government to what was seen as the enduring social problem of New Age travellers, and the kind of nuisance and anti-social behaviour associated with travellers, as described by Jeremy in the quotation above. Accordingly, certain provisions of the Act were aimed specifically at curtailing the activities of New Age travellers, and those provisions – which placed limits on the number of vehicles that could gather in one place – also applied to ravers. While some travellers decided to move abroad to Ireland and Europe (Martin 1998: 751–2), others fought the legislation, as did activists connected to the UK anti-road protests (see McKay 1996: Ch. 6; 1998 for discussion). Indeed, campaigning against the *Criminal Justice Act* 'united previously disparate groups' (Rietveld 1998: 247), and that included ravers. However, perhaps because they were the least politically motivated of the three groups, the involvement of ravers in anti-*Criminal Justice Act* campaigning was likely more reactive than born of a radical politics. In some ways, this answers McKay's (1996: 104) question posed at the beginning of his chapter on rave culture – namely where are the politics? To be sure, a central problem for many analysts of rave has been to consider its contribution to a culture of resistance, asking whether rave culture is simply hedonistic or whether it can be seen as a form of political activism. Answering that question requires attention to be focused on both the progressive and conservative elements of rave and rave culture, which is a distinction that will become apparent in the following discussion.

Some commentators argue that rave was devoid of politics with a capital 'P'. In fact, researchers at the Manchester Institute of Popular Culture (the 'Manchester School') tended to see the mixing of hitherto discrete subcultures (New Age traveller, football, Indie) on the same dance floor as a sign of the postmodern politics of rave culture and acid house music (Redhead 1990: 75; 1993: 3–4; see also McKay 1996: 105), which reached its zenith at the Castlemorton festival/ rave in 1992 (McKay 1996: 120, 123; see also Malyon 1998: 192–3). Thus, like the traveller lifestyle, the emergence of rave heralded a shift away from class-bound, coherent youth subcultures (e.g. Hall and Jefferson 1976; Hebdige 1979), towards more plural, fluid, eclectic and elective social identities and 'neo-tribes'

(Bennett 1999; see also Martin 2009 for discussion) – a transition captured in the phrase 'subculture to clubcultures' (Redhead 1998).

To some extent, rave's contribution to a culture of resistance could be found in a 'cultural politics of the provinces' (McKay 1996: 107), such as that found in the Manchester (or Madchester) scene, which was 'working against a London-centred internationalism and perceived privilege' (McKay 1996: 107). Other progressive aspects of rave included the democratic status of house events wherein dominant modes of musical organization and consumption were rejected (Hesmondhalgh 1995), and the cultural politics of sampling, which was a relatively accessible technology that enabled people to produce music cheaply (McKay 1996: 116, 117). The 'club', as one of the places of the dance scene side of rave, was also presented as a 'libertarian utopian space, packed with transformative possibility' (McKay 1996: 117).

Adopting this more positive view, and rejecting Hesmondhalgh's (1995) depiction of rave as defined by individual retreat into music and a lack of social collectivism, Rietveld (1998: 258–9) argues that, above all, raves were tactile-acoustic events where people congregated to be physically close, despite the law. However, like members of the Manchester School, she says rave was less about opposition and resistance than it was about decontextualized (postmodern) pleasure (Rietveld 1993; see also McKay 1996: 114). Indeed, it has been argued that rave culture exhibited some quite conservative qualities entirely consistent with the Thatcherite 'enterprise culture' that grew in Britain during the 1980s and 1990s (Martin 1998: 753). According to this interpretation, raves were a form of 'deviant enterprise' analogous to Thatcherite philosophy around entrepreneurialism and self-help. Raver entrepreneurs therefore accepted the more mainstream notion of enterprise as profit-making, although they operated (as travellers did at free festivals) outside of the formal economy (see Redhead 1993: 22). However, '[t]he dance scene split into those who saw an opportunity to cash in, those willing to cough up and those who valued it as an escape from those priorities' (Wright 1998: 238). Thus, while some of the new rave entrepreneurs were accused of selling out to capitalism, ripping off punters and pulling off scams (Wright 1998: 238), it has been argued that for the most part raves and acid house clubs offered punters 'an escapist hedonist leisure activity in an increasingly commercialised rave scene' (Rietveld 1998: 255). But that is a long way from saying ravers and rave culture offered a radical and oppositional alternative to the mainstream in ways similar to New Age travellers and anti-road protestors. Indeed, it might be suggested that ravers were furthest removed from a wider culture of resistance simply because, unlike the other two groups, they were always closest to – and sometimes central players in – the commercial mainstream.

Interestingly, it has been argued that travellers forced to develop survival strategies during the Thatcher years were, like ravers, also engaged in a version of 'deviant enterprise', thus providing an example of the exercise of 'subterranean values' – 'values, that is to say, which are in conflict or in competition with other deeply held values but which are still recognised and accepted by many' (Matza and Sykes 1961: 716). Thus some young travellers (often dubbed 'Thatcher's children') who took the Thatcherite values of self-help and entrepreneurialism literally, argued that they were solving their homeless and other housing problems in an enterprising way, which is why many expressed exasperation and alarm at the government's harsh treatment of them and the ultimate criminalization of their lifestyle via the *Criminal Justice Act* (Martin 1998: 747). In a sense, then – and although most may never have articulated it as such – the way of life of these travellers was itself a form of protest or resistance – a radical alternative to 'straight' society – which was how many anti-road protestors viewed themselves and their cultural politics.

Anti-road Protestors

While New Age travellers and ravers articulated politics through pleasure or lifestyle, anti-road protestors expressed their politics through direct action, although sometimes that political strategy was combined with pleasure and the adoption of alternative ways of living (McKay 1996: 131). In accordance with other novel forms of social activism, including new social movements, DIY protest and direct action around the UK government's road-building policies were largely a response to disillusionment with parliamentary politics and a rejection of old politics (McKay 1996: 128; Jordan 1998: 131) – although it has been noted some involved in Reclaim the Streets (RTS), for instance, still talk in terms of state, capital and class (Aufheben 1998: 125). The two particular aspects of the anti-road/anti-automotive movement examined in this section are the Dongas' fight to stop the building of a motorway in the south of England, and the struggle by RTS and other groups to prevent the M11 link road through London.

The Dongas Tribe was formed on Twyford Down in Hampshire as a spontaneous response to the final stage of a road-building project, 'partly inspired by the direct action protest of a few local Greenham Common veterans against the first damage to the Itchen Navigation waterway in early 1992' (McKay 1996: 139). The aim of the Dongas was to prevent the construction of the extension of the M3, which would destroy a Site of Special Scientific Interest. The Dongas have been described as 'traveller-style road protestors' (McKay 1996: 132). However, just as the older, hippie generation of travellers dissociated themselves from the younger, 'crusty' travellers, so the Dongas distinguished themselves from New Age travellers of all ages. Moreover, while values/ethics/spirituality informed the politics of the Dongas (and continues to do so for other groups such as Friends of the Earth and Earth First! (EF!)), they distanced themselves from a 'New Age' philosophy, simply because the New Age perspective privileges individual change over social change. As Donga Alex states: 'It is the translation of ethics into political action that goes beyond the personal which differentiates EF! values from those of New Agers' (Plows 1998: 170).

Another point of distinction between groups like the Dongas and New Age travellers is that, while for the latter 'the road is a special space that somehow encapsulates the sense of freedom they seek', for the former 'roads have been constructed as site [sic] of all that's wrong with Britain' (McKay 1996: 134–5). Notwithstanding these divergences, there were affinities between travellers and the Dongas. For example, both groups shared an admiration for tribal and nomadic peoples with respectful attitudes to the land, as evidenced by the Native American influence in the establishment from the mid-1970s of Tipi Valley in Wales. Thus there was a definite homology between the Donga lifestyle and politics, which has been called 'practical paganism' or 'political paganism':

> For example, their mundane yet practical micro approach to environmental respect is evident 'every time we shit in the earth where it becomes fertilizer and do not flush it out to the sea where it becomes a poison'. The Dongas are an amazing mixture of the wildly New Age (Sam: 'if you play music around a stone circle ... you do have this aura of really powerful energy with you and everything you do from there on becomes really magical) and the eminently and stubbornly practical (as with the huge kick-start they gave road protest). (McKay 1996: 138)

So the Dongas combined a political strategy of non-violent direct action, withdrawal and refusal – squatting the land to be dug up for the motorway, using their bodies as sites of resistance – with a kind of New Age spirituality. The Donga lifestyle also contained creative and performative elements. For instance, there was a Donga play featuring dragons, and they developed rituals and festivals to celebrate the seasons (McKay 1996: 139). Interestingly, the Dongas revived the tradition of the fairs, holding the Tan Hill Fayre in 1994 after a 20-year break (McKay 1996: 145–6).

It is important to realize that the anti-roads movement did not revolve around a single issue, but rather embraced 'issues of land ownership, environmentalism, health and pollution, technology, big business, regional and self-empowerment and self-development, the power of the law itself' (McKay 1996: 135), which is one of the reasons why direct action campaigners like the Dongas were able to form unlikely coalitions with 'respectable' middle-class people in local communities (McKay 1996: 132). This is also another feature of the 'new politics' of contemporary protest movements, whereby 'the conflict is not staged by one class but by a social alliance that consists, in varying proportions, of elements coming from different classes and "nonclasses"' (Offe 1985: 835).

Just as Tactical Frivolity significantly influenced the roads protests and large-scale carnivalesque collective actions in the United Kingdom during the 1990s (Chesters and Welsh 2004: 329), so the Dongas have been seen not only as instrumental in inspiring a protest culture against roads but, it is argued, also able to 'claim responsibility for the extraordinary upsurge in direct action politics seen in the 1990s in Britain' (McKay 1996: 45). While some Dongas became a tribe in a more nomadic/travelling sense, others became concerned with developing links with local communities and connecting social and environmental issues, such as bad housing and the impact of roads on residents' health, safety and quality of life (Plows 1998: 161), demonstrating that 'Donga ideals are far removed from the perceived hedonism and pose of youth subcultures' (McKay 1996: 145). Indeed, the Dongas positioned themselves at the other extreme of ravers and rave culture (with New Age travellers lying somewhere in between), and in May 1993 they even refused to allow techno outfit Spiral Tribe access to their camp to hold a free party for their benefit (McKay 1996: 147).

Rather than seeing protest as a way of life, the Dongas saw their way of life as a form of protest, which confirms Melucci's (1984: 830, original emphasis) argument that: 'Since the action is focused on cultural codes, the *form* of the movement is a message, a symbolic challenge to the dominant patterns' and so: 'The medium, the movement itself is a new medium, is the message'. This was also true of other anti-road protests, such as the campaign against the construction of the M11 link road through London. Like the Dongas' protest, this was not about a single issue but a whole way (or ways) of life (McKay 1996: 152). Centring on Claremont Road, the protest entailed regular Sunday parties that attracted a diversity of groups from environmentalists to ravers to activists against the Criminal Justice Bill. Direct action was also viewed as a performance: 'Closing the road to cars, they built barricades, towers, art installations, and tunnels – and converted the street itself into a room for living and partying, complete with furniture, snooker tables, dining areas, and a stage' (Ferrell 2001: 132; see also McKay 1996: 151). Just like the Dongas' 'practical/political paganism' (see above), the occupation of Claremont Road was a case in which '"direct action" becomes "performance where the poetic and pragmatic join hands"' (Ferrell 2001: 136; see also Jordan 1998: 132). In this way, the 'theatrical function' of the direct action 'is that it is enacted in front of an audience, not only the media, but for local passers-by, who are often awestruck by what they see and are thus brought into dialogue with the issues' (Jordan 1998: 133).

The action at Claremont Road revitalized RTS, a 'disorganized' anti-automotive movement that emerged in the early 1990s alongside the wider anti-road protests (Ferrell 2001: 132). The direct action by RTS represented, at once, the 'festival of the oppressed' – people formerly excluded from streets now celebrated down the middle of them – and the 'festival of resistance' whereby this reclaimed 'celebratory space spawned new "living rooms" in the street, new interactions and pleasures, even new forms of practical resistance' (Ferrell 2001: 136–7). Here, direct action effects change not via the mediation of professional politicians, but 'by individual and collective participation in social affairs' (Jordan 1998: 148). Importantly, RTS activists were also acutely aware of how their direct action carried on a tradition of carnival, which 'celebrates temporary liberation from the prevailing truth and the established order', and they thus recognized 'their role in breathing new life into old subversions' (Ferrell 2001: 137). As both poetic and pragmatic performance, direct action such as this involves the use of the body as a site of 'creative resistance':

> To engage in direct action you have to feel enough passion to put your values into practice; it is literally embodying your feelings, performing your politics. The body has been marginalised by our technocratic culture. This is dangerous: it further reveals a society completely out of touch with itself and its environment; a society which prefers to use the metaphor of the machine – hard, unconnected

parts – rather than the body – interconnected, fluid and soft. Direct action makes visible the devastation of industrial culture's machinery and returns the body to the centre of politics, of cultural practice. (Jordan 1998: 134)

In particular, it is via the festival of resistance and 'immersion in the edgy dangers of direct action' (Ferrell 2001: 138) that RTS and other similar (dis)organizations show how, while the car is a deadly problem, it is actually 'symptomatic of a larger set of contemporary problems regarding the mass extermination of human spontaneity [and] the routinization of everyday existence' (Ferrell 2004: 288). Indeed, like the Dongas and the broader anti-road movement, RTS combines pleasure and politics – which, according to Jeff Ferrell (2001: 139), means it 'introduces a particularly playful politics' or, in the words of one RTS group, 'a determination to turn "the pavement into a playground"'.

Conclusion

The foregoing analysis of New Age travellers, ravers and anti-road protestors has certain implications for (new) social movement studies. For example, the activism of anti-road protestors is similar to what Melucci (1984) sees as being a symbolic function of new movements – namely that their direct action 'revealed' or *made visible* the devastation of industrial-technocratic culture (Jordan 1998: 134). Similarly, Melucci's ideas about contemporary movements posing symbolic challenges to dominant norms have been applied to rave culture, and in particular the 'ecstasy revolution', because the use of ecstasy transforms personal attitudes and provides new orientations of social action such that 'dance culture can be classed as a contemporary movement which can be seen to demonstrate to society that alternatives are possible' (Wright 1998: 240–41).

While opinion remains divided as to the precise nature (and efficacy) of the cultural politics of rave, commentators are less equivocal about the anti-roads movement. As shown earlier, the Dongas not only kick-started a protest culture against roads and road building, but also sparked an upsurge in direct-action politics in Britain during the 1990s (McKay 1996: 45). Importantly, the Dongas and other protest groups were instrumental in ending the British government's road-building programme via a unique combination of politics, pleasure and performance: 'The subversive imaginations of the M11 campaign and Reclaim the Streets have succeeded in creating acts of resistance which are both powerful poetic gestures and effective political strategies' (Jordan 1998: 151).

As with new social movements generally, the direct action protest repertoire of anti-road protestors was born of disillusionment with parliamentary politics and the perceived failure of established pressure groups (McKay 1996: 128). However, contrary to what new social movement theory postulates, all three cultures examined here were not entirely insulated from the broader political system. In fact, each culture became politicized – and many activists were forced to engage directly with traditional political actors – when the *Criminal Justice Act* was introduced (Martin 1998, 2002). In one fell swoop, this piece of legislation effectively criminalized, and in turn extinguished, the way of life of New Age travellers, the holding of outdoor rave parties and the activities of anti-road protestors.

As stated at the beginning of this chapter, the performative, festival or festival-like elements of the culture and politics of New Age travellers, ravers and anti-road protestors constituted only a part – albeit an integral one – of their lifestyles and forms of protest. Moreover, while carnival, performance and so on continue to be incorporated into contemporary repertoires of collective action (as people like Chesters and Welsh 2004 have shown), questions remain about the wider cultural influence and 'political' significance of festivals and festivalization processes. For, although festivals clearly open up possibilities for some people to experience and consume culture in radical, counter-cultural ways – or, to use Melucci's (1989: 60) term, act as 'cultural laboratories' for experimentation in alternative living and personal transformation – they nevertheless do so within certain limits. Indeed, according to Presdee (2000: 47), the predominance of commodification and commercialization in the current period means 'authentic' carnival or carnivalesque in the classic Bakhtinian sense is increasingly experienced as 'carnival fragments' or 'secondary carnival'. But it was ever thus. Festivals and carnivals operate within the confines of the larger society, and are not supposed, in social movement parlance, to break the system limits. Therefore, it may be argued that contemporary festivals, whether commercial or non-commercial, carry on this tradition: performing a release or safety value function, acting as a sanctioned hiatus from the humdrum of everyday life.

References

Anderton, C. 2008. Commercializing the carnivalesque: The V Festival and image/ risk management. *Event Management*, 12, 39–51.

Aufheben 1998. The politics of anti-road struggle and the struggles of anti-road politics: The case of the No. M11 Link Road Campaign, in *DiY Culture: Party and Protest in Nineties Britain*, edited by G. McKay. London: Verso, 100–28.

Bakhtin, M. 1968. *Rabelais and His World*, translated by H. Iswolsky. Cambridge, MA: MIT Press.

Bartholomew, A. and Mayer, M. 1992. Nomads of the present: Melucci's contribution to 'new social movement' theory. *Theory, Culture and Society*, 9(4), 141–59.

Benford, R.D. and Hunt, S.A. 1992. Dramaturgy of social movements: The social construction and communication of power. *Sociological Inquiry*, 62(1), 37–55.

Bennett, A. 1999. Subcultures or neo-tribes? Rethinking the relationship between youth, style and musical taste. *Sociology*, 33(3), 599–617.

Bodnar, C. 2006. Taking it to the streets: French cultural workers' resistance and the creation of the precariat movement. *Canadian Journal of Communication*, 31(3), 675–94.

Calhoun, C. 1994. Social theory and the politics of identity, in *Social Theory and the Politics of Identity*, edited by C. Calhoun. Oxford: Blackwell, 9–36.

Calhoun, C. 1995. 'New social movements' of the early nineteenth century, in *Repertoires and Cycles of Collective Action*, edited by M. Traugott. Durham, NC: Duke University Press, 173–215.

Chesters, G. and Welsh, I. 2004. Rebel colours: 'Framing' in global social movements. *The Sociological Review*, 52(3), 314–35.

Cummings, J. 2006. More than just a t-shirt: Neo-tribal sociality and linking images at Australian indie music festivals. *Perfect Beat*, 8(1), 69–84.

Cummings, J. 2008. Trade mark registered: Sponsorship within the Australian indie music festival scene. *Continuuum*, 22(5), 675–85.

De Sario, B. 2007. 'Precari su marte': An experiment in activism against precarity. *Feminist Review*, 87, 21–39.

Doerr, N. 2010. Politicizing precarity, producing visual dialogues on migration: Transnational public spaces in social movements. *Forum: Qualitative Sozialforschung*, 11(2), Art. 30, May.

Ferrell, J. 2001. *Tearing Down the Streets: Adventures in Urban Anarchy*. New York: Palgrave.

Ferrell, J. 2004. Boredom, crime and criminology. *Theoretical Criminology*, 8(3), 287–302.

Freedman, J. and Tarr, C. 2000. The *sans-papièrs*: An Interview with Madjiguène Cissé, in *Women, Immigration and Identities in France*, edited by J. Freedman and C. Tarr. Oxford: Berg, 29–38.

Giddens, A. 1991. *Modernity and Self-Identity*. Cambridge: Polity Press.

Hall, S. and Jefferson, T. 1976 (eds). *Resistance Through Rituals: Youth Subcultures in Post-war Britain*. London: Hutchinson.

Hebdige, D. 1979. *Subculture: The Meaning of Style*. London: Methuen.

Hesmondhalgh, D. 1995. Technoprophecy: A response to Tagg. *Popular Music*, 14(2), 261–3.

Hetherington, K. 1992. Stonehenge and its festival: Spaces of consumption, in *Lifestyle Shopping: The Subject of Consumption*, edited by R. Shields. London: Routledge, 83–98.

Hetherington, K. 1994. The contemporary significance of Schmalenbach's concept of the *Bünd*. *The Sociological Review*, 42(1), 1–25.

Hetherington, K. 1996. Identity formation, space and social centrality. *Theory, Culture and Society*, 13(4), 33–52.

Hetherington, K. 2000. *New Age Travellers: Vanloads of Uproarious Humanity*. London: Cassell.

Inglehart, R. 1977. *The Silent Revolution: Changing Values and Political Styles Among Western Publics*. Princeton, NJ: Princeton University Press.

Jordan, J. 1998. The art of necessity: The subversive imagination of anti-road protest and Reclaim the Streets, in *DiY Culture: Party and Protest in Nineties Britain*, edited by G. McKay. London: Verso, 129–51.

Lowe, R. and Shaw, R. 1993. *Travellers: Voices of the New Age Nomads*. London: Fourth Estate.

Maddison, S. and Martin, G. 2010. Introduction to 'Surviving Neoliberalism: The Persistence of Australian Social Movements'. *Social Movement Studies*, 9(2), 101–20.

Maffesoli, M. 1996. *The Time of the Tribes*. London: Sage.

Malyon, T. 1998. Tossed in the fire and they never got burned: The Exodus Collective, in *DiY Culture: Party and Protest in Nineties Britain*, edited by G. McKay. London: Verso, 187–207.

Martin, G. 1998. Generational Differences Amongst New Age Travellers. *The Sociological Review*, 46(4), 735–56.

Martin, G. 2001. Social movements, welfare and social policy: A critical analysis. *Critical Social Policy*, 21(3), 361–83.

Martin, G. 2002a. Conceptualising cultural politics in subcultural and social movements studies. *Social Movement Studies*, 1(1), 73–88.

Martin, G. 2002b. New Age travellers: Uproarious or uprooted? *Sociology*, 36(3), 723–35.

Martin, G. 2004. New social movements and democracy, in *Democracy and Participation: Popular Protest and New Social Movements*, edited by M.J. Todd and G. Taylor. London: Merlin Press, 29–54.

Martin, G. 2009. Subculture, style, chavs and consumer capitalism: Towards a critical cultural criminology of youth. *Crime Media Culture*, 5(2), 123–45.

Mattoni, A. and Doerr, N. 2007. Images within the precarity movement in Italy. *Feminist Review*, 87, 130–35.

Matza, D and Sykes, G.M. 1961. Juvenile delinquency and subterranean values. *American Sociological Review*, 26(5), 712–19.

McKay, G. 1996. *Senseless Acts of Beauty: Cultures of Resistance Since the Sixties*. London: Verso.

McKay, G. (ed.) 1998. *DiY Culture: Party and Protest in Nineties Britain*. London: Verso.

McNevin, A. 2006. Political belonging in a neoliberal era: The struggle of the *sans-papièrs*. *Citizenship Studies*, 10(2), 135–51.

Measham, F. 2004. Drug and alcohol research: The case for cultural criminology, in *Cultural Criminology Unleashed*, edited by J. Ferrell, K. Hayward, W. Morrison and M. Presdee. London: Glasshouse Press, 207–18.

Melucci, A. 1984. An end to social movements? *Social Science Information*, 23(4/5), 819–35.

Melucci, A. 1985. The symbolic challenge of contemporary movements. *Social Research*, 52(4), 789–816.

Melucci, A. 1989. *Nomads of the Present: Social Movements and Individual Needs in Contemporary Society*. London: Hutchinson Radius.

Melucci, A. 1996. *Challenging Codes: Collective Action in the Information Age*. Cambridge: Cambridge University Press.

Neilson, B. and Rossiter, N. 2008. Precarity as a political concept, or, Fordism as exception. *Theory, Culture and Society*, 25(7–8), 51–72.

Offe, C. 1985. New social movements: Challenging the boundaries of institutional politics. *Social Research*, 52(4), 789–816.

Plows, A. 1998. Earth first! Defending Mother Earth, direct-style, in *DiY Culture: Party and Protest in Nineties Britain*, edited by G. McKay. London: Verso, 152–73.

Presdee, M. 2000. *Cultural Criminology and the Carnival of Crime*. London: Routledge.

Purdue, D., Dürrschmidt, J., Jowers, P. and O'Doherty, R. 1997. DIY culture and extended milieux: LETS, veggie boxes and festivals. *The Sociological Review*, 45(4), 645–67.

Redhead, S. 1990. *The End-of-the-century Party: Youth and Pop Towards 2000*. Manchester: Manchester University Press.

Redhead, S. (ed.) 1993. *Rave Off: Politics and Deviance in Contemporary Youth Culture*. Aldershot: Avebury.

Redhead, S. 1995. *Unpopular Cultures: The Birth of Law and Popular Culture*. Manchester: Manchester University Press.

Redhead, S. 1998. *Subculture to Clubcultures: An Introduction to Popular Cultural Studies*. Oxford: Blackwell.

Rietveld, H. 1993. Living the dream, in *Rave Off: Politics and Deviance in Contemporary Youth Culture*, edited by S. Redhead. Aldershot: Avebury, 41–78.

Rietveld, H. 1998. Repetitive beats: Free parties and the politics of contemporary DiY dance culture in Britain, in *DiY Culture: Party and Protest in Nineties Britain*, edited by G. McKay. London: Verso, 243–67.

Rojek, C. 2000. *Leisure and Culture*. Basingstoke: Macmillan.

Sandbrook, D. 2011. Eat, drink, and empty your pockets. *New Statesman*, 20 June, 40–41.

Sharpe, E.K. 2008. Festivals and social change: Intersections of pleasure and politics at a community music festival. *Leisure Sciences*, 30, 217–34.

St John, G. 2008. Protestival: Global days of action and carnivalized politics in the present. *Social Movement Studies*, 7(2), 167–90.

Stallybrass, P. and White, A. 1986. *The Politics and Poetics of Transgression*. London: Methuen.

Taylor, V. 1989. Social movement continuity: The women's movement in abeyance. *American Sociological Review*, 54(5), 761–75.

Tucker, K.H. 1991. How new are the new social movements? *Theory, Culture and Society*, 8(2), 75–98.

Turner, V. 1969. *The Ritual Process: Structure and Anti-Structure*. London: Routledge and Kegan Paul.

Trilling, D. 2011. Can pay, won't pay. *New Statesman*, 20 June, 43.

Wright, M.A. 1998. The great British ecstasy revolution, in *DiY Culture: Party and Protest in Nineties Britain*, edited by G. McKay. London: Verso, 228–42.

PART II
Local and Global Communities

Chapter 6

Varieties of Cosmopolitanism in Art Festivals

Jasper Chalcraft, Gerard Delanty and Monica Sassatelli

Cosmopolitanism, internationalism, multiculturalism, transnationalism: these terms have all – to some extent – been presented as varieties of a contemporary preoccupation with the limits of identity, and the possibilities that new imaginaries present for a contemporary world characterized by inequality. The art worlds examined here are as embroiled in these preoccupations and possibilities as other aspects of society; their difference is that they do not so much debate and develop them as display and perform them. We are concerned with how cosmopolitanism – as distinct from the other terms above (see Delanty 2009) – is part of, and results from, these displays (Papastergiadis 2007). As this chapter will show, art festivals demonstrate that what has sometimes been identified and denigrated as *aesthetic cosmopolitanism* (Tomlinson 1999; Sassatelli 2012) may more usefully be repositioned within the more encompassing *cosmopolitanism* and brought to bear on how new types of communities can be created beyond the constraints of localities.

The chapter draws on case studies of several festivals by the authors and other researchers with a collaborative European Euro-Festival project.[1] The project took 13 case-studies covering music (WOMAD, Sonar, Umbria Jazz), literature (Berlin, Hay, Borderlands), film (Berlin, Cannes, Venice and Vienna Jewish Film Festival) and urban mixed-arts festivals (Brighton, Venice Biennale, Vienna) to investigate their role in transnational identification and a cultural public sphere in Europe. In what follows, we address key issues that emerged from our research concerning cosmopolitanism in festivals. To take our observations beyond the art worlds themselves, we need to plot them against what we call here *varieties of cosmopolitanism*, as the result of four cosmopolitan relationships, and the related dispositions that are variously expressed in these varied cultural events, but also found in cosmopolitanism at large. The chapter concludes by re-evaluating cosmopolitanism in art festivals by returning to key questions that inform the chapter: How is cosmopolitanism expressed within art festivals? And what role do the varieties of cosmopolitanism present in art festivals represent for broader society?

---

1   Details of the project's partners and 13 case-studies can be found on its website, www.euro-festival.org. In what follows, we draw from our extensive body of interviews with organizers, artists and other stakeholders, document analysis, observation and focus groups with audiences. For a fuller account, see in particular the final reports edited by Sassatelli (2008), Segal and Giorgi (2009), Giorgi (2010) and Santoro (2010). See also Giorgi, Sassatelli and Delanty (2011).

Cosmopolitanism and Festivals

The Euro-Festival project was born as a reaction to a dismissive mainstream view of contemporary festivals that sees them trapped between the poles of dichotomies such as the authentic versus standardized and engaged versus commercial: our aim has been to explain their cultural significance. Within this, an important dimension has been how they relate to cosmopolitanism, conceived of as a wider societal condition; the cultural significance of festivals might be seen as an expression of cosmopolitan trends in social and cultural transformation. To develop a nuanced analysis of festivals, we also needed a nuanced one of cosmopolitanism.

One of the problems with cosmopolitanism is that it is both an empirical and a normative concept – that is, as is increasingly being recognized in the literature, it is both an experience of reality, in the sense of a lived experience and a measurable empirical condition, and an interpretation of one's experience. Insofar as it is an interpretation, normative aspects enter into it.[2] Cosmopolitan arguments are primarily critical assessments relating to particular kinds of human experiences that arise as a result of new ways of seeing the world. The emergence of cosmopolitan orientations derives from the relations of a plurality of social actors who, encountering each other, critically engage with their situations. The cosmopolitan condition is shaped by the logic of the encounter, exchange and dialogue. Cosmopolitan dispositions/attitudes or orientations and values should be seen in the context of particular kinds of relationships, which are the focus of analysis rather than specific social actors. They are embodied in cultural forms, such as frames, socio-cognitive structures, cultural repertoires, discourses and quasi-objective cultural phenomena. In these cultural forms, universalistic meta-rules are present to varying degrees. All involve different levels of reflexivity.

The first cosmopolitan relationship is the relativization of one's own identity: a reinterpretation of culture occurs as a result of the encounter of one culture with another. The use of the Other to reinterpret one's own culture has been a feature of many forms of everyday cosmopolitanism, such as what is often called 'cultural omnivorousness' based on consumption, but it also includes 'soft' kinds of cosmopolitanism around curiosity/appreciation of other cultures, which are often found in educational programmes.

The second is the positive recognition of the Other. This is a type of relationship in which self–Other encounters take a stronger form, involving political and ethical commitments. In this instance, a step in the direction of cosmopolitan citizenship occurs whereby universalistic meta-rules play a greater role. It is a stronger reflexive relationship, entailing the inclusion of the Other, not just awareness as in the previous type of relationship. One major expression of cosmopolitanism on this level is in the internationalization of law.

---

2   The literature on cosmopolitanism is now huge and interdisciplinary. Here we do not attempt a synthesis, but will distil from it a rough definition (for an overview, see Delanty and Inglis 2010; Delanty 2009).

The third type of relationship concerns the mutual evaluation of cultures or identities – both one's own and that of the Other. This is a self-reflexive mode of relationship that is based on cultural distance, scepticism and critique, and makes possible for people to mediate between cultures. It will typically be found in dialogic encounters and is sustained by deliberative-style communication. Such reflexivity can be found in varieties of post-nationalism and what are often referred to as rooted or embedded forms of cosmopolitanism.

The fourth type of cosmopolitan relationship is a shared normative culture in which self–Other relations are mediated through an orientation towards world consciousness. In this case, global issues are predominant. This kind of cosmopolitanism entails the formation of a moral consciousness rooted in emotional responses to global issues, concern with global ethics based on shared values, putting the non-national interest before the national interest. One of the main expressions of such kinds of relationship is in new forms of civil society, such as global or cosmopolitan civil society.

It should be noted that these four levels are not necessarily preconditions of each other, for they can be combined in different ways and one level may not presuppose another. It has also been noted in research on cosmopolitanism that people are not cosmopolitan equally in all levels. However, as 'ideal typifications' of cosmopolitanism, they represent generic forms of relationships and varying degrees of 'thinness' and 'thickness'. The four types of cosmopolitan relationship are not to be read as a scale, but rather as key nodes in a (virtuous) circle. This (with no moral weight given to *virtuous*) helps to visualize the interlinked dependency of our varieties of cosmopolitanism, trying to avoid the linearity and hierarchy of a 'scale' while still addressing the link between festivals as cultural sites and wider societal trends. We approach the question of cosmopolitan challenges for festivals in terms of an account that distinguishes between cosmopolitanism as a particular condition that may be present in arts festivals in different varieties, and that sees cosmopolitanism less as a condition than as a process. As sites of cosmopolitanism, festivals embody cosmopolitan orientations, relationships, dispositions and so on in concrete social contexts; they allow us to understand the cosmopolitan condition as an existing trend in society as reflected in arts festivals. However, arts festivals do not simply *reflect* cosmopolitan currents, they can seen as having an active role in bringing about cultural change. As the case studies presented in this chapter show, festivals may appear in particular occurrences as agents of cosmopolitan relationships, and in others as products of these; most often, they are good symbols of them, through which it is possible to interpret varieties of cosmopolitanism.

Place

That 'festivals must be rooted in either a place or a theme' (Organizer, Vienna Jewish Film Festival, Euro-festival interview) is a statement that would probably find most of our festival directors in agreement – although that they represent alternatives may need questioning in order to understand how *both* theme and place work in 'making' a festival. Even if it is difficult to pin down, and given the multifarious incarnations that a 'festival space' can take – from gated, tented one-day events that create a temporary place of their own to programmes stretching across time and space, drawing on existing, mostly urban locales – an attention to the situatedness of the festivals as cultural artefacts and organizations appears fundamental, especially to avoid interpreting them in the light of their position within a specific genre or art world only, which would mean missing their specificity as festivals. That means paying attention to the social and spatial organization – and therefore the related cultural politics – of the places that host them. In short, this means a focus on the festival's 'topography' as a key to inquiring into how cultural practice, social identity and place relate (see also Willems-Braun 1994). This issue is one especially conducive to a discussion of cosmopolitanism, particularly given the latter's common association with an overcoming of placedness.

Particularly for urban festivals, we have often found in the field a synergistic relationship between the festival and the place – something like a chemical reaction difficult to unpack or 'artificially' reproduce as if in a laboratory – as many not so successful attempts spurred in recent decades by the exponential growth of festivals have realized the hard way (Sassatelli and Delanty 2010).[3] The trigger for the reaction seems to lie in how a strong focus on the city hosting the festival – on its specificity and 'sense of place' – combines with an intense encounter with outside artists, cultures and even publics. These may not quantitatively dominate the scene, but may act as the active ingredient that, even in small quantities, activates and flavours the final mix and makes it 'work'. To grasp this, rather than place as a static container and cosmopolitanism as a dispositional construct, we need to view both relationally.

The multiplicity and seemingly paradoxical configuration of festivals – holding together and at the same time exposing key dichotomies in cultural life such as production/consumption, economic/aesthetic value, local/global – meant that we

---

3   It may be worth acknowledging that 'place' is not an interpretative key that is valid for all festivals (as 'cultural content' is). However, both from those festivals that draw on place and from those which do not, the indication is that a sensibility for a (rethought) notion of place is needed, rather than a cutting negation or affirmation of its relevance. It is telling of a dichotomous view lacking in nuance that some critiques of festivals – and the general vulgata of festivals as increasingly commercialized and inauthentic, especially in comparison to 'traditional festivals' (Robinson and Picard 2006) – have seen them almost in terms of what Augé (1993) terms non-places: standardized, empty spaces, characterized by a lack of those relational, historical connections concerned with identity that make a place. But here is an interesting contradiction: the two least 'placed' and urban festivals – Borderlands and WOMAD, which describe themselves as travelling nomadic festivals – are at the same time those most explicitly about the placedness of culture, about where music comes from (WOMAD), about a space for debate in a particular area, the borderland area between Western and Eastern Europe for the literatures emerging in that context (Borderlands).

had to consider this 'topography' not in an exclusively material sense, but in more heterotopic (Foucault 1984) and relational (Massey 1992) terms. As such, far from being static, as the objectifying opposition of place and time within a Newtonian physics would suggest, Massey suggests turning to modern physics, where 'the identity of things is *constituted through* interactions ... space is not absolute, it is relational' (Massey 1992: 76–7). What is relevant for a renewed concept of place that the study of festivals both requires and advances is to consider the 'geography of external relations' on which identities – including identities of place – depend (Massey 2006). Within this new relational spatial logic, local and global need not any more be in contrast – or 'placedness' and 'placelessness' – and we may be somewhat nearer to seeing how, in practice, cosmopolitanism finds its space. That may allow us to see non-locally bounded communities as those – perhaps not permanent but yet not ephemeral either (to pre-empt a recurrent critique against cultural consumption, although convincingly rebutted already in Bianchini and Parkinson 1993: 203–4) – generated in festival settings.

One first step in disassociating place with stasis is to relink the divide with time, and consider a four-dimensional space–time continuum. The idea of 'atmosphere' – a recurring metaphor used by our interviewees struggling to single out the 'essence' of a festival – emerged in the field. For festival participants and organizers, often waxing lyrical about the physical and spiritual signs of the festival on place – from flags going up to the 'magic in the air' – the particular identity and distinctiveness of a festival are about a certain *atmosphere*. We observed this in all our festivals, and found that it both confirmed Falassi's (1987) famous characterization as 'time out of time' and required a fuller interpretation beyond this mere observation. Indeed, a recurrent festival creates within its location a sort of 'seasonal' atmosphere with its own calendar, somehow also reminding us of the never totally severed connection that even post-traditional festivals maintain with similarly totalizing religious festivities. The festival atmosphere – or 'swing', feel or 'air' – varies in its specific traits. Our research indicates that these can be grouped into the two main factors of 'immersion' and of 'permanence in variation'. Immersion is the result of the separate calendar and 'map', lived experience and synesthesia. Permanence in variation is obtained through a plurality of markers that are not constant, but that never change all at once: the build-up of expectations based on previous years' experiences or novices' eagerness, recurrent festival sections and rituals (e.g. prizes) that are both familiar and novel each year.[4]

---

4   As a term that addresses a 'strange weave of space and time', an interpretation of 'atmosphere' can evoke Benjamin's (1936) famous 'aura' of high art. In Chalcraft, Delanty and Sassatelli (2010), we explore this a little further, noting how it is important to distinguish the two, and in particular not to be tempted by the suggestive theory of the 'decay of the aura': mainstream dichotomic visions of festivals as either authentic or commercial may be flawed precisely in assuming (dis)enchantment and commodity fetishism – Benjamin's as well as later critiques of cultural industry ultimate targets – as an exhaustive explanatory key for contemporary festivals.

What comes closer to the festivals atmosphere is that of the places that host them. It is the fortunate (or cunning) combination of both that the festivals participants – especially the organizers – are eager to stress. A revealing quotation comes from Perugia (Umbria Jazz):

> Here [in Perugia] people used to breathe a completely different air if compared to all the other Italian cities ... Pagnotta [festival founder] has decidedly breathed this air as well! ... You couldn't help but look at the miracle of this city ... It can't be denied that this environment has had an influence. Pagnotta breathed this air, too. Definitely a multicultural air. (Festival organizer, Euro-festival interview)

This extract is also indicative of our recurring finding that festivals and cities seem to elicit the same type of strong, local feeling of ownership. The festival is seen as fundamental for the city profile, and vice versa (or at least contributive to it, in the case of capital cities like Berlin and Vienna, whose sheer wealth of cultural events, institutions and programming dilute the impact of one festival): they are linked by a symbolic (rather than causal) relationship. And, as the quote shows, place can draw its specificity from certain types of relationships with the external or Other – what we would call cosmopolitan relationships. If it is 'local', it is certainly not so at the expense of the 'global' (rather, it is precisely because of it). So, especially in our globalized era of digital reproduction and communication, the traditional or early modern festival function of bringing events and cultures closer (the lineage here is with world fairs) may somehow be made banal and easily exploited, but the sociability function of creating an immersive and evolving experience is not. And this experience is based on exchange, encounter and dialogue with the Other, in such a pervasive way as to become taken for granted.

Given this combination of atmosphere and sense of ownership, it is not surprising that a recurrent theme is that of the *brand*. As we observed for urban festivals (Sassatelli and Delanty 2010), branding the city and branding the festival go hand in hand, and festival organizers themselves often speak explicitly of the 'brand':

> [T]he festival is actually developing the *recognition of the Brighton brand*. So that's a very important part of its activity. (Local marketing researcher, Brighton Festival, Euro-festival interview)

> Therefore they [the festival] are also known in other cities, just like a brand. We are talking globally. (Organizer, Sonar, Euro-festival interview)

As used by the organizers, and linked to marketing activities, what emerges is a rather superficial, city-marketing notion of place branding. This emphasizes the exploitation of a city's (and festival's) identity in terms of consolidated traditions or heritage – a key theme in local cultural policies seeking to promote place specificity, ironically often pursuing 'regeneration' strategies that increasingly are seen as imposing standardization (Quinn 2005). However, to stick to this superficial interpretation may miss the importance of this branding component for a cultural sociology of festivals. Instead, following sociological exploration into the notion of branding and its role in the global culture industry (Lury 2004; Lash and Lury 2007), to conceptualize the festival as brand allows an analysis of phenomena of commoditization (or commercialization) without simply reducing the festival to a commodity being produced, sold and consumed. Like a brand, the festival is not for sale – although it is really what people are buying into. And this is linked to its multi-form, 'poietic' (productive, rather than produced), narrative (part of a 'story' of the city), singular (as opposed to the exchangeability of the commodity form) nature. In line with the atmospheric immersion and above all permanence in variation, 'The brand is like an organism, self-modifying, with a memory' (Lash and Lury 2007: 6). The value it brings is a sign-value dependent on relations and experience.

However, it is also important to see festivals (and places) as *peculiar* brands. By spilling over outside the corporate domain, and being associated with a 'place' (as a cultural object), the brand itself may not go unchanged. A city (or a festival) as a brand is not a *corporate* brand; it cannot be subsumed by a single, corporate 'identity' or intentional strategy – and, in fact, the sense of ownership that festivals elicit also means that everybody has different ideas of what the festival should be and represent. More interesting for the issues at hand, is festivals being *global* cultural brands – at least allegedly. The very assumption that a festival's programme can be understood, chosen and enjoyed across the globe (which is particularly true for those festivals that have 'branded' satellites in several locations, such as Hay and WOMAD), or conversely that a 'global' offering can be brought to the local audience of a festival, implicitly or explicitly draws on an idea that there is a 'global taste' and an 'omnivorous' desire for being exposed to different experiences, made intelligible within the festival frame itself. Thanks to this dimension, a festival's placedness does not rank it near a 'local' pole on a local-to-cosmopolitan scale; rather, it displaces such a scale and suggests that we find ways of representing 'place' that are not based on such linear models – see, for instance, the idea of global localities, derived from two of our music case studies in Chalcraft and Magaudda (2011).

If, as social scientists, we still struggle to *place* cosmopolitanism, festival organizers sometimes face similar dilemmas. This can be seen in the very idea that a balance should be struck between 'local' and 'international' artists, as the programme design and presentation in festival publications show. This balance seems to be difficult to conceptualize (as, admittedly, we prompted them to do by specifically asking about 'local' and 'international' artists), but in practice the festival thrives on the tension:

> I think there is a paradox and there is a tension there [between concentrating on local artists or on international ones], but I think, you know, I don't think it's

too much of an issue. I think it's only an issue when you think about it in terms of, sort of, theoretically, because, actually, it does work, you know, and that's the proof of the pudding, really, in a way. (City Council officer, Brighton Festival, Euro-Festival interview)

The increasing complexity of artists' place affiliation is also indicative. Artists now are not simply 'from' somewhere. As any Venice Art Biennale catalogue will show, the world is still unequal, and certain locales are much more likely to produce artists than others (Wu 2009). Still, one does notice the struggle to adapt classifications designed when 'national pavilions' could, allegedly, much more adequately represent places and cultures. So today artists in the catalogue are not just 'from' a place, they are all 'born in …' and 'live and work in …' Maybe soon 'live' and 'work in' will be separated too. Not only has territorial belonging become multi-dimensional and dynamic, but this also means that 'place' is less a passive backdrop for culture *taking place* and more an active ingredient in both the production and consumption of culture. Festivals, with their particular focus on live events, may not only foreground this awareness of how the festival space is socially constructed, but also of how conversely its social relations are spatially constructed. And this beyond any simple idea of the 'local' and beyond old spatial metaphors of top-down or bottom-up, suggesting that we may need revised, more lateral and horizontal metaphors, able to grasp parallel, heterotopic (Foucault 1967) places. From this point of view, one of the stumbling blocks in cosmopolitan theory, and in a rendering of its practical relevance beyond normative theory – that is the reluctant but seemingly inevitable conclusion that cosmopolitan openness and dwelling in a place are irreconcilable – may begin to be overcome as a solution is performed in festivals.

Cultural Content

What is the cultural content of cosmopolitanism in festivals? Given our typology of cosmopolitanism, it ought to explicitly privilege *encounter, exchange* and *dialogue.* Many contemporary cultural forms can be seen as exploring and expressing these, but does this amount to a 'world culture'? If some art festivals express cosmopolitanism, is this because their cultural content is cosmopolitan? Are cosmopolitans made in the same way everywhere, or are there culturally and socially specific ways in which these relationships can be cultivated? For example, does the wealthy, well-educated reader at a literature festival in Berlin require a different type of cosmopolitan content from the dance music fan lost in the beats of Barcelona's Sonar? Or is the cosmopolitan nature of cultural content effectively determined by the festival itself, by its audience, how they behave, how the material is presented and so on?

The Euro-Festival case studies suggest that content ultimately derives its meaning from the total festival experience, rather than being an inalienable quality of the cultural form, object or performance itself. This is obvious to artists who recognize differences between their audiences, and frequently present their work in ways sensitive to the context of performance and/or display. Some directors are also very aware of the differences between audiences, and seek to adapt their cultural offerings accordingly, and these choices were explicitly discussed by arts professionals. For example, the French director of a music agency whose groups regularly played at various WOMAD festivals discussed in interview how some audiences are more interested in the broader backgrounds of artists than others. For example, in the United States, people

> want to know everything about the geography, economy, culture. This is more an Anglo-Saxon way to approach cultural information. We don't speak only about the artistic act, the music, the emotion that goes through the music ... Japanese people are a little bit like this, too ... a bit like the Anglo-Saxons. They want really precise things. This is more barbarian in my country, and maybe in the Latin countries. We trust more in the emotion of the music even if we don't know exactly from where he's coming, this musician. The organizer [too], they want less information about the things around the music. (Euro-festival interview)

Clearly, the levels of encounter, exchange and dialogue that help constitute a cosmopolitan disposition can be hugely varied: cultural producers have to recognize and cater for these types of disposition, these desires for contextual information about the background of a given artist. Most of the festivals studied demonstrate a desire for encounter on the part of audiences, but exchange and dialogue are more complicated. Some festival audiences – in this case, a broad categorization of Anglo-Saxons and Japanese versus Latin cultures – *appear* to be more instinctively cosmopolitan than others. But this is only when one ignores their broader cultural dispositions and contexts – for example, of Anglo-Saxons (and Japanese) often being less well-informed than French audiences who already know the history and aesthetics of Mbalax and Qawwali.

Increasing professionalization of festivals has played a role here, particularly when they have been closely tied to the diffusion and institutionalization of artistic genres (for example, Sonar and electronic music; WOMAD and world music). They sometimes view this close association between their festival and genre as part of a recognizably shared global culture. For example, one of the organizers of Sonar said:

> Therefore [the festival is] known in other cities, just like a brand. We are talking globally. If you would like to do something that goes beyond your neighbourhood, you have to establish a relationship not with your continent, which is Europe, but with the world. You should address to the international market, because the aesthetics is being standardized, and the forms to produce, create and compose are the same in Japan and in Bilbao. (Euro-Festival interview)

Festival organizers are often keen to promote the level of internationalism inherent to their festivals. Both the Venice Biennale and the Internationales Literaturfestival Berlin (ILB) provide an ethnic breakdown of their artists – for example, the ILB's own statistics have between 50 and 60 per cent of invited British, American and French authors coming from a migration or mixed ethnic background.

Such a quantitative approach to a festival's degree of cosmopolitanism, to the sheer breadth of alterity (delineated by nationality and ethnicity) on offer, demonstrates a need to satisfy sponsors and institutional partners (through matching the rhetoric of multicultural cultural policy and national discourses of inclusion), as well as a perceived appeal to audiences. The media, too, tend to trumpet such statistics, but members of the public and some academics question this approach.

Generally, ideas about a particularly cosmopolitan or 'world culture' were not forthcoming from interviewees, though some – such as the director of the ILB – were particularly insightful. Speaking of the literary goals of the festival, he described how:

> The festival is both about 'world literature' (*Weltliteratur* as in Goethe to represent the small circle of extraordinary literature of universal appeal regardless of origin) and about the literatures of the world (*die Literaturen der Welt*), that is the literatures that arise from specific contexts. It tries to balance the two ... (Euro-festival interview)

Applying this more generally to cultural content that includes niche musics, high art, local artists, classical fiction and popular non-fiction, we find a similar problem. Balancing what one might define as being of 'universal appeal' with the rather different appeal of the culturally specific is something many festivals attempt. Crucially, appreciating the latter presupposes a cosmopolitan disposition, an existing omnivorousness that can look beyond what is lost to what is shared. Given the nature of transcultural exchange, sharing requires a technical intervention: translation.

In emphasizing the crucial *human* contact that festivals bring, in contrast to interactions that are increasingly virtual, a translator of the Borderlands festival makes the case that this human contact makes a different kind of exchange and understanding possible:

> For poets, also, when you just hear their poems read in the original, you understand so much more even if you don't understand the words. *You hear the beauty of what is not lost in translation.* (Euro-Festival interview, emphasis added)

This is the crucial point regarding cultural content: in one form or another, these cultural manifestations are all *translated*. What is shared, at the intellectual as well as the visceral and emotive aesthetic level, is that which is not lost in translation. Thus translation emerges as a key theme: metaphorically within performing and visual art based festivals, and literally in literary festivals. Interestingly, how translation emerges is a very good example to help us visualize the 'dialectical' dimension of cosmopolitan tendencies – that is, their being always predicated on a tension between local (and notably national) and global (or 'transcendental' with respect to territorial boundaries). On the one hand, the idea that 'supporting translation is the means to create world literature' suggests not only sensibility for otherness, but also capacity for positive recognition and possibly even mutual evaluation of 'foreign' content (our second and third cosmopolitan capacities). On the other hand, as languages are still clearly national languages (their gatekeepers remain national institutes, schools, academies, etc.), this seems to point to how the cosmopolitan edifice is still firmly based on national foundations. Nevertheless, the increasing presence (especially in literary festivals) of diaspora authors, authors writing in languages 'other' than their mother-tongue and so on also shows that displacements exist.

People

Neither of the two key elements detailed above makes much sense without the third: people, the audiences that make festivals events with an impact beyond the inner circle of an art world. The audience is both the public and the broader context of collective representation that art festivals offer: host communities, national arts bodies, Europe/Europeans, the world, artists. These are different spaces and moments from those offered by galleries, museums, auditoriums, theatres and cinemas. Increasing audience numbers at festivals, and an increasing number of festivals (*Performing Arts Yearbook for Europe* 2008), demonstrate that there is a market, taste, disposition for consuming art in this format.

One of the ways in which art festivals offer the opportunity for developing and expressing a cosmopolitan condition is in the nature of audiences' encounter with the Other. Primarily, this is through the art works themselves, though some of the festivals offer a more tangible and visceral opportunity for active engagement. Literary festivals – in particular, Hay-on-Wye – provide events where direct questions can be asked of authors, journalists and thinkers: the similarity to the ideals of the nineteenth-century Parisian salon is evident. Other genres exploit similar strategies, with Brighton Festival's 'Debates' drawing sell-out crowds, creating a palpably electric atmosphere and attracting incisive audience participation. Interestingly, the audience focus groups we conducted in Brighton were not responsive to the issue of participation when narrowly conceived as critical debate around the festival. They did not read reviews before choosing events, and few participated actively on blogs or other social media. But the way they talked about this revealed a clear sense of ownership of the festival, displaying pride in its growing national media coverage. And because of that sense of ownership, everyone felt entitled to discuss the festival as an expert – something that favoured taking up an attitude of responsibility itself. This seems to take shape in a welcoming attitude among festivalgoers, a cultural curiosity that spills over into a social curiosity:

> [E]veryone in Brighton is very chatty and friendly anyway, but people actually talk to you and say, you know, have you been to this before, what do you think of it, ... you chat a lot more to people that you wouldn't normally talk to. So you're much more part of the community if you go out and do festivally things.

> I would rather be exposed to all of that variety of life, than be closed off, and I think the Festival really heightens all that diversity. (Brighton resident, Euro-Festival Focus Group)

These acts of heightened sociability and communication across class and other divides (which is implied by the British focus group attendee above), also help people transcend other divides in some festivals, like that of artist and audience. So, while talking about art, culture and society is one obvious means of engaging with the Other, WOMAD provides another: cooking with the artists. Local specialties are prepared by artists in constant dialogue with the audience, and occasional musical accompaniment. Sometimes this dialogue provides just a general gloss of the artists' cultural backgrounds or culinary traditions, or often deep insights into their societies and biographies. In this performance space, artists are able to exchange their stories, and to feed the crowds a literal sample of their broader culture.

Breaking down the artist–audience boundary happens in other festivals also – for instance, with Umbria Jazz:

> [T]he international jazz scene is all there. The city keeps on living, nothing is compromised by the event. And while you keep on going to work, to your office, as usual, you can meet Cecil Taylor, Stan Getz, Count Basie or Art Blakey, and all the greatest jazz players, at a bar on Corso Vannucci in the city centre, drinking a glass of wine or eating an ice-cream! Where else can you find anything like that? Nowhere else! (Music critic, Euro-festival interview, cited in Magaudda et al. 2011)

In this way, the organization of festivals favours kinds of exchange that take us beyond the aesthetic and into the shared banal aspects of everyday life. Not quite a shared normative culture as such, but a clear demonstration to audiences and artists of how apparent differences rest on similar shared needs.

The European Union has clear objectives regarding the participation of its citizens in the arts. For example, the European Commission's 2007 European Agenda for Culture is 'founded on three common sets of objectives: cultural diversity and intercultural dialogue; culture as a catalyst for creativity; and culture as a key component in international relations'. Here it is worth noting that, while the first objective effectively encapsulates the three logics which we see as crucial to developing and sustaining a cosmopolitan disposition (encounter, exchange, dialogue), the other two objectives of the Commission simply demonstrate culture's renewed political expediency. In the past, culture's role in international diplomacy has often been a form of moral rearmament, a tool or weapon through which a nation pursues its national interest and position within the firmament of 'civilized nations' (e.g. see Prevots 1998 on US–Soviet cultural diplomacy during the Cold War).

While the sentiments behind the European Commission's Agenda may be well meant, they fail to address one crucial element that influences its citizens' access to and participation in arts programmes which should improve 'the development of the intercultural competences of citizens': cost. Art festivals range from free (as is the case for WOMAD in Spain) to relatively cheap (VJFF; Berlinale; Brighton Festival fringe events; Umbria Jazz) or quite expensive (Brighton Festival main events; Venice Biennale; WOMAD in the United Kingdom, Sonar, Umbria Jazz). Cost, structure and reputation serve to promote and encourage certain audiences above truly open access. Consequently, the audiences engaged in encounters, exchange and dialogue are often those already engaged with the wider world through an existing cosmopolitan disposition.

The project's data on audiences support this view. The most detailed data came from three audience surveys, and from three focus groups. For example, confirming expectations of an educated, white, middle-aged and middle-class art festival audience, the average festivalgoer to Umbria Jazz is 39 years old, with 50 per cent of them possessing a degree; at the ILB, 46 per cent are aged between 26 and 50, with 75 per cent of the audience having a degree; and although the Vienna Jewish Film Festival displays a notable age range,[5] 60 per cent of this almost entirely local Viennese audience have a degree, with two-thirds of these having a postgraduate qualification.[6]

In our case studies, the socio-demographic and political orientations remain remarkably similar. Generally, the 'cultural omnivore' can be considered the default profile for most art festival audiences, so trying to understand particular tastes among a general omnivorousness may delineate which kind of diversity contemporary audiences consider essential to their identities. Our audience survey data are only partial, with detailed research on only three of the 13 festivals, but they still give some idea of how art festivals are viewed by those who pay to attend them.

For example, more than 40 per cent of the Umbria Jazz sample consider the festival to be an expression of multiculturalism, though only 20 per cent believe it to be cosmopolitan (thus revealing how the term itself is not used or understood by audiences), while almost no one believed that the festival had any political

---

5   See Segal and Giorgi (2010: 210–13).

6   A recent survey from the National Endowment of Arts (2010: 50) suggests that the situation is broadly similar in the United States. Its statistics on 'outdoor arts festivals' give an audience aged 35–54, 73 per cent of whom are Caucasian, and predominantly graduates.

functions (Santoro and Solaroli 2010: 88–93). Unsurprisingly, perhaps – given the nature of jazz music – only a small percentage of this sample (under 15 per cent) thought the festival was a good opportunity to learn about the arts of other countries. Unlike Umbria Jazz, where most attendees come from outside Perugia, the ILB attracts a predominantly local audience. A further difference between it and Umbria Jazz is the large percentage of the ILB audience who view the festival as an expression of multiculturalism and of cosmopolitan culture: 87 per cent and 62 per cent respectively. Audience opinions of the ILB collected by Giorgi (2010) show how cosmopolitanism appears to be seen both positively and negatively, with some of the ILB audience seeing cosmopolitanism as 'something associated with humanistic ideals, [while] for others it is rather linked to economic liberalism as a political ideology' (2010: 62).

Meanwhile, respondents to the project's survey of the Vienna Jewish Film Festival, as with the ILB, were locals.[7] Also similar to the ILB is the high number of respondents who see the festival as multicultural (95 per cent) and cosmopolitan (80 per cent). The difference between these two festivals and Umbria Jazz appears to be attributable to the genres with which they deal: serious literature and serious cinema versus a musical genre with a long-established niche global market. It is also not surprising that the well-educated cultural cognoscenti of Germany and Austria's capitals would confirm their own multicultural/cosmopolitan ethos in a questionnaire. The dynamics of a music festival are experienced differently, and the aesthetic experience is perhaps more visceral and less overtly reflexive. Nevertheless, we can see a clear link between the socio-economic and educational background of these audiences, and the degree to which they identify their respective festivals with cosmopolitan and multicultural qualities.

There are differences between how different genres of festival engage their publics, and in particular in the way that festivals choose to separate audience from artists (and organizers). How exactly a festival is *staged* provides a clear symbolic expression of its degree of dialogue and exchange (rather than the statement of these intentions found in almost all promotional material), and it also provides a practical one. Engaging with the Other, and engaging with each other, is something that festivals orchestrate – intentionally or otherwise – through the spaces and opportunities for contact that they create. The nature of performance is a further obvious factor, but other elements contribute to how contact and exchange are experienced. For example, festivals like the ILB and VJFF, being attended mostly by residents of Berlin and Vienna, who attend just one or a few events rather than a whole weekend, tend to be less steeped in the shared transformative experiences that characterize music festivals like WOMAD and Sonar. Yet a festival like Cannes, which is the antithesis of inclusive, still manages to generate a transformative atmosphere of participation.

The significant shared aspects of art festivals are not exclusively artistic, or explicitly political. In fact, it is at least as much through the shared experience

---

7   See Santoro (2010: 210) for detail on socio-demographic background.

of mundane activities like queuing for toilets, cooking or buying food, and congregating in bars, refreshment tents and the general spaces of the festival that the virtuous circle of cosmopolitan qualities is created. While each of these may be 'banal' or superficial, together they outline a whole lived experience, beyond the disembodied, cursory one that starts and finishes with a movement of stage curtains – and this may be conducive of more embodied forms of cosmopolitanism too. The crucial element here is that while audiences may have their options reduced in festivals that are more immersive, they ironically have more agency over the off-programme content of the festival. The professionalization of festival organization means the key ingredients for this social effervescence are increasingly well understood and catered for – organizers recognize that the total experience is as important to their success as an exciting programme; European audiences have become festival connoisseurs, something reflected in their expansion and attention from the mainstream press (for example, UK quality newspapers as sponsors of WOMAD and Hay-on-Wye) – but intangibles remain. The atmosphere of some festivals is thus effectively driven by the communal self-realizing, self-perpetuating spirit that the festival fans create year after year. Sometimes this is linked to place; at other times it is to the cultural content and the ways audiences experience it; WOMAD is a good example, having maintained its loyal fan base and atmosphere despite a recent change in site from an urban park to a rural country estate, and developing this ethos in its multiple global editions. Sonar and Hay-on-Wye have also been able to expand their festival experiences beyond their original homes.

Unravelling, discovering and theorizing cosmopolitanism in contemporary art festivals carries with it one particular challenge. The words 'cosmopolitan' and 'cosmopolitanism' are rarely used spontaneously by interviewees – or indeed by participants in focus groups – to describe aspects of the festivals studied. This is not surprising, given that cosmopolitan theory has yet to properly enter the vocabulary of everyday policy-making, or popular discourses of social harmony. Yet it remains problematic when other terms that dominate cultural policy throughout Europe (and beyond) have recently been contested – multiculturalism being the best example. In fact, as the audience surveys mentioned above indicate, art festival audiences strongly identify themselves – and the festivals they choose to attend – with the 'multicultural', 'transnational' and 'international', and it is the last of these that is most consistently positively used and understood. Most festival directors do not see 'cosmopolitanism' as a useful way of describing what they do, and it is the 'international' element that is seen to be the most positive characteristic. However, when pressed for their opinions on these terms and their meanings, some directors gave insightful perspectives on how arts professionals see their festivals and their social role. For example, the Greek director of WOMAD in Abu Dhabi responded to a question on festivals as opportunities for experimenting with hybrid or transnational identities and cosmopolitanism, as instances of internationalization or globalization, with the following answer:

> Well, I am unconvinced about this. I know such thinking is very prevalent in
> visual arts biennials, the conceptual exploration of globalization, etc. How
> accessible is this thinking to the audience/public and how far does it contribute
> to the success or not of the event? To me a festival is a festival. The sub-context
> and different layers of interpretation belong to the sphere of the few and the very
> definition of a festival is that there has to be broad appeal.
>
> Cosmopolitanism, for me personally means openness. An open perception of
> otherness, a certain lack of fear … In the context of arts festivals in general, it is
> the foundation of everything. I do not believe in defining boundaries of ethnicity,
> artistic identity, national or cultural or other – and not even of art forms … I
> also think underlying value judgments are dangerous, like transnational equals
> 'good', national(ist) equals 'bad'. Yet I get caught up in those definitions all
> the time. I have to do it, because in one way or another a festival does not exist
> in a vacuum and it has to have a certain identity in order to be appealing and
> sustainable. So, a bit of a catch 22 here. (Euro-Festival interview)

One of the dilemmas, then – and one especially evidenced in the accounts of other
directors who favour the term 'international' – is that the 'national' remains the
frame through which the interactions between selves and others, between insiders
and outsiders, are explored. There are many obvious reasons why this is the case,
not least practical issues: visas for international artists, funding from state-level arts
organizations, national pavilions, the basic recognition and delineation of difference
in festival programmes and cultural content through nationality. All of these ensure
that festivals find themselves reifying the national even when they explicitly seek to
move beyond it, to focus on interaction, boundary-crossing and so on.

It is unsurprising that literature festivals are the most explicitly reflexive
about such issues, as with the rationale of the Borderlands festival detailed in its
programmes – for example, from the 2008 programme:

> Borders may be spaces of contact, but also of friction. However Europe has yet
> to learn to experience its old and new borders as something positive – as spaces
> where different cultures coalesce and mix, spaces which create something new.

Fundamental to the questions that Borderlands asks is a focus on the literal border
spaces that previously have divided Europe's East and West. Meanwhile, the
opening speech from the 2006 edition of the ILB dealt with the global South:

> The welcome and maybe even the integration of immigrants can be 'successful'
> only on the basis of a *politics of relation*, which has still to be invented …
> [I]dentitarian mutual slaughters will not end until these same humanities have
> agreed to consider the identity of everyone, individual or group, as both
> inalienable and changeable in its relation to the other. *I can change by exchanging*
> *with the other, without losing or distorting myself.* To drum in these repetitions is

an act of faith that frontiers will be reanimated, becoming places of agreement and exchange ... (ILB Opening Speech, 200)

Notable in these unashamedly ideological speeches – designed to set the tone of the particular edition of the festival – is the lack of cosmopolitanism as an explicit leitmotif or goal. Nevertheless, reaching out to a public with a broad international political agenda indicates that – for the organizers, at the very least – a shared normative culture (one of the four cosmopolitan conditions) is perceived to exist, as well as being an aspiration for a positive and politically relevant recognition of the other (our second type). Borderlands and ILB audiences are looking for solutions, actively engaged in thinking through global issues rather than escaping into the imaginative escapism that literature *can* offer. Significantly, in the ILB's opening speech of 2003, we see the same thing, with the arts trumpeted as a crucial element in achieving greater social cohesion and equality: the world's diversity needs to be fought for by guaranteeing 'that all ideas and forms of art are enabled to flourish'.

The predominant sentiment behind the overtly anti-parochial representations of the world through which most art festivals present themselves is one of exchange: identities (like places) are relativized, Others are positively recognized and dialogue occurs. However, it is hard to describe this as a shared normative culture, or to understand how far this might extend beyond the bounds of the festival itself without a greater understanding of art festival publics. Focus groups tend to draw in enthusiasts and stakeholders. Their accounts tell us much about how a festival is used and perceived by its fans, but give us little idea of why some sectors of the population do not attend these events. Audience surveys are useful indicators, but depend on the help of festival organizers to be successful. Publics remain the core of art festivals, for without large numbers of genuine non-professional enthusiasts, festivals are effectively just trade fairs, catering for insiders and the professionally interested. Where there are large numbers of genuine non-professional enthusiasts – as the Euro-Festival case studies demonstrate – art festivals contain great transformative potential, though whether other factors outside of this art world may impact negatively on this remains unclear. Art festivals and their publics may be cosmopolitan, even if they never use the term, but their broader impact is harder to assess.

Conclusions

How is cosmopolitanism expressed within art festivals? In answering, it is worth looking beyond the explicit rhetoric played out within the festivals that often lead not only academic critics but also audiences to knowingly and ironically raise their eyebrows – the visible expressions of a cosmopolitan disposition that almost all festival directors, and most of those professionals involved (artists, programmers, etc.), avow through key words like 'international', 'multicultural' and 'exchange'. In fact, as we described in this chapter, it is often in the off-programme activities of art festivals that a shared normative culture grounded in those relationships we identify as cosmopolitan can be found germinating. Indeed, if we go back to our four cosmopolitan relationships – relativization of one's own identity, positive recognition of the other, mutual evaluation of cultures and shared normative culture – and recall our findings in previous sections, we can see how they all emerge, although to different degrees. Not surprisingly, the first type is most easily singled out, whereas the fourth type emerges more as an ultimate goal in certain reflexive accounts rather than being embodied in the festivals themselves (although this might have been different had we considered more openly political or engaged festivals, such as the recent and growing phenomenon of anti-racism festivals).

It is important to address the overall predominance of the first type, especially given that a possible – and indeed actual – criticism is that this is simply a *banal* form of cosmopolitanism. This is the type that is more often dismissed as banal in the sense of *inconsequential*, with no real political or ethical purchase beyond the fleeting and separated experiences that originate it, a merely *aesthetic* cosmopolitanism – a critique that first emerged about cosmopolitanism in tourist experience (e.g. Urry 1995). However, we hope that our findings can indicate a different interpretation. This is related to our second, but intimately connected, question: What role do the varieties of cosmopolitanism present in art festivals represent for broader society? We can offer a broad answer that finds as many specific incarnations as there are festivals in our diverse sample. Our distinction into four relationships allowed us to see how the spill-over of one into the other was even more noticeable than the prevalence of one or the other in specific instances. This is what the idea of the 'virtuous circle', rather than a scale, addressed: the fact that once you relativize your culture because of exposure to other cultures, you may be induced to positively recognize the other, and/or to start to re-evaluate your own culture, which in turn may affect your openness and capacity of code-switching between different cultural repertoires. This includes, importantly, spilling over beyond the festivals' settings that first stimulated the relationship (as we have partly seen, a theme in the Brighton focus group was how the cultural risk-taking attitude stimulated by the festival also translated into openness in social terms). In providing a 'culture medium' for the virtuous circle of these cosmopolitan relationships, festivals can be seen not only as interesting in themselves, but as generative of cosmopolitan relationships. If the cosmopolitanism that so emerges is *banal*, it is so in the sense of being increasingly 'taken for granted' – a social reality, available to people. In the current, widely accepted celebration of openness to cultural diversity, the analytical framework of varieties of cosmopolitanism is useful because it can help us to appreciate their interconnectedness, and thus value varieties otherwise deemed banal, practical or even indifferent. Similarly, cultural omnivorousness (as openness to cultural diversity) has been critiqued as a renewed logic of distinction, effectively reproducing old structural inequalities (Ollivier 2008). Although not political or ethical in a direct manner, the aesthetic cosmopolitanism found in festivals is not only a more or less interesting condition present in these festivals, and relevant for their analysis only; it carries a broader cultural significance. The risk of irrelevance, banality or commercial exploitation is there – and indeed people involved in festivals often have shown a high level of reflexivity about these contradictions. As contradictions, these are best interpreted as the result of conflicting trends, rather than a linear narrative of decadence from a golden past of authentic, traditional festivals. Cosmopolitan varieties within festivals are thus not reducible to such a narrative – as, for instance, in Chaney's (2002) influential vision of cosmopolitanism within avant-garde art losing its critical edge to commercialization. Rather, art festivals are a series of multifaceted processes and relationships that take us closer to the complexity of our contemporary culture. Their increasing popularity is helping to engineer the fading of an 'emancipative' function of aesthetic (high) culture (Jones 2007: 76), and instead favours the artistic exploration of the possibilities of the democratization of culture.

References

Augé, M. 1995. *Non-places: Introduction to an Anthropology of Super-modernity*. London: Verso.

Beck, U. 2006. *The Cosmopolitan Outlook*. Cambridge: Polity Press.

Benjamin, W. 1969 [1936]. The work of art in the age of mechanical reproduction. *Illuminations*. New York: Schocken Books.

Bianchini, F. and Parkinson, M. (eds) 1993. *Cultural Policy and Urban Regeneration: The West European Experience*. Manchester: Manchester University Press.

Chalcraft, M., Sassatelli, M. and Delanty, G. 2010. Varieties of cosmopolitanism in art festivals, in *European Arts Festivals: Creativity, Culture & Democracy*, edited by M. Santoro. Available at: www.euro-festival.org/publications.html [accessed: 20 November 2012].

Chalcraft, J. and Magaudda, P. 2011. Space is the place. The global localities of Sònar and WOMAD music festivals, in *Arts Festivals and the Cultural Public Sphere*, edited by G. Delanty, L. Giorgi and M. Sassatelli. London: Routledge, n.p.

Chaney, D. 2002. Cosmopolitan art and cultural citizenship. *Theory, Culture and Society*, 19(1–2), 157–74.

Delanty, G. 2009. *The Cosmopolitan Imagination: The Renewal of Critical Social Theory*. Cambridge: Cambridge University Press.

Delanty, G. and Inglis, D. (eds) 2010. *Cosmopolitanism: Critical Concepts in the Social Sciences*, 4 vols. London: Routledge.

Emirbayer, M. 1997. A manifesto for a relational sociology. *American Journal of Sociology*, 103, 281–317.

Falassi, A. 1987. *Time Out of Time: Essays on the Festival*. Albuquerque, NM: University of New Mexico Press.

Foucault, M. 1984 [1967]. Of other spaces: Utopias and heterotopias, translated by J. Miskowiec. *Architecture/Mouvement/Continuité*, October.

Giorgi, L. 2010. *European Arts Festivals: Cultural Pragmatics and Discursive Identity Frames*. Euro-festival Project, Deliverable 3.1. Available at: www.euro-festival.org [accessed: 20 November 2012].

Jones, P. 2007. Cultural sociology and an aesthetic public sphere. *Cultural Sociology*, 1(1), 73–95.

Kendall, G., Woodward, I. and Skribis, Z. 2009. *The Sociology of Cosmopolitanism*. London: Sage.

Lash, S. and Lury, C. 2007. *Global Culture Industry: The Mediation of Things*. Cambridge: Polity Press.

Lury, C. 2004. *Brands: The Logos of the Global Economy*. London: Routledge.

Magaudda, P., Solaroli, M., Chalcraft, J. and Santoro, M. 2011. Music festivals and local identities, in *Art Festivals and the European Public Culture*, edited by L. Giorgi. Brussels: European Commission.

Massey, D. 1992. Politics and space/time. *New Left Review*, 1(196), 65–84.

Massey, D. 2006. London inside-out. *Soundings: A Journal of Politics and Culture*, 32, 62–71.

National Endowment for the Arts 2010. *Live from Your Neighbourhood: A National Study of Outdoors Arts Festivals. Volume 1: Summary Report*. Research Report 51. Washington, DC: NEA.

Ollivier, M. 2008. Modes of openness to cultural diversity: Humanist, populist, practical, and indifferent. *Poetics*, 36, 120–47.

Paperstagiadis, N. 2007. Glimpses of cosmopolitanism in the hospitality of art. *European Journal of Social Theory*, 10(1), 139–52.

Performing Arts Yearbook for Europe (PAYE) 2008. Manchester: Impromptu Publishing.

Prevots, N. 1998. *Dance for Export: Cultural Diplomacy and the Cold War*. Middletown, CT: Wesleyan University Press.

Quinn, B. 2005. Arts festivals and the city. *Urban Studies*, 42(5/6), 927–43.

Robinson, M. and Picard, D. 2006. *Tourism, Culture & Sustainable Development*. Paris: UNESCO.

Santoro, M. (ed.) 2010. *European Art Festivals: Creativity, Culture and Democracy*. Euro-festival Project, Deliverable 4.1. Available at: www.euro-festival.org/publications.html [accessed: 20 November 2012].

Santoro, M. and Solaroli, M. 2010. The institutional ecology of a festival: The case of Umbria Jazz. Available at: www.rivisteweb.it/doi/10.1424/73166 [accessed 20 November 2012].

Sassatelli, M. (ed.) 2008. *European Public Culture and Aesthetic Cosmopolitanism*. Euro-festival Project, Deliverable 1.1. Available at: www.euro-festival.org [accessed: 20 November 2012].

Sassatelli, M. and Delanty, G. 2010. Cities in festivals, festivals in cities, in *Art Festivals and the European Public Culture*, edited by L. Giorgi. Euro-festival Project, Deliverable 3.1. Brussels: European Commission.

Segal, J. and Giorgi, L. 2009. *European Arts Festivals from a Historical Perspective*. Euro-festival Project, Deliverable 2.1. Available at: www.euro-festival.org [accessed: 20 November 2012].

Szerszynski, B. and Urry, J. 2002. Cultures of cosmopolitanism. *Sociological Review*, 50, 461–81.

Szerszynski, B. and Urry, J. 2006. Visuality, mobility and the cosmopolitan: Inhabiting the world from afar. *British Journal of Sociology*, 57, 113–31.

Tomlinson, J. 1999. *Globalization and Culture*. Cambridge: Polity Press.

Urry, J. 1995. *Consuming Places*. London: Routledge.

Willems-Braun, B. 1994. Situating cultural politics: Fringe festivals and the production of spaces of intersubjectivity. *Environment and Planning D: Society and Space*, 12(1), 75–104.

Wu, C-T. 2009. Biennials without borders? *New Left Review*, 57, 107–15.

Wuthnow, R. 1989, *Communities of Discourse: Ideology and Social Structure in the Reformation, the Enlightenment, and European Socialism*. Cambridge, MA: Harvard University Press.

Chapter 7

Sovereign Bodies: Australian Indigenous Cultural Festivals and Flourishing Lifeworlds

Lisa Slater

In 2008, I was an observer at a two-day workshop concerned with the future of the Laura Aboriginal Dance Festival.[1] The delegates were Aboriginal and Torres Strait Islander peoples from across Cape York Peninsula, representing communities (Indigenous townships) that dance at this long-running event. There was an open-floor discussion; following cultural protocols, one by one elders got to their feet to speak for country.[2] A highly respected elder told of how he and his family cared for country – walked, talked, sung, hunted, burned – to keep their ancestral lands healthy, as the land looked after them. He then passionately implored his audience to understand that dancing at the Laura festival is the same. My memory is of the old man becoming animated and agile, made young as his feet stomped the floor, his traditional country manifest in the room. As someone who has been to many Indigenous festivals, I saw dust rising, that old man dancing.[3] After him, elders stressed their support for the festival and its role in gathering people from across the region to strengthen and affirm the Cape as a multicultural Aboriginal domain, and as a means to maintain and develop strong culture for the Cape and surrounding communities. All the participants then undertook an exercise to arrive at the festival purpose or mission statement. Despite the range of people and communities in the room, it did not take long for consensus to emerge. The countrymen were unanimous that the Laura Festival is a significant event for

---

1 The Laura Aboriginal Dance Festival is held biennially 15 kilometres from Laura, at the Ang-Gnarra Festival Grounds, Cape York Peninsula, Queensland (330 kilometres from Cairns). The workshop was an initiative of the Aboriginal and Torres Strait Islander Arts Board (ATSIAB), and was held over two days in Cairns, on 5–6 May 2008.

2 Throughout this chapter, 'country' refers to the Indigenous concept of traditional or customary lands that hold multi-dimensional relationships, networks, history and law.

3 I use the general term Indigenous to refer to the diverse nations and clan groups that comprise Aboriginal and Torres Strait Islander Australians.

maintaining cultural integrity and passing on tradition to young people.[4] That old man does not dance alone.

There are hundreds of Indigenous festivals across Australia, from small community gatherings to large-scale productions complete with rock star stages, and the corresponding talent. Since colonization, there has been a history of Indigenous public performances for non-Indigenous audiences. My focus here is on what are readily called Indigenous cultural festivals, and more so those events that are innovations of the 'traditional' ceremonial life that now unfolds in settler, liberal Australia. They are public performances, manifestations of a sacred, ritual world. In particular, I am drawing my observations and analysis from festivals I have attended and researched (but absolutely not limited to these examples, or excluding events in urban Australia), such as Garma (Northern Territory), Laura Aboriginal Dance (Far North Queensland) and KALACC festivals (Kimberley, Western Australia). These festivals are held on lands that are recognized under forms of land rights and native title, and 'traditional' culture is practised and is acknowledged by, and affects, state and corporate activities. Like many Indigenous festivals, they have a similar purpose: to maintain and strengthen culture. Yet it is Indigenous culture that worries so many people in the mainstream. In this chapter, I examine Indigenous cultural festivals as creative commitments to the ontological primacy of land and non-Western sociality and ritual life, which emerges in a deeply intercultural world dominated by settler liberalism. A hope and aim of these events is to compose anti-colonial relations, arguably whereby 'culture' is not a commodity to be scrutinized and judged but rather recognized as emanating from complex lifeworlds.

In the same month as the 2011 Laura Festival was staged, academic John Morton (2011) wrote an opinion piece for *The Australian* newspaper, entitled 'Threadbare paradigms hamper Indigenous progress'. He wrote that since the new millennium, there has been a 'dramatic' shift in Australian public intellectual debates addressing Indigenous issues. Previously, Indigenous difference – here identified as 'culture' – was the vehicle for achieving Indigenous rights and political recognition; currently, the reigning public discourse – promulgated and popularized by Aboriginal public intellectual Noel Pearson – is the need for Indigenous people to engage with the 'real economy'. Put simply, political responses to Indigenous socio-economic issues have been directed largely towards mainstreaming. Morton (2011: 2) goes on to argue that Pearson and his supporters are not opposed to difference, but rather to 'those who wish to sustain a culture of victimhood'. By drawing on Marcia Langton's attack on the 'old Left', he associates 'victimhood' with keeping 'Aborigines in a non-modern place'. Putting aside whether he is correct to suggest that there has ever been such an easy division between left and right, and previous steadfast support for 'culture' (and his un-nuanced use of the term 'difference'), if Morton is discussing an intellectual debate, it is one that has been had in the disciplines of anthropology and Indigenous studies,

---

4   Countrymen is a gender neutral term for Indigenous traditional owners, readily used in northern Australia.

surrounding Peter Sutton's (2009) book *The Politics of Suffering*. He worries over the politicization of the academy, and wants to defend Sutton's work (and person) from what Morton sees an as an ideological attack by some on the academic left. But he is most troubled by Aboriginal 'culture'. Morton took the opportunity to reiterate Sutton's thesis:

> [C]ertain forms of Aboriginal tradition, when corrupted in the context of modernisation, led to distress and dysfunction. Aboriginal child-rearing practices, strategic recourse to legitimate violence and the articulation of extended kin obligations were placed under the microscope and found to be inconsistent with the encroachment of imposed regimes of schooling, policing and welfare, which relied on other *rationalities* for potential good effect. (2011: 2, emphasis added)

The problem identified by Sutton is one of differing rationalities: realities or ontology. Broadly speaking, Indigenous and settler colonials have ontological differences. Yet Morton advocates for a neat middle ground. Relinquishing ontology is a very different proposition from setting aside ideological differences. However, for the moment I will put aside these criticisms to return to culture. If somewhat tentatively, Morton weighed into the 'culture wars' or the politics of engagement with Indigenous policy and its role in the imagined futures of and for Indigenous peoples (Hinkson 2010: 1). While Morton suggested an ideological slanging match, Altman and Hinkson's (2010) edited collection, *Culture Crisis*, which contains diverse scholarship, notes that 'culture' has become an object of critical attention – a 'site of intense, future focused contestation' (Hinkson 2010: xiv).

What is this thing called Aboriginal culture, which is simultaneously revered and deplored? Indigenous visual arts – that is, paintings from remote Australia, not urban art – are close to universally admired. Even the most conservative politicians are photographed in their offices with a desert dot painting – or an Arnhem Land bark or the subtle red earth tones of the Kimberley – as backdrop, roundly praised as good culture. At the same time, kinship systems and obligations to extended family are readily, with bipartisan support, condemned as 'an impediment to progress'. Maybe this is to confuse the question, or even to ask the wrong question. A specific practice only becomes 'Indigenous Culture', as Eric Michaels (1994) points out, once it is taken out of local networks of production, circulation and exchange. My above example works, as Morton does, with mainstream formulations of 'culture' or cultural difference as an object or processes abstracted from its material and discursive relations. It is an arrangement that, on one hand, commodifies Indigenous culture as an aspect of the mainstream economy and, on the other, essentializes it as unchanging traditional practices that are a bad fit with modernity. To produce good culture, it must be disarticulated from bad culture.

But why does that old man dance? What are the forces or assemblages to which he binds himself when he – like his countrymen – speaks of the vital role of cultural maintenance, and the place of festivals in this process? In drawing readers' attention to Morton's article, I am not only taking the temperature of an ongoing debate, but more importantly I think he publicly discloses presumptions that are foundational to the popular construction of 'Indigenous culture' and the 'Indigenous problem'. Before continuing, I know I risk making Morton into a straw man (or worse, a whipping boy), and this is not my intention. Rather, I am arguing that public discourse – or what passes as political debate – is hampered by 'threadbare paradigms', but the same cannot be said of much scholarship in the broad fields concerned with Indigenous issues. It is a rich resource – as is to be found elsewhere, such as in local programs and initiatives such as festivals – for understanding our present, and realizing just and desired futures. I want to propose that there are vastly different articulations of culture being expressed by that old man and Morton. Or, to be more accurate, what is at play is ontological politics. Indigenous cultural festivals, I argue, are an innovative responses to keeping culture alive – meaningful lifeworlds comprised local networks of production, circulation, exchange, sociality and law, embedded in settler, liberal modernity.

Indigenous and non-Indigenous Australians live in entangled and interdependent lifeworlds. All Australians are influenced by government policies and bureaucratic decisions, yet Indigenous people and communities are marked by cultural, historical, socio-economic (more often perceived, but sometimes geographical) differences and, despite processes of colonization and assimilation, they continue to assert sovereignty. These apparent differences between lifeworlds play out in political and social fields. The questions of how to theorize such difference-yet-relatedness within an increasingly expanding and complex social field, Hinkson and Smith (2005: 157) argue, is a crucial challenge for accounts of 'Indigenous Australia' and anthropology in general.

Wrestling with this very material dilemma, they propose the 'intercultural' as a productive concept. There are not, they argue, separate Indigenous/non-Indigenous spheres that meet at an 'interface'; rather, their approach is one that considers 'Indigenous and non-Indigenous social forms to be necessarily relational, and to occupy a single socio-cultural field' (Hinkson and Smith 2005: 158). Sympathizing with their intellectual project, Patrick Sullivan (2005) is wary of the term 'intercultural', arguing that the concept emerges from, and is limited by, the modernist project of 'caught between two worlds'. He calls for the development of relational anthropology, which accounts for the fluidity and contestation privileged by many Indigenous peoples, and which reveals complex fields of interrelations and co-location. In this sense, he proposes that cultures should primarily be understood as effects of strategic and political relationships (Sullivan 2005: 184).

There are cultural differences, but they emerge in a relational field: the reproduction of cultural differences is in a field of interdependencies, imbrications and relatedness (Preaud 2009: 119). Importantly, there is no site of neat convergence, for example, where state policies and bureaucracy and local difference and divergence unite; rather, it is in the thickness of everyday life that people navigate the effects of power-laden relational processes – be they familial, local, regional, national or global. In this shared social domain, socio-economic disadvantage – or what is too commonly thought of as the 'problem' (and sometimes the promise) of Indigenous culture – emerges. It is in *our* present that so-called traditional culture is harnessed as a resource for ameliorating social issues. Why? Because strong, healthy life is made from, among other things, a world that is meaningful, shared and valued by self and others. The festivals that are the focus of this chapter represent a public space within contemporary Australia where 'traditional' or customary culture takes precedence and structures exchanges and events – with, I would argue, the express purpose of enlivening and enriching life.

The association of non-Indigenous people (particularly settler colonials) with 'modernity' and Indigenous people with 'tradition' or 'not modern' (yet) is commonplace. Arguably, it is particular practices or performances of Indigeneity that are categorized as the pre-modern, to which liberal settler societies then attribute aesthetic-moral value. As Weiner and Glaskin (2006, quoted in Preaud 2009: 42) write:

> The emergence of a domain called (variously) the 'customary', the 'traditional' and/or 'the Indigenous' is made visible chiefly in the bi-cultural context of the modern nation-state. The 'invention' of tradition is not, as the phrase might suggest, an essentially autogenously generated transformation from within a community perceived to be spatially and culturally distinct. It is a gloss for a particular moment in inter-cultural relations, especially of an asymmetric nature.

We are in a particular intercultural moment – albeit a long one – whereby commentators, public intellectuals and politicians alike worry that traditional culture is limiting and delaying Indigenous people's entry into modernity. To return to Morton (2011: 5) as one such example, he finishes his article with 'as we move beyond the era of what Pearson calls 'the campaign blackfella', we will be more ready to accept that the most important problem shaping research is the desirability of Aborigines entering more fully into modernity'. For many, I think this would be perceived as a reasonable expectation of research and, more generally, public policy. However, the underlying assumption is that there are two separate social domains – the Indigenous and non-Indigenous – with the former either outside or standing at the threshold of modernity. I would contend that the more pressing scholarly concern should be the study and conceptual unravelling of this damaging false binary.

The intellectual project of Elizabeth Povinelli's (2006) monograph *The Empire of Love* is to critique the accompanying discourses of individual freedom and social constraint that circulate in settler-colonial societies. The idea of freedom, the fantasy of individual choice, in Povinelli's theoretical arrangement, is produced within a liberal assemblage of conflicting cultural modes of modernity and tradition – or what she refers to as autological and genealogical imaginaries (also see Probyn 2008):

By the *autological subject*, I am referring to discourse, practices, and fantasies
about self-making, self-sovereignty, and the value of individual freedom
associated with the Enlightenment project of contractual constitutional
democracy and capitalism. By *genealogical society*, I am referring to discourses,
practices, and fantasies about social constraints placed on the autological subject
by various kinds of inheritances. (Povinelli 2006: 4)

She sets herself the assignment of understanding how these discourses animate
and enflesh ethical and normative claims about the governance of love, sociality
and bodies, and in so doing operate as strategies of power that contribute to the
material conditions that over-invest in some to live prosperous and optimistic
lives, while others are diminished – 'the power to cripple and rot certain worlds'
(Povinelli 2006: 9). Despite the fact that socialities can be radically different,
I would argue that there are not two competing cultural modes. The genealogical
web of kinship relations to human and non-human worlds, ancestral traditions and
attendant obligations give life deep meaning to many Indigenous peoples, while
settler liberal subjects are largely formed within social systems that privilege
self-fashioning discourses. The reality, as Elspeth Probyn (2008: 235) writes,
is that 'we live viscerally between interpellation and freedom'. Settler liberal
governance promulgates freedom and choice, while responsibility is not only
to the self but bears the traces of genealogical constraint: self-fashioning within
the limits of family and community values makes a good and proper citizen.
However, the state recognizes autological – modern – subjects if they conform to
the Western imaginary of agency, citizenship and responsibility (Preaud 2009: 57).
Concurrently, the state perceives others – in this case, many Indigenous peoples,
whose agency, responsibilities and humanness derive from alternative sociality
and order, human and more-than-human world – as beholden to tradition, so thus
not being autonomous, fully modern agents. The discourses of autological subject
and genealogical society are a claim on what makes us human, and they contribute
to securing settler liberal power and reproducing it as normative (Povinelli 2006).

The discourses of modernity and tradition obscure the distribution of power and
value within the Australian state, and the complex navigations and inventiveness
that compose the quotidian for minorities in intercultural domains. My concern here
is the dilemma for Indigenous people of negotiating the discourses of autological
subject and genealogical society, and how this impacts upon their everyday lives.
These very lifeworlds are routinely not taken into account when 'culture' is
abstracted from its material and discursive relations – be it to praise or problematize.
These discourses cannot be understood outside of people's familiar lives. They
are not a set of rules that one applies to life; rather, Indigeneity enfolds in dense
social worlds (Povinelli 2006: 85). Lifeworlds – or thick life, to borrow from
Povinelli – generate sociality, which has its own local obligations, responsibilities,
social identities, agency and hierarchies. Povinelli's goal is to understand how the
discourses of modernity and tradition shape social life, so we can begin to 'formulate
a positive political program' – a politics of thick life – 'in which the density of social

representation is increased to meet the density of actual social worlds' (2006: 21). I wish to follow her. Arguably, what are commonly referred to as customary or traditional cultural practices are Indigenous relational ontologies, being privileged and performed in shared social domains.[5] Where else are the spaces of enunciation or performance of contemporary Indigeneity if not here and now? What are the experiments in living that emerge from Indigenous peoples contesting modernity?

To quarrel with and expose the inequitable power of Western visions of modernity, post-colonial scholars are attentive to alternative or hybrid modernities. If modernity is best understood as an attitude of questioning the present, as Gaonkar (1999: 13) assumes, then modernity is everywhere. All modernities are contextual. Western modernity, with its distinctive moral and scientific vision, distinguished from its own ancient past and non-Western societies, is associated with the development of industrial capitalism, which ushered in social and economic transformations, and with them the production of new forms of subjectivity (Gaonkar 1999: 15; Knauft 2002). As others have argued, this is not modernity but the history of the West, which is also a history of exploitation and domination of Indigenous peoples justified by racial logics of primitivism and tribalism (Chakrabarty 2000; Povinelli 2006). The intellectual, political terrain from which I draw is that of postcolonial, African, Indigenous and subaltern studies organizations, artists, writers and thinkers, who have interrogated the Western construction of modernity as power-laden, secular, disembodied and separate from the non-human world (e.g. see Ahluwalia 2010; Arabena 2006; Fanon 1963; Kimberley Aboriginal Law and Culture Centre 2007; Marika 1999; Mbembe 2001; Moreton-Robinson 2007; Povinelli 2002). Critiquing the commitment of European political thought to the human as ontologically singular, Chakrabarty writes:

> I take gods and spirits to be existentially coeval with the human, and think from the assumption that the question of being human involves the question of being with gods and spirits. Being human means ... Discovering 'the possibility of calling upon God [or gods] without being under an obligation to first establish his [or their] reality'. (2000: 16)

The agency, love, wiliness and creativity of spirits, ancestors, country – the more-than-human world – are called upon, or rather made manifest in the

---

5   According to Preaud, relational ontology refers to 'each person or agency is uniquely articulating constellations of relationships that define his/her/its being: here singularities do not derive from individual internal characteristics but from the ordering of a particular network (or rather sets of networks if we add to kinships networks of places, histories, and myth) and ways of navigating through it: each agent thus appears as a moving node of a network and, indeed, it is the very condition of their *being*' (2009: 123–4). He goes on to argue that relational ontology is a 'general property of living systems and not specifically attached to particular segments of the human population and it is from a relational nexus of heterogeneous elements that singular positions are articulated' (2009: 134).

world, because they are vital to many Indigenous people's relational ontology. If a meaningful relationship with a particular 'country' is constitutive of being and self, then it cannot be left out or put aside for the so-called prize of secular modernity (Preaud 2009: 29). Articulating maligned or largely unrecognized (or unrecognizable) alternative ontologies into spaces dominated and mediated by the liberal settler state produces contestation and creativity. In this sense, Indigenous cultural festivals are expressions and generation of, as well as experiments in, Indigenous modernity.

Across Australia, and globally, Indigenous cultural festivals are growing in number and influence, ranging from small community events to those of national and international reach and significance (Phipps and Slater 2010). There are literally hundreds of Indigenous festivals and celebrations in Australia, most of which are local events driven by community organizations and individuals, with very little funding or outside support, with a focus on contemporary cultural practices: sport, music, art or 'traditional' culture. The driving force of these events is often, in mainstream speak, community well-being: the gathering together of people to celebrate, share and remember, and clear a public space that is dedicated to the values and aspirations of the people and place. Notably, as Michelle Duffy (2005) suggests, because festivals are structured events, they bring groups and communities together to mark out particular socio-political, historical and cultural affiliations. Like mainstream festivals, Indigenous festivals are deployed as a means to enhance community creativity, belonging and well-being, and thus nourish community resilience. Scholars have recognized festivals and community celebrations as important events that provide both material and symbolic means of responding to and coping with change (Gibson and Connell 2011; Gibson and Stewart 2009; Mulligan et al. 2006). And many Indigenous Australians face relentless change.

Historically, Indigenous people have participated in festivals commemorating nationhood, and staged counter-festivals to protest colonization and to celebrate survival. They are a means of entering into dialogue with mainstream Australia and testimony to ongoing political struggles (Kleinert 1999: 345). The annual Survival Day concerts staged across Australia unsettle and challenge official Australia Day celebrations, and have grown out of a long history of utilizing public performance to remind broader Australia of the continuing Indigenous presence. For contemporary audiences, performance has become an increasingly familiar aspect of cultural practice among Indigenous peoples. Such events are a testimony to ongoing political struggles, and for both Indigenous performers and their audience they provide an important context for the contemporary negotiation and transmission of Indigenous people's, and more broadly Australian, identities (Myers, quoted in Kleinert 1999).

In recent years, several major Indigenous festivals have emerged, including Garma Festival (North-East Arnhem Land, Northern Territory), The Dreaming (South-East Queensland), Barunga Festival (Northern Territory), Laura Aboriginal Dance Festival (Cape York, Queensland), Coming of the Light (Thursday Island, Torres Strait Islands) and KALACC Festival (Kimberley, Western Australia).

In 2003, in recognition of the vibrancy and significance of Indigenous festivals, the Department of Foreign Affairs and Trade funded a touring photographic exhibition, *Kickin' up Dust: Contemporary Festivals of Indigenous Australia*, featuring images of the Torres Strait Cultural Festival (Thursday Island), Stompem Ground (Broome, Western Australia), Larapuna (Tasmania) and Garma festivals (Payne 2003). The lineage of all of these festivals is extremely intercultural: from ceremony practised on country to rodeos, sports days and country shows, to the glamour of international arts festivals and a long history of arts and culture being deployed to ameliorate social issues.

In recent years, there has been an increasing academic, government and philanthropic interest in community celebrations, and particularly in the relationship between community art and well-being (see Mulligan et al. 2006; Phipps and Slater 2010). In turn, philanthropic and government agencies increasingly are receiving applications for funding for Indigenous festivals. Notably, the Australia Council's Aboriginal and Torres Strait Islander Arts Board (ATSIAB) (2008), as a part of its industry development strategy, Celebrations, is supporting festival events in recognition of their artistic, cultural and economic benefits for Indigenous peoples.

Telstra Foundation, the philanthropic arm of the Australian telco, Telstra, initiated the three-year research project for which I was primary researcher, after identifying a need for evidence-based research.[6] The foundation was receiving numerous funding applications that relied upon anecdotal evidence to demonstrate the connection between Indigenous celebrations and strengthening social well-being (Phipps and Slater 2010). What became clear during the research was the number of government and non-government bodies that were initiating, or responding to, the thirst for Indigenous community celebrations and events. However, differing pressures, ambitions and agendas often drive funding agencies and Indigenous communities. Add to this the fact that festivals are run by diverse and divergent bodies – be they community agencies, such as sport and recreational or arts workers, Indigenous organizations or councils, professional events managers, or energized and passionate individuals – all with varied capacities and resources. All events, no matter how big or small, rely on volunteers – be they local or from elsewhere – and the goodwill of community – individuals and organizations – elders' and traditional owners' approval and support, compliance with council regulations and some form of sponsorship, even if it is the local shop. This is quite apart from, as any arts/community sector worker knows, the relentless demands of applying for funds, reporting and acquittal. This is all to say that Indigenous festivals are complex contemporary events, which makes them captivating to study – and no doubt challenging and rewarding work.

---

6 This project started in 2007 and won the support of the Australian Research Council under the Linkage grants scheme, 'Globalising Indigeneity: Indigenous cultural festivals and wellbeing in Australia and the Asia-Pacific' (LP0882877, 2008–10), partner organization Telstra Foundation (see Phipps and Slater 2010).

Indigenous festivals, as Rosita Henry (2008) writes, have grown in tandem with state policies that foster the celebration of culture as a further means to govern people. For all the positive aspects of Indigenous festivals – like all arenas of Indigenous lives – they operate within a web of government and non-governmental agencies and corporate agendas, values and power relations. Indeed, funding and supporting such events could be regarded, in some instances, as cunning forms of governmentality. Henry (2008: 53) points out that 'the state deceptively asserts its presence *within* the festivals. Indeed, agents and agencies of the state colonize the festivals, so that the festivals become prime sites for recognition of the "effects" of the state'.

This can most readily be observed in what events and programs are funded. For example, at the Barunga Festival, the Department of Lands and Planning's Road Safety Branch sponsors the 'Road Safety Song Competition'. Local bands become the medium to deliver government directives 'about safe and appropriate behaviour for drivers, passengers and pedestrians' (Barunga Festival 2010). Most of the bands perform their usual repertoire with the addition of lyrics such as 'don't drink and drive', 'wear your seatbelt' and so on. For all the import of road safety awareness, the means of delivery are paternalistic, and it is assumed that the problem is one of 'education and promotion', and that people only need to learn 'proper' conduct and they will adjust their behaviour. (Notably, the competition is popular but that might have little to do with the 'awareness' campaign and much more to do with the opportunity it affords to perform in front of countrymen.) However, partaking in such events should not simply be interpreted as submitting to the process of assimilation or naivety. Indigenous festivals and public performances have long been creative means to negotiate and intervene in forms of state power, to mark out a continuing presence and legitimacy, and to assert some agency in a rapidly changing world dominated by mainstream values and bureaucratic power (Henry 2008: 54).

Since colonization, there has been a history of Aboriginal public performance for non-Indigenous people. However, they have been received primarily as modes of 'cultural' tourism or entertainment, representative of a 'primitive' age or dying culture. Kleinert (1999: 347) writes that:

> Colonial history is replete with a rich history of such performances. However, the importance of these cultural representations has been largely overlooked, either bracketed off from history as anthropology ... appropriated as theatre, viewed primarily as a form of entertainment and a spectacle of an exotic primitive Other.

Françoise Dussart (2000: 76) argues that the forced sedentarization of Central Desert Aborigines, which imposed inter-group residency on various Aboriginal societies, resulted in public ritual becoming an important tool for inter-Aboriginal engagement. At this time, non-Indigenous viewers other than anthropologists were rare. During the Protectionist era, mainstream community festivals and events, such as rodeos and rural shows, provided an opportunity for Indigenous peoples to embrace the performative potential of such events for political engagement with settler society (Henry 2000: 587). However, with the introduction of various *Aboriginal*

Land Rights Acts, public performance became a 'kind of legal tool', due to the legislation requiring proof of genealogical and religious connections to the land (Dussart 2000: 76). Government officials thus became a new audience for public ceremonies. The socio-political role and effectiveness of these cultural performances for Indigenous people went largely unacknowledged by non-Indigenous audiences until the last two decades, when the Australian public more broadly began to appreciate aspects of 'traditional culture'. More importantly, however, the state's recognition of the continuance of Indigenous land ownership and governance saw the emergence of Indigenous organizations – such as land councils and various cultural-political bodies – in which customary law became further entangled with bureaucracy and state-based process. As discussed earlier, this produces fields of interrelation and co-location, or the intercultural, in which Indigenous people must navigate asymmetrical political power and competing social identities and boundaries. Settler liberal governments' intrusion into, and bureaucratization of, Indigenous lifeworlds, alongside mainstream embracing of Indigenous cultural performance, produces new contexts for the articulation (and transfiguration) of 'Indigeneity' into the Australian political space (Preaud 2009: 32). Festivals might also be thought of as experiments in and expressions of the agency of 'country'.

The Indigenous cultural festivals to which I wish to draw attention are those that I understand to be an innovative extension of what is known as ritual or ceremonial life, within the transmutations and constraints of settler liberal colonialism (Preaud 2009: 49). As noted, festivals I have attended and researched, such as Garma, Laura Aboriginal Dance and KALACC festivals, inform my analysis. These three festivals are held in regions where there are discrete Aboriginal lands recognized by the state, and where ceremonial life and 'traditional' culture and languages remain strong and exert significant influence on state and corporate activities. Broadly speaking, they have a similar purpose: to keep culture strong. KALACC festival is held every few years in different locations across the Kimberley, Western Australia. It takes place over five days, and attracts up to 3,000 people. The Kimberley Aboriginal Law and Cultural Centre (KALACC), whose objective is to strengthen Kimberley Aboriginal social, cultural and legal values, organizes the event. The event gathers Indigenous people from across the Kimberley to learn and maintain songs and dances, to sustain culture and to demonstrate sovereignty. The event is closed to tourists and visitors, and only a few select influential people from outside the region are invited (KALACC 2011). The annual Garma Festival of Traditional Culture is one of Australia's premier Indigenous cultural festivals. It is an initiative of the Yolŋu Indigenous people of North-East Arnhem Land, and is held on traditional lands, Gulkula, near the mining town of Nhulunbuy in the Northern Territory. At Garma, Yolhu culture is practised and shared through visual arts, Bunggul (traditional dance), Manikay (traditional song), contemporary music, workshops and forums, and men and women's cultural tourism programs. Garma is open to tourists and visitors, but only through an application and invitation process (Slater 2006). Laura Aboriginal Dance Festival began over 30 years ago, and is held biannually 15 kilometres from the township of Laura, Cape York, Queensland, on

Kuku Yalanji land. The three-day program is a celebration of the region's Indigenous cultures, primarily featuring dance groups from across Cape York and into the Torres Strait, and has become one of the largest gatherings of Indigenous people in Australia. It is open to tourists (Slater 2010).

There are, as mentioned, hundreds of events scattered across the country, many of them small, local festivals with the express purpose of cultural maintenance and transmission. Notably, as much as they are highly intercultural events, festivals are not only showcases for or spectacles of the remnants of Indigenous traditions or contemporary artistic expression, but in many cases are temporal, material and socio-cultural spaces in which Indigenous people affirm and maintain the ontological primacy and agency of ancestral lands and beings. There are different categories or levels of Indigenous knowledge – public, sacred or secret-sacred – often referred to as inside/outside, which designates the appropriate level of access and openness of the knowledge to 'outsiders' or those who are not holders of the law. The manifestations of ancestral beings or country at festivals – be it through song, dance, designs, objects or stories – are at the level of public knowledge (Preaud 2009: 44; Magowan 2000). The KALACC festival, Preaud (2009: 45) writes, 'can be seen as an extension of the movement of secularization of ritual power or, to put it differently, the projection of ritual practices into novel situations and sets of relationships'. Festivals are another means by which Australia, on the local, regional and national levels, is affirmed, contested and reproduced as Indigenous country. An alternative modernity is actualized, and the more-than-human world of country, spirits and ancestors materializes in shared social domains, where it can test the secular modern commitment to and desire for a world of the ontologically singular.

Cultural festivals reterritorialize the state and non-Indigenous peoples into an alternative sociality. One of the express purposes of festivals is as agents for transforming relationships with settler Australia – be it government or citizens. In these spaces, Indigenous and mainstream Australians are positioned as equivalent, and 'our' lifeworlds are co-located and entangled. What distinguishes and gathers 'us' is Indigenous law and governance, largely made prominent in these spaces through ceremony, but it is also asserted in a variety of other ways, such as meetings, talks and workshops. For a few days, the imaginary notion of 'we' is re-composed. Countrymen are the hosts, all others are guests and 'we' are interpolated into an assemblage in which 'country' is a, if not *the*, primary actor; power relations shape-shift. I am not suggesting that the significance, or affect, of this is recognized or responded to in the same way by all: if one has little experience in particular forms of sociality, then attentiveness and humility might just be one of the best options. What does it feel like? What are the possibilities? How are notions such as respect, reconciliation and equality tested in these places? I am proposing that the festivals to which I draw attention here are an experiment in anti-colonial relationality.

Cultural festivals are creative, and I would especially argue very generous, ways in which Indigenous people have made themselves present in the world and continue to challenge a history that had rendered them absent (Henry 2000: 586). To be 'rendered absent' from history is to be made marginal to the civic body, which reinforces the values of the settler colonial culture. In turn, Indigenous people's incorporation into the national body too often comes at the cost of their being subject to and limited by mainstream discourses and representations of modernity and tradition. In so doing, the socio-cultural differences that are life-sustaining and generative do not inform the very government policies that are being created to improve Indigenous lives. Indigenous peoples and cultures have long been denigrated, misunderstood, discounted and appropriated, made meaningful or meaningless through a colonial lens, but rarely recognized as material expressions of world-views and sociality that anchor and tend life. I am in no way suggesting that festivals are the only or remaining space where 'culture' is performed – of course, this is in no way true: culture is lived in the everyday. Furthermore, there are an abundance of 'cultural' programs and initiatives that are developed and supported by government and non-government agencies in conjunction with Indigenous communities as a means of addressing social issues. However, what is well documented – and most especially etched into the lives of Indigenous people – is the assimilative pressures upon peoples who are embedded within a dominant culture. A vital component of sustaining and supporting socio-cultural well-being is the creation of public spaces in which Indigenous values, hopes, ambitions and imagined futures can be asserted over and against the social construction of reality by state practices and the mainstream (Morrissey et al. 2007: 245).

Scholars have noted the importance of performance for Indigenous cultural politics, most especially knowledge transfer, and the renewal and assertion of Indigenous identity (Henry 2008; Myers 1994; Phipps and Slater 2010; Slater 2007). In public discourse, it has become distressingly familiar to hear of inter-generational breakdown in Indigenous communities, and the associated social and cultural distress. It is well understood that a sense of identity is a prerequisite for mental health and, as Morrissey (2007: 249) and others argue, cultural identity depends not only on access to culture and heritage, but also on opportunities for cultural expression and cultural endorsement within society's institutions. Groundbreaking reports such as the national report of the Royal Commission into Aboriginal Deaths in Custody (1991) and *Bringing Them Home* (National Inquiry into the Separation of Aboriginal and Torres Strait Islander Children from Their Families 1997) have highlighted the devastating role that fractured or lost cultural identity has played in the lives of Indigenous people. When I refer to cultural transmission, I am not only discussing the teaching of particular practices, such as traditional dance or painting, but much more importantly the inter-generational transfer of social relations and worlds of meaning. Here I follow Tim Ingold (2000) and Martin Preaud, who conceptualize the transmission of cultural knowledge 'not in terms of a set of contents passed on from one generation to the next but as a nexus of relations generated in the immanent field of country, or the environment' (Ingold, quoted in Preuad 2009: 101). To return to an earlier discussion, if one's social identity – one's 'beingness' – is constitutive of meaningful relationship with 'country', and networks of kinship with the human and non-human – that is, a particular cosmological order – then it is vital to life itself. In the context about which I write, the import of cultural transmission is to maintain, bind and actualize social relations to 'country' in ever-transforming social fields, not to return to a mythical, pristine, pre-colonial past (Preaud 2009: 109). Cultural festivals are one such *route* for reinvigorating significant relationships and social identities, with the express purpose of strengthening young people's capacity to navigate the demands of a deeply intercultural world, and to be innovators and agents of the new roles and possibilities generated in our shared present.

If I were to attempt an answer to my own question, 'Why does that old man dance?', I could simply answer, 'So his children's children can also dance, or be known by, their country'. But this is to say little if one separates particular practices from local networks, relations and conditions of production. Public formulations of Indigenous culture often have it as practices somehow exercised in discrete social domains, subject to corruption by modernity but not of modernity. The discourse of the conflicting cultural modes of modernity and tradition operates to obscure complex fields of interrelation, co-location and power relations in which people's lives are embedded. It produces the 'Indigenous problem', and the solution as a movement more fully into secular, liberal modernity. In so doing, we fail to attend to the complex navigations and experiments in living that constitute marginalized peoples every day, and more so to care for their hopes, values, pain, love and desired futures. Cultural festivals are creative assemblages composed of and from the pressures and promise of a globalizing, intercultural world. That old man, I would contend, was affirming festivals as contemporary practices for nurturing the ontological primacy of land and alternative forms of sociality. Why? Because it constitutes social reality, and people will fight (however tactically) for their worlds of meaning. In this sense, I am arguing that cultural festivals are peaceful weapons in a continuing ontological political contest.

References

Aboriginal and Torres Strait Islander Arts Board 2008. *A New Landscape*. Sydney: Australia Council.

Ahluwalia, P. 2010. *Out of Africa: Post-structuralism's Colonial Roots*. London: Routledge.

Altman, J. and Hinkson, M. (eds) 2010. *Cultural Crisis: Anthropology and Politics in Aboriginal Australia*. Sydney: UNSW Press.

Arabena, K. 2006. *Not Fit for Modern Australian Society: Aboriginal and Torres Strait Islander People and the New Administration for Indigenous Affairs*. AIATSIS Research Discussion Paper No 16. Canberra: AIATSIS.

Barunga Festival. 2010. *Barunga Sports and Culture Festival* [Online]. Available at: www.barungafestival.com.au [accessed: 19 September 2010].

Chakrabarty, D. 2000. *Provincializing Europe: Postcolonial Thought and Historical Difference*. Princeton, NJ: Princeton University Press.

Duffy, M. 2005. Performing identity within the multicultural framework. *Social and Cultural Geography*, 6, 677–92.

Dussart, F. 2000. The politics of representation: Kinship and gender in the performance of public ritual, in *The Oxford Companion to Aboriginal Art and Culture*, edited by S. Kleinert and M. Neale. Oxford: Oxford University Press, 75–8.

Fanon, F. 1963. *The Wretched of the Earth.* New York: Grove Press.

Gaonkar, D.P. 1999. On alternative modernities. *Public Culture*, 11, 1–18.

Gibson, C. and Connell, J. (eds) 2011. *Festival Places: Revitalising Rural Australia.* Bristol: Channel View.

Gibson, C. and Stewart, A. 2009. *Reinventing Rural Places: The Extent and Significance of Rural and Regional Festivals in Australia.* Wollongong: University of Wollongong.

Henry, R. 2000. Festivals, in *The Oxford Companion to Aboriginal Art and Culture*, edited by S. Kleinert and M. Neale. Oxford: Oxford University Press, 586–87.

Henry, R. 2008. Engaging with history by performing tradition: The poetics politics of Indigenous Australian festivals, in *The State and the Arts: Articulating Power and Subversion*, edited by J. Kapfler. New York: Berghahn Books, 52–69.

Hinkson, M. 2010. Introduction: Anthropology and the culture wars, in *Culture Crisis: Anthropology and Politics in Aboriginal Australia*, edited by J. Altman and M. Hinkson. Sydney: UNSW Press, 1–14.

Hinkson, M. and Smith, B. 2005. Introduction: Conceptual moves towards an intercultural analysis. *Oceania*, 75, 157–66.

Ingold, T. 2000. *The Perception of the Environment: Essays on Livelihood, Dwelling and Skill.* London: Routledge.

Kimberley Aboriginal Law and Culture Centre 2007. *New Legend: A Story of Law and Culture and the Fight for Self-Determination in the Kimberley.* Fitzroy Crossing: Kimberley Aboriginal Law and Culture Centre (KALACC).

Kimberley Aboriginal Law and Culture Centre 2011. *KALACC Festival.* Available at: www.kalacc.org.au/festivals.htm [accessed: 20 July 2011].

Kleinert, S. 1999. An Aboriginal Moomba: Remaking history. *Continuum*, 13, 345–57.

Knauft, B. 2002. Critically modern: An introduction, in *Critically Modern: Alternatives, Alterities, Anthropologies*, edited by B.M. Knauft. Bloomington, IN: Indiana University Press, 1–54.

Magowan, F. 2000. Dancing with difference: Reconfiguring the poetic politics of Aboriginal ritual as national spectacle. *Australian Journal of Anthropology*, 11, 308–21.

Marika, R. 1999. 1998 Wentworth Lecture. *Australian Aboriginal Studies*, 1, 3–9.

Mbembe, A. 2001. *On the Postcolony.* Berkeley, CA: University of California Press.

Michaels, E. 1994. *Bad Aboriginal Art: Tradition, Media and Technological Horizons.* Sydney: Allen & Unwin.

Moreton-Robinson, A. (ed.) 2007. *Sovereign Subjects: Indigenous Sovereignty Matters.* Sydney: Allen & Unwin.

Morrissey, M., Pepua, R., Brown, A. and Latif, A. 2007. Culture as a determinant of Aboriginal health, in *Beyond Bandaids: Exploring the Underlying Social Determinants of Aboriginal Health*, edited by I. Anderson, F. Baum and M. Bentley. Darwin: Cooperative Research Centre for Aboriginal Health, 239–54.

Morton, J. 2011. Threadbare paradigms hamper Indigenous progress. *The Australian*, 1 June, 1–5. Available at: www.theaustralian.com.au/news/arts/threadbare-paradigms-hamper-indigenous-progress/story-e6frg8nf-1226064600224 [accessed: 14 July 2011].

Mulligan, M., Humphrey, K., James, P., Scanlon, C., Smith, P. and Welsh, N. 2006. *Creating Communities: Celebrations, Arts and Wellbeing Within and Across Local Communities*. Melbourne: Globalism Institute, RMIT University

Myers, F. 1994. Culture-making: Performing Aboriginality at the Asia Society Gallery. *American Ethnologist*, 24, 679–99.

National Inquiry into the Separation of Aboriginal and Torres Strait Islander Children from Their Families 1997. *Bringing Them Home: Report of the National Inquiry into the Separation of Aboriginal and Torres Strait Islander Children from Their Families*. Sydney: Human Rights and Equal Opportunity Commission.

Payne, S. 2003. *Kickin' Up Dust: Australian Contemporary Indigenous Cultural Festivals*. Canberra: Department of Foreign Affairs and Trade.

Phipps, P. and Slater, L. 2010. *Indigenous Cultural Festivals: Evaluating the Impact on Community Health and Wellbeing*. Melbourne: Globalism Research Centre, RMIT.

Povinelli, E.A. 2002. *The Cunning of Recognition: Indigenous Alterities and the Making of Australian Multiculturalism*. Durham, NC: Duke University Press.

Povinelli, E.A. 2006. *The Empire of Love: Toward a Theory of Intimacy, Genealogy, and Carnality*. Durham, NC: Duke University Press.

Preaud, M. 2009. Country, Law and Culture: Anthropology of Indigenous Networks from the Kimberley. PhD thesis, James Cook University, North Queensland.

Probyn, E. 2008. Troubling safe choices: Girls, friendship, constraint, and freedom. *South Atlantic Quarterly*, 107, 231–49.

Royal Commission into Aboriginal Deaths in Custody 1991. *National Report*. Canberra: AGPS.

Slater, L. 2006. An end to forgetting. *Meanjin*, 65, 29–34.

Slater, L. 2007. My island home is waiting for me: The Dreaming Festival and archipelago Australia. *Continuum*, 21, 571–82.

Slater, L. 2010. Calling our spirits home: Indigenous cultural festivals and the making of a good life. *Cultural Studies Review*, 16, 143–54.

Sullivan, P. 2005. Searching for the intercultural, searching for the culture. *Oceania*, 75, 183–94.

Sutton, P. 2009. *The Politics of Suffering: Indigenous Australia and the End of the Liberal Consensus*. Melbourne: Melbourne University Press.

Chapter 8

Music Festivals as Trans-national Scenes: The Case of Progressive Rock in the Late Twentieth and Early Twenty-First Centuries

Timothy J. Dowd

This chapter deals with the linkage between music festivals and music scenes – in this instance, the scene devoted to progressive rock. The term 'music festival' sometimes refers to mammoth events that can enjoy extensive corporate sponsorship (Laing 2004). However, mammoth festivals have not been found in the progressive rock scene of recent decades. Although this scene is large in terms of the territory it spans – crossing both oceans and continents – it is notably small in terms of the number of participants it has. This small size is matched by a lack of attention from mainstream actors: corporations, critics and others have mostly ignored this recent scene and its music. Consequently, the global proliferation of 'prog' rock festivals from the 1990s onwards was due mainly to the efforts of scene members themselves – with musicians, owners of small businesses (such as online record shops) and fans mobilizing to launch and support festivals that occurred well outside the mainstream.

Progressive rock has not always been outside of the mainstream, however. Like other types of rock music, prog rock had its roots in the counter-culture and political turmoil of the 1960s (Dowd forthcoming 2013, 2014). This genre would be marked by two elements: the *intention* to create a rock music that was 'art' rather than mere entertainment (e.g. rock music meant for serious listening rather than for dancing) and the *infusion* of rock music with elements from classical music, jazz, folk, the avant garde and so on. As the 1960s gave way to the 1970s and 1980s, some prog rock gained considerable commercial appeal – becoming what Lena and Peterson (2008) label an 'industry-based' genre. In particular, multinational record corporations promoted (and benefited from) the sales of recordings by six bands from the United Kingdom – Emerson, Lake & Palmer, Genesis, Jethro Tull, King Crimson, Pink Floyd and Yes – as well as recordings by prog bands in other nations, such as Rush (Canada), Premiata Forneria Marconi (Italy) and Kansas (United States). Yet, amid the commercial success of a few prog bands in the 1970s and 1980s, progressive rock was also a 'scene-based' genre operating at the grassroots level (see Lena and Peterson 2008) – such as the so-called 'Canterbury Sound' in the United Kingdom, with its little-known prog bands like Hatfield and the North and National Health (see Bennett 2002, 2004).

This mixture of mainstream (for example, Genesis) and underground (for example, Hatfield and the North) would eventually disappear in prog rock, especially when its commercial appeal fell dramatically after the 1980s. As it retreated from the mainstream, those elements already underground moved progressive rock into the twenty-first century.

While many readers are probably unfamiliar with recent progressive rock, it nonetheless provides a helpful case through which to approach music scenes in general, and music festivals in particular. We can conceive of a music scene as 'a focused social activity that takes place in a delimited space and specific span of time in which clusters of producers, musicians and fans realize their common musical taste and collectively distinguish themselves from others' (Peterson and Bennett 2004: 1). Peterson and Bennett note that this 'delimited space' can be of various types – such as the 'local' activity found in particular cities (e.g. Grazian 2005), the 'trans-local' activity that spans multiple cities (e.g. Dowd, Liddle and Nelson 2004) and the 'virtual' activity that occurs online (e.g. Nieckarz 2005). Of course, a given scene can encompass all three types of activities – such as the straight-edge and indie music scenes of various locales that are linked by online communities and 'in place' events (Cummings 2008; Williams 2006). Although we can think of the 'focused social activity' of scenes in terms of interaction – such as when individuals come together to discuss their common musical tastes – it is also important to acknowledge the 'infrastructure' of scenes (specialty shops, publications, venues, websites and so on) that enables and supports such interaction (see Bennett 2002, 2004; Cvetičanin and Popescu 2010; Williams 2006). Indeed, music festivals are an important element of this infrastructure (Dowd, Liddle and Nelson 2004; Gardner 2004; Kahn-Harris 2007), and they have been particularly important for the progressive rock scene of the late twentieth and early twenty-first centuries.

Rather than offer a case study of a particular prog rock festival, I approach the festival–scene linkage by analysing prog rock festivals as a whole. Tracking the activity that unfolded at 124 festivals from the 1990s to the present, I show how they collectively forged connections that crossed Europe, the Americas and Australasia. Some scholars have focused on the globalization of music by understandably taking a 'top-down' approach that heeds the impact of powerful entities (such as multinational recording corporations that circulate their products around the world – Hitters and van den Kamp 2010) or the influence of well-situated actors (for example, critics at high-profile periodicals who call attention to international music – Janssen, Kuipers and Verboord 2008). I take a 'bottom-up' approach here. Like other scholars, I reveal how grassroots activities – including festivals – have created a scene that is not limited to a single locale but instead is trans-local (Cummings 2008; Gardner 2004; Kahn-Harris 2007).

This chapter proceeds in two broad sections. I first situate the progressive rock scene of recent decades, describing the scene's infrastructure, of which festivals are a key component. I then show how festivals play a key role in linking the scene's participants in trans-local fashion, as they routinely bring together prog bands from near and far. In addition to the festivals data gathered for this chapter,

I also rely on information from scholarly and media sources, as well as my long-term participation in this scene.

The Current Progressive Rock Scene

It might seem that the currently underground nature of progressive rock would result in a fragmented scene – with participants from, say, Italy disconnected from those in Poland and Sweden. However, some suggest that mainstream inattention to this broad genre has prompted enthusiasts to engage prog rock in collective fashion (Atton 2001; Bennett 2002, 2009). Indeed, Bennett uses the terms 'scene writing', 'excavation' and 'heritage' to denote how scene members come together both to explore and celebrate progressive rock. Such efforts are facilitated by the scene's 'infrastructure' that has developed over the years. This includes small businesses that help circulate this music (for example, independent record labels, retailers); magazines and online forums devoted specifically to progressive rock; and prog rock festivals that serve as pilgrimage sites for scene participants (Anderton 2009; Covach 1997).

Regarding the festivals themselves, what Covach (1997) observed in a previous decade is still true today: these festivals are highly international in focus. Consequently, they promote connections that can offset scene fragmentation. At a festival I attended in the small town of Gettysburg, Pennsylvania, for example, 524 fans from Canada and parts of Europe shared three days with bands from the United States (District 97, Epiicycle, Galactive Collective, Mars Hollow, Phideaux), as well as those from the United Kingdom (The Reasoning, Tinyfish), Italy (Daemonia), Poland (Osada Vida, Quidam) and Sweden (Moon Safari) (Collinge 2011b). These three days included the concerts themselves, as well as much socializing among fans and bands that occurred in the festival venue (for example, in the merchandise room) and in the festival hotel (with the latter sometimes lasting into the small hours). In other words, this 2011 Rites of Spring Festival (ROSFest) offered an important site at which scene participants could momentarily overcome the physical distances that normally separated them – bringing together scene participants from such places as Italy, Poland and Sweden. Let us first consider the infrastructure of which these festivals are a part before turning to their trans-local nature.

The Global Infrastructure in Action

The current infrastructure of progressive rock is partly shaped by the (in)action of major record labels (such as EMI, Sony and Universal), those entities that are owned by multinational corporations and have a tremendous impact on the popular music business in general (see Dowd 2004; Hitters and van den Kamp 2010). Whereas major labels were the champions of progressive rock in the 1970s and 1980s – signing and distributing a range of prog bands – they have since dropped bands from previous decades, like Yes (*Classic Artists: Yes* 2007; Collinge 2006b), and have dabbled briefly with only a few of the more recent bands, such as Iona, Porcupine Tree and Pure Reason Revolution (Bollenberg and Collinge 2006; Ewing 2011c; Scharf 2010). Rather than dealing with any current prog, the majors now exploit the back-catalogues of prog's one-time superstars and near-stars. This involves the re-release of albums in new formats (such as CD, 5.1 Surround) and the release of compilation after compilation. This is not without its frustration for some: 'Do we really need another *Pink Floyd Best Of?*' (Ewing 2011b: 104), asks one prog enthusiast when confronted with EMI's latest compilation, *A Foot in the Door: The Best of Pink Floyd* (2011); another wonders whether EMI's 40th anniversary edition of Jethro Tull's *Aqualung* (2011) is necessary when a 25th anniversary edition is already available (Wilding 2011).

Entrepreneurs have filled the prog gap left by the majors. On the one hand, some have established small companies that address prog's historical roots by focusing on the past music that the major labels now overlook. As the founder of Esoteric Records (Mark Powell) observed, 'I was a consultant for both EMI and Universal. But the problem was that there were a lot of cult albums that they weren't interested in reissuing, because they weren't cost effective' (Donlevy 2011: 16). Hence Esoteric (www.cherryred.co.uk/esoteric.asp) – and other small companies like the ProgQuébec label (www.progquebec.com – see Lucky 2009), Voiceprint Records (www.voiceprint.co.uk) and Wayside Music (www.waysidemusic.com) – serve as prog 'archivists' by re-releasing obscure vinyl albums in digital formats and by unearthing and making available concert and rehearsal performances of early prog acts (Anderton 2009; Bennett 2009; Covach 1997). On the other hand, entrepreneurs have also established specialized record labels to deal primarily with the prog of the present – which includes recent bands, as well as prog performers from previous decades who continue to make music years after their respective debuts. One of these entrepreneurs (Peter Morticelli) reminisced:

> I recall looking around at bands active at the time [in 1989], and feeling that the only ones with true staying power were of the same ilk – Pink Floyd, Genesis, Tull, Genesis, Rush, etc. And thought, well, if there is a common denominator there, why doesn't anyone who runs a record company seem to care? (Collinge 2006b: 75)

Morticelli thus founded Magna Carta Records (www.magnacarta.net/home5. html), a small US label that became home to veteran (for example, Kansas) and rookie (for example, Magellan) prog bands and that had international distribution. It was one of many prog labels/distributors that emerged – like Anon Islet Records of Australia (www.anonisletrecords.com), Cuneiform Records of the United States (www.cuneiformrecords.com – see *Romantic Warriors* 2010), Inside Out Music of Germany (www.insideoutmusic.com/index.aspx), K-Scope Records of the United Kingdom (www.kscopemusic.com – see Murphy 2010) and Poseidon of Japan (www.facebook.com/PoseidonRecords?v=info).

Both types of record company – archivists and specialists – would benefit from another development in the infrastructure: the rise of specialized shops dealing in progressive rock. Started initially as mail-order establishments, and then going online, these shops would offer fans a convenient 'one-stop' site where progressive acts of all types – be they acts from the distant past or immediate present, and acts from near or far – could be found. Greg Walker's Syn-Phonic Music (www.synphonic.8m.com) is one example. Fans shop there for prog rock CDs by the nationality of the acts – with 64 nations represented, from Algeria and Bahrain to Uzbekistan and the former Yugoslavia.

As progressive rock became less a market segment for major record corporations to exploit, it became more a 'little world' of creators, entrepreneurs and enthusiasts (see Atton 2001). This had ramifications for the musicians themselves. Even though certain musicians from previous decades have remained active in the progressive rock scene, their presence has not crowded out new bands seeking to enter the scene. Indeed, the costs of entry for contemporary musicians have been very low – particularly when compared with costs associated with the mainstream music market, dominated by the majors and their superstars (Dowd 2004). It would be tempting to attribute those low costs to the 'democratization' of music made possible by the post-1995 proliferation of online music distribution and consumption (Schmutz 2009; Young and Collins 2010). However, that would overlook another important development that preceded and fostered online music: the digital revolution in both musical instruments and musical recording that put once prohibitively expensive technologies commandeered by major corporations and superstars into the hands and homes of musicians with modest means (Merrill 2010; Ryan and Peterson 1993). Prior to the explosion of online music, for instance, Spock's Beard (a US-based band) spent some $3,500 to record and release its debut album, *The Light* (1995). Initially selling some 8,000 copies of this independently released and distributed album, Spock's Beard would go on to become a leading band in prog rock (Collinge 2008; Popke 2002; Shilton 2011). That said, entry costs have fallen considerably in recent times, with online distribution of music (on Facebook and through online stores) greatly reducing the expenses formerly associated with the manufacture and shipment of physical copies (that is, CDs) (*Romantic Warriors* 2010). As one member of Bubblemath effused:

> Bands that would have never seen even the tiniest spark of sunlight ten years ago are now able to reach, and maintain, a global fan base thanks to the internet … That was science fiction comedy even a decade ago … We're an unsigned independent band from Minneapolis, Minn. – and we're selling really well in Japan! Unbelievably cool! (Harabadian 2003–04: 61)

While costs for prog bands are now relatively low, that does not mean that they are absent – especially when album sales are in numbers in keeping with a 'little world', and consequently require many musicians to maintain other jobs to subsidize their musical efforts (Gardiner 2008; *Romantic Warriors* 2010). 'We're not in it for the money,' notes one member of UK group Oceansize, 'but if you can't pay your rent then you're going to start questioning it' (Moon 2010: 64). This issue of cost has spurred an informal side to the scene's infrastructure – one where fans sometimes subsidize bands in interesting ways. A UK band from the 1980s offers a notable example. With album sales now at 5 per cent of the levels enjoyed during the band's 1980s heyday, Marillion asked its fans to purchase albums prior to completion in order to cover the recording costs of the *Anoraknophobia* (2001) album and the marketing costs of the *Marbles* (2004) album (with more than 13,000 fans placing orders for the latter album). Their fans have also made donations that made concerts in the United States possible. Marillion has reciprocated by, among other things, offering fans limited-edition CDs (complete with a listing in the liner-notes of those who made advanced orders), as well as a weekend event for fans that drew nearly 2000 people from 27 countries (Feehery 2002; Gardiner 2002). Spock's Beard intentionally followed the 'Marillion model', but with the following twist: not only did they get some 2,000 pre-orders for a limited edition of their tenth album, *X* (2010), but those 130 fans buying the expensive 'Ultra Package' had their names sung in the lyrics of the album's sixth song, 'Their Names Escape Me' (Moon 2010). While The Flower Kings of Sweden likewise have close relations with their fans, the band has turned to them directly for logistical, rather than financial, support. Thus their fans have helped by moving equipment for concerts and tours (that is, acting as 'roadies'), staffing merchandise desks at venues, and serving as sound engineers and road managers (Gardiner 2002). As tokens of their appreciation, the Flower Kings have provided their fans with CDs not meant for retail establishments – such as the *Édition Limitée Québec 1998* and *Harvest Fanclub CD 2005*.

Fans are able to engage with progressive rock bands in such a direct fashion because of another aspect of this scene's infrastructure that reduced the distance between bands and fans: the proliferation of prog-specific information sources. Offering a corrective to growing mainstream inattention, entrepreneurs have established specialist magazines that provide journalistic and critical coverage of progressive rock (some of which remain in paper format to this day), thereby keeping scene members apprised of prog's roots and recent developments. Such magazines include *Acid Dragon* of France (est. 1988 – see aciddragon.eu), *Eclipsed* of Germany (est. 1992 – see www. eclipsed.de), *Progression* of the United States (est. 1992 – see progressionmagazine. com), *Prog-Résiste* of Belgium (est. 1995 – see www.progresiste.com), *iO Pages* of the Netherlands (est. 1996 – see www.iopages.nl), and *Classic Rock Presents Prog* of the United Kingdom (est. 2008 – see www.classicrockmagazine.com/tag/ classic-rock-presents-prog). Fans themselves have also produced information sources by creating fanzines – including zines devoted to Emerson, Lake & Palmer (*ELP Digest*), Jethro Tull (*A New Day*), King Crimson (*Elephant Talk*), Yes (*Notes from the Edge*) and the so-called Canterbury bands (*Calyx* and *Facelift*) (Atton 2001; Bennett 2002). Having originated in print form, such fanzines are now commonly found online – for instance, *Notes from the Edge* is available on Facebook (www. facebook.com/NotesFromtheEdge). Like their close-cousins of online fan forums, these fanzines provide an easy way for enthusiasts to discuss the past and present situation of particular bands. The movement of fanzines and forums online is part of a virtual explosion of prog-related websites occurring from the mid-1990s onwards. Some of these websites are general resources that provide a wealth of materials (for example, breaking news, discographies, reviews) about prog rock around the world (Anderton 2009, 2010) – including the *Dutch Progressive Rock Page* (www.dprp.net), the *Gibraltar Encyclopedia of Progressive Rock* (www.gepr.net), and *Prog Archives* (www.progarchives.com). Other websites provide a detailed view of prog music in particular places – such as in Brazil (www.rockprogressivo.com.br), Israel (www. mitkadem.co.il), Italy (www.arlequins.it), Montréal (www.progmontreal.com), Norway (www.progrock.no), and Spain (www.dlsi.ua.es/%7Einesta/Prog). These information sources complement the now commonplace websites and Facebook pages that bands themselves host – information sources that facilitate communication within the scene, as evidenced by the successful requests for help coming from Marillion, Spock's Beard and The Flower Kings.

The infrastructure discussed so far could lead to a scene that is more virtual than physical (see Bennett 2002, 2004). By simply going online, fans can locate, discuss and enjoy prog rock without leaving the comfort of their homes. However, other elements of the infrastructure work against this scene devolving completely into a virtual one. These include the few venues that regularly champion progressive rock concerts – such as Orion Studios in the United States and Spirit of '66 in Belgium (Bollenberg 2006; *Romantic Warriors* 2010) – and progressive rock festivals that can (and do) prompt fans to leave their homes by travelling both near (locally) and far (trans-locally).

Music Festivals as Infrastructure

These prog festivals are grassroots in nature, springing forth from the small scene itself. This is evident when considering the founders of the festivals from the 1990s onwards. One group of founders comprises the prog musicians who took it upon themselves to establish and stage festivals. For example, Alfonso Vidales of Cast, a Mexican band, was responsible for the Baja Prog Festival held annually in Mexicali from 1997 to 2008 (Collinge 2006a); meanwhile, members of a Dutch group, Flamborough Head, enticed both bands and fans to attend a festival at a small farm near Bakkeveen from 1997 to 2010 – appropriately named ProgFarm (www.flamboroughhead.nl/Doc.aspx?docId=812). Entrepreneurs have also started festivals. In 1993, for instance, Greg Walker of Syn-Phonic Music joined with two others to create one of the first prog festivals in the United States, ProgFest – the very festival that later helped launch Spock's Beard (Borella 1993; Collinge 2008). The founders of the ProgQuébec label, Sean McFee and Stephen Takacsy, established the Festival des Musiques Progressives de Montreal (FMPM) that ran from 2006 to 2009 (Collinge 2010; Lucky 2009; www.fmpm.net). Prog-oriented magazines have also played an important role, such as when *iO Pages* and *Classic Rock Presents Prog* have each sponsored festivals – the former's

ProgdecenniO of 2006 and *iO Pages* Festival from 2007 to 2011 (see van der Vost and Kikkert 2006) and the latter's High Voltage Festival in 2010 and 2011 (Ewing 2011a). Indeed, one magazine (*Prog-Résiste*) has worked with a Belgian music club, The Spirit of '66, to offer the Convention *Prog-Résiste* that has run from 2001 to 2011 (Bollenberg 2006; www.spiritof66.be). The efforts of fans have also proven pivotal because they have (co)founded such festivals as ProgDay (1995–2011; see Collinge 2007) and NEARFest (1999–2010 – see Collinge 2002a) in the United States, Le Festival Crescendo in France (1999–2011; www.festival-crescendo.com/en/festival/history) and the Winter's End Festival in the United Kingdom (2010–11 – see BBC 2010).

The grassroots nature of prog festivals is also evident in terms of their size.[1] Some festivals are located in small towns (for example, ROSFest, Winter's End), small clubs (for example, Convention *Prog-Résiste*, FMPM, ProgdecenniO) or even small structures like barns in the hinterlands (for example, ProgFarm). Not surprisingly, the restricted capacity of their venues leads to audiences that number in the (low) hundreds. Hence, ProgDay – which is the longest-running prog festival in the United States and occurs on a tiny farm in North Carolina – typically has some 200+ people in attendance and sometimes tops out with more than 300. Other festivals take place in moderate-sized venues – such as those found in urban areas (for example, BajaProg), on university campuses (for example, NEARFest) or in open-air settings with limited space (for example, Le Crescendo Festival). It is not unusual for them to reach audiences in the (low) thousands. More unusual are the prog festivals that draw audiences in the tens of thousands. I have only identified one that does this: the High Voltage Festival that has occurred in London's Victoria Park and that has stages devoted, respectively, to prog, metal and classic rock. Thus, while it has drawn more than 30,000 festival-goers, we should not assume that all are there for progressive rock. A co-organizer of the North East Art Rock Festival (NEARFest) put these numbers into perspective:

> It is also extremely important to recognize that the scene is still very small. So, 1,800 people is not all that many if you consider the number of fans that attend a Billy Joel/Elton John concert. The attendance of one of their shows equals nearly 10 NEARFests! (Collinge 2002a: 70)

The smallness of these festivals does not mean that their costs are unimportant: In fact, two costs can have tremendous impact: the financial costs associated with not selling a sufficient number of tickets to subsidize the event, and the physical and mental costs associated with organizing an event that is a labour of love rather than one's actual job (see Collinge 2002a, 2006a; *Romantic Warriors* 2010). While such costs are somewhat temporary for festivals that are one-off affairs – such as ProgdecenniO, which was staged to celebrate the 10th anniversary of the *iO Pages*

---

1   The citations in the previous paragraph serve as the information sources for this and the next one.

magazine – they are pressing for those festivals that are regular events. A number of multi-year festivals have failed to satisfactorily address one or both of these costs and, as a result, have ceased operating – including BajaProg, FMPM, ProgFarm and ProgFest (Collinge 2010, 2011a; Collinge and Patrick 2008). NEARFest is particularly notable in this regard because its organizers abruptly cancelled its 2011 incarnation some three months before the festival; seeking a satisfactory ending, the organizers put together a farewell festival for 2012, the NEARFest Apocalypse (www.nearfest.com/news.asp). This tenuous situation of prog festivals – especially in times of economic downturn – has prompted some organizers to invoke the title of a Supertramp (1975) album: 'Crisis? What Crisis?' (www.myspace.com/symforce; www.flamboroughhead.nl/PF08Booklet.zip).

Nonetheless, this crisis is not beyond addressing. On the one hand, some festivals have weathered this crisis and remain in operation in the long term. Perhaps this is due to their enticing locales, like the beachfront venue of Le Festival Crescendo or the thriving club at which Convention *Prog-Résiste* occurs. Or perhaps it is due to groups of altruistic fans – such as those at ROSFest and ProgDay, 'who put up the front money in order to finance things in advance of tickets going on sale. These people also cover any losses to the bottom line in the end. These are people who love progressive rock and are willing to put their money up for basically no return' (Collinge 2007: 80; Collinge 2011b). On the other hand, when certain prog festivals end their run in one locale, others rise to take their place elsewhere. Noting the demise of some long-running festivals in the United States (such as NEARFest), one writer points fellow prog-enthusiasts to thriving possibilities in Italy: its 2011 summer-season yielded at least four prog festivals, two of which were new – the Civitella Progressive Rock Festival and the We Love Vintage Festival (Berry 2011).[2] That writer's comments suggest not only the trans-local nature of the prog rock scene but also the importance of viewing festivals in the aggregate rather than in isolation.

The Trans-local Aspect of Prog Festivals

While there are many ways to investigate the trans-local nature of prog festivals as a group, I take an approach that is in keeping with the above discussion: tracking the location of the festivals, and especially the nationalities of the musical acts that they feature. If the global scene is connected (trans-local) versus fragmented (local), then festivals should feature a healthy number of prog acts from abroad.

I documented these festivals in three broad steps. First, lacking any comprehensive list of prog festivals occurring around the world in the last two decades, I ploughed

---

2 Italian prog sometimes thrives in terms of attention, as well – with some its concerts and festivals having drawn audiences of between 10,000 and 13,000 (donatozoppo.blogspot.com/2010_06_27_archive.html and www.musicalnews.com/stampa.php?codice=3595&sz=7).

through numerous sources to identify 'festivals' that bring multiple prog acts together on single days, or over successive days. These sources were prog magazines like *Progression*, online resources like the *Dutch Progressive Rock Pages* and *Prog Archives*, fan forums, 'gigographies' of prog musicians and, of course, Google and Yahoo search engines. In many instances, information that I gleaned about one festival led me to discover another festival. Thus my sample of festivals resembles the 'snowball' sample of some qualitative researchers in which one respondent leads to another and then another, and so on (Small 2009). In constructing this sample, it became clear that some prog festivals are known throughout the progressive rock scene (such as the BajaProg festival in Mexico), while others are known only in their immediate locales (for example, the Colorado Creative Rock Festival in the United States). I worked hard to identify a sample of festivals that ranged from the obvious to the obscure, so as to capture nuances. Second, I omitted those festivals devoted to other musical genres (such as avant-garde and folk) and topics (for example, beer) that occasionally included prog rock acts. Most notably, I excluded festivals that addressed rock music in general without providing distinctive stages for prog rock – such as the Burg Herzberg festival in Germany (www.burgherzberg-festival.de/index_e.html). While rock festivals have long featured particular prog bands (see Stump 1997), they tend towards the mammoth events that elude the bulk of current prog musicians and veer sharply away from the do-it-yourself (DIY) character of prog festivals. I also excluded festivals devoted to progressive metal – like the Prog Power festivals in the Netherlands (progpower.eu) and United States (www.progpowerusa.com). Although progressive rock and metal are close cousins and had blurry boundaries between them in the 1970s (see Walser 1993)[3] – and while a few groups like Dream Theater and Opeth comfortably occupy their intersection (see Ewing 2012) – they now tend to be separate scenes with their own respective infrastructures (see Kahn-Harris 2007). Indeed, prog scene members sometimes make sharp distinctions between the two – such as begrudgingly acknowledging the broader commercial appeal of metal (e.g. Popke 2002) or noting their divergent audiences (e.g. Collinge 2002a). Still, I do include festivals that deal both in progressive rock/metal – for example, Australia's ProgFest (O'Toole 2011; www.facebook.com/Progfest?sk=info).

The third step involved compiling information on the performers featured at a given festival. In many instances, this was relatively straightforward because promotional materials (such as festival posters) and reviews typically listed the performers and their respective nationalities. However, given the grassroots natures of these festivals, some did not leave any trace of information for a given year – particularly those obscure festivals that did not attract attention beyond their immediate locale. Furthermore, I suspect that I missed some prog festivals that were detailed only in Cyrillic script (for example, Russian) or in non-Western

---

3   Metal arose around the same time as prog, and it likewise emphasized instrumental virtuosity – drawing explicitly on such Baroque composers as Antonio Vivaldi and J.S. Bach to do so (Walser 1993).

characters (for example, Japanese). As a result, the festivals that I consider here are neither the total population – as I know of some that occurred but for which I lack information – nor a representative sample in the statistical sense. That is not a problem because my goal here was not the pursuit of statistical generalization, but rather analytical generalization – whereby lessons gleaned from a snowball sample and from retrievable historical materials can help us work through concepts and arguments, such as those involving the trans-local (see Haveman 2004; Small 2009).

The appendix at the end of the chapter lists the 124 festivals that comprise my sample. Some of these festivals occurred only once and then disappeared (for example, the Subtacto Festival in Norway), while others ran for more than 10 years (for example, the Rio Art Rock Festival in Brazil). For those lasting beyond a single year, some offered multiple events within a single year (for example, the InProg Festival in Russia), while others had events sporadically (rather than regularly) across the years (for example, the Rock in Opposition Festival in France). Given such patterns, it is helpful to think in terms of 'festival-events' – the actual gatherings associated with a given festival. In fact, these 124 festivals resulted in 468 festival-events from 1993 to 2012. The number of festival-events started off low in 1993 at two, but rose quickly thereafter – topping 10 in 1997, exceeding 20 in 2001 and passing 50 in 2011. Indeed, the global prog scene enjoyed at least 30 festivals annually from 2003 to 2011, with new ones taking the places of defunct festivals. 'Global' is the operative word here, as 29 nations hosted these festival-events. While the United States was clearly a hub of activity during this span – with 77 festival-events in the sample – so too were France (34 festival-events), Germany (39), Italy (29), the Netherlands (34) and the United Kingdom (35). Meanwhile, Scandinavian and South American countries accounted collectively for 34 and 38 festival-events respectively.

These festival-events varied considerably in terms of both the number and nationalities of acts that they each featured. Sixteen of the 468 festival-events brought to the stage only two prog performing acts – that is, bands or individuals – while the Australian ProgFest of 2011 used three stages to offer an astounding 31 performing acts in a single day, garnering an attendance of some 1,000 people in the process (O'Toole 2011). Of course, most of the 468 festival-events fell somewhere in between – averaging some seven performing acts per event, with four being the most common number. Taken together, the festival-events had 3240 instances in which prog musicians performed. As Table 8.1 reveals, these performance represent numerous countries.

Here again we see the global nature of the prog festivals – with musicians from 45 nations appearing at prog rock festivals. Indeed, the 'multinational' acts in Table 8.1 offer additional evidence in that regard. One example of such an act is the aptly named group Transatlantic, the four members of which were drawn from the following prog bands: Dream Theater and Spock's Beard (United States), The Flower Kings (Sweden) and Marillion (United Kingdom). Performances by UK acts easily out-distanced those from the United States, Italy, Sweden and France.

**Table 8.1   Number of Festival Performances by Nationality of
                Acts, 1993–2012**

Argentina: 73	Armenia: 1	Australia: 88
Austria: 4	Belarus: 10	Belgium: 61
Brazil: 44	Canada: 106	Chile: 51
Cuba: 1	Czech Republic: 2	Denmark: 3
Ecuador: 1	Estonia: 1	Finland: 40
France: 196	French Guiana: 2	Germany: 144
Hungary: 25	Indonesia: 20	Iran: 1
Ireland: 3	Israel: 5	Italy: 262
Japan: 98	Latvia: 5	Lithuania: 18
Luxembourg: 1	Mexico: 56	Multinational: 68
Netherlands: 124	Norway: 98	Panama: 3
Peru: 47	Poland: 66	Portugal: 8
Russia: 77	Spain: 57	Sweden: 231
Switzerland: 27	Tunisia: 1	UK: 634
Ukraine: 3	USA: 468	Venezuela: 6

However, that British advantage is reduced considerably when we move from examining sheer numbers to looking at specific prog bands.

The low entry barriers that musicians face in the progressive rock scene in general (see above) are also at play in prog festivals. More than 2000 bands have less than five festival performances to their credit, with one being the most common number. The UK advantage in Table 8.1, then, partly comes from the large supply of British bands who are 'one-and-done' among prog rock festivals. The global nature of these festivals comes to the fore, however, if we look at the bands who secure the most performances, as shown in Table 8.2.

Table 8.2 shows that the top 20 bands hailed from nine different nations. Note the absence of the big six prog bands mentioned at the outset of the chapter: Emerson, Lake & Palmer, Genesis, Jethro Tull, King Crimson, Pink Floyd and Yes. It is not the case that these early exemplars are inconsequential in the now-underground scene of progressive rock. Jethro Tull and Emerson, Lake & Palmer have both performed at recent festivals, while (ex-)members of all six groups have also appeared at festivals over the past two decades. Furthermore, tribute bands that perform the music of the six exemplars are commonplace in the post-1993 festivals. In fact, one of the acts in Table 8.2 (RPWL) began as a tribute band playing covers of Pink Floyd songs before morphing into an entity emphasizing original music (Bollenberg 2003–04). Nonetheless, it is clear that progressive rock encompasses far more than those early exemplars. Indeed, it is a scene with much 'churn' in that the Top 20 acts account for just 11 per cent of festival performances from 1993 onwards, while hundreds – if not thousands – of other bands make only a few appearances at prog festivals around the world.

Table 8.2   Performing Acts with the Most Festival Appearances, 1993–2012

Cast (Mexico): 26	Mostly Autumn (UK): 19
The Flower Kings (Sweden): 25	Pendragon (UK): 19
The Watch (Italy): 24	Lazuli (France): 18
Flamborough Head (Netherlands): 23	Magenta (UK): 18
Anekdoten (Sweden): 22	After Crying (Hungary): 16
RPWL (Germany): 22	Pallas (UK): 16
Sylvan (Germany): 22	Riverside (Poland): 16
Galahad (UK): 20	Quidam (Poland): 15
IQ (UK): 20	Arena (UK): 14
Eclat (France): 19	Le Orme (Italy): 14

Given the churn that marks the progressive rock scene, a pressing question remains: do prog festivals simply occur among disconnected locales or do they serve to create trans-local connections? While the top 20 bands Cast and Flamborough Head clearly benefited from hosting long-running festivals in their own backyards (BajaProg and ProgFarm, respectively), their high performance numbers also stem from performing in nations other than their own – something that is true for all of the 'top 20' acts in Table 8.2. Such international flows are not simply coincidence. Just as the city of Canterbury sponsored festivals that celebrated the so-called Canterbury Sound of bands like Caravan (see Bennett 2004), so too did organizers in Seattle (ProgMan Cometh 2002–03; rpursuit.com/ GlassBros/AymericLeroyProgmanReview.asp) and Tokyo (Canterbury Week Japan 2004; www.poseidon.jp/cwj/index.htm) put together events that celebrated the Canterbury Sound – and included performances by noted Canterbury musicians far from the United Kingdom. Exchanges between French and Japanese prog musicians – namely those associated with the bands Eclat (France) and Wappa Gappa (Japan) – fostered the rise of the Prog 'Sud Festival in France. Running from 2000 to the present, this festival seeks both to promote regional bands and to build trans-national ties between progressive rock bands – with more than half of the festival's bands originating from beyond France (www.progsudfestival. fr). Moving from anecdotes to simple numbers, 368 of the 468 festival-events featured at least one performer who crossed international borders (such as a Japanese band performing in France). Indeed, 54 of these festival-events featured *only* international acts.

Such numbers do not adequately capture the trans-local nature of prog rock festivals. To get at that, I turn to the particular connections made at festivals featuring international performers. Consider the 2011 ROSFest mentioned earlier. Its program included performers from Italy, Poland, Sweden, the United Kingdom and the United States. Thus, in bringing together bands, personnel, fans and merchandise from these nations, ROSFest 2011 facilitated 10 distinct connections among nations: Poland/Italy; Sweden/Italy; Sweden/Poland; United Kingdom/ Italy; United Kingdom/Poland; United Kingdom/Sweden; United States/Italy;

United States/Poland; United States/Sweden; and United States/United Kingdom. Now consider the 368 festivals that had at least one international performer. My analysis shows that, in bringing together performers of divergent nationalities, they created 2,784 distinct connections between various nations – forging trans-local ties at various festival-events. As such, it is evident that there exists a range of trans-local ties, and that to ignore the trans-local nature of the prog rock scene would constitute a significant error.

Indeed, there is a plethora of ties between performers of different nationalities. While some performers have relatively few ties to those of other nationalities – such as those from Cuba, Iran and Tunisia – other performers benefit from very dense ties. Indeed, a measure known as 'the degree of centrality' (Knoke and Young 2008) reveals that the musicians from the following nations are the most connected to musicians from other nations: Italy (93.1), the United States (86.4), Sweden (84.1), France (81.8) and the United Kingdom (81.8).

Despite their small and grassroots character, prog rock festivals are not solely focused on their immediate locales. Instead, the majority of festival-events in my sample are oriented towards progressive rock bands that come from different nations. By frequently offering programs that combine performers of different nationalities, these prog rock festivals spark connections that span numerous locales. These connections enliven a small scene by making it a trans-local one where people from far-flung places come together to talk, listen and play, thus ensuring that it does not devolve into a virtual scene devoid of such face-to-face activity. In fact, many scene members view these trans-local connections at festivals as desirable – as shown by the following review:

> [NEARFest 2002] did a good job of filling the slots according to the established formula. Day one had the requisite Italian and Swedish acts (La Torre dell'Alchimista and Isuldur's Bane, respectively), an avant-garde entry (Canada's Miriodor), a contemporary American group in the critically hailed Echolyn, and a reunited classic '70s band, Nektar. Day two, Sunday, brought us progressive fusion (Canada's Spaced Out), hard-driving symphonic instrumental (Japan's Gerard) and another youthful American entry in hard-edged neo-progressive band Enchant. The British 'old guard' capped things off, represented by Caravan and Genesis guitar legend Steve Hackett. (Collinge 2002b: 61)

Conclusions

As Bennett (2002, 2009) notes, members of music scenes can engage in considerable activity to offset the mainstream inattention afforded to the music they love. This has been the case in progressive rock. From the 1990s, scene participants built a 'little world' of sorts. This world included a global infrastructure of specialized entities dealing in the recording, distribution and evaluation of progressive rock of the past and present. It also included progressive rock festivals that brought all those elements together – doing so more than 30 times a year from the early 2000s onwards.

While Bennett's (2002, 2004) work suggests that elements of this progressive rock scene (such as the Canterbury Sound) are more virtual (online) than local (face-to-face), I maintain that the progressive rock scene is a trans-local one. Just as prog enthusiasts use online forums to arrange meetings at concerts and gatherings (Atton 2001), they do so for prog festivals as well (e.g. see http://bit.ly/1ptGp8W). Often lacking the funds to mount tours of distant countries, current prog musicians are attracted to the festival setting, which provides them with equipment and probably an enthusiastic audience (see *Romantic Warriors* 2010). Festivals likewise provide specialized magazines and fanzines with events worthy of coverage (peruse the pages of *Progression* and *Classic Rock Presents Prog*, for instance). They also are important sites at which vendors offer such wares as t-shirts, CDs and artwork. In fact, the merchandise areas are often the second most crowded places at festivals – following the concert stage (Covach 2004). Scene members typically have to travel in order to attend a festival. When they do, as this chapter shows, they often will encounter bands (and associated personnel) from other nations. While attendance figures suggest most fans are not present, festivals nevertheless serve as catalytic events that mobilize the most enthusiastic fans and thus help this highly global genre take root in various places.

While this chapter has emphasized the trans-local nature of the progressive rock scene, Bennett (2009) and Schmutz (2005) remind us that, for many genres, the celebration of the past is an important way to invigorate the present. That is, music scenes can span physical distance as well as span time. Festivals play an important role in the latter, too. In other research (Dowd 2014), I address how prog festivals are also sites of what Bennett (2009) calls 'heritage work'. Given that these events routinely feature the 'old guard' and tribute bands that pay homage to that guard, music festivals are important places not only for moving prog into the twenty-first century but also for taking the twentieth century along for the ride. Hence, while progressive rock is no longer the most visible of scenes, it nonetheless shows the vital role that festivals can play.

Acknowledgements

I presented versions of this chapter to audiences in Italy, the Netherlands and the United States. I thank them for their generous feedback – as well as Pauwke Berkers, Jinwon Chung, Susanne Janssen, Danny Kaplan, Sonal Nalkur, Marco Santoro, Vaughn Schmutz, Tracy Scott, Yun Tai, Marc Verboord and especially Laura Braden. I also thank Andy Bennett for all he has done to improve this chapter.

References

Anderton, C. 2009. 'Full grown from the head of Jupiter'? Lay discourses and Italian progressive rock, in *Canonizing Music History*, edited by V. Kurkela and L. Vakeva. Newcastle-upon-Tyne: Cambridge Scholars, 97–112.

Anderton, C. 2010. A many-headed beast: Progressive rock as European mega-genre. *Popular Music* 29(3), 417–35.

Atton, C. 2001. 'Living in the past'? Value discourses in progressive rock fanzines. *Popular Music*, 20(1), 29–46.

BBC 2010. Prog rocking all over Stroud. Available at: http://bbc.in/1sX170a [accessed: 20 November 2013].

Bennett, A. 2002. Music, media and urban mythscapes: A study of the 'Canterbury Sound'. *Media, Culture & Society*, 24(1), 87–100.

Bennett, A. 2004. New tales from Canterbury: The making of a virtual scene, in *Music Scenes: Local, Trans-local, and Virtual*, edited by A. Bennett and R.A. Peterson. Nashville, TN: Vanderbilt University Press, 205–20.

Bennett, A. 2009. 'Heritage rock': Rock music, representation, and heritage discourse. *Poetics*, 37(5–6), 474–89.

Berry, R. 2011. Live news: An Italian summer of prog. Available at: www.prog-sphere.com/2011/06/30/live-news-an-italian-summer-of-prog [accessed: 20 January 2013].

Bollenberg, J. 2003–04. RPWL: from *The Dark Side of the Moon* to the bright side of the sun. *Progression*, 4(Fall/Winter), 52–6.

Bollenberg J. 2006. Meet you at the Spirit of '66: Small Belgian venue is home away from home for progressive rock acts, and fans, the world over. *Progression*, 50(Summer/Fall), 74–6.

Bollenberg, J. and Collinge, J. 2006. Transcending a religious pigeonhole: The peace and serenity of Iona in 5.1 Surround. *Progression*, 50(Summer/Fall), 18–21.

Borrella, M. 1993. ProgFest '93: A Tale of Two Parties. *Expose* 1. Available at: www.expose.org/archive/exp01/ProgFest1Review.html [accessed: 20 February 2013].

Collinge, J. 2002a. Doing it right: NEARFest organizers Chad Hutchinson and Rob Laduca share the secrets behind progressive rock's most successful ongoing festival. *Progression* 40(Spring), 69–72.

Collinge, J. 2002b. A Jersey delight: NEARFest '02 hits a high note with largest crowd ever. *Progression* 41(Summer/Fall), 61–3.

Collinge, J. 2006a. Baja Prog: Tacos, tecladas, and 20 bands! *Progression*, 50(Summer/Fall), 66–9.

Collinge, J. 2006b. Sweeter the second time around. *Progression*, 49(Winter), 11–19.

Collinge, J. 2007. ProgDay '06: Splendor in the grass. *Progression*, 51(Spring/Summer), 78–81.

Collinge, J. 2008. Going the way they go. *Progression*, 55(Fall/Winter), 22–9.

Collinge, J. 2010. Progressive festival roundup. *Progression*, 59(Spring), 116–20.

Collinge, J. 2011a. Prelude. *Progression*, 62(Autumn), 7.

Collinge, J. 2011b. Rites of Spring Festival 2011. *Progression*, 62(Autumn), 72–5.

Collinge, J. and Patrick, J. 2008. Festival happenings 2008. *Progression*, 55(Fall/Winter), 104–8.

Covach, J. 1997. Progressive rock, 'Close to the edge' and boundaries of style, in *Understanding Rock: Essays in Musical Analysis*, edited by J. Covach and G.M. Boones. New York: Oxford University Press, 3–31.

Covach, J. 2004. The professor's seminar. *Progression* 46(Spring/Summer), 75–6.

Cvetičanin, P., and Popescu, M. 2011. The art of making classes in Serbia: Another particular case of the popular. *Poetics*, 39, 444–68.

Cummings, J. 2008. Trade mark registered: Sponsorship within the Australian indie music festival scene. *Continuum*, 22(5), 675–85.

Donlevy, M. 2011. Esoteric records. *Classic Rock Presents Prog*, 14(February), 16.

Dowd, T.J. 2004. Concentration and diversity revisited: Production logics and the U.S. mainstream recording market, 1940–1990. *Social Forces*, 82(4), 1411–55.

Dowd, T.J. 2013. Music travels: The transnational circulation of Italian progressive rock at small-scale music festivals, 1984–2012. *Polis*, 27(1), 125–58.

Dowd, T.J. 2014. The remembering: Heritage work at progressive-rock festivals 1983–2012, in *Sites of Popular Music Heritage*, edited by S. Cohen, R. Knifton, M. Leonard and L. Roberts. London: Routledge.

Dowd, T.J., Liddle, K. and Nelson, J. 2004. Music festivals as scenes: Examples from serious music, womyn's music, and skate punk, in *Music Scenes: Local, Trans-local, and Virtual*, edited by A. Bennett and R.A. Peterson. Nashville, TN: Vanderbilt University Press, 149–67.

Ewing, J. 2011a. Anderson & Co are go! *Classic Rock Presents Prog*, 14 (February), 12–13.

Ewing, J. 2011b. Hits and misses. *Classic Rock Presents Prog*, 21 (November), 104.

Ewing, J. 2011c. A view to a quill. *Classic Rock Presents Prog*, 14 (February), 46–54.

Ewing, J. 2012. 2011 readers' poll results. *Classic Rock Presents Prog*, 23 (February), 34–43.

Feehery, M. 2002. Marillion makes a brave move. *Progression*, 41(Summer/Fall), 56–7.

Gardiner, M.A. 2002. Takin' it to the people. *Progression*, 41 (Summer/Fall), 27–9.

Gardiner, M. 2008. Heritage, or heresy? *Progression*, 53 (Spring), 20–26.

Gardner, R.O. 2004. The portable community: Mobility and modernization in bluegrass festival life. *Symbolic Interaction*, 27(2), 155–78.

Gibraltar Encyclopedia of Progressive Rock 2011. RIO. Available at: www.gepr.net/genre2.html#RIO [accessed: 20 December 2012].

Grazian, D. 2005. *Blue Chicago: The Search for Authenticity in Urban Blues Clubs*. Chicago, IL: University of Chicago Press.

Harabadian, E. 2003–04. It all adds up for Bubblemath: Irreverent Midwestern band rides the internet wave. *Progression*, 44(Fall/Winter), 58–61.

Haveman, H.A. 2004. Antebellum literary culture and the evolution of American magazines. *Poetics*, 32(1), 5–28.

Hitters, E. and van de Kamp, M. 2010. Tune in, fade out: Music companies and the classification of domestic music products in the Netherlands. *Poetics*, 38(5), 461–80.

Janssen, S., Kuipers, G. and Verboord, M. 2008. Cultural globalization and journalism: The international orientation of arts coverage. *American Sociological Review*, 73(5), 719–40.

Kahn-Harris, K. 2007. *Extreme Metal: Music and Culture on the Edge*. Oxford: Berg.

Knoke, D. and Yang, S. 2008. *Social Network Analysis*. Thousand Oaks, CA: Sage.

Laing, D. 2004. The three Woodstocks and the live music scene, in *Remembering Woodstock*, edited by A. Bennett. Aldershot: Ashgate, 1–17.

Lena, J. and Peterson, R.A. 2008. Classification as culture: Types and trajectories of music genres. *American Sociological Review*, 73, 697–718.

Lucky, J. 2009. Sean McFee. Available at: www.jerrylucky.com/interviews_020. htm [accessed 20 November 2012].

Merrill, B. 2010. Music to remember me by: Technologies of memory in home recording. *Symbolic Interaction*, 33(3), 456–74.

Moon, G. 2010. Suspended animation. *Classic Rock Presents Prog*, 18(October), 62–4.

Murphy, I. 2010. Scoping out K-Scope. *Progression*, 60(Autumn), 78–9.

Nieckarz, P.P. Jr. 2005. Community in cyber space? The role of the internet in facilitating and maintaining a community of live music collecting and trading. *City & Community*, 4(4), 403–23.

O'Toole, D. 2011. Progfest 4. *Classic Rock Presents Prog*, 20(October), 125.

Peterson, R.A. and Bennett, A. 2004. Introducing music scenes, in *Music Scenes: Local, Trans-local, and Virtual*, edited by A. Bennett and R.A. Peterson. Nashville, TN: Vanderbilt University Press, 1–15.

Popke, M. 2002. Morse code. *Progression*, 41(Summer/Fall), 32–5.

Ryan, J. and Peterson, R.A. 1993. Occupational and organizational consequences of the digital revolution in music-making. *Current Research on Occupations and Professions*, 8, 173–201.

Scharf, N. 2010. Forging ahead. *Classic Rock Presents Prog*, 12(December), 86–8.

Schmutz, V. 2005. Retrospective cultural consecration in popular music: *Rolling Stone*'s greatest albums of all time. *American Behavioral Scientist*, 48(11), 1510–23.

Schmutz, V. 2009. Social and symbolic boundaries in newspaper coverage of music, 1955–2005: Gender and genre in the US, France, Germany and the Netherlands. *Poetics*, 37(4), 298–314.

Shilton, N. 2011. Spock's Beard's *Snow. Classic Rock Presents Prog*, 18(August), 74–7.

Small, M.L. 2009. 'How many cases do I need?': On science and the logic of case selection in field-based research. *Ethnography*, 10(1), 5–38.

Stump, P. 1997. *The Music's All That Matters: A History of Progressive Rock*. London: Quartet Books.

van der Vost, B.J. and Kikkert, M. 2006. ProgdecenniO. *Dutch Progressive Rock Pages.* Available at: www.dprp.net/concrev/2006progdecennio.php [accessed: 20 November 2012].

Walser, R. 1993. *Running with the Devil: Power, Gender and Madness in Heavy Metal Music.* Hanover: Wesleyan University Press.

Wilding, P. 2011. Another lungful. *Classic Rock Presents Prog,* 21(November), 106.

Williams, J.P. 2006. Authentic identities: Straightedge subculture, music and the internet. *Journal of Contemporary Ethnography,* 35(2), 173–200.

Young, S. and Collins, S. 2010. A view from the trenches of music 2.0. *Popular Music and Society,* 33(3), 339–55.

Videography

Classic Artists: Yes (dir. Jon Brewer, 2007).

Romantic Warriors: A Progressive Music Saga (dir. Adele Schmidt and Jose Zegarrra Holder, 2010).

Appendix: The Sample of 124 Progressive Rock Festivals

2Days Prog Festival (Italy, 2009–11)
3Rivers Progressive Rock Festival (USA, 2008–09)
Art Rock Bahia de Cadiz Festival Internacional (Spain, 2003)
Art Rock Festival (Poland, 2007)
Austral Sinfonica (2004, Argentina)
Baja Prog Festival (Mexico, 1997–2008)
Baltic Prog Fest (Lithuania, 2007–10)
Bay Area Rock Fest (USA, 2007–08)
Buenos Aires Prog '99 (Argentina, 1999)
CalProg (USA, 2005–10)
Canterbury Sound Festival (UK, 2000–02)
Canterbury Week Japan (Japan, 2004)
Civitella Progressive Rock Festival (Italy, 2011)
Classic Rock Society Progday (UK, 2002)
Classic Rock Society Spring Progfest (UK, 1997–2002)
Classic Rock Society Rotheram Rocks (2001–09)
Close to the Edge Buenos Aires Prog Fest (Argentina, 2010–11)
Colorado Creative Rock Festival (USA, 2008–10)
Convention Prog-Résiste (Belgium, 2001–11)
Crescendo Festival (France, 1999–2011)
Crescendo Festival Guyana (French Guiana, 2011)
Colossus '99 (Finland, 1999)
Cuneifest (USA, 2011)

Ecco Prog Fest (Russia, 2008)
Eclipsed Festival (Germany, 2001–11)
Electric Garden (UK, 2010)
EthelFest (USA, 2010–11)
Festival de la Associacion de Rock Progresivo (Argentina, 1998)
Festival de Rock Progresivo Ciudad de La Plata (Argentina, 2010–11)
Festival Eclipse (France, 2002–03)
Festival Internacional de Rock Progresivo (Mexico, 1999)
Festival Mexprog (Mexico, 2000)
Festival Panprog (Panama, 2002)
Festival Progresivo de Tiana (Spain, 1999–2008)
Festival Progressif Avec (Canada, 1994)
Festival Progressif de Sarlat (France, 2000, 2003–04)
Festival Progresivo Minorisa (Spain, 2002)
Finisterrae Festival (Spain, 2010–11)
Freakshow Art Rock Festival (Germany, 2001, 2003–11)
Freak Parade (Germany, 2007–09)
Generation Prog Festival (Germany, 2011)
German Progressive Rock Festival (Germany, 1997)
Gong Rock in Progress Festival (Italy, 2009)
Go Progfest (Portugal, 2009–10)
Göteborg Artrock Festival (Sweden, 1994–95)
Gouveia Art Rock (Portugal, 2003–11)
High Voltage Festival Prog Stage (UK, 2010–11)
Indonesian Progressive Festival (Indonesia, 2001–02)
Inexistence Festival – Festival de Musiques Progressive (Canada, 2009)
InProg (on the Hills) (Russia, 2001, 2003–06, 2008–11)
Interart Rock Festival (Finland, 2006)
iO Pages Festival (Netherlands, 2007–11)
Italian Progressive Rock Festival (Japan, 2011–12)
Le Festival des Musiques Progressives de Montreal (Canada, 2006–09)
Les Tritonales – Festival des Musiques Progressives (France, 2003–10)
Lima Prog Fest (Peru, 2011)
Madrid Art Music Festival (2008–09)
MARPROG Festival (USA, 2009–10)
Milwaukee Art Rock Showcase (USA, 2007)
MiniProg Festival (Hungary, 2007)
Minnuendö Festival Internacional Art Rock (Spain, 2004–11)
Montreux Prog Nights Festival (Switzerland, 2006–08)
Motstöy Festival (Norway, 2006–07)
NEARFest (1999–2010)
Night of the Prog (Germany, 2006–11)
Oskar Art Rock Festival (Poland, 2006–11)
OsloProg (Norway, 2002–10)

Planet Pul Festival (Netherlands, 1994–99)
Poseidon Festival (Japan, 2003–06)
pROCKfest (Germany, 2006–07)
ProGBury (UK, 2010)
Progday (USA, 1995–2011)
ProgdecenniO (Netherlands, 2006)
Progeny Festival (UK, 2003–04, 2010)
ProgEst Festival (Canada, 1997–98)
Prog Exhibition (Italy, 2010–11)
ProgFarm (Netherlands, 1997–2010)
Prog Fest (Australia, 2008–11)
Progfest (USA, 1993–95, 1999, 2000)
Progfever (Netherlands, 2003)
Prog Fury (USA, 2010)
Prog in the Park (USA, 2004–06)
ProG Liguria (Italy, 2012)
Progman Cometh (USA, 2002–03)
Progmeister (UK, 2011)
Prog-Nose (Belgium, 2004–05)
Prog Passion Festival (Netherlands, 2005–06)
Progressivamente (Rock) Festival (Italy, 1994, 1997, 2003–05, 2011)
Progressive Promotion Festival (Germany, 2011)
Progressive Rock Fes (Japan, 2010–11)
Progrock 2009 (Poland, 2009)
Progrock Festival (Finland, 1996)
Progscape (USA, 1994, 1996)
Progsfest (UK, 2004)
Progsol Festival (Switzerland, 2003–07)
Prog 'Sud (France, 2000–11)
Progtoberfest (Canada, 2005–09)
Progtopia (Australia, 2011)
Progvention (Italy, 2010–11)
Progwest (USA, 2001–02)
Progworld '99 (Netherlands, 1999)
Rio Art Rock Festival (Brazil, 1999–2009)
ROSFest (USA, 2004–11)
Rock in Opposition Festival (France, 2007, 2009–11)
Rogue Fest (USA, 2002–06)
Rota-Prog Festival (Spain, 2001)
Santiago Art Rock Festival (Chile, 2002–11)
Sesto Art Rock Festival (Italy, 2005, 2007–08)
Slottsskogen Goes Progressive (Sweden, 2000–11)
Somerset Prog Festival (UK, 2007–08)
Stockholm Progressive Festival (Sweden, 1997)

Subtacto Progfest (Norway, 2007)
Summer's End Festival (UK, 2005–11)
Sweden Prog Fest (Sweden, 2011)
Symforce Festival (Netherlands, 2007–09)
Terra Incognita Convention (Canada, 2006–11)
Trieste Live Music Rock Festival (Italy, 2004)
Trieste Summer Rock Festival (Italy, 2009–11)
Una Noche de Rock Progresivo (Peru, 2009–11)
Uppsala Progressive Rock Festival (Sweden, 2007–11)
Vigevano Progressive Rock Festival (Italy, 1998–2000)
We Love Vintage (Italy, 2011)
Whitchurch Music Convention (UK, 1999)
Whitchurch Music Festival (1999–2003)
Winter's End Festival (UK, 2010)

Chapter 9

The Greening of the Music Festival Scene: An Exploration of Sustainable Practices and Their Influence on Youth Culture

Joanne Cummings

This chapter explores the 'greening' of the contemporary music festival scene by reviewing the environmentally sustainable practices engaged in by festival organizers and examining how this may influence young people. It is argued that contemporary music festivals play an important role as sites for raising public awareness and education of eco-political issues, especially for young people. Music festivals may serve as sites within which a global consciousness of environmental issues and global awareness are displayed and further developed among a trans-local youth audience. As part of local and global music scenes[1] within which groups of like-minded people come together to celebrate, festivals allow young people to represent, understand and perform their identities simultaneously in a multitude of ways (Cummings 2006). Focusing on the literature surrounding the 'greening' of the contemporary music festival, the chapter argues that, as custodians of the planet's future, young people will be active participants in 'green governance', whereby corporate business and industry increasingly seek to promote themselves as environmentally friendly. The music festival industry attempts to reconcile a business model with an approach to environmental sustainability. Drawing on examples of well-known American, British and Australian music festivals, the chapter examines the important role played by festival organizers in moving towards more sustainable festival practices. Festival organizers realize that despite the economic and social benefits of hosting festivals, considerable waste and other negative environmental impacts often result. The growing awareness of festivals as sites of waste and potential sites of addressing such issues provides the opportunity to remake or form communities beyond the constraints of locality and within the particular settings of the festival. Significantly, the chapter will address the contradiction between the 'for profit' nature of the contemporary music festival and the promotion of environmentally sustainable lifestyles in everyday life.

---

1   A festival scene is a social milieu within which groups of producers, musicians and fans come together to as a group to share their common musical tastes and distinguish themselves from others (Cummings 2008).

The 'Greening' of the Music Festival

In response to the increasing global awareness of environmental issues – particularly climate change (Gibson and Stewart 2009) – the music festival industry has begun to stage 'environmentally friendly' and carbon-neutral events to promote sustainable lifestyles ('green governance') to young people. The term 'greening' has been defined by the music festival industry as 'investment in environmentally friendly facilities and practices' (Laing and Frost 2010; Mair and Laing 2012: 2). The World Commission on Environment and Development (1987: 24) defines sustainability as 'development that meets the needs of the present without compromising the ability of future generations to meet their needs'. In recent years, there has been growing interest from researchers in investigating the environmental impacts of events, yet research projects are still in their early stages, and more comprehensive studies are yet to be done (O'Sullivan and Jackson 2002; Doyle and Doherty 2006; Giblett and Lester 2008; Getz and Andersson 2009; Brooks, Magnin and O'Halloran 2010; Laing and Frost 2010; Henderson 2011; O'Rourke, Irwin and Straker 2011; Pelham 2011; Mair and Laing 2012).

The contemporary music festival had its origins in the 1960s British and American outdoor rock and pop festivals in terms of physical layout, style and content. British examples of these events included Reading, Glastonbury, Hyde Park and Isle of Wight, while American examples of early music festivals included Monterey and Woodstock. Anderton (2009) argues that such festivals display a preference for rural or 'greenfield' sites (including urban green spaces), which are not otherwise used for musical performances and the provision of onsite camping. The festivals also have a variety of musical arts in the program, and feature numerous bars and catering outlets as well as a range of other cultural activities such as carnival games, rides, street theatre, circus skills, children's activities, alternative therapies, workshops and a retail market (Anderton 2009: 40).

Over time, music festivals have been connected to political agendas with a 'counter-cultural' hippie, alternative, anti-corporate, New Age heritage (Martin 1998; Anderton 2009). This counter-culture partly inspired the environmental movement, eco-friendly youth cultures and festivals (McKay 1998, 2000). However, as Gibson and Connell (2005: 242) note, while festivals may claim to 'increase environmental awareness they may unintentionally threaten the very nature that they sought to celebrate, as environmental damage is caused by large numbers of people living, dancing and performing in a small area for several days' (2005: 242). An example of this is the 1970 open-air festival of Peace Love and Music held in Ourimbah, New South Wales, Australia, which Cockington (2001: 144–5) maintains had 'all the features that made Woodstock successful including a village-fair atmosphere and a ready availability of LSD, the official festival drug … [But] despite their supposed love of nature, hippies at a festival would often turn a pristine paddock into a garbage dump, leaving their trash behind, for the pixies to clean up'. Similarly, the 2004 Woodstock Festival was described after the event as: 'Hillsides strewn with garbage and abandoned tents, beside a creek bed littered with lawn chairs, underwear and rotting scraps of food' (Arneman 2008). In 2007, the *Independent* reported that 'a stream running through the Glastonbury festival grounds was cordoned off to prevent festival goers peeing in it. Ammonia levels from human urine became so high that they were endangering fish' (Arneman 2008).

Although these early festivals can be seen as hedonistic and waste-producing, the mini-village atmosphere that is created at music festivals provides an opportunity for these festivals to act as avenues for fostering social change. The problem with the early festivals was that they failed to engage their audiences in the environmental messages and eco-political issues that were often mixed in with the music. For example, over the last three decades, Glastonbury[2] has been involved with a range of socio-political issues and organizations, including the Campaign for Nuclear Disarmament (CND) (1981–90), Greenpeace (1992 onwards) and Oxfam, as well as the establishment of the Green Fields, which is a regular and expanding eco-feature of the festival (from 1984 onwards) (see McKay 2000). As Glastonbury Festival organizer Michael Eavis commented on the introduction of green initiatives to the festival, 'you cannot force people to believe the issue' (BBC 2007). Eavis does not see Glastonbury as an eco-festival, but it is trying to be greener. The Green Fields space within the festival is like a festival within a festival, promoting sustainability, pedal-power, permaculture, alternative energy and biodiversity. Glastonbury employs an army of volunteers to clean up the site on the completion of the festival. Most volunteers see the rubbish left behind at the festival, such as tents, as a reflection on today's 'throw away' society.

Through the introduction of green initiatives and the promotion of 'green values', festival organizers are trying to change festival-goers' attitudes towards the environment. Due to the temporal nature of festival spaces, they allow people the opportunity to experiment with new identities, explore new practices and often create an atmosphere of togetherness (Cummings 2006, 2007). This is important, as 'when this occurs, individuals more readily adopt practices of others at an event whether that be waving, chanting or following codes of environmental care such as recycling waste' (O'Rourke, Irwin and Straker 2011).

Anderton (2008) argues that the reality of the business constraints within which festival organizers operate should not be ignored but rather considered in relation to the cultural milieu within which the event is established and the personal beliefs of the organizers themselves. Further, a draft report by the United Nations' Music and Environment Initiative recognizes the potential influence that festival organizers have to:

> Reduce impacts of their production through adjusting their operations, greening their supply chain along with the purchasing decisions. These festivals also have the opportunity to communicate environmental issues through having a captured and most likely engaged and receptive audience. Televised music events, either

---

2   Glastonbury is an annual summer festival held in Wiltshire, United Kingdom, which began in 1970.

in-studio of televised live outdoor events have enormous reach and the potential
to be successful conduits to disseminating environmental messaging. (Jones and
Scalon 2010)

Getz (1997: 36, cited in Laing 2010) comments that prevailing social values
now require that all events be environmentally friendly and hopefully proactive
about 'green' management and operations. Organizers of mega-events like music
festivals increasingly are using 'green strategies' when bidding for events – for
example, the Sydney 2000 Olympic Games. This creates interesting partnerships,
or 'strategic collaborations', between high-polluting and green events – for
example, the 2009 Formula 1 race and Earth Hour (Laing 2010). Interestingly, in
a recent large-scale literature review of festival-related articles, Getz (2010) found
that articles on the environmental impact of events were lacking. Getz (2008, cited
in Laing 2010) acknowledges that attention to the environmental outcomes of
events is a priority area for research.

This direction in research is consistent with a global push to introduce new
policies and laws on climate change (see Doyle and Doherty 2006). In 2010, the
United Kingdom introduced the *Climate Change Act*, which commits the country
to an 80 per cent reduction in carbon dioxide emissions by 2050, with a further
commitment to cut them by 34 per cent from 1990s levels by 2020 (O'Neil 2009).
Australia introduced a carbon-pricing scheme in June 2012, which initially caused
much public debate and concern about the associated increased cost of living.

It is mainly young people (aged 18–26) who attend music festivals. As
custodians of the future, as well as the target of campaigns aimed at promoting
green sensibilities and sustainable lifestyles, it is important to understand how
(and why) young people engage in environmental activities. The Australian-
based National Youth Affairs Research Scheme (NYARS) report on sustainable
consumption and young Australians as agents of social change (Bentley, Fien and
Neil 2004) highlights the fact that musicians play a key role in the symbolism and
narrative around sustainable lifestyles, and can be used as a means to promote
such lifestyles. The report acknowledges the role music festivals may play as a
way for young people to become involved with their community and act as agents
of social change (2004: 60). However, it fails to acknowledge the important role of
festivals as sites for raising environmental awareness and promoting wider 'social
responsibility' around sustainable lifestyles. Significantly, the NYARS report calls
for further qualitative research on youth and sustainable consumption, suggesting
an exploration of 'the disconnection between social concern and personal action
and levels of happiness derived from different levels of consumption' (2004: 85).

The contemporary music festival plays an important role in engaging young
people with environmentalism. Festivals incorporate music, dance, play and other
creative elements. This festive and creative style of 'activism' is indicative of
the politics of 'new social movements' (Martin 2002), which appeals to young
people because it is 'imaginative, envisionary and fun to do' (Sharpe 2008: 228).
On a more serious note, it may also inspire young people to adopt sustainable

lifestyle practices. Music festivals are social spaces in which social responsibility meets commerciality, providing a role for festivals in any future configuration of 'green governance'. Festivals may be highly commercialized events, but that does not mean festival-goers are politically disengaged or inactive. However, further research is needed to elicit qualitatively rich data from young people about their attitudes and practices with respect to environmental sustainability with a view to understanding their role as *active citizens*.

The music festival industry acknowledges that, despite the economic and social benefits of hosting events, considerable waste and other negative environmental impacts often result from them. While there has been a British Standard (BS 8901) specifically designed to assist the events industry move towards greater sustainability, until now there has not been a similar Standard geared towards the international events industry. In 2012, the International Organization for Standardization aimed to release a new Management System Specification Standard for Sustainability in event management, which was to be concerned primarily with event organizers but would also be able to be used by the whole supply chain of an event, including the venue and the service providers. The standard ISO 20121 (Sustainable Event Management Systems) will take a management systems approach requiring identification of key sustainability issues, such as venue selection, operating procedures, supply chain management, procurement, communications and transport, among others. Like BS 8901, the global standard will be suitable for all sizes and types of events. In addition, implementing the recommended systems will not only help to reduce a company's social and environmental impact, but is also likely to increase business efficiency and cut costs. ISO 2012 was expected to be finalized in 2012 to coincide with the London Olympics (Sound Emissions 2011). To date, there are no similar Australian standards. At this stage, the international standards are voluntary and there are no guarantees that Australian festivals will comply.

The Festival Organizer's Role in Creating Green Events

Increasingly, festival organizers are marketing events with 'green credentials' and becoming more knowledgeable about sustainability practices (Laing 2010). This is important, as festival organizers play a crucial role in the boundary work of the festival (Dowd, Liddle and Nelson 2004). Brooks, O'Halloran and Magnin (2007) recommend five ways to make music festivals more sustainable. First, through education about how to strategically plan for sustainability, festival organizers will develop the capacity and confidence to enthusiastically share their vision, goals and actions with suppliers and artists, and will bring the message to the audience more generally. Second, festival organizers need to be the supply chain intermediaries, as they are the point of contact for all the stakeholders, including the festival organization itself, the audience, artists and suppliers (including transport and energy systems). For the festival to become sustainable, the organizers depend on the cooperation and creativity of their supply chain. Education and capacity become particularly important in this context, as the festival organizer conveys the sustainability message in a way that seems achievable in the short term and beneficial in the long term. Third, festival organizers need to form strategic alliances, as there is great potential for them to join together to shift the attitudes of their key stakeholders and society at large. Festival organizers joining together could send a clear message to stakeholders that 'this is the direction in which the industry is going'. Fourth, it is essential that the festivals are profitable, which will give the wider community confidence that sustainable initiatives and modifications to supply chain practices are viable. Finally, it is necessary for there to be a realization of potential through the resonation of messages promoted at the festival in the broader community. With music festivals at the cutting edge of social and artistic expression, there is great potential for stakeholders – particularly artists and audiences – to receive and act upon sustainable ideas and initiatives. It is important to note that, although the environmental impacts of the festival can be managed by the festival organizers, ultimately it is up to the festival-goers to be 'clean and green' and to put the messages into practice (BBC 2007).

Creating Green Festival Policy and Practice in the Music Festival Scene

Getz (2009: 70, cited in Laing 2010) notes that sustainable events are not just those that can endure indefinitely; they are also events that fulfil important social, cultural, economic and environmental roles. In this way, they become institutions that are permanently supported in a community or nation. The music festival industry today is beginning to consider the environmental impacts of festivals and is creating policies accordingly.

In 2006, A Greener Festival was set up to promote sustainable events and environmentally friendly music and arts festivals. This not-for-profit organization promotes the annual awards scheme in collaboration with the UK festival awards. The awards are based on a seven-part questionnaire, which covers event management, travel and transport plans, carbon dioxide emissions, fair trade, waste management and recycling, water management and noise pollution. Points are awarded for festivals that can show an active plan to promote public transport, reduce on-site waste, recycle and compost wherever possible, reuse water and use sustainable power. Festivals are expected to have a coherent environmental policy, and A Greener Festival has environmental auditors who visit as many festival sites around the world as possible to assess how festivals implement their plans (A Greener Festival 2008).

Although there has been vibrant discussion relating to the capacity of music festivals to promote 'green governance' on issues pertaining to the environment and sustainability among young audiences, to date no research has comprehensively documented the effectiveness of music festivals in promoting eco-awareness and sustainable lifestyles among young people. The chapter will now explore some of the green initiatives currently being utilized on the Australian music festival scene, including Peat's Ridge Festival, Big Day Out and Splendour in the Grass, the Falls Festival and Homebake. Research conducted within this festival scene has indicated that the music festival is a forerunner in experimenting with using 'sustainable' sources of energy and promoting a carbon-neutral cause as part of a festival's green credentials. The research further suggests that the music festival industry is now actively engaging in 'green governance' that is promoting corporate and community responsibility by improving the status and attraction of sustainable lifestyles for young people.

The 'green' policies adopted by these festivals will now be examined in turn. The following section will cover environmental audits, green tickets, recycling and waste management programs, website promotion of the festivals' green initiatives and ways in which festival-goers can lead more environmentally sustainable lifestyles, as well as eco-cops and green space. The following is based on the festival organizers' own advertising, public statements, independent websites and my previous ethnographic research.

Environmental Audits

An environmental audit is a way of assessing which particular areas of a business impact on the environment and to what extent. An audit is an effective risk-management tool enabling festival organizers to check how well they comply with their organization's environmental objectives, targets and environmental legislation. An environmental audit assesses the likelihood of causing environmental harm based on the policies, procedures and systems put in place to negate such impacts. Knowing where the festival's weak spots lie is a critical component of effective risk management, and also provides a high level of due diligence. Environmental auditing can help festival organizers to: (1) assess how effectively they manage those aspects of the festival that have an ability to impact on the environment; (2) prioritize what actions they can take to reduce the impact on the environment; and (3) demonstrate accountability and due diligence to third parties such as government, customers and shareholders (Global Protection Agency 2011b).

Environmental audits can save festival organizers money through the early detection of potential environmental impacts. They may also reduce the costs associated with energy use, resource consumption and the generation of waste. An environmental audit should be independent, objective and based on agreed clear audit goals and processes. Audits should also be regular and ongoing, and conducted against a benchmark or initial assessment – generally detailed in the festival's environmental plan. An environmental audit will generally provide the starting point for any other environmental measures, and can provide a valuable tool for festivals' performance management and planning. It can be an effective risk-management tool for assessing compliance with environmental legislation, and can also be used to identify areas for improvements and efficiencies (Global Protection Agency 2011b).

In 2006, an environmental audit of the Peat's Ridge festival[3] was undertaken by the University of New South Wales' Eco Living Centre, which examined the ways in which the festival approached sustainability and environmental management. The results of this audit were used for the first time at the 2008 festival. Peat's Ridge aims to become a 'model event' and a template for other festivals. The 2009 website contained detailed information on how the festival implemented sustainable practices, including the types of intervention (for example, composting toilets and solar power), costs, logistics, information and resources, tips and supplier details (Peats Ridge Festival 2008). The festival utilizes a range of sustainable products, including 100 per cent bio-diesel generators, odour-free composting toilets, grey-water management, a container deposit system, organic waste composting, reclaimed materials for decoration, certified organic food at the stalls, biodegradable cutlery, onsite bike couriers, natural ink printing and chemical-free cleaning products (Peats Ridge Festival 2011). Peats Ridge encourages festival-goers to change their behavior; however the festival's goal is not to educate festival-goers in any didactic way, but rather to lead by example.

The problem with the Peats Ridge festival environmental audit was that there was no follow-up. The results from the audit were not made available to the public. Therefore, it is difficult to say whether the festival was successful in its implementation of the findings of the audit and the how festival-goers responded.

Prior to the 2007 Big Day Out, event organizers conducted two energy audits (similar to an environmental audit) of the festival to understand the greenhouse gas emissions caused by patrons' energy usage. First, the festival sought to reduce energy use where possible, and then made a commitment to 'carbon offset' the show. They achieved this through the planting of native trees. In 2007, organizers planted 6,735 trees, in 2008 they planted 9,248 trees and in 2009 they planted 5,876 trees. The reason the festival organizers gave for choosing a tree plantation for creating carbon credits was because it created jobs, had sound conservation benefits, reduced soil salinity and improved farm viability in marginal areas. Trees also convert the greenhouse gas carbon dioxide to oxygen for us to breathe. These trees are now permanent plantings on farm reserves, and produce oxygen and capture carbon using a sophisticated model developed collaboratively by several leading research agencies, including the Cooperative Research Centre for Sustainable Production Forestry. The plantings are consistent with the technical guidelines provided by the Australian Greenhouse Office and the carbon credit is recouped over a 30-year lifespan (Big Day Out 2011).

Big Day Out organizers reported on their 2011 website that the 2009 energy audit found the festival had reduced its carbon emissions directly related to waste from the 2008 event by 5 per cent. The majority of this reduction was through

---

3   The Peats Ridge festival is held annually on a farm in Glenworth Valley, New South Wales. It began in 2004, and is a leading example of how to produce a sustainable festival.

having better managed waste bins at each site and an enthusiastic audience taking the time and care to dispose of their waste accordingly, along with the waste management organizations contracted at each site to assist (Big Day Out 2011). The problem is that the results of energy or environmental audits undertaken by the festivals are usually self-reported, and hence are most likely to only report positive information. Full public disclosure of audit results is needed so festival-goers are able to make choices based on facts rather than festival hype. Further research is needed into the implementation of environmental audits and festival-goers' response.

Green Tickets and Carbon-neutral Events

Climate Friendly[4] is a company that provides carbon-management solutions to businesses and individuals; it offers festival organizers the opportunity to offset audiences' carbon emissions for one day, using a green ticketing scheme. Most emissions associated with events are the result of people travelling to and from the venue. Food, drink and waste emissions also contribute significantly to the overall carbon footprint. The Climate Friendly ticket helps cover these impacts and more through making each audience member a climate 'offsetter' for the entire day of the festival.[5] The ticket covers festival-goer transport, food, drink and waste emissions. For approximately $3.50,[6] festival-goers invest in international renewable energy projects to balance out their impact for the day of the event. The benefit of using a Climate Friendly ticket is that it demonstrates the process and benefits of carbon offsetting to a wide audience. It is an educational and meaningful way of creating significant greenhouse savings at no cost to the festival organizer (Global Protection Agency 2011a).

There are two ticket options available to festival organizers. With the first option, the Climate Friendly fee is built into ticket pricing. This means that the cost of offsetting each festival-goer's emissions for the day is included in their ticket price. This option achieves the greatest carbon dioxide emissions reductions and entitles the festival organizers to publicize the fact on their website, in advertisements, and on tickets, t-shirts and other media that each person attending the event is climate neutral for the entire day of the show.

The second option is a voluntary Climate Friendly Ticket at point of sale (opt-in). This option provides the ticket buyer with the choice of offsetting their emissions for the day at the ticket point of sale. The resulting carbon offset will depend on the percentage of tickets sold. The contribution from the climate-friendly

---

4   See https://climatefriendly.com/who-we-are.

5   Based on Australian national per capita emissions data (Global Protection Agency 2011).

6   $3.50 (GST inclusive) reflects the current cost of carbon credits and may be subject to fluctuation (Global Protection Agency 2011).

tickets is invested in renewable energy projects (clean energy credits) that save an amount of carbon dioxide equivalent to that which an Australian citizen emits per day (Global Protection Agency 2011a). Splendour in the Grass[7] has used voluntary Climate Friendly ticketing since 2007 (Global Protection Agency 2011a). In 2007, the festival sold 5,425 green tickets (31 per cent of the audience); in 2008, this decreased to 4,091 green tickets (23 per cent of the audience) (Global Protection Agency 2008). The festival reported problems with the ticketing system, which may have accounted for the decrease in green tickets sold. Splendour in the Grass festival-goers who did not purchase green tickets were still able to offset their carbon emissions through the purchase of an 'I like my music loud and green' patch made from recycled, ethically made fabric.

Another Australian festival that uses a green ticketing system is Big Day Out[8] (BDO). In 2008, the festival organizers decided to go 'carbon neutral'. They planted 6,750 trees, which earned them carbon credits, and they aim to continue the event as 'carbon neutral' in the future. In 2009 BDO patrons were offered the chance to reduce their carbon emissions for the day through the purchase of a green ticket. The carbon offset is achieved through the planting of native eucalyptus trees. The green ticketing system uses a company called CO_2 Australia. In 2010, a total of 32,231 festival-goers (percentage of audience unknown) participated in a carbon-free day and offset 3,097.42 tonnes of carbon dioxide. This was down from 2009, when a total of 34,050 festival-goers participated in a carbon-free day, offsetting a total of 2641 tonnes of carbon dioxide (Big Day Out 2011). It is difficult to compare these figures, as the percentage of the audience buying the green tickets and total audience numbers are unknown, and may differ from year to year.

Promoting Green Credentials in Cyberspace

Music festivals are an example of what Mair (2011) refers to as type 2 events that take place for another reason but have a strong green focus. These events are very much focused on offering leisure and entertainment experience, but the festival organizers feel that they can play a role in encouraging sustainable behaviour by leading by example. They do this primarily by demonstrating their commitment to environmental issues on their website.

The majority of contemporary music festivals in Australia have part of their website dedicated to explaining the green initiatives or sustainable practices employed by the festival. This is their way of promoting their 'green credentials' to festival-goers. For example BDO's 'Clean and Green' promotion used the

---

7   Splendour in the Grass is an annual winter music festival held in Byron Bay, New South Wales, Australia.

8   Big Day Out is an annual national touring festival that was first held in 1992.

catchphrase 'reduce, recycle and offset'. The festival website encouraged festival-goers to 'reduce, recycle and offset' in their everyday lives, including:

> Use less power, cut down on your car use, talk it up (vote/political action), buy less, compost all organic waste, support local, global and national environmental group, and offset your personal emissions. (Big Day Out 2008)

Recycling and Waste-management Programs

The music festival industry still relies on outdated and ineffective public place recycling systems to reduce waste being directed to landfill and/or recovering valuable resources. In some cases, there are no public place recycling systems, with all material being sent to landfill. Traditional public place recycling systems typically use two bins (one for waste and one for recycling), which are placed together to create a waste/recycling station. This approach requires double the number of bins to be placed around the event and additional cleaning staff to place and empty bins. It is in fact a costly and ineffective waste and recycling system to implement and operate. For example, a typical 20,000-person event will generate approximately 80,000 to 100,000 drink containers. With current public place recycling rates of 10–40 per cent, this means that up to 70,000 containers end up in landfill per event. With hundreds of major events, festivals and tours in Australia each year, this is an enormous and unsustainable waste of resources. BDO uses this type of recycling system. It aimed to have 80 per cent recyclability across all shows by 2010. As this is self-reported by the festival, it is not possible to know whether this goal was achieved. Homebake employed this type of recycling system but this proved to be less effective than the drink ticket system due to cross-contamination of the bins (Global Protection Agency 2011c).

The Global Protection Agency (GPA) recycling system used at Australian festivals, including Splendour in the Grass and Homebake,[9] uses simple economics to increase the amount recycled at the event. By placing an economic value on the container (in the form of a deposit), festival-goers are financially encouraged to do the right thing and return their empty containers to one of the festival's recycling centres.

The system specifically covers aluminium cans and PET plastic beverage containers. By placing a deposit (usually $1.00) on the container at the point of sale, festival-goers have an incentive to return their empty cans or plastic bottles to one of the event's recycling centres to redeem their deposit. Each container represents $1.00, and the economic value cycles from festival-goer to bar to festival-goer. According to the GPA website, the results have been outstanding, with recycling rates ranging from 80 to 95 per cent (Global Protection Agency 2011c), and the system has been extremely well received by audience members. If a festival-goer

---

9 Homebake is an annual Sydney-based festival.

complies with the system, they will always redeem their original deposit, and will not be out of pocket. Likewise, if festival-goers want to collect discarded containers, then they stand to make money out of the system (and help keep the event clean).

The only time a festival-goer will be out of pocket is if they make a conscious decision not to recycle, thereby discarding the container and the associated $1.00 deposit (Global Protection Agency 2011c). GPA reports that the number of containers recycled at Splendour in the Grass in 2008 was 180,000, while at Homebake in 2007 it was 124,000 and increased to 125,000 in 2008.

The Falls Festival has developed its own recycling program, which is very similar the GPA recycling system used at Splendour in the Grass and Homebake. In addition, the organizers of the Falls Festival have created a policy that caterers and other stallholders must supply biodegradable cutlery and recyclable packaging.

Green Space

Some festivals include a 'green space' within the festival grounds for the promotion and education of sustainable lifestyles to festival-goers. For example, in 2008 Splendour in the Grass, along with its sponsor Climate Friendly, hosted a 'Green Space' at the festival, which included recycled bean-bags, free cups of Fair Trade organic tea, the latest in sustainable gadgets, soaps, bags and information from influential climate change organizations like Friends of the Earth, the Wilderness Society, Greenpeace, the World Wildlife Fund and the Australian Conservation Foundation. In comparison, at the Canadian Hillside festival – which has been promoted as an eco-festival with strong political views – organizers decided against 'embedding the festival with a political agenda as it is disruptive to the festival atmosphere and an intrusion on the patron's freedom of choice'. Instead, they have tents such as the 'envirotent' and 'community tent'; these spaces are enclosed and need to be actively entered into by the festival-goers (Sharpe 2008).

Eco-Cops

Eco-cops are a group of volunteers – usually students – who patrol the festival grounds to encourage festival-goers to recycle and provide them with information about the green policies of the festival. Both Glastonbury (UK) and Splendour in the Grass have eco-cops. At Splendour in the Grass, the eco-cops promote the festival's Binyabutt campaign, which encourages people not to litter with their cigarette butts by giving away free pocket-size ashtrays made from recycled film canisters.

Connecting to the Local Community

The Falls Festival aims to create a positive environmental impact by applying extensive environmental practices to a significant population over three days. The festival aims to minimize the impact of the festival on the local environment and make improvements to existing conditions where possible. Organizers also aim to reach beyond the festival by using it as an opportunity to pass on important information and ideas to the wider community. The festival supports ongoing enhancement and protection projects on the festival site and surrounding areas (including tree planting, fencing and track work). Surveys are carried out to identify threatened or protected wildlife and flora in the surrounding areas so they can be monitored and protected from human disturbance. The festival also promotes educational activities for developing awareness and respect, and the ongoing protection of both the local and global environment. During the event, festival organizers aim to give festival-goers as much information as they can through their website, the event guide, signs, the super screen and specially trained staff.

Green governance seems to have become an integral part of the contemporary music festival scene, and appears to have been welcomed by festival-goers. In 2008, Buckinghamshire New University surveyed festival-goers about green events. Researchers surveyed 1,407 festival-goers across Europe (500 British fans, 600 from Finland, 330 from Germany and the Netherlands). When asked about environmental issues, over 80 per cent of festival-goers thought that noise, waste and traffic had a negative impact. Festival-goers were also aware of a rise in carbon dioxide emissions, and 48 per cent of festival-goers said they would pay more for greener events, while 36 per cent said having a green policy was important to them when buying a ticket. Overall, the British festival-goers were found to be greener than European festival-goers (A Greener Festival 2008).

In 2009, A Greener Festival surveyed festival organizers about their events and found that 22 per cent believed their festivals' environmental credentials had an influence on ticket buyers, with 36 per cent thinking they had a huge or definite influence. They concluded that it was festival-goers' opinions that where encouraging the move towards greener festivals (O'Neil 2009). This is yet to be researched in Australia.

This was further supported by Virtual Festivals (VF), which asked British and European festival-goers how important environmental initiatives were when they were choosing which festival to attend (this question was also asked in 2006 by A Greener Festival, and in 2008 by Buckinghamshire New University). They found that in 2009, 59.4 per cent of festival-goers said it was 'very or fairly important', an increase from the 2008 survey which found that only 36 per cent of festival-goers said it was important when they were considering which event to go to. Surprisingly, the 2009 result is more than double the 2006 results, when only 27 per cent of festival-goers thought it was important (O'Neil 2009). O'Neil's (2009) article also reports the change in festivals' use of sustainable energy sources and changes in audience travel to festivals. This research provides a good starting point for further studies to be conducted on festival-goers' reception of green issues and the eco-political content within festivals.

Conclusion

As yet, no research has comprehensively documented the effectiveness of music festivals in promoting eco-awareness and sustainable lifestyles among young people. To date, the majority of the literature on festivals has been dominated by 'festival tourism' and the socio-economic impacts of festivals on localities, as well as marketing and operational issues (see O'Sullivan and Jackson 2002; Gibson and Connell 2005; Quinn 2006; Cummings 2008; Cummings, Woodward and Bennett, 2011). Getz (2008, cited in Laing 2010) has acknowledged that attention to environmental outcomes of events is a priority area for research.

While some initial quantitative research has been conducted in relation to European festivals, festival-goers and green events, there has been no research of this type done in Australia. In particular, there is a need for further qualitative research that investigates festivals as sites for raising awareness about social issues and promoting political consciousness, particularly exploring young people's attitudes to the disjunction between their environmental concerns, personal action and consumption practices (Martin 2009).

Further research needs to be undertaken to address the connection between music festivals and environmental sustainability. Though it represents an intriguing topical empirical and theoretical question, until now sociological research into the issue of youth, music festivals and environmentalism has been lacking. Further research is needed to investigate whether there is a connection between 'green' music festivals and young people's decision-making when it comes to alternative consumption and sustainable lifestyles. That is, to what extent are a festival's green credentials an issue for attendees that could influence their attendance patterns? Also, in line with recommendations from the NYARS report, further research needs to explore the link between young people's consumption practices and sustainable lifestyles (Bentley, Fien and Neil 2004: 86). Thus the longer-term impact of the greening of festivals in terms of its association with broader patterns of green and ethical consumption is a pertinent topic. How might the greening process affect the way festivals are managed and organized? Are the discourses and narratives associated with festivals – particularly youth festivals – changing to accommodate greening imperatives, and how might this alter the types of festivals that take place into the future? Finally, might it be that attendance at music festivals becomes an important site for the generation of an ethics of green consumption among young people?

Over the last decade, the post-subcultural turn in youth cultural research (e.g. see Bennett 1999; Bennett and Kahn-Harris 2004; Muggleton 2000) has emphasized the increasing diversity and fluidity of youth cultural groups, in which aspects of musical taste and attendant aesthetically informed cultural practices provide platforms for sociality. In this context, the contemporary music festival becomes an important site for the coming together of an audience. This critical transition in the ways that youth cultural practice is now understood currently lacks any clear political dimension in terms of its mode of inquiry and explanation. The issues explored in this chapter offer a insight into how a post-subcultural politics of youth may begin to take shape – a shape in which a series of pertinent issues, relating to environment, sustainability and global citizenship are centrally placed.

Acknowledgement

Parts of this chapter are based on a previously published chapter (Cummings, Woodward and Bennett 2011).

References

Anderton, C. 2009. Commercializing the carnivalesque: The V Festival and image/ risk management. *Event Management*, 12, 39–51.

Arneman, K. 2008. Greening the groove: Festivals and the environment. *G-Online*. Available at: www.gmagazine.com.au/node/676/full [accessed: 13 March 2009].

Bennett, A. 2009. 'Heritage rock': Rock music, re-presentation and heritage discourse. *Poetics*, 37(5–6), 474–89.

Bennett, A. and Kahn-Harris, K. (eds) 2004. *Music Scenes: Local, Translocal and Virtual*. Nashville, TN: Vanderbilt University Press.

BBC 2007. *Glastonbury*. London: BBC.

Bentley, M., Fien, J. and Neil, C. 2004. *Sustainable Consumption: Young Australians as Agents of Change*. Canberra: National Youth Affairs Research Scheme, Department of Family Community Services.

Big Day Out 2008. Ambience. Clean and green-BDO statement. Available at: www. bigdayout.com/ambience/cleangreenbdostatement.php [accessed:4 August2008].

Big Day Out 2011. Big Day Out clean and green statement. Available at: www.bigdayout.com/ambience/clean-and-green---bdo-statement.php [accessed 18 July 2011].

Brooks, S., Magnin, A. and O'Halloran, D. 2010. Rock On33: Bringing strategic sustainable development to music festivals. *Progress in Industrial Ecology: An International Journal*, 6(3), 285–306.

Brooks, S., O'Halloran, D. and Magnin, A. 2007. Rock on! Bringing Strategic Sustainable Development to Music Festivals. MA thesis, Blekinge Institute of Technology.

Cockington, J. 2001. *Long Way to the Top: Stories of Australian Rock and Roll*. Sydney: ABC Books.

Cummings, J. 2006. It's more than a t-shirt: Neo-tribal sociality and linking images at Australian indie music festivals. *Perfect Beat*, 8(1), 69–84.

Cummings, J. 2007. We're all in this together: The meanings Australian festivalgoers attribute to their music festival participation, in *History of Stardom Reconsidered: The Refereed Proceedings of the Inaugural Conference of IIPC*, edited by K. Kallioniemi, K. Kärki, J. Mäkelä and H. Salmi. Turku: International Institute for Popular Culture, University of Turku, 153–7.

Cummings, J. 2008. Trade mark registered: Sponsorship within the Australian Indie music festival scene. *Continuum*, 22(5), 675–85.

Cummings, J., Woodward, I. and Bennett, A. 2011. Festival spaces, green sensibilities and youth culture, in *Festivals and the Cultural Public Sphere*, edited by G. Delanty, L. Giorgi and M. Sassatelli. London: Routledge, 142–55.

Dowd, T.J., Liddle, K. and Nelson, J. 2004. Music festivals as scenes: Examples from serious music, womyn's music and skate punk. *Music Scenes: Local, Translocal and Virtual*, edited by A. Bennett and K. Kahn-Harris. Nashville, TN: Vanderbilt University Press, 149–67.

Doyle, T. and Doherty, B. 2006. Green public spheres and the green governance state: The politics of emancipation and ecological conditionality. *Environmental Politics*, 15(5), 881–92.

Getz, D. 2010, The nature and scope of festival studies. *International Journal of Event Management Research*, 5(1), 1–47.

Getz, D. and Andersson, T.D. 2009. Sustainable festivals: On becoming an institution. *Event Management*, 12, 1–17.

Giblett, R. and Lester, L. 2008. Environmental sustainability. *Continuum*, 22(2), 167–70.

Gibson, C. and Connell, J. 2005. Festivals: Community, identity and capital, in *Music and Tourism*, edited by C. Gibson and J. Connell. Clevedon: Channel View Press, 214–69.

Gibson, C. and Stewart, A. 2009, *Reinventing Rural Places: The Extent and Impact of Festivals in Rural and Regional Australia*. Wollongong: University of Wollongong.

Global Protection Agency 2008. Case Study: Climate friendly and Splendour in the Grass music festival. Available from: www.globalprotectionagency.com.au/Splendour_case_study.pdf [accessed: 24 June 2011].

Global Protection Agency 2011a. Climate friendly tickets™ – helping you make your audience climate neutral. Available at: www.globalprotectionagency.com.au/carbon/climate_tickets.htm [accessed: 23 June 2011].

Global Protection Agency 2011b. Environmental auditing. Available from: www.globalprotectionagency.com.au/environmental_auditing.html [accessed: 27 June 2011].

Global Protection Agency 2011c. Recycling systems. Available at: www.globalprotectionagency.com.au/recycling/system_works.html [accessed: 27 June 2011].

A Greener Festival 2008. Music fans want green events. Available from: www.agreenerfestival.com/newsletters/Music%20Fans%20Want%20Green%20Events.pdf [accessed: 24 October 2008].

Henderson, S. 2011. The development of competitive advantage through sustainable event management. *Worldwide Hospitality and Tourism Themes*, 3(3), 245–57.

Jones, M. and Scalon, X. 2010. Singing to a greener tune: Current status of the music industry in addressing environmental sustainability [electronic draft]. Available from: www.grida.no/files/workshops/music-environment/Singing%20to%20a%20Greener%20Tune%20DRAFT%20REPORT.pdf [accessed: 18 January 2012].

Laing, J. and Frost, W. 2010. How green was my festival: Exploring challenges and opportunities associated with staging green events. *International Journal of Hospitality Management*, 29(2), 261–67.

Mair, J. 2011, Towards a research agenda for environmentally sustainable events, paper presented to 7th Biennial Symposium of Consumer Psychology of Tourism, Hospitality, and Leisure of the International Academy of Culture, Tourism, and Hospitality Research, Chiang Mai, Thailand.

Mair, J. and Laing, J. 2012, The greening of music festivals: Motivations, barriers and outcomes – applying the Mair and Jago model. *Journal of Sustainable Tourism*, 20(5), 683–700.

Martin, G. 1998, Generational differences amongst New Age travellers. *The Sociological Review*, 46(4), 735–56.

Martin, G. 2002. Conceptualizing cultural politics in subcultural and social movement studies. *Social Movement Studies*, 1, 73–88.

Martin, G. 2009. Subculture, style, Chavs and consumer capitalism: Towards a critical criminology of youth. *Crime, Media, Culture*, 5(2), 123–45.

McKay, G. 1998. *DIY Culture: Party and Protest in Nineties Britain*. London: Verso.

McKay, G. 2000. *Glastonbury: A Very English Fair*. London: Victor Gollancz.

Muggleton, D. 2000. *Inside Subculture: The Postmodern Meaning of Style*, Oxford: Berg.

O'Neil, C. 2009. Green shots. *IQ*, Q4, 22–3.

O'Rourke, S., Irwin, D. and Straker, J. 2011. Dancing to sustainable tunes: An exploration of music festivals and sustainable practices in Aotearoa. *Annals of Leisure Research*, 14(4), 341–54.

O'Sullivan, D. and Jackson, M.J. 2002. Festival tourism: A contributor to sustainable local economic development? *Journal of Sustainable Tourism*, 10(4), 325–42.

Peats Ridge Festival 2008. Sustainability. Available at: www.peatsridgefestival.com.au/home.asp?pageid=E7504F407896B639 [accessed: 21 October 2008].

Peats Ridge Festival 2011. Sustainability. Available at: www.peatsridgefestival.com.au/home.asp?pageid=E7504F407896B639 [accessed: 18 July 2011].

Pelham, F. 2011. Will sustainability change the business model of the event industry? *Worldwide Hospitality and Tourism Themes*, 3(3), 187–92.

Quinn, B. 2006. Problematising 'festival tourism': Arts festivals and sustainable development in Ireland. *Journal of Sustainable Tourism*, 14(3), 288–306.

Sharpe, E.K. 2008. Festivals and social change: Intersections of pleasure and politics at a community music festival. *Leisure Sciences: An Interdisciplinary Journal*, 30(3), 217–34.

Sound Emissions 2011. New sustainability in events management standard. Available at: www.soundemissions.com.au/site/index.php?option=com_conten t&view=category&layout=blog&id=68&Itemid=175 [accessed: 25 July 2011].

World Commission on Environment and Development. 1987. *Our Common Future. The World Commission on Environment and Development.* Oxford: Oxford University Press.

PART III
Spatial and Temporal Narratives

Chapter 10

Location, Spatiality and Liminality at Outdoor Music Festivals: Doofs as Journey

Susan Luckman

In an article published in *The Guardian* in July 2009, British commentator Simon Jenkins discusses the ongoing success of the outdoor festival in the United Kingdom in the face of the then emerging Global Financial Crisis. Framed within a debate about an apparent dearth of interest in and money for the arts – at least as measured against how many new buildings dedicated to it are being built, the author makes the point that, 'From the vales of Glastonbury to the tent city of Hay-on-Wye, from Latitude to the Glade, from V at Weston to T in the Park, from Womad to Wycheood, from Reading to Leeds, festival promoters are having a year without compare'. These are not all music festivals, nor are they particularly cheap – indeed, many are quite expensive – and not all of them are outdoor, but it is clear that music and 'being in the open air, rather than entombed in concrete' continues to offer people an experience in which they are willing to invest their time and hard-earned cash.

Reflecting upon research undertaken into the Australian outdoor dance music scene (and doof festivals in particular) at the turn of the millennium and into the first part of this decade, in this chapter I offer some insights into the enduring popularity of the outdoor music event. To do so, I focus upon how the spatiality of outdoor dance music festivals – both internally and in terms of the journey to the site – operates upon the affective experience of the event. Inspired in part by the theoretical work of Victor Turner, I argue that, given the degree of immersion and associated participant involvement that travel to a distant outdoor site necessitates, the festival can be perceived as a crossing – literal and figurative – that deepens the experience and facilitates the creation of a secular 'liminal culture' (St John 2010a). The first part of the chapter establishes the centrality of the spatial as an important organizing frame for many music festivals. Then, after the outdoor doof festival is introduced, the discussion moves into a deeper examination of this in relation to Turner's conceptualization of the liminal.

Figure 10.1   **'Where am I and where do I want to be?'**
at WOMADelaide, March 2010

Guidelines for Getting 'Away from It All': Maps as Ironic Tools of Escape

In many ways, my thinking about the importance of place to outdoor music festivals starts exactly where many a participant's journey into a music festival does: with a map. Nowhere is the overt spatiality of many outdoor music festivals so directly apparent as in the prominence of the need for directions either to or within the festival site. Whether it is the iconic directions to a clandestine rave site provided either by a recorded telephone message or via convoy once vehicles have met up somewhere by the side of the M25 London ring road, site maps with directions on outdoor doof festival fliers, the directions required to negotiate the journey to the Nevada desert and the attention to spatial planning detail as Black Rock City arises out of the playa annually at Burning Man, or the informational map guide to the WOMADelaide site in the city's Botanic Gardens (see Figure 10.1), maps figure prominently as a feature of outdoor music festivals. Be it a single or multi-day event, rural or urban, given the attention paid by both organizers and participants to such festivals' spatial organization as part of a holistic experience, maps operate as key entry tools for making sense of the forthcoming journey. Like the so-called 'sandbox' video game where the joy is in exploring an unknown space provided for your enjoyment or challenge, festival maps offer the promise of a space to be explored.

But maps are not simply tools of possibility – something to which critiques of them as a technology of control in geography and other disciplines attest. Historically and into the present day, maps retain a key role in processes of conquest, colonialism, governance, ownership, occupation and exploitation. Geographer, cartographer and map historian Brian Harley offers a particularly critical vision of the role of maps:

> As much as guns and warships, maps have been the weapons of imperialism. Insofar as maps were used in colonial promotion, and lands claimed on paper before they were effectively occupied, maps anticipated empire. Surveyors marched alongside soldiers, initially mapping for reconnaissance, then for general information, and eventually as a tool of pacification, civilization, and exploitation in the defined colonies ... Maps were used to legitimise the reality of conquest and empire. They helped create myths which would assist in the maintenance of the territorial *status quo*. (Harley 1988: 282)

Certainly, in a (post)colonial settler society like Australia, evidence of the colonizing role of mapping is ever present: they are a powerful colonial tool, when used to '"desocialise" the territory they represent ... [Fostering] the notion of a socially empty space' (Harley 1988: 303). The colonial project would certainly bear out the thesis that 'every map presages some form of exploitation' (Hall 1993, quoted in Pickles 1995: 21). However, the presence of maps as tools of possibility at politically, socially and environmentally conscious music festivals such as WOMAD problematize the conception of Harley and others that maps have no redeeming qualities and that they speak 'pre-eminently a language of power, not of protest' (Harley 1988: 301–2). The very fluidity of the various 'truths' that maps represent, above and beyond physical space, reveals their capacity to operate as ideological tools representing alternative visions as well as hegemonic ones:

> Such a relationship is possible because all maps are, in some sense, maps of imaginary worlds in that all of them involve a process of selection, representation, and conceptualization that inevitably falsifies the territory they

represent, even as they communicate valuable information about that territory. In this way, the production of a map introduces the values and the prejudices, the perceptions and the misconceptions, the insights and the blind spots, the ideology and the culture, of the mapmaker into the representation of the territory. (Padrón 2007: 284)

As is also evident in fiction, not to mention childhood imaginations, maps allow us to dream of other worlds. They further appeal to us in their ability to render the world simpler and more knowable than it actually is (Goodchild 1995: 48). As already mentioned, the exploratory space of the festival *qua* 'sandbox' game realizes this in the emphasis upon thoughtful organization of its internal ludic space.

Doof as Outdoor Music Festival

Before venturing any deeper into this particular journey, the outdoor doof festival itself needs to be introduced. Australia's rave-derived dance music scene is just one localized manifestation of a global cultural movement (or moment), the overseas family tree of which has been thoroughly chronicled (cf. Malbon 1999; Pini 1997; Redhead 1990, 1993, 1997; Redhead, Wynne and O'Connor 1997; Rietveld 1998; St John 2009, 2010b; Thornton 1995). Itself increasingly the focus of academic work (cf. Bollen 1996; Chan 1999; Gibson 1999; Gibson and Pagan 1999; Luckman 1998, 2001a, 2001b, 2003, 2008; Murphie and Scheer 1992; St John 2001a, 2005; Tramacchi 2000), contemporary dance music culture in Australia has erupted out of the meeting of these international influences and sounds with already present local communities and practices. While significant similarities exist between aspects of the Australian scene and other sites in what we may call electronic music's cultural diaspora, local manifestations of dance music exist within a global network of practice but have evolved in their own unique fashion (Straw 1991: 369). In Australia, this global spirit fuelled the small and relatively exclusive 'private' parties that emerged as a local outgrowth of rave as a transnational cultural practice in the late 1980s/early 1990s – in particular, the doof, 'a type of autonomous space where an evolution seem[s] to be taking place' (Strong 2001: 73).

    While the exact origin of the term 'doof' is not clear, the most widely accepted story traces it back to a 1992 gathering organized by members of the activist sound collectives Non Bossy Posse and Vibe Tribe in the inner Sydney suburb of Newtown. A middle-aged neighbour in the terrace house next door to the party is now famously quoted as having knocked on the door to ask, 'What is all this "doof", "doof", "doof" music?' in reference to the sound the bass made on the other side of the double brick wall. Before long, the term gained currency and was used to denote events located physically and/or conceptually outside of the club mainstream. The term 'doof' thus remains strongly linked to those scenes within the contemporary Australian dance music milieu that are constructed as 'alternative' or 'subcultural', either through their actions (political activism) or their generic character (psytrance), or by means of their articulated – though challenged – self-promotion (major festivals).

While doofs are not inherently conducted in the countryside (bush or desert) – especially given that the word by its very onomatopoetic nature hails from inner-city Sydney – doof diverges somewhat from the British model of raving, and has found a more companionable consciousness in the hippie spirit of Goa or psytrance. As a result, doof as a 'journey' or 'transcendent' experience is grounded in trance as a genre, a technique and a state of mind. As a result, doof events as outdoor festivals have been a logical home for the kind of experience sought here, one whereby, as St John writes, 'remote, interior ["outback"/desert] and hinterland bush locales have occasioned new techno rituals ("doofs"), with trance-oriented events establishing particular popularity in Australia' (2001b: 5). Or, in the words of Ken Gelder (2001: xvi) in his foreword to St John's *FreeNRG* anthology, 'This [doof-centred] new Australian counter culture's aim is essentially one of re-enchantment ... Everything is hybridised and hyphenated: these are future-primitives, techno-shamans producing eco-rapture'.

Trance music has thus been embraced by the Australian rave-derived scene. Its particular model for outdoor dance communion resonates in a country blessed with a sunny climate, and large swathes of undeveloped land fringed by beaches. Psytrance-inspired doof has furnished Australia's alternative party people with the vehicle *par excellence* by which to realize the famous rave dream of PLUR ('peace, love, unity and respect') and community. Here, in the words of techno zine maker Kathleen Williamson, underground techno culture has helped 'co-create magical spaces for community and personal transformation' (St John 2001a: xi). These spaces prominently feature the Australian landscape, not its cities. Notably, too, they are not pristine landscapes – wildernesses empty of occupation. The doof rituals discussed here acknowledge the prior and ongoing occupation of the land by Indigenous Australians. Doof culture, informed as it is by its own sense of tribalism, makes explicit overtures to those who have been 'dancing this land' for millennia.

British ravers' innovative use of the structural detritus of industrialization and beyond is now the stuff of well-worn legend: raves in disused warehouses, aircraft hangers, squatted homes, and so forth. Similarly, doofs in Australia have sought to (re)claim a form of common access to officially circumscribed spaces in the nation's cities and towns. This said, while it may be slightly less the case in inner Sydney than elsewhere, doof's spiritual home has evolved beyond the term's urban birthplace to claim the bush and the desert beyond the city limits. In a country still relatively well-endowed with natural expanses, it is here that participants are apparently more able to realize fully a desire to transcend, if only intermittently, the organizing temporality of contemporary urban life:

> The main difference between the city and bush parties is the atmosphere and the drugs of choice. Bush parties are more psychedelically oriented! This is my experience anyway – they also tend to go longer – no noise restrictions, etc. and many people show up just for the sunrise onwards. Some of the warehouse parties I went to went through the morning but not all. [Being outdoors works for these kinds of events as] claustrophobia can be a bit of a problem for those in a psychedelic state. (personal communication)

Going bush, and therefore taking people out of the familiar, has its own specific effects that are linked back to the desire to dislocate from the everyday – literally, pharmacologically and/or psychically. For electronic dance participants within the doof scene, nature and escape become entwined. The Australian landscape is thus metaphorically perceived as the ideal site within which to unpack and unburden the self. In the words of a local dance street press writer, '[At an outdoor party] the separation between nature and culture becomes blurred especially once we're all covered in a light film of dust which has risen from the dance floor throughout the night. We are to feel that nature isn't something separate from us, we are a part of it' (Shell 1998).

Spatial Journeys: Festivals as Road Trips

But all too frequently on a large, sparsely populated land mass, one needs to put effort into getting to these outdoor music festival sites. In terms of Michel Callon and Bruno Latour's ideas, which have coalesced under the term actor-network theory, time is rendered into a narrative journey within the event frame, and becomes a powerful actor in the network, circumscribing any given event. So too the journey to a dance festival's physical location is a notable 'event' in and of itself, circumscribing the 'headline' event. It is in this stage of journeying to a festival that maps really come into their own as a way-finding device. As map specialist and curator Robert Karrow asserts, 'maps through time and space have been made to address certain core questions', namely:

- Where am I and how do I get where I want to be?
- What does my world look like, and what is my place in it?
- What does my part of the world look like, and how do I belong there?
- What happened here, what will happen here, and how are these events important to me?
- How can maps help me comprehend things I can't even see?
- How can maps enhance my literary and artistic experiences?
- How can I get access to maps, acquire and use them? (2007: 13)

Therefore maps not only guide us once on journeys, but can give rise to the kind of questioning that puts us in motion, physically and existentially, in the first place.

Given this, how might the journey to an outdoor doof festival space figure in the overall affective experience of the event? How does the road trip feature in the overall event frame? As I have written elsewhere (Luckman 2010), consistently in the literature on road movies, the road is seen as representing a journey – both literal and figurative – a space of self-discovery. Similarly, and more particularly, road movies clearly also signal the possibility of escape; the road as metonym for freedom can be seen every day in pseudo-cinematic car advertisements, where the road is a mythical space of escape from suburbia, employment and family responsibilities, all cast as predictable and cloying or claustrophobic. Or, sometimes more simply, it represents a 'getting away from it all', a respite from the stresses of life in the city. Thus uprooted and removed from the normal rituals, networks and psychological crutches that keep one's monotonous life in place, the individual is free to explore paths not (yet) travelled: to rewrite their stories anew against the blank canvas of a thinly inhabited landscape, to see where the journey takes them. In this figuration, the road becomes a metaphor for life itself (Eyerman and Löfgren 1995: 67): a journey where many people and experiences are encountered and a different person emerges at the end. On the screen this is realized as a romanticized existential personal experience where the protagonists '[s]tripped of all their possessions, as well as the niceties of society' find a road that offers the 'chance to recast the die of life' (Eyerman and Löfgren 1995: 61). Typically, the protagonist becomes transformed by the journey and people they meet on the road. Thus there can never truly be a neat return; some characters simply do not make it, and for the others the person who re-enters the world away from the road must always be different from the person who set out along the journey.

In her book on the Burning Man Festival, Rachel Bowditch (2010: 21) draws upon the work of Victor and Edith Turner to suggest that the 'tourist is half a pilgrim and a pilgrim is half a tourist'. Signalling the shift to a recognition of the profound significance of travel to secular destinations to which this work gave rise, she continues:

> Secular pilgrimage sites such as Burning Man create a temporary transient community of pilgrims who enter into a liminal state of spontaneous bonding, what Victor Turner called *spontaneous communitas*. Through the journey to a distant place, the pilgrim is separated from everyday social life, temporarily becoming geographically and socially marginal. (Bowditch 2010: 21–2)

How people approach an event – the thoughts and expectations they bring with them – can have a profound effect on how they experience it and the degree to which they engage as a contributor to the festival, rather than simply opting for the more passive role of consuming that on offer from other people. The effort and planning required to attend an event outside of one's immediate location, especially where you have to plan ahead to meet your basic needs for transport, food, shelter and warmth, reinforce how the negotiation of space creates a deep sense of commitment to and immersion in an event.

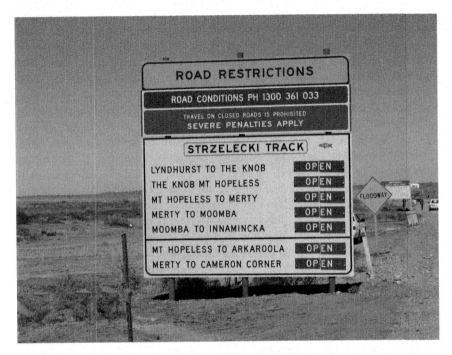

Figure 10.2   On the road to the Outback Eclipse Festival, December 2002

Marking off Festive Space from the Quotidian: Preparation, 'Ownership' and Immersion at Outdoor Dance Events

The kind of festive space I have been talking about is by no means unique to outdoor doof festivals. For example, Bowditch (2010), following on from the work of de Certeau ('walking the city'), and especially Pearson and Shanks (2001) and their idea of 'desire mapping', observes that the lovingly rebuilt space of the temporary city itself looms large as a key to the ongoing success of the annual Burning Man Festival. Here, the site's spatial organization and material realities (weather extremes – hot during the day, chilly at night – not to mention the regular dust storms) enliven the location with agency within the overall experience of each year's event. Given that the purpose-built site needs to be planned out in advance to accommodate the complex event infrastructure, it is most certainly not a massive, unplanned free-for-all. Indeed, quite a bit of Bowditch's book examines the labour and thinking around utopic city arrangement and how this unfolds experimentally in the desert. She identifies the two main discourses running through the festival as ritual and performance, and analyses the ways in which physically moving into, occupying and leaving the site are conducted within a frame that sees each stage of this process as a psychic movement too, with 'rituals' of welcome, return and initiation built into the immersive experience.

Similar spatial planning can frequently be found in the planning of dedicated festive dance music spaces: 'in the rave or dance party, "music is an *environment*"' (Hemment 1996: 29). At a structural level, raving and the incarnations that have spun out from it involve far more than just music and dancing; it is, for its participants, an experience 'which is greater than the sum of its parts' (Critcher 2000: 158). In keeping with raving's sense of ritual, care is taken to construct the event arena. Be it indoors or out, themed or generic, contemporary dance spaces are conceptualized in terms of sound quality, lighting and light shows, props, sets, visuals (computer-generated graphics, edited video and film), games and other stimuli, separate 'rooms' (including chill-out spaces), smell, smoke and even bubbles. While not essential, most events purport to have, if not a full-blown theme, at least a certain 'vibe' or look. An event's thematic identity is more than just a gimmick or marketing tool: it provides a focal point for participants' preparations and expectations. As Bollen (1996: 176) writes, theming 'provides design impetus for the advertising campaign and for scenic installations at the party site; it serves as a cultural reference for staged performances; and it offers partygoers the opportunity to focus their participation in the event through fashion and body-styling'.

A well-structured and engaging forum is essential for the creation of a positive 'vibe' and the facilitation of the desired experience of the event is also thoroughly spatialized within the doof festival. For example, Primal Elements, Earthcore's 2000–01 '5 day international dance music and lifestyle extravaganza' at Mitchell River in eastern Victoria, Australia was ordered around five zones, four of which thematically represented earth, fire, water and air; these were organized around the fifth central (market) zone, where 'the 5th primal element [coffee] will be available' (*Earthcore News*, 29 December 2000). In a gesture pointing to a limited, though poetically ludic, interactive engagement with participants, the organizers invite people to join the zone that most resonates with their hopes for the event or other commitments to self and community identification:

> When you arrive at the site, you will have the option to camp in one of these given areas, but be warned – choose carefully!!
>
> Fire – The main floor will be situated here, so if you are into pounding music, flame-throwers and too much action this is the place for you.
>
> Water – Situated closer to the river with a really mellow vibe – no pounding music here, but instead the DRG Tech crew with their 5 domes and only chill music, the Healing Arts zone and wheatgrass garden, and the chai shop. One of the paths leading to the Mitchell River begins at this zone.
>
> Air – Higher on the hill overlooking the rest of the site. This zone will be the home of two Renegade Floors/Villages 2001 – A Space Conspiracy, and the EAZE Multimedia Performance Arts Zone ...

Earth – Deep down in the grotto you will find the Electric Egg Mutation
Parlour – with tactile tunnels, the pit and other under- and other-worldly delights
and horrors.

... The aim of the game here is to maximise your enjoyment and become a part
of the festival as a whole. (*Earthcore News*, 29 December 2000)

During its 15-year run between 1993 and 2008, Earthcore's promotional
material – like other textual material generated for and at doofs – is laden with
spatial iconography and directions.

As with many other outdoor dance music festive spaces, the doof event is
approached by many participants with great care. Trouble is taken before, after
and during the event to facilitate the desired positive experience. Much effort goes
into preparations, and a large part of the pleasure derived from the festival arises
from the knowledge that the community created the space itself: 'many of these
bush doofs are multi-day events, and that completely changes prep requirements
for attending. There are services, but by the last day supplies may have run dry at
whatever stalls there were' (personal communication). Thus, in Australia – with its
vast distances and large areas of country with sparse population – preparation is
particularly important, not just for the 'bells and whistles' of an event (costumes,
decorations, and so forth) but also for basic necessities (food, water and ... coffee,
for example):

In Oz I think prep is more significant than say the UK where civilisation is never
too far away. State forests where many of these events were and are held are,
though accessible, often over an hour's drive from any sort of facilities during
the night. Hence bringing something to eat, drink, etc. is important – and there
is no ground for the organizers saying must buy from their bar or whatever!
(Though to be honest many warehouse parties had none – but bringing some
cheese and wine for brekkie would be difficult – also coffee of course!).
(Personal communication)

A sense of ownership of the conduct of the event – in the form of a commitment
to thoughtful self-preparation, responsibility for other people, for the 'vibe' or for
cleaning up afterwards in order to minimize environmental impact – is even felt by
participants at some of the larger quasi- or wholly commercial bush events, where
the demarcation is somewhat institutionalized:

Many of the festivals in the bush now have means for you to earn the price
of your ticket by working the entry point, or clean up, etc. ... People show
up at bush parties and decorate their campsites adding extra lighting and
artwork to the event. Unless a city/warehouse party is privately organized, it's
unlikely people will contribute to the space other than costumes and attitude.
(Personal communication)

Tying directly in with the degree of preparation and effort put into attending these distant doof festivals – not to mention the emphasis put on performative engagement underpinning the scene – in its emails to participants, Earthcore invites participants to augment, or even to populate as 'citizens', the spatial structure it has set up for its commercial events. The evocation of citizenship recurs in the Earthcore organizers' public discourse regarding their large-scale events. For example, *The Age* newspaper featured an article in the lead-up to the 10,000-strong party Earthcore organized around the beginning of the year 2000, where Pip Darvall metaphorically compared Earthcore to a city that is 'bent', a parallel universe consisting of 'a normal city put through a blender': 'We liken our events to creating a small city in the middle of nowhere, with all necessary services provided … Roads, parking areas, camping villages, entertainment zones, a market for food and clothing, security staff, the Red Cross, police, the CFA, a water supply system and so on' (Crawford 1999: T1). Later on, this invitation to contribute to the same event was extended even more clearly: 'Those camping within each zone are encouraged to participate in their happenings. Choose your quadrant before you arrive or be assigned one upon arrival. Get a group together and work out how you can contribute and extract the most possible enjoyment out of your festival' (*Earthcore News*, 29 December 2000).

Outdoor dance events are an eagerly awaited opportunity to go out into the bush or desert camping with friends, which brings us to one of the fundamental reasons for their popularity. Repeatedly, both the organizers I interviewed and other people to whom I spoke regarding the Australian doof scene referred to the pleasure they derive from spending a number of nights outdoors with friends: 'I always preferred bush parties, and felt more at ease wandering to campsites of mates or just off for a bit of quiet (so to speak) in the trees, so my bias is that warehouses parties are less fulfilling' (personal communication).

Multi-day outdoor doof festivals are, among other things, a focal point around which to organize a group camp, where the act of camping itself is understood, not just here but more broadly, as something greater than a holiday experience, signifying as it does the experience of 'getting away from it all' to some purer place. Having escaped to the outdoors, these travellers are now also out of their everyday comfort zones – albeit in an environment embraced for its invigorating and renewing qualities. So, psychically as well as physically located, the scene is felt to be ideally set for the 'more than the everyday' event ahead. Even in commercial bush doofs, this temporal and subjective dislocation is a fundamental part of the participants' enjoyment. As Earthcore's Spiro Boursine elaborates:

> [There's a] tribal element in the sense of, it's obviously back out in nature, etc. So there's obviously there's tribal roots to nature, so therefore there's a tribal element. Also the community … I think the reason why Earthcore is so different from the other [high-profile commercial] events is that when you put people into an environment they're not accustomed to, which their day-to-day lives don't

correspond to, they feel slightly freshened, because they're not accustomed to this strange environment they're at. So therefore their social inhibitions, and their ego, and their hierarchic structures between their own personal social groups sort of dissipate, and that's why Earthcore's really good in the sense of we get such a huge cross-section of the community of people that go out to entertainment. (Interview)

Displaced and hence apparently rendered open to new experiences, participants are now set for a communion centred upon a sense of reconnecting with natural and pre-industrial worlds. As I have critically examined elsewhere (Luckman 2003), organizers and participants both capitalize upon this, employing hybridized imagery and discursive frameworks drawn from myriad Indigenous, traditional, New Age or just generally counter-cultural belief systems. Therefore, I would like to argue here that it is precisely this ability for the outdoor music festival to take people on a journey outside the quotidian that is one of the key reasons for its ongoing appeal.

Displacement, Liminality and the Festive Outdoors

My interest in how space and a journey to it come together in an intense and concentrated experience has led me to draw on the work of sociologist Victor Turner. Turner is well known for his argument that, in the contemporary secular milieu, highly prized leisure time has 'inherited the function of the ritual frame' (Turner 1987: 77). That is, secular play has become a more serious, structured and self-reflexive endeavour precisely because of the decline in the significance of previous forms of sacred, particularly religious, ritual. Further, 'People in all cultures recognize the need to set aside certain times and spaces for celebratory use, in which the possibility of personal and communal creativity may arise' (Turner 1982b: 11–12). Placed into this historical context, the kind of 'pilgrimage' or journey to a place beyond the everyday required by outdoor music events is hardly new. Indeed, as Turner (among many others) has argued, anthropologically they are among human beings' earliest cultural practices; nothing could be greater evidence of the ongoing and deep human appeal of music experienced in the outdoors, and for this reason Turner's work has informed many recent accounts of electronic dance music cultures globally (cf. St John 2008a, 2010a).

In contemporary Australian doof culture, too, 'ritual' is both an implicit and literal function of the structuring of time and space. Thus, like similar festivals, doof events mark one of the few spaces in industrialized society where 'play' is sanctioned for adults. Though the event may be limited in time, the effects of the experience are not similarly containable. As Tramacchi notes of the doof experience, weekends may provide the space for people to get to a bush party but within 'rave and *doof* culture, the regenerative bliss of liminal togetherness is seen more as a means of simply becoming more human, more meaningfully engaged, when, on Monday morning, one eventually resumes a position in a structural/ institutional matrix' (2000: 210). Further tying them back anthropologically to deep social practices of shared reciprocity, outdoor doof festivals are ideally 'full of practices of hospitality, kindness and giving (drink, dope, food, etc). In other words, it is deeply based on the "gift economy"' (2000: 100–101). These markers of this space resonate with the kinds of gift economies, 'participant not audience' directive and a sense of empowered inspiration for action beyond the event underpinning the remote, US desert-based Burning Man Festival – as well as, I would imagine, other events where the journey away from the familiar requires high levels of commitment and immersion on the part of participants.

As sociologist Sarah Pink (2009: 24) argues, one of the strengths of Turner's work is that he 'argued that we should distinguish between "mere experience" and "an experience". In this formulation "mere experience" is the continuous flow of events that we passively accept, while "an experience" is a defined and reflected on event that has a beginning and an end'. The journey to the outdoor doof festival helps to frame this particular event precisely as 'an experience', something clearly more than – and definitively framed off from – the everyday flow of events. It therefore has far greater impact than a dance music event held within commuting distance of home, and requiring only the most quotidian of journeys: taxi, bike, walking or public transport. This is not to say that such events cannot loom large in people's personal histories as an important event in their lives, but I would maintain that, in terms of the experience, there is something qualitatively and quantitatively different about 'an experience' requiring an extended journey, which has the facility for disjuncture from the everyday strongly built into the fundamental concept of the event *qua* immersive commitment.

In this way, outdoor doof festivals are indeed manifestations of Turner's liminal: an 'in between' space where new possibilities of individual identity and social organization and being are opened up. Turner's thinking regarding the liminal was heavily influenced by the work of fellow anthropologist Arnold van Gennep, and in particular his work on rites of passage (Turner 1982a: 24). While I am not arguing here that the dance music festival constitutes the kind of profound, frequently pre-industrial, ritualistic, life-changing event marked out by the rite of passage in van Gennep and Turner's work, there are elements present in these experiences that can illuminate the profound ongoing value of outdoor music and dance events as both leisure experience and, frequently, politically charged rendering of an alternative utopic vision of individual life and collective organization. Of particular relevance here, Turner notes that van Gennep 'distinguishes three phases in a rite of passage: *separation, transition, and incorporation*' (1982a: 24). The first two of these stages – *separation* and *transition* – provide insight into the contemporary significance of the journey beyond the quotidian to a special event:

Figure 10.3   Outback Eclipse Festival, December 2002

> The first phase of *separation* clearly demarcates sacred space and time from
> profane or secular space and time (it is more than just entering a temple – there
> must be in addition a rite which changes the quality of *time* also, or constructs a
> cultural realm which is defined as 'out of time,' i.e. beyond or outside the time
> which measures secular processes and routines). (Turner 1982a: 24)

The road trip to a multi-day festival, for example, signifies time away from work
and home. In the second phase, that of *transition*: 'The ritual subjects pass through
a period and area of ambiguity, a sort of social limbo which has few ... of the
attributes of either the preceding or subsequent profane social statuses or cultural
states' (Turner 1982a: 24). It is from this 'margin' or 'limen' state that Turner
further develops his thinking around the liminal.

As I mentioned above, much has already been written about dance music cultures,
rites of passage and Turner's work on liminality, and it is not the purpose of this
chapter to retrace over this ground. Further I agree with St John (2010a: 224) that
researchers laying claim to the dance party as a profound rite of passage frequently
appear to be unable to back up the claim with evidence, and that Turner's original
'liminal'–'liminoid' distinction, which largely limited the former to the 'agrarian
and tribal cultures' (Turner 1982a) and the latter to industrial,[1] seems somewhat

---

1   Or, as St John writes elsewhere (2008b: 8), liminal (ritual) and liminoid (leisure).

outdated and hence it may be best to speak of liminal cultures (St John 2010a: 226). But the road less travelled here is the enabling role geography, distance and journey play in facilitating the experiences of disjuncture and immersion, even if this is not experienced at a spiritual or deeply felt level as in anthropological studies of the role of ritual in pre-industrial societies. Nonetheless, the journey still marks off the outdoor dance music festival as 'an experience'. Despite the apparent grounding provided by festival maps, ironically perhaps the festive destination is the very liminality this in-between journey space presages – an in-between space of release from everyday responsibility in which *potentially* to map out other visions of the self and society, to varying degrees of commitment and veracity. This is an individual experience, but one – importantly – facilitated collectively within a heterotopic liminal cultural space. In this way, not only are new spatial maps being laid out, but it is also hoped that new personal ones can also be imagined if not actually drawn.

Acknowledgements

A big thank you to Graham Browne, Ken Miller, Kate Leeson, Lisa Slater and the interviewees.

References

Bollen, J. 1996. Sexing the dance at Sleaze Ball 1994. *The Drama Review*, 40(3), 166–91.
Bowditch, R. 2010. *On the Edge of Utopia: Performance and Ritual at Burning Man*. London: Seagull Books.
Chan, S. 1999. Bubbling acid: Sydney's techno underground, in *Australian Youth Subcultures: On the Margins and in the Mainstream*, edited by R. White. Hobart: Australian Clearinghouse for Youth Studies, 65–73.
Crawford, A. 1999. Earthcore – party like it's 2000: It's all the rave. *The Age*, 27 December, Today, 1, 3.
Critcher, C. 2000. 'Still raving': Social reaction to ecstasy. *Leisure Studies*, 19(3), 145–62.
Eyerman, R. and Löfgren, O. 1995. Romancing the road: Road movies and images of mobility. *Theory, Culture and Society*, 12, 53–79.
Gelder, K. 2001. Foreword, in *FreeNRG: Notes from the Edge of the Dance Floor*, edited by G. St John. Melbourne: Common Ground, xv–xvii.
Gibson, C. 1999. Subversive sites: rave culture, spatial politics and the internet in Sydney, Australia. *Area*, 31(1), 19–33.
Gibson, C. and Pagan, R. 1999. *Rave Culture in Sydney, Australia: Mapping Youth Spaces in Media Discourse*. Available at: www.snarl.org/youth/chrispagan2.pdf [accessed: 29 July 2011].

Goodchild, M. 1995. Geographic information systems and geographic research, in *Ground Truth: The Social Implications of Geographic Information Systems*, edited by J. Pickles. New York: Guilford Press, 31–50.

Harley, J.B. 1988. Maps, knowledge, and power, in *The Iconography of Landscape*, edited by D. Cosgrove and S. Daniels. Cambridge: Cambridge University Press, 277–312.

Hemment, D. 1996. E is for ekstasis. *New Formations*, 31, 23–38.

Jenkins, S. 2009. Let the elite's building funds dry up. Outside, cultural Britain is flourishing. *The Guardian*, 23 July. Available at: www.guardian.co.uk/commentisfree/2009/jul/23/arts-funding-elitism-policy [accessed: 25 July 2009].

Karrow, R. Jr. 2007. Introduction, in *Maps: Finding our Place in the World*, edited by J.R. Akerman and R.W. Karrow Jr. Chicago, IL: University of Chicago Press, 1–17.

Luckman, S. 1998. Rave cultures and the academy. *Social Alternatives*, 17(4), 45–9.

Luckman, S. 2001a. 'Sorted'? Mapping the regulation of dance parties in Australia. *Journal of Australian Studies*, 64, 217–23.

Luckman, S. 2001b. 'What are they raving on about?': Temporary autonomous zones and reclaiming the streets. *Perfect Beat*, 5(2), 49–68.

Luckman, S. 2003. Going bush and finding one's 'tribe': Raving, doof and the Australian landscape. *Continuum: A Journal of Media and Cultural Studies*, 17(3), 318–32.

Luckman, S. 2008. Doof, dance and rave culture, in *Sounds of Then, Sounds of Now: Popular Music in Australia*, edited by S. Homan and T. Mitchell. Hobart: Australian Clearinghouse for Youth Studies, 131–50.

Luckman, S. 2010. Road movies, national myths and the threat of the road: the shifting transformative space of the road in Australian film. *International Journal of the Humanities*, 8(1), 113–25.

Malbon, B. 1999. *Clubbing: Dancing, Ecstasy and Vitality*. London: Routledge.

Murphie, A. and Scheer, E. 1992. Dance parties: Capital, culture and simulation, in *From Pop to Punk to Postmodernism: Popular Music and Australian Culture From the 1960s to the 1990s*, edited by P. Hayward. Sydney: Allen & Unwin, 172–84.

Padrón, R. 2007. Mapping imaginary worlds, in *Maps: Finding our Place in the World*, edited by J.R. Akerman and R.W. Karrow Jr. Chicago, IL: University of Chicago Press, 255–87.

Pickles, J. 1995. Representations in an electronic age, in *Ground Truth: The Social Implications of Geographic Information Systems*, edited by J. Pickles. New York: Guildford Press, 1–30.

Pearson, M. and Shanks, M. 2001. *Theatre/Archaeology*. New York: Routledge.

Pini, M. 1997. Women and the early British rave scene, in *Back to Reality? Social Experience and Cultural Studies*, edited by A. McRobbie. Manchester: Manchester University Press, 152–69.

Pink, S. 2009. *Doing Sensory Ethnography*. London: Sage.

Redhead, S. 1990. *The End-of-the-Century Party: Youth and Pop Towards 2000.* Manchester: Manchester University Press.

Redhead, S., ed. 1993. *Rave Off: Politics and Deviance in Contemporary Youth Culture.* Aldershot: Avebury.

Redhead, S. 1997. *Subculture to Clubcultures: An Introduction to Popular Cultural Studies.* Oxford: Blackwell.

Redhead, S., Wynne, D. and O'Connor, J. eds. 1997. *The Clubcultures Reader: Readings in Popular Cultural Studies.* Oxford: Blackwell.

Rietveld, H. 1998. *This is Our House: House Music, Cultural Spaces and Technologies.* Aldershot: Ashgate.

Shell. 1998. Let the chaos begin. *Tekno Renegade*, December, n.p.

St John, G. ed. 2001a. *FreeNRG: Notes from the Edge of the Dance Floor.* Melbourne: Common Ground.

St John, G. 2001b. Introduction: techno inferno, in *FreeNRG: Notes from the Edge of the Dance Floor*, edited by G. St John. Melbourne: Common Ground, 1–6.

St John, G. 2005. Outback vibes: sound systems on the road to legitimacy. *Postcolonial Studies*, 8(3), 321–36.

St John, G. (ed.) 2008a. *Victor Turner and Contemporary Cultural Performance.* New York: Berghahn Books.

St John, G. 2008b. Victor Turner and contemporary cultural performance: An introduction, in *Victor Turner and Contemporary Cultural Performance*, edited by G. St John. New York: Berghahn Books, 1–37.

St John, G. 2009. *Technomad: Global Raving Countercultures.* London: Equinox.

St John, G. 2010a. Liminal culture and global movement: the transitional world of psytrance, in *The Local Scenes and Global Culture of Psytrance*, edited by G. St John. New York: Routledge, 220–46.

St John, G. (ed.) 2010b. *The Local Scenes and Global Culture of Psytrance.* New York: Routledge.

Straw, W. 1991. Systems of articulation, logics of change: Communities and scenes in popular music. *Cultural Studies*, 15(3), 368–88.

Strong, P. 2001. Doofstory: Sydney Park to the desert, in *FreeNRG: Notes from the Edge of the Dance Floor*, edited by G. St John. Melbourne: Common Ground, 71–89.

Thornton, S. 1995. *Club Cultures: Music, Media and Subcultural Capital.* Cambridge: Polity Press.

Tramacchi, D. 2000. Field tripping: psychedelic *communitas* and ritual in the Australian bush. *Journal of Contemporary Religion*, 15(2), 201–13.

Turner, V. 1982a. *From Ritual to Theatre: The Human Seriousness of Play.* New York: Performing Arts Journal Publications.

Turner, V. 1982b. Introduction, in *Celebration: Studies in Festivity and Ritual*, edited by V. Turner. Washington, DC: Smithsonian Institution Press, 11–30.

Turner, V. 1987. Carnival, ritual, and play in Rio de Janeiro, in *Time Out of Time: Essays on the Festival*, edited by A. Falassi. Albuquerque, NM: University of New Mexico Press, 74–90.

Chapter 11

Performing the Promised Land: The Festivalizing of Multi-cultures in the Margate Exodus Project

Michael Balfour

What is a festival? It's something exceptional, something out of the ordinary ... something that must create a special atmosphere which stems not only from the quality of the art and the production, but from the countryside, the ambience of a city and the traditions ... of a region. (de Rougement, quoted in Isar 1976: 131)

The use of festivals as a way to promote cultural and economic regeneration has been widespread in the United States and many European cities, particularly following World War II (Bassett 1993; Hiller 1990; Hudson 1995; Levin 1982: 10–18; Ley and Olds 1988, 1992; Whitt 1987). International festivals such as Edinburgh in 1947, Dartington in 1948 and the Festival of Britain in 1951 were attempts to use culture and the arts to promote optimism and 'provide a platform for the flowering of the human spirit' (Henderson 1991: 26). The link between culture and new economies was also important, with a conscious use of art to increase tourism and economic development. There are, however, obvious tensions between the aims of *economic* regeneration, with its focus on property development, tourism and investment in infrastructure, and *cultural* regeneration, more concerned with specific communities' self-development and abilities to draw on the arts as a way to represent themselves and their stories. As Waterman (1998: 64) notes: 'Prestige projects and place-marketing do not necessarily contribute to cultural regeneration and are more inclined to benefit the local middle class and cultural tourists'.

Over the past two decades, there has been a remarkable rise in the number of arts festivals worldwide (Quinn 2005). As urban centres have moved from nodes of production to service-oriented consumption, there has been a need to reposition and differentiate cities in an increasingly competitive world. Drawing on Paddison (1993), cities and urban areas have increasingly used entrepreneurial displays that employ arts festivals, conferences and trade shows as key constituents in attracting investment needed for regenerating and restructuring old urban areas (e.g. the European City of Culture initiative). Cities compete with each other in generating ever more sophisticated place-marketing events and strategies that span the calendar year. The impact of the competitive and economic nature of the festivalization of culture is far from clear, and it has been argued that it can lead to 'serial reproduction' (Richards and Wilson 2004: 1932) and, ironically, a certain homegenization of place that pays lip-service to local distinctiveness:

> Now it's festivals, festivals everywhere. Big ones, small ones, wild ones, silly ones, dutiful ones, pretentious ones, phony ones. Many have lost purpose and direction, not to mention individual profile. Place a potted plant near the box office, double the ticket prices and – whoopee – we have a festival. (Bernheimer 2003: 21)

The double bind of homogenization and a top-down 'culture is good for you' approach to festivals is not the only tactic in evidence. A number of precedents exist for festivals that seek to represent counter-narratives and/or explore the particularities of local community interests. As Turner (1982) notes, communal creativity, celebration and festivals are significant ways for communities to express the close relationship between identity and place. While many arts festivals have been sited in major cities, there has been a corresponding growth and development in more regional contexts. As Frey (1994) argues, regional and decentralized festivals often emerged as reactionary attempts to represent other voices and perspectives that often were not represented by keystone arts festivals in the main capitals – for example, Avignon. As Quinn (2005: 929) argues:

> [These] festival initiatives have shown themselves to be highly reflective, as well as constitutive, of the resources, circumstances and people existing in particular places. They emerged in response to artistic needs lacking within that place and crystallised the key resources available there.

Clearly, there is a strong genealogy with alternative and counter-culture festivals from the 1960s and 1970s, in which grassroots social movements explored a range of themes through arts festivals, happenings and protests with themes of anti-war, feminism, environmentalism and gay rights. It is not the focus of this chapter to explore this period in detail; I merely note that there is a strong lineage of community-based festivals that are driven by the imperatives of creating culture by, for and with local communities. The nature of the 'alternative' festival event is that it challenges the form and content of traditional arts festivals (in the mould of Edinburgh, etc.) in placing an equal emphasis on processes of community engagement and ownership and/or investment in the final outcome. The intent of these more localized festivals is to privilege the communal and participative dimension that is so key to the origins of the festival, and to use the arts as a vehicle for the community to talk to itself, to reflect, to celebrate and to reinforce the distinction of place. A good example of this type of festival is the Caribbean carnival now found in most North American and British cities. The considerable economic and tourism benefits of these celebrations do not outweigh the strong connections they still have with their specific diasporic networks. The carnivals maintain their position as hybrid sites (Bhaba 1994), where 'cultural identities, notions of belonging and values systems are celebrated, contested and negotiated' (Quinn 2005: 935).

Diasporic and Refugee Festivals

> Displacements of whole populations. Refugees from famine and war. Wave after wave of emigrants, emigrating for either political or economic reasons but emigrating for survival. Ours in the century of enforced travel ... the century of disappearances. (Berger 1992: 12)

The number of people forcibly uprooted by conflict and persecution worldwide stood at 42 million at the end of 2008. The total includes 16 million refugees and asylum seekers, and 26 million internally displaced people uprooted within their own countries (UNHCR 2009). The settlement experience for many refugees in new host countries can be a very difficult time. Some 25–30 per cent of refugees have recognized conditions such as post-traumatic stress disorder (PTSD) and a further 40 per cent have experienced extremely traumatic pasts before arriving in Australia (DIMA 2006). Around 80 per cent of entrants have not rented a house, paid a bill or gone to work, and have had no experience of engaging with institutions such as banks, real estate agents or government departments in the previous decade (DIAC 2009). Significant settlement issues include high rates of unemployment, housing issues, English-language barriers, effects of torture and trauma, and general health issues (DIMA 2006).

War and displacement create breaks from cultures of origin in which an individual's sense of self and identity has been formed and is embedded. Displacement can cause alienation from and questioning of basic assumptions about self and one's place in the world. Contact with other places, people and cultures challenges notions of our own culture as 'original' or 'authentic' – and presents ideas about new ways of life, identity and cultural expression. There can be a profound sense of loss with the destruction (often violent) of economic and social infrastructure, and consequently the cultural activities and values that once made life meaningful. However, cultural practices are embodied and reconstructed in sites of refuge, often to facilitate a sense of connection with history and previous lives. As such, theatre and performance activities in these contexts express both a sense of cultural dislocation and a means of rebuilding a sense of identity. There has been a growth in diasporic and refugee-themed festivals over the last 10 years (Thompson, Hughes and Balfour 2009), with local government and community agencies trying to find creative responses to settlement that promote a resource-based rather than deficit-based approach to the settlement of new arrivals into local cultures. Conquergood reports from his experience working as a theatre consultant in a Hmong refugee camp on the Thai border:

Refugee camps are liminal zones where people displaced by trauma and crisis – usually war or famine – must try to regroup and salvage what is left of their lives. Their world has been shattered. They are in passage, no longer Laotian, certainly not Thai, and not quite sure where they will end up or what their lives will become. Betwixt and between worlds, suspended between past and future, they fall back on the performance of their traditions as an empowering way of securing continuity and some semblance of stability. Moreover, through performative flexibility, they can play with new identities, new strategies for adaptation and survival. The playful creativity of performance enables them to experiment with and invent a new 'camp culture' that is part affirmation of the past and part adaptive response to the exigencies of the present. Performance participates in the recreation of self and society that emerges within refugee camps. Through its reflexive capacities, performance enables people to take stock of their situation and, through this self-knowledge, to cope better. (Conquergood 1988: 180)

Contemporary cultural theorists have highlighted the role of performance and arts festivals in creating identity on both an individual and social level – so a person can create and adopt new identities through acts of speech and performance in everyday life. In some of this work, there is a similar positive gloss given to the creative possibilities of the 'border' in bringing about new forms of identity and relationships between people:

[T]hese 'in-between' spaces provide the terrain for elaborating strategies of selfhood – singular and communal – that initiate news signs of identity, and innovative sites of collaboration, and contestation, in the act of defining society itself. (Bhabha 1994: 2)

While refugee festivals and celebratory events are designed to acknowledge new cultures, there has been an equal emphasis on the need to create bridges with local communities. This chapter focuses on the ways in which refugee and migrant groups have been dispersed into areas that are often characterized by low socio-economic contexts, and the resulting tensions that exist within complex, fluid and multi-ethnic communities. How do artists work within and transcend these complex environments? The Margate Exodus project serves as an example of how artists can employ a range of tactics to combine the needs of community arts festivals to work with local communities, but at the same time devise aesthetic strategies that transcend the micro-politics of ethnic tensions in a specific context.

Margate

In 1887, John Bartholomew's *Gazetteer of the British Isles* described Margate in the following terms:

Margate, seaside resort, Kent, in Isle of Thanet, 5 miles NW. of Ramsgate and 74 miles E. of London by rail. The place was formerly known as Mergate, meaning a passage to the sea ... Margate is undoubtedly the most familiar seaside resort of Londoners, of whom many thousands visit the place every year ... Much has been done in the town for the convenience and comfort of visitors; piers and esplanades especially have been constructed at great expense. The town is well known for its fine hotels and its hospitals for the reception of invalids.

In stark contrast is Will Self's (2006) description of Margate 119 years later:

Next to the station stands the enormous, wrinkled digit of Arlington House, a Brutalist 20-storey block of flats that seems to waggle a warning at all asylum seekers: 'Enter this land of promise, and you'll be banged up in here forever'. Or worse, in the decaying terrace of the Nayland Rock refugee hostel. Once this was a luxury hotel, now it houses Roma on the run from central Europe, Congolese fleeing the meltdown of central Africa, Iraqis evading the maelstrom of the Middle East. Strange, that so many people escaping the dread gravity of these landmasses, should find themselves clinging on to the very tip of the Isle of Thanet, which in turn is like a cold sore on the Kentish lip of old England.

Thanet is the easternmost district of the County of Kent, United Kingdom. It has a population of approximately 127,000, the majority of whom live in the three seaside towns of Margate, Broadstairs and Ramsgate. Thanet suffers from acute social and economic deprivation. The Audit Commission (2005) notes that, 'Thanet contains some of the most deprived areas in Kent, including the two most deprived wards in south-east England, both of which are in the top 2% of deprived areas in England'.

Margate has been a destination for different waves of migratory forces, and has high levels of refugees, asylum seekers and economic migrants from all over the world. Margate's faded past as a promised land is echoed in the ageing grandeur of its infrastructure and buildings, 'an ideal context, then, geographically, historically and emotionally, in which to revisit the greatest migration story ever told' (Morris 2006: 15). Once a popular seaside resort in the 1960s and 1970s, Margate has been marred by multiple social and economic problems, dwindling resources and a shrinking tourism industry. Many former Victorian hotels and B&Bs have been converted into care homes and bed-sits for an influx of immigrants, giving the resort the cruel nickname of Benefits-on-Sea. The transience of the population is reflected in one of the local primary schools having a 44 per cent mobility rate (turnover of pupils) (TES survey, 2000). Tracy Emin (2008), the conceptual artist, grew up in the town and recently reflected:

It's strange to witness the death of a town. In some ways there is a melancholy romance. It's like the tragic set of a film, but the sad thing is that the star is

Margate. Margate has become Britain's tragic Norma Desmond from *Sunset Boulevard*, almost nothing can save her.

Arts regeneration has been one of the key areas of investment as a way to redevelop and reimagine the town. A multi-agency partnership between Thanet District Council, Kent County Council, the South East Development Agency (SEEDA), the Arts Council England, the Government Office of the South East (GOSE), the Heritage Lottery Fund, English Partnerships and English Heritage was set up in 2005 and secured over £35 million to kick-start the initiative. The partnership invested in cultural activities as part of a campaign to change perceptions and raise the profile of Margate, quoting a mission statement:

> By 2015, Margate will become a dynamic, thriving and successful town. It will be a major hub and driving force of creativity and culture that excites and inspires residents and visitors alike. It will embrace and celebrate its traditions as a place of relaxation, leisure and seaside fun.

The partnership presents its regeneration plan, making use of existing infrastructure of buildings and the coastline:

> These natural assets, coupled with an embryonic creative sector, a large number of major development opportunities in and around the town centre, and the Turner Contemporary, all create the platform to place Margate firmly back on the map as a successful town by the sea and a thriving visitor destination.

In many ways, Margate represents the quintessential site of arts regeneration. The place-making initiatives of beautification and cosmopolitanism – the attraction of outside 'creatives' and cappuccino bars – erode and displace character and local distinctiveness, but bring with them cash, investment and kudos (city types slumming it in Margate for a kitsch experience and a visit to the new Turner gallery). This is not a celebration of what Margate is, but a re-branding of its history and an attempt to put it on the 'cool list'. Its deeper histories and its ongoing attempts to deal with tensions derived from its ethnic diversity are skirted around and marginalized, in an attempt to present a frontality of experience driven by a contemporary vision of 'seaside fun'. The projected image and the actual reality construct a cultural chasm between economic regeneration and social regeneration. Each new cultural initiative walks a tightrope between social and economic inclusivity, balancing the need for outside perspectives and investment with the need to value and understand the local.

In this chapter, I utilize the Margate Exodus festival as an example of a way to sneak up on the paradox of balancing both social and economic needs. The festival was a relatively small event, created early on in the rejuvenation plans of the town. In 2002, Michael Morris from the London-based international arts organization Artangel became intrigued by the possibility of commissioning a number of artists to develop a festival project exploring themes of migration in collaboration with the residents of Margate. The result was the Margate Exodus project, a one-day outdoor festival. The festival consisted of a promenade performance, a rock concert, an outdoor photography show and a 25-metre wooden Burning Man sculpture. In this chapter, I explore how Artangel used the festivalization process to foreground the impact of the migration experience through diverse aesthetic means. The festival was designed as a way to initiate a dialogue in the town about the grander narratives of history and economic circumstances, and how these impact on individual lives in distinct but interconnected ways.

In the Beginning

> Thou shalt not oppress a stranger, for ye know the heart of a stranger, seeing ye were strangers in the land of Egypt. (Exodus, 23.9)

The festival day commenced in Margate's central shopping area with a performance by a newly elected politician, Pharoah Mann, giving his victory speech. The promenade performance then continued in a series of site-specific scenarios staged throughout the town, filmed by British National broadcaster Channel 4. Penny Woolcock, the director, developed the story from the Exodus tale, and re-staged it in collaboration with a number of the town's residents, who acted, made costumes and props, or were part of the crowds following the actions.

The festival continued in the evening with a cycle of Plague Songs at Margate's Winter Gardens. The free concert featured local singers and musicians performing their own versions of songs written exclusively for Exodus by Brian Eno and Robert Wyatt, Laurie Anderson, The Tiger Lillies, Scott Walker, Rufus Wainwright and others, who based the songs on one of the ten biblical plagues – Blood, Frogs, Lice, Flies, Death of Livestock, Boils, Hailstones, Locusts, Darkness and Death of the Firstborn. Each of the local singers and musicians had been working with a composer and voice coach over the summer in preparation for the performance. Over in the former Dreamland funfair, Antony Gormley's massive-scale *Waste Man*, created in collaboration with a team from Margate and the Isle of Thanet, was a 25-metre figure tightly packed with unwanted detritus. The spirit of Exodus threaded its way across the town with *Towards a Promised Land*, Wendy Ewald's large-scale banner photographs of children newly arrived in Margate. The photographs formed an audio-visual trail of the children's migration stories.

As a festival, the Exodus day existed as a hybrid event: part arts extravaganza brought in from outside and part community festival reflecting the distinctive and diverse nature of Margate. Interestingly, as a festival it did not focus on one ethnic group – typical in other refugee festivals (Thompson, Hughes and Balfour 2009). Instead, it took a universal approach to the story of migration as a common emotional experience that might 'cut across the divisions of race, faith, politics and circumstance' (Morris 2006: 16). The unifying experience of forced migration (economic and/or political) was what held the disparate elements of the project together. Given the simmering context of racial tensions in the town, this was both an elegant and progressive way to include the town in a conversation about itself and the different forms of migration it had experienced. By situating the exodus motif either in biblical history, or obliquely through images that included participants from the United Kingdom and Ireland as well as Africa and Afghanistan, the artists tried to explore the experience and impact of dislocation in myriad ways.

The Exodus project can be seen to draw on the traditions of the community play movement, particularly from the 1960s, 1970s and 1980s (Kershaw 1992). There are strong connections here with localism, and with responsiveness to community issues. Companies such as Medium Fair, Welfare State, EMMA (UK), Bread and Puppet (US), as well as – more recently – the work of Lyndon Terracini's development of regional festivals, provide a context for the Exodus project. There are also more extended lineages back to the 'town play' initiatives that drew in people – not only actors, but a whole range of informal, voluntary labour – as a means of both maximizing the 'localness' of the event and promoting inclusion. Like the earlier community play movement, the Margate Exodus used a range of performance styles and modes with considerable sophistication in order to match the show to a specific audience. It also developed carefully structured approaches to participatory practices that echoed influences as different as Ann Jellicoe, Augusto Boal and the European experiment of Odin Theatre.

As an artist-led collaborative project, Margate Exodus explored what Hauptfleisch (2007) defines as key elements in a festival, including diverse non-traditional and temporary spaces, the use of different forms (music, photography, theatre, film, ritual) and different levels of engagement (some audience members followed the whole day of activities, while others saw only some of the events). The range of arts activities was important in situating the festival as a meta-event encompassing a series of individual but linked performances. The loose coalition of performances was meant to invoke meaning-making that would transcend one specific event and create a 'flow' of experience (Schoenmakers 2007: 34).

The Margate Exodus project attempted to make a connection between multiple ethnic communities. Its creators were not avowedly community activists, but were more interested in the affective challenges of staging projects in a marginalized space. In their previous work, all artists were linked to work that had strong participatory elements or employed community members, or they were progressive public artists attuned to creating work for a broad audience. In structuring the Margate Exodus project as a series of distinct but interlinked events (sharing of place, community, theme), the artists created a complex 'poly-systemic' theatrical event (Cremona 2007: 5). Although conceived of as a whole, the project did not constitute a single event, but rather something more fractured and complex, a series of sub-events containing a blend of competing but complementary activities. The focus in this chapter is on two of these elements: Wendy Ewald's *Towards a Promised Land* and Anthony Gormley's *Waste Man*, as I think they demonstrate how these artists sought to explore issues in an affective way to communicate the fragility of belonging to any one place, and the tentative nature of identity and migration.

Lives, Words, Pictures

> Children have taught me that art is not a realm where only the trained and the accredited may dwell. The truly unsettling thing about children's imagery is that, despite their inexperience with what adults might call rational thinking their images tap into certain universal feelings with undeniable force and subtlety.
> (Ewald, quoted in Neri 2006: 30)

In *Towards a Promised Land*, Wendy Ewald worked with 22 young people who had arrived in Margate from diverse locations, including Iraq, Belarus, Egypt and the Congo, as well as London, Derby, Belfast and Germany. Ewald is an experienced 'participatory' photographer. She strives to develop close working relationships with her co-photographers, helping them develop camera skills and a strong sense of ownership over the material. Her portraits are of the children, taken from locations of their choosing around Margate, as well as images of their possessions, selected from belongings brought with them. The possessions are designed to evoke memories of home and lives left behind, as well as the here and now. The images were used for an exhibition in the local library, and made into large-scale banner images displayed along Margate's seawall, as well as smaller images shown in the Dreamland Amusement Arcade, a cinema, a pub, a fish and chip shop and a domestic home. A downloaded audio 'banner trail' was created around the multi-site gallery; this included interviews and moving testimonies by the young people. Visitors followed a map and were guided by the stories of the children, and the places and possessions they had chosen.

Ewald's participatory approach to making images began in 1969, with a project working with Naskapi children on a First Nation reservation in Canada. The raw beauty of the images the children created galvanized Ewald to explore more collaborative art projects, and she travelled and worked in Colombia, Mexico and India over the next decade. Increasingly, her work became a fusion of aesthetics, skills empowerment and cultural negotiation. This work led her to explore binaries of difference, particularly around issues of race, as with her noted project examining the effects of apartheid on Afrikaner children in Johannesburg and African children in Soweto. Part of her developing praxis is taking the time to understand and negotiate the realities of different cultural norms. Her work in Islamic cultures (Morocco and Saudi Arabia), for example, involved Ewald undergoing intensive cultural dialogue about what could and could not be represented, and how to explore different models of selfhood. During her career, Ewald has striven to 'articulate and integrate marginalized parts of the social body by educating those parts, via the reflective processes of word and image, to observe themselves then record and display those observations' (Neri 2006: 32).

The intimacy created in Ewald's work between artist and co-artist/participant is governed by a shared respect for the artistry in the process. The Margate Exodus project further developed her interest in complex cultural negotiations and translations. The process enabled the young people to develop skills and reflect on life in Margate and the experiences through which they had gone; these included feelings of loss and hopes for a new life. The negotiation of the portrait, and the selection of possessions, neatly encompassed the link between two versions of home: one lost, the other in transition. Ewald views teaching as an open praxis, 'a political act that enables people to understand the powers that use them and the powers that they use' (Ewald, quoted in Neri 2006: 33).

The visitor/gallery experience brought into stark relief the different experiences and feelings associated with the exodus theme: the children's excitement, sadness, longing and anxiety about displacement. While some of the children disclosed the background to their exile, others did not. Within this ambiguity, the categories of refugee, migrant, asylum seeker and transient became superfluous. The project deliberately explored the theme of exodus from the children's different experiences of enforced as well as economic and circumstantial relocation: 'All children have an ability to tell their stories in a very direct or revealing way. Their language is their own, and they don't censor themselves, so their observations can shift from sweet to violent in a moment' (Ewald 2006: 33). For example, one of the accompanying narratives (part of the audio guide and printed gallery guide) for the children's images read as follows:

> I thought it would be beautiful and safe here. I'm scared of bandits. I'm afraid of the police. Everyday there are police that pass by, always, 'eee oow eee oow eee oou eeeoow'. There's no space for playing here. (Celeste, born 1997, Democratic Republic of Congo; arrived in Margate 2004, current whereabouts unknown) (Ewald 2006: 59)

The diversity of cultural backgrounds of the exiles, ranging from the Middle East to Belfast, also helped to loosen expectations of what or who a refugee/migrant might be. It splintered the 'secure knowing' of the listener/viewer, and interpolated them in the stories as broad human experiences, away from categories and victim narratives.

The process of walking through the town, with the headphones, searching for the next image, also brought the context of the town into play. The children's commentaries talked about their favourite places in the town, or first impressions of arriving, as well as aspects about themselves. However, the listener/viewer following the map and audio commentary was involved in an active and dynamic way with the town, as they inevitably had to navigate unexpected changes and encounters. Myers (2008: 174), who has used similar site-specific modes of walking tours with refugee participants, describes the process, drawing on Ingold, as 'wayfaring'. Ingold (cited in Myers 2008: 174) distinguishes the ways in which wayfaring relates not to 'placeless nor place-bound, but place making'. Myers (2008: 176) states that, 'These contexts and environments of enactment can be understood as relative and as developing, coming into being through a process of discovery and attunement of attention and perception rather than through a mental construction'.

Figure 11.1   A portrait from the Margate Exodus project

Source: Copyright Wendy Ewald, *Towards a Promised Land*. Reprinted with kind permission.

The process undertaken by the viewer/listener while wayfaring their way to view the photographs around Margate, and listening to the children's commentaries, emplaces them in the contextual layers of the town. *Towards a Promised Land* demonstrated how the children have contributed to the formation of place, made accessible the ways in which their lives coexist and co-inhabit the other identities of the town, and articulated 'a plurality of forms of place and provide mechanisms for passing on knowledge and experience to others in similar situations' (Myers 2008: 177).

Ewald's project seems to offer another tactic for dealing with the unwavering paradox of migrant representation. Although the children do discuss personal stories related to exile, the stories are contextualized within a complex set of frames that serve to disorientate a viewer/listener from secure knowing. The selection of stories from a broad cultural base – for example, Belfast, London, Iraq and the Congo – sets up questions about who or what is an exile. The content of the children's contributions ranges from discussions about special possessions to significant (positive and negative) places in Margate and episodic accounts of home and the journey to the United Kingdom. These stories surprise, and also act to extend any fixed notion of refugee. The diverse locations of the images around the town (from the seawall to a fish and chip shop) force the viewer/listener to engage with and at times actively negotiate the plurality of place. The viewer/listener is therefore able to encounter the ways in which the children's stories and lives interpolate with other experiences and perspectives.

Figure 11.2   Part of the Margate Exodus project, near the Giant Wheel

Source: Copyright Wendy Ewald, *Towards a Promised Land*, reprinted with kind permission.

In Ewald's work, the narratives of the children offer a collage of impressions of the town, likes and dislikes, favourite objects and reflections on different ways of being at home. The paradox of migrant performance is that it can imply the production of a secure map of experience by fixing testimonial points and coordinates, which make an encounter with alterity more elusive. These examples offer tactics about how to 'sneak up' on the paradox, by exploring 'the other' in different ways:

This is ... not necessarily so much about knowledge of the other, or information about their situation ... as [it] is about the ethical quality of the experience itself, about a certain kind of affect. It is not perhaps even about, in the first instance, empathy or sympathy with the other, as these forms of relationship may be more about seeing in the other what is like oneself (what Levinas calls the Same). It is perhaps something more purely embodied than that, less explicit. (Burvill 2008: 236)

The imperative of the Margate Exodus is drawn from delivering an aesthetic festival project about a broad human issue, rather than responding to or being initiated by the needs of a specific community (refugee or otherwise). Nevertheless, it was determined by a social perspective and, as Cremona (2007: 14) notes, is typical of social-ethnic festivals in which artists and communities collaborate to 'juxtapose [themselves] to the prevailing culture in order to strengthen and confront it'.

The use of diverse places and transformed locations in Margate was essential to festivalizing the everyday into potentially liminal environments. The spilling out of the Margate Exodus from the first street promenade performances to the children's blown-up images on familiar buildings and landmarks was an important indicator of the event's visibility and ability to temporarily transform the town.

The Margate Exodus deployed multifarious festivalizing techniques to involve and engage the town in a conversation with itself. Ewald's work features the deliberate use of formal and informal spaces. The exhibition took place in a gallery, and enabled the children's work to be valued and appreciated in an official site. The spilling out of the images on to the side of the bingo hall, and also more intimate spaces (Fish and Chip shop, someone's house) provided an opportunity for more intimate and informal social spaces to develop in response to the work. The isolation of walking the audio tour was combined with unexpected moments and encounters with locals, and free-flowing discussions ensued, provoked by the images and their positioning. Admittedly, these are small and transient moments of liminality, but still powerful in their own way. As small episodic moments that linked into the broader experience of the day – particularly the *Waste Man* event (more on this below) – they served to disrupt the normal everyday flow of existence in promising ways. What enhanced the potential of *Towards a Promised Land* was its positioning within the broader festival events. Schoenmakers' (2007) distillation of the 'flow' concept as used by Csikszentmihalyi (1992) is defined to 'indicate an experience in which the borderlines between activities may become less clear and become part of an integrated experience'. Williams (1974) discusses how the emotional experience of viewers who watch different single programs during a television night perceive the night as a whole event. This translates to the festival participant, who may perceive distinct performances as part of an integrated meta-event. The sum of each makes up for a richer overall experience. Obviously the degree to which the organizers have collated a density of events contributes to the 'flow', just as the level of engagement of the participant/festival-goer has an impact on the intensity of the experience.

The concept of flow is also related to the emotional experience of events, in particular the way in which emotional energy is transferred between different performances. Zillmann (1972) discusses the ways in which there is an excitation transfer, even between events that have no casual or thematic connection. Therefore, if there is a density of a events in a festival, there is likely to be a flow of emotions between the diverse activities, building into a concentrated focusing (or 'flow') that minimizes disturbances and more acutely accentuates the 'playing culture' (Sauter 2007: 20). In the Margate Exodus festival, this can be identified through the multiple forms and approaches to performance that saturated the town for the day. The intention of the organizers was to explore the nature of transience and belonging within the context of a mobile, fragile and somewhat tense ecology. The emphasis on aesthetic projects meant that these themes were explored in non-confrontational ways that were designed to be inclusive but not falsely unifying narratives. The festival's efficacy lay in the diffuse and ambiguous denial of moral certainties, and the exploration of what displacement actually *feels* like. Ewald did this very simply in the use of imagery, and the careful and bold placing of these photographs around the town. Gormley built on this sensuality of experience by creating the burning of the *Waste Man* in a fiery ritualistic culmination to the day. Although very different in process and outcome, the events certainly created an opportunity to capitalize on the previous singular events, and complete the festival in an appropriately celebratory and affective way.

The Waste Man

I have to say, the stated aims of Exodus – to call attention both to foreign incomers and the internal exile of Margate's disadvantaged – struck me as just a little patronizing when I heard about them. Nor could I envision the burning of a lot of old chairs becoming the fire from which the phoenix of Margate's civic beauty would be reborn. But that was before I saw *Waste Man* in all his fleshly, wooden glory, towering up above the defunct rollercoasters of Margate's Dreamland Funfair. His peculiar, 3D collage of a body was reminiscent of a giant Arcimboldo, devised to remind us all that all is vanity. (Self 2006)

Anthony Gormley's sculpture was created over six weeks with over 30 tonnes of waste materials collected by Thanet council and local people. The debris was deposited in 'Dreamland', an empty wasteland next to the sea that had been the former site of a vast funfair. Gormley's (2008: 62) sculpture was 'a sign of those who had been dispossessed or refused a place, standing up defiantly to be recognised'.

The process of constructing the *Waste Man* enabled a wide range of people to engage at whatever level they wanted. The work was a collective body made from the raw materials of people's home lives: beds, tables, dining chairs, toilet seats, desks, pianos and rubbish (all the limiting baggage of the householder), 'transformed into energy' (Gormley 2008: 62). Volunteers donated waste from the bottom of their gardens, the contents of their sheds, old furniture, documents,

Figure 11.3 The *Waste Man*

Source: Copyright Anthony Gormley, *The Waste Man*, reprinted with kind permission.

photos and mementos they wanted – for whatever reason – to see ignited. Unlike Ewald's process, in which participation and negotiation were key philosophical components, Gormley took a different approach. The process of local residents helping to build the *Waste Man* meant that the sculpture was filled with the town's debris, purged from attics, sheds and furtive hiding places. The expunging of unwanted objects and mementos, piled up into a beautiful and awe-inspiring structure that was then burned to the ground, seemed to literally embody Margate's secrets and material secretions. The depositing of the waste had been an individual act. The residents had turned up with stuff in the boots of their cars, wheelbarrows pushed across the town, and large transit vans. The contents of the structure were implicated into the town's identity. The statue was not a representation of Margate or its community politics; it was an embodied performance of the town. The audience for the burning represented a full and varied demographic of Margate town. It was unusual to have such a range of people present for a single event. The burning became an odd form of communion – more than a collective response to something like a council-funded fireworks display, it was imbued with a certain wordless significance. The transition from following the play's promenade through the town to the Dreamland site moved from a performance about the morality of exile to one that created an embodied symbolism – a moment of shared collective emotion:

> with a sudden 'crack', smoke began to pour from his belly and lick up his chest. He was on fire – and so were we. I have no paradigm for what it's like to watch an enormous wooden figure burn – save perhaps the film of the *Wicker Man*. But without fear of hyperbole, let me tell you, it was a beautiful sight. The silence of the crowd transformed from being surly, to being awed, and we were all moved. Perhaps that was the mystery of the Margate Exodus? A voluntary exile, away for them quotidian ills of the early 21st century, and towards some deeper, darker, more chthonic place and time. (Self 2006)

The *Waste Man* offers a possible instance of how an exposure to the Other might be created most effectively as an indirect experience, an 'ethical performance whose essence cannot be caught in constative propositions. It is a performative doing' (Critchely 1992: 7).

As Burvill (2008) argues, such ethical performative encounters with the Other often appear fleetingly. The openness and responsiveness to alterity are bounded by the more constant fixed ways of knowing. Performance might seek to dislodge or destabilize, but often these tactics fall short. In escaping the paradox of victimhood narrative and understanding refugee experiences, the Margate Exodus seems to set up a fresh contradiction, in that the meaningful, corporeal encounter with alterity is often accidental and momentary; therefore, the closer the art moves to trying to create a comportment towards the other, the more quickly the meaningful experience disperses.

In constructing a festival about migration for a town with all the symptoms of dislocation and transience, the artists were always going to be fighting against the fragmentary nature of its audience. The Margate Exodus festival was unlike other specialized or commercial festivals, which give rise to a particular community that defines or at least recognizes itself in the very act of attending the event. Such festivals create the condition for communitas through the shared interest in, for example, the same genre of music (opera, hip hop, jazz, folk) that will cut across other diverse elements of the audience (age, gender, nationality). In

Figure 11.4   The *Waste Man* burning

Source: Copyright Anthony Gormley, *The Waste Man*, reprinted with kind permission.

contrast, the Margate Exodus defined its audience by the very tensions that existed in the town: the issues of race and otherness, and a struggle over degenerating resources (housing, schools, even a sense of national identity). Self (2006) rightly calls attention to the potential of the festival to be patronizing: 'It hardly seemed likely that the furious – often quasi-fascistic – denizens of Thanet were going to respond to the art-house filmic conceit by throwing their arms around the inmates of Nayland Rock in a gesture of human solidarity'.

One of the areas of efficacy that might be expected in 'Others festivals' is the degree to which diverse individuals are brought together to form a single homogeneous group and be enriched by a temporary communitas:

> This type of festival goes far beyond purely commercial aims, and often seeks out to 'eventify' salient aspects of the life of a particular society, or to celebrate the culture, beliefs or value system which distinguish it from other societies. Warstat shows how the festivalising process in working-class celebrations in Germany after World War I was aimed at inducing a community framework, in order to secure adhesion by conferring a sense of belonging. (Cremona 2007: 11)

Cremona further notes that the ways in which the community prioritizes particular aspects of its culture influence the focus of an event – for example, the Little Karoo National Arts Festival emphasizes the 'verbal aspect of the productions, which is a way of reaffirming and regenerating interest in the language and the culture behind it'. The festivalization of culture tends towards a process of identification and (re-)construction of a specific group, and can have an isolating effect on individuals who do not identify with or feel connected to the group. The 'art-house conceit' of the Margate Exodus festival may have alienated (and probably did) some of the Margate population. Artangel's tactic was to ensure a diversity of art forms from popular culture (local rock bands) to the crowd-pleasing spectacle of the *Waste Man*. The profile of the artists and the presence of film crews also lent a certain prestige to the town – a sense of 'putting us on the map'. The preparation leading up to the festival was also critical in amassing a growing participation and ownership over elements of the event. Although Margate Exodus was never conceived of as a community festival, its component parts all shared a differing need for local contributions.

Perhaps the real efficacy of Exodus lies in its bold approach to traversing the complex terrain of multiculturalism in its most concrete and hardest manifestations. The deliberate grounding of the festival in a town like Margate, with its simmering racial tensions brought on by years of immigration, was always going to be a disavowal of the myth of one culture for all – or, as Hauptfleisch (2007: 41) argues, 'the rather antiquated idea that there is some kind of "universal" norm of what constitutes art and culture across the globe, but the notion that there can be a single cultural system in a country'. The ideal of Exodus was not to construct a festival for all, or to reflect an aspired-for ideal of a diverse population becoming a unity-culture through a festivalizing process, but to reflect on the shared experience of the modern malaise of forced and economic dislocation:

> Depending on one's definition of it, multiculturalism is – increasingly – a basic condition of nationhood in the vast majority of countries and any attempt to attain nationhood must deal with the complexities posed by a diverse population. So too must any festival seeking to express the 'soul' of the particular nation. Hauptfleisch 2007: 42

Hauptfleisch refers to this new complex as a cultural poly-system, borrowing a term from Even-Zohar (1979) to refer to a web of interlinked but different cultural systems. The emphasis is on distinctive cultural, social and religious systems existing in complex coexistence with each other. The added complexity with multiculturalism is that within each diaspora group there are complex relationships, with their own value systems and tensions between traditional and hybrid forms of culture influenced by its displacement from homelands.

Hauptfleisch (2007) uses the poly-system term to investigate the multifarious and competing elements of a festival, regarding each individual event as something that may disturb as well as feed into an overall thematic conceptual conceit. The poly-system is therefore more likely to be a series of 'linked sub-festivals – an uneasy composite of (potentially) competing activities' (Hauptfleisch 2007: 42). If we accept that festivals deploy meaning through fragmentary and complex systems of interpretation, then the Margate Exodus's spread of activities has a double benefit: to critique any unifying principle of migration, and to explore connections and experiences diffusely and ambiguously through diverse aesthetic languages.

Self (2006) draws attention to the ritualism in Gormley's *Waste Man*, and reminds us of the deep connection between the origins of the festival as a holy or religious activity that generated the conditions for communitas. The trope of communitas is easy to invoke, but less easy to identify and understand. Nevertheless, in intention at least, the feast of migration stories (photographs, performance, music, ritual and symbolism) was designed as an intervention into the everyday. The festival was like an agnostic series of Mediaeval mystery plays, stripped of narrative and morality but celebrating and exploring the theme of transience in a community that was defined by its own chronic sense of dislocation. The Margate Exodus was an exploration of the human residue of modern border controls and economic migration. Through multiple art forms, the festival presented the eddies and circulating promiscuity of mass migration, and linked it back to biblical and historical movements. It represented these universal themes through contemporary individual stories, snapshots and macro-case studies of how the network of national and transnational globalized forces create victims and forced travellers in search of security and stability. The Margate Exodus project importantly attempted to create a connection not simply through promoting a singular culture (or even a single type of migratory story – for example, refugee), but by linking the theme to the ways in which everyone in Margate was subject to the same forces. This was a key consideration for the local 'white' population and the tensions that waves of new arrivals had created. The generalized theme broadened its base and its range of encounters and interactions to take the Margate Exodus from a festival that was for its own audience (a specific ethnic group) to an event of cultural interaction and (to some extent) exchange (an appeal to the experiences of multiple ethno-cultural audiences).

Conclusion

Klaic, Bollo and Bacchella (n.d.: 48) argue that festivals can and should serve a social function as well as an artistic and commercial one. They suggest that a festival enables the residents to create a new vision, a way of looking at the place where they live from another point of view. It can improve the quality of communication among the residents and enhance the mutual understanding of social, ethnic, age and cultural groups.

The *Margate Exodus* provides an important example of a performance festival that helped to create/reinforce the efficacy of local communities while at the same time impacting on the perception of the area within and outside that area. Drawing inspiration from a long tradition of community arts festivals, street plays and the original tenets of carnival and celebration, the Margate Exodus commissioned artists who could both create art and connect it with the local context. The festival positioned the residents as participants *and* spectators – an essential element if concepts of urban regeneration are to take root. Festivals that have a social intention need to be characterized by multiple levels of engagement. Far too often, the economic priorities of regeneration supplant local distinctiveness with a glossy veneer of cosmopolitanism. There is a marginalization of cultural practice that may reflect multiple meanings and the conflicting realities of in situ communities. In the case of the Margate Exodus, the balancing of community participation with a strong and innovative aesthetic agenda can be seen to, at the very least, facilitate a dialogue about the local and global impact of mass migration (we are all travellers …). In doing so, the festival may be viewed – albeit tentatively – as having contributed to an affective construction of hope, which could be shared, discussed and owned by those residents who accepted the invitation to reimagine their sense of place.

References

Audit Commission. 2005. *Cliftonville West and Newington Wards, Thanet.* London: Audit Commission. Available at: www.audit-commission.gov.uk/ neighbourhoodcrime/downloads/example5.doc [accessed: 14 July 2011].

Bassett, K. 1993. Urban cultural strategies and urban regeneration: A case study and critique. *Environment and Planning* A25, 1773–88.

Berger, J. 1992. *Keeping a Rendezvous.* London: Granta Books.

Bernheimer, M. 2003. Beyond the big three. *Financial Times*, 28 June, 2.

Bhaba, H. 1994. *The Location of Culture.* London: Routledge.

Burvill, T. 2008. 'Politics begins as ethics': Levinasian ethics and Australian performances concerning refugees. *Research in Drama Education: The Journal of Applied Theatre and Performance*, 13(2), 233–43.

Conquergood, D. 1998. Health theatre in a Hmong refugee camp: Performance, communication, and culture, *TDR*, 32(3), 174–208.

Cremona, V.A. 2007. Introduction: The festivalising process, in *Festivalising! Theatrical Events, Politics and Culture*, edited by T. Hauptfleisch, S. Lev-Aladgem, J. Martin, W. Sauter and H. Schoenmakers. Rodopi, Amsterdam, 5–13.

Critchely, S. 1992. *The Ethics of Deconstruction.* Oxford: Blackwell.

Csikszentmihalyi, M. 1992. *Flow: The Psychology of Happiness.* London: Rider.

Department of Immigration and Multicultural Affairs (DIMA) 2006. *Settlement Needs of New Arrivals.* Canberra: Commonwealth of Australia.

Department of Immigration and Citizenship (DIAC) 2009. *Longitudinal Survey of Immigrants to Australia.* Canberra: Commonwealth of Australia.

Emin, T. 2008. My life in a column. *The Independent,* 18 April. Available at: www.independent.co.uk/opinion/columnists/tracey-emin/tracey-emin-my-life-in-a-column-811091.html [accessed: 28 August 2011].

Ewald, W. 2006. *Towards a Promised Land.* Gottingen: Steidl.

Even-Zohar, I. 1979. Polysystem theory. *Poetics Today,* l(1–2), 287–310.

Frey, B.S. 2000. *The Rise and Fall of Festivals: Reflections on the Salzburg Festival.* Zurich: Institute for Empirical Research in Economics, University of Zurich.

Gormley, A. 2008. *The Waste Man.* Available at: www.antonygormley.com/viewproject.php?projectid=62&page=1 [accessed: 14 December 2008].

Hauptfleisch, T. 2007. Festivals as eventifying systems, in *Festivalising! Theatrical Events, Politics and Culture,* edited by T. Hauptfleisch, S. Lev-Aladgem, J. Martin, W. Sauter and H. Schoenmakers. Amsterdam: Rodopi, 39–47.

Hauptfleisch, T., Lev-Aladgem, S., Martin, J., Sauter, W. and Schoenmakers, H. 2007. *Festivalising! Theatrical Events, Politics and Culture.* Amsterdam: Rodopi.

Henderson, G. 1991. *Large-scale Festivals. Discussion Document, National Arts and Media Strategy Unit.* London: Arts Council of Great Britain.

Hiller, H.H. 1990. The urban transformation of a landmark event: The 1988 Calgary Winter Olympics. *Urban Affairs Quarterly,* 26, 118–37.

Hudson, R. 1995. Making music work? Alternative regeneration strategies in a deindustrialized locality: The case of Derwentside. *Transactions, Institute of British Geographers,* 20, 460–73.

Isar, R.F. 1976. Culture and the arts festival of the twentieth century. *Cultures,* 3, 125–45.

Klaic, D., Bollo, A. and Bacchella, U. n.d. *Festivals: Challenges of Growth, Distinction, Support Base and Internationalization.* Tartu: Department of Culture, Tartu City Government.

Levin, B. 1982. *Conducted Tour: A Journey Through Twelve Music Festivals of Europe and Australia.* London: Coronet.

Ley, D. and Olds, K. 1988. Landscape as spectacle: World's fairs and the culture of heroic consumption. *Environment and Planning Development: Society and Space,* 6, 191–212.

Ley, D. and Olds, K. 1992. World's fairs and the culture of consumption in the contemporary city, in *Inventing Places,* edited by K. Anderson and F. Gale. Melbourne: Longman Cheshire, 178–93.

Margate Renewal Partnership 2011. *This is Margate.* Available at: www.thisismargate.co.uk/margate_renewal_partnership.aspx [accessed: 15 November 2011].

Miller, M. 2006. Prologue. *Towards a Promised Land.* Gottingen: Steidl.

Myers, M. 2008. Situations for living: Performing emplacement. *Research in Drama Education: The Journal of Applied Theatre and Performance,* 13(2), 171–80.

Neri, L. 2006. Wendy Ewald: Portrait of a praxis. *Towards a Promised Land.* Gottingen: Steidl.

Paddison, R. 1993. City marketing: Image reconstruction and urban regeneration. *Urban Studies*, 30(2), 339–50.

Quinn, B. 2005. Arts festivals and the city. *Urban Studies*, 42(5/6), 927–43.

Richards, G. and Wilson, J. 2004. The impact of cultural events on city image: Rotterdam, Cultural Capital of Europe 2001. *Urban Studies*, 41(10), 1931–51.

Sauter, W. 2007. Festivals as theatrical events: Building theories, in *Festivalising! Theatrical Events, Politics and Culture*, edited by T. Hauptfleisch, S. Lev-Aladgem, J. Martin, W. Sauter and H. Schoenmakers. Amsterdam: Rodopi.

Schoenmakers, H. 2007. Festivals, theatrical events and communicative interactions, in *Festivalising! Theatrical Events, Politics and Culture*, edited by T. Hauptfleisch, S. Lev-Aladgem, J. Martin, W. Sauter and H. Schoenmakers. Amsterdam: Rodopi.

Self, W. 2006. Psychogeography. The wicker chair man. *The Independent*, 14 October. Available at: www.independent.co.uk/opinion/columnists/will-self/will-self-psychogeography-419792.html [accessed: 2 December 2008].

TES 2007, Survey. Available at: www.tes.co.uk [accessed 12 December 2010].

Thompson, J. Hughes, J. and Balfour, M. 2009. *Performance in Place of War.* London: Seagull Press.

Times Education Supplement 2000. Seaside Haven. Available at: www.tes.co.uk/article.aspx?storycode=339383 [accessed: 28 August 2011].

United Nations High Commissioner for Refugees (UNHCR) 2009. *Global Trends: Refugees, Asylum-seekers, Returnees, Internally Displaced and Stateless Persons.* Geneva: Division of Operational Services, Field Information and Coordination Support Section.

Waterman, S. 1998. Carnivals for elites? The cultural politics of arts festivals. *Progress in Human Geography*, 22, 54.

Whitt, J.A. 1987. Mozart in the metropolis: The arts coalition and the urban growth machine. *Urban Affairs Quarterly*, 23, 15–36.

Williams, R. 1974. *Television: Technology and Cultural Form.* London: Fontana.

Woolcock, P. 2008. Interview about Exodus. Available at: www.channel4.com/fourdocs/papers/penny_int.html [accessed: 19 December 2008].

Zillmann, D. 1972. The role of excitation in aggressive behavior. *Proceedings of the Seventeenth International Congress of Applied Psychology, 1971*, Vol. 1. Brussels: The Congress, 925–36.

Chapter 12

The Emotional Ecologies of Festivals

Michelle Duffy

When asked to talk about what it means to participate in one of Melbourne's multicultural festivals, a member of a Middle Eastern and West African music and dance group responded:

> I particularly enjoy playing at a street party in my suburb because it changes the nature of the place where I conduct my daily life. Where I walk to pay bills or do the shopping becomes a place infused with memories of people dancing, playing music, sitting in the sunshine chatting, meeting friends. It adds to the quality of life by adding a new and pleasant dimension to what Sydney Road means to me. (interview 1998)

This comment – 'it changes the nature of the place' – is striking in terms of what a festival can do. We hear very clearly how a festival creates and entangles subjects within notions of identity, place and community. Moreover, this response reveals two significant and related processes inherent within festivals that will be explored in this chapter: festivals are transformative; and this capacity to transform arises out of affective relations facilitated by the festival between people and place.

Much of the festival literature explores the ways in which these events mediate and express ideas about the identity of a place or community through distinctive cultural artefacts and activities, including music, costume, dance and food (Derrett 2003; Duffy, Waitt and Gibson 2007; Duffy and Waitt 2011; Gibson and Connell 2005; Quinn, 2003). This body of research has approached the relationships between arts practices, festival participation and engagement, place and community through the lens of representation (Cohen 1993; Connell and Gibson 2003; Kong 1996). For example, in the case of music festivals, the music genres performed – the song lyrics, instrumentation, melodic structures or performance styles – are understood as constructions of identity that are associated with specific cultural groups or lifestyles. This approach can tell us much about place-based belonging – cultural practices such as music do help forge place-based identifications – but it does not help in understanding and articulating the *experiential* processes involved – the ways in which participation in music activities has an impact on our bodies and what this may mean in terms of processes of subjectivity, identity and hence notions of community building and belonging (Ehrenreich 2008; Thrift 2008). Moreover, this formulation of the festival disregards the ways in which emotional and affective responses are integral to other processes of identity-formation and social connection – how the body and its responses to the sights, sounds, smells, experiences and feelings aroused by the festival event are all fundamental to what has been suggested as a festivalization of the everyday.

While the festival can be conceived as a form of public culture that mediates certain ideas about community, such an event also offers a means to challenge ideas of who belongs and who is excluded (Browne 2007, 2011). This paradoxical nature of festivals – which operate simultaneously as a set of inclusionary and exclusionary practices – has been complicated further by the processes of globalization and the consequent tensions between local and global cultures and practices. Some scholars have argued that globalization and the increased importance of the market and the cultural industry have lessened the Durkheimian notion of festival as an event that binds people together (Giorgi and Sassatelli 2011). Instead, festivals are more likely to be considered as a form of cultural tourism, and as such increasingly are used in local government policies and organizational strategies for initiating economic renewal as an integral component of reinvigorating a place and community (Connell and McManus 2011; Dunphy 2009, Gibson and Connell 2011). In this framework, a range of factors such as cultural planning, leisure and lifestyle sampling – the so-called creative industries – are used to influence the branding of a particular place as a desirable destination for investment and expenditure. The festival is used as a means to commodify traditions and cultural products in order to construct certain representations that then promote the uniqueness of that place or community. In this framework, we are all tourists (Urry 1995), and increasingly we find it difficult to differentiate between representation and 'reality' (Jansson 2002).

In a similar way, the boundaries between the festival event and its geographical and social context have also increasingly become the focus for understanding the influences and effects of the festival event as it spills out beyond its temporal and spatial boundaries – a process called festivalization (Cremona 2007; Roche 2011; Yardimci 2007). As Maurice Roche (2011) argues, festivalization processes draw on collective understandings and practices of space, time and agency, which are then deployed so as to shape communal notions of identity and belonging. Moreover, these events are interpellated into a community's calendar of 'memorable and narratable pasts, with the sociocultural rhythm of life in the present, and with anticipated futures' (Roche 2011: 127–8; see also Duffy et al. 2011). Festivals, rather than transcending the everyday, are now examined for the ways in which they are intimately embedded within the public sphere as normative and at times transformative processes (Giorgi and Sassatelli 2011), an experience so vividly described in the participant's quote that opens this discussion.

The ideas presented in this chapter are grounded in empirical research conducted on music festivals – research that has sought to understand the role of emotional responses and affective qualities in creating these events as sites of belonging (see Duffy 2009, 2010; Duffy and Waitt 2010; Duffy et al. 2011; Duffy, Waitt and Gibson 2007; Waitt and Duffy 2011). One important focus has been to consider the ways in which music taps into our affective, emotional and intuitive selves, as this opens up a means through which to examine how affect and emotion influence social interactions (DeNora 2000; Gilbert 2004; Juslin and Sloboda 2001; Smith 2000). Music organizes experience, and does so through the ways in which its affects are registered not just through cognitive processes but also through its impact on the physical body (Gilbert 2004). A number of researchers have pointed to the distinct roles sound has within the social realm (Attali 1992; DeNora 2000; Frith 1996; Gibson and Connell 2005; Leyshon, Matless and Revill 1998; Martin 1995; Small 1998, to name a few). While culturally based (Attali 1992), music and sound are usually understood as having the capacity to bring people together. We respond in this way because, as Barbara Ehrenreich (2008: 24) argues, 'to submit, bodily, to the music through dance is to be incorporated into the community in a way far deeper than shared myth or common custom can achieve'. Charles Keil and Steven Feld (1994: 167) more concisely describe this as a feeling of 'being in the groove together'. These physical effects alter our perception of places and of others as we are immersed in music's properties, and thus we can either be drawn into its 'participatory discrepancies, [which] gives you that participation consciousness' (Keil and Feld 1994: 22) or we can be left feeling alienated, separate – even violated. These arguments suggest that listening plays a key role in creating community – it requires some level of concentration and engagement – but it also suggests a bodily way of being in the world. This is not to suggest that the goal of a music festival is to lose one's self through sound in some euphoric event (although this may be so for some participants attending certain types of festival events – see Saldanha 2007; St John 2010). While the rhythmic, tonal and tactile qualities of sound and music do facilitate and enable personal and social things 'to happen' (Ansdell 2004: 72), sound can equally be intrusive, disruptive and alienating.

While the research discussed here has focused on music festivals in particular, these findings have led to thinking more carefully about the broader sonic qualities of festivals and community places. By drawing attention to our affective and emotional responses to music and sound, we can uncover the power dynamics of the interactions and relationships of bodies in space, and of how these are important in shaping relations within and beyond communities (Duffy 2005). Recent work in a range of disciplines has drawn attention to listening practices because this offers 'important insights as to how festival spaces may create an affective ambience that encourages an openness to others, and sustain a social identification through the intangible feeling that encompasses an emotional space of belonging together' (Waitt and Duffy 2011: 458; see also Ansdell 2004; Benzon 2001; Ehrenreich 2007). Hence listening is an integral factor to what it means to belong or to be excluded, but requires a different approach to thinking about what occurs in these shared spaces of meaning (Nancy 2007). What is proposed in this chapter is that a focus on sound – and not just music – brings our attention to the body as it inhabits place in ways that are intuitive, emotional and *connected* (Thrift 2008). Sound brings our attention back to the flesh of our bodies, and how they respond to rhythms, melodies and timbres, and to others likewise engaged (Benzon 2001; Duffy, Waitt and Gibson 2007; Ehrenreich 2008; Wood, Duffy and Smith 2007). It is not simply that music and sound represent identity, and therefore notions of belonging, as some researchers have suggested; rather, it is that subjectivities are constituted within the very *unfolding* of the sonic event (Ansdell 2004; Hall 1996; Jazeel 2005).

This chapter suggests that an important means for conceptualizing these socio-spatial relations is in terms of these sonic processes, and for seeking out how these operate, draws on the work of Nigel Thrift's (1999) notion of an ecology of place and Jean-Paul Thibaud's (2002) ecological approach to perception, both of which use the earlier work of James Gibson (1986). The significance of these approaches is threefold: it lies in their concern with the situatedness of our knowing, the role of our senses in constituting knowledge (about who we are, how we belong, what our 'place' is) and the affordances attributed to these sensory perceptions (what Thibaud calls the ambience or quality of a situation). Bringing these approaches together, a framework of listening is offered as a means to re-examine and rethink the processes of belonging in and through the festival event.

To begin to address the role of these experiential processes in constituting community and belonging, this chapter is organized as follows. First, it provides a discussion of material from two festival events, and critically explores ethnographic and interview material from two different music festivals: the Swiss-Italian Festa held in the twin towns of Daylesford-Hepburn Springs about a 90-minute drive north-west of Melbourne, and the classical music Four Winds Festival held in the New South Wales coastal town of Bermagui, and about 400 kilometres south of Sydney. Both festival locations are characterized by diverse socio-economic groups – the result of various migrations into these locations; an initial European settlement displacing Indigenous people in the late nineteenth century; loggers, farmers (as well as fisherman in the Bermagui area) settling in the early twentieth century; then the hippies and other alternative groups arriving from the 1960s. More recently, both towns have been redefined as 'tree-' and 'sea-change' towns due to the influx of particularly older residents from nearby capital cities. However, while these festivals celebrated distinct forms of communal identity, the focus of both research projects involved paying close attention to how bodily responses to the sound and music of these festivals enabled participants to feel connected to a particular place and community. In both examples, the framework of listening points to reciprocal and ephemeral, but nonetheless intense, relationships between the body, sound and place. This leads to the question of what can be uncovered about the processes of belonging and community-making using this framework.

To answer this, the final section discusses the practices of listening. Listening practices and affective responses are brought together in a discussion of the concept of emotional ecology – a concept that draws on the work of Thrift (1999) and Thibaud (2002) – and offered as a means to assist in understanding festivalization processes and their role in constituting notions of community, not just in the time-space of the festival event but also in shaping our relations in and of place as we go about our daily lives.

Festival Bodies and Affective Spaces

The Swiss Italian Festa: (Re)imagined Connections

The Swiss Italian Festa was first held in 1993 in the twin towns of Daylesford-Hepburn Springs, just over an hour's drive north-west from Melbourne, as a community initiative to encourage and celebrate the region's links to the Swiss and Italian settlers of the district, who followed the search for gold in the 1850s. Held in April–May at the time of this research (although since 2009 the festival has been held in October), and commencing with a street parade along the main road between the two towns, residents young and old participate in a range of song and dance, and the wearing of diverse costumes, as well as the waving of banners covered with drawings created by local schoolchildren, all of which combine to represent various aspects of a specifically Swiss-Italian heritage.

However, any such reference to this particular regional identity is woven through with contradictions. While many of these residents are fourth- and fifth-generation Swiss Italians who can trace their heritage back to the cantons of Ticino and Grigione, most are no longer able perform this region's folk music and dance repertoire, nor do they even speak its dialect (Keller 2007). Instead, much of this repertoire is provided by German-Swiss performers – something that musicologist Marcello Sorce Keller points out is difficult to imagine in Switzerland itself, as 'the Germanic-sounding *Schweizerische Volksmusik* is generally abhorred' (Keller 2007: 195). Yet also accepted are more generalized representations of both Swiss-Italian and Italian culture, and these break any conventional notion of a single ethnic or cultural repertoire; Swiss German yodellers, a Swiss didjeridu player and primary school renditions of popular Dean Martin tunes are all enthusiastically watched and applauded. Alongside these cultural hybrids, some adults and children choose to wear masks, referencing both the carnivalesque and the historical links to public culture in Northern Europe. As the 2009 Festa president Rob McDonald commented, 'You would be hard pressed to find a more exuberant and vibrant display of community participation in a local event' (www.hepburnadvocate.com.au). This riotous mix does enchant, and in *looking* at this event, what is emphasized is a rediscovery and claiming of a European heritage, albeit via a chaotic mix of identities – Swiss-Italianness, Swissness, Italianness, pop Italianness, Daylesford localness, Swiss-Germanness – and many varied combinations. But how does such an event create and perhaps reaffirm connection to the *contemporary* place and community of Daylesford-Hepburn Springs? That is, how do the rhythmic, tonal and tactile qualities of sound and music facilitate and enable the constitution of community 'to happen' (Ansdell 2004)?

In exploring this particular festival, the methodological focus was of the researcher as a listening body. This meant using a method of participant sensing and drawing on the significance of the researcher's own embodied experiences and how these might contribute to making sense of (other) bodily interaction with festival places (Longhurst, Ho and Johnston 2008; Wood, Duffy and Smith 2007). The decision was taken to focus on the Festa's opening event, the street parade, in order to consider how its sounds triggered bodily responses and connections; this was determined by paying attention to the researcher's emotions, pulse, gestures and bodily affects. To gain some sense of how audience members were affected by the sounds of the parade, and in turn how this may affect others, a record of observations was made, including photographs, sound and video recordings (for a more detailed discussion of the methodology used, refer to Duffy et al. 2011). Research notes taken of this event attempt to capture these individual and group affects:

> I hear the very excited shouts and squeals of school children as harried officials try to get them to fall in line behind banners. They've started! A silent clown (he never speaks the entire time of the event) swings his arms around in imitation of the flag bearers, joining in with them as they lead the parade down to the Reserve. Many of us line the footpaths on either side of the road, some walking alongside the costumed groups who keep in time with the musicians. Many others fall in behind the marchers, strolling along to the sounds of the Festa's theme song. Those who remain on the footpaths laugh, greet and call out to those walking past. The parade flows on; dogs barking, members of the Swiss Yodel Choir Matterhorn carrying their large ringing cowbells, some bystanders clap and cheer as the procession makes its way along the street. I, too, join in the parade. We turn and head off the street, and so end up winding our way through the park and towards the reserve. I overhear two women: 'Isn't there supposed to be lanterns?' 'No, that's tomorrow evening, to end the Festa. It will be like the New Year's Eve parade'. 'Ah! Yes, New Year's Eve! Isn't that great! A real community feel'. Although the bands are only dimly heard where I'm walking, we keep up the pace they initiated, weaving between goats, dogs, children in costume, adults wearing masks, but all of us happily making our way, following those ahead. When we all finally arrive at the Hepburn Recreation Reserve, the school marching gives a final flourish, and then we are welcomed by the Festa organisers. After these official greetings, we all settle down into the familiar activities of concert attendance. (Research diary notes, April 2006)

While many of the festival participants were not necessarily direct descendants of Swiss Italian migrants, the visual cues incorporated into the parade, such as costumes and masks, and the sounds of the parade, such as the choir of cow bells or the marching band, did locate the performances more broadly within a Northern European heritage. However, the parade's sonic qualities gave rise to a different experience of connection and belonging, an experiential shaping of place that worked across these more varied and combined cultural identities. And through *listening* to the Swiss-Italian Festa parade, very obvious aural rhythmic clues

Figure 12.1 Waiting for the Swiss Italian Festa Parade to start, April 2006

Source: Photograph by author.

emerged that then located and interpellated these various people and identities within this one place.

Prior to starting, the bodies of those present moved in separate and less organized rhythms – excited school children, harried officials, those waiting along the footpaths talking among themselves. Once the parade music started, this very quickly changed. Many of those who lined the footpaths on either side of the road started to walk alongside the costumed groups, who were moving in time with the musicians. Those who remained on the footpaths laughed and called out to those walking past. The parade flowed on amidst a soundscape directed towards the parade's movement: dogs barking, cowbells still ringing, bystanders clapping and cheering as the procession made its way. The sonic, rhythmic qualities of the parade brought the event together into a sense of coherence, facilitating relations between bodies in ways that emphasized connection. From a physiological level, this point of connection was observed through the ways in which participants were affected by the rhythm, tempo and simple melodic riff specially written for the parade, and played by the school marching band.

Even before the actual parade started to move down the main street, band members had played the beat and melody, and onlookers perhaps involuntarily became familiar with its shape and mood. And, although performed in a somewhat carelessly structured tempo, its repetition nonetheless generated and sustained some sense of an ongoing marching beat. As the parade gained momentum, the steady flow of parade participants created a rhythm of interconnected bodily movement. Those in the parade moved past those on the footpath, and many of the onlookers caught up in these rhythms chose to tag onto the end of the parade, so augmenting and expanding this communal body, enveloped in the sonorities brought together – however chaotically – and enabling even further points of connection, such as the reference to the New Year's Eve parade and exclamations at various points of 'Isn't this great! A real community feel!'

Figure 12.2   Final destination of the Swiss Italian Festa parade, April 2006

Source: Photograph by author.

An analysis of this material in terms of rhythm, and more specifically the methodology of rhythmanalysis proposed by Henri Lefebvre (2004), assists in understanding how these feelings of community and connection are being constituted. Rhythm simply means regular repetition, yet we attribute meaning to these recurring patterns, be they inherent in the environment (such as seasonal and diurnal patterns) or used to depict forms of cultural identity (as in percussive and sonic elements we come to associate with, for example, the dance beats of Latin America or the cross-rhythms of various Sudanese genres). However, rhythm is more than a representational mode; the term effectively captures the sense of impact and change *between* things. Pulses quicken, hearts race, our interest is momentarily caught. Thus rhythm influences our individual bodily rhythms and tempos that can in turn ripple out again to other bodies, so engaging people (music, place, things) within a network of affect 'as potential and emergent' (Clough 2010: 209; see also Gilbert 2004). The potential for change inherent in this affective sonic network is vital to understanding the processes of festivals. As Lefebvre suggests, the conscious and unconscious perceptions we have of our bodily rhythms mean that we think with our bodies 'not in the abstract, but in lived temporality' (Lefebvre 2004: 21). Hence rhythm organizes relations within the space and time of the festival. These ongoing fluid co-constitutions of communal bodies arising in response to rhythmic structures – keeping in mind the porosity of the body to sound waves that are experienced as a pulse (Kahn 1999) – in turn help give rise to the constitution of bodily spatial belongings and spatial subjectivities.

In this way, the capacity of the body to sense rhythm, and our affective and emotional responses to this, have a role in the emergence of processes that regulate the dynamics of social interaction. As Lefebvre argues, the creation of a space through music 'presupposes a unity of time and space, an alliance' (2004: 60), which he then suggests occurs in and through this rhythmic framework. In this instance, the rhythms of the parade, because of the ways in which they give coherence to the unfolding of the Festa event, anchor the everyday, lived time of those present. Yet the affective connections made in and through rhythm and its associated bodily movement are only one way of constituting a sense of belonging. Bodily affectivity and the body's capacity to act also operate within more intimate but nonetheless threshold spaces between the body and what is beyond the body's borders. What this focus can uncover is taken up in the study of the Four Winds festival.

The Four Winds Festival: Feeling in Place

The biannual Four Winds Festival is held at Bermagui, a coastal town of around 2000 people, located about 400 kilometres south of Sydney. First staged in 1991, this event began when a group of private landowners came together with the aim of generating an Australian classical music 'scene' outside the eastern seaboard's metropolitan regions. Since then, far from the handful of friends that attended the first festival, the weekend festival now draws around 1000 attendees each day to the ticketed program held over the Easter long weekend, primarily from the hinterland of Bega Valley Shire (30 per cent), Canberra (30 per cent) and Sydney (30 per cent). Those who attend are predominantly people aged over 40 years, many tertiary educated and often semi-retired. The main festival venue is approximately 9 kilometres outside the township of Bermagui in a natural amphitheatre, and the program offers a repertoire of mostly Western classical music traditions, along with carefully chosen non-Western (or 'world music') traditional performances, such as Middle Eastern, Turkish and South Indian music genres. Since 2008, this two-day ticketed event has been preceded by a free afternoon concert held in a public park on the town's foreshore.

The research discussed here originated in an invitation from one sea-changer very much involved with the festival and the local community, who asked us to examine the 2008 festival for ways in which festival attendees made connections to place and community through the sounds and music of the festival. The method used to consider this was based on solicited diary methodologies, but it was one that asked participants to explore the more sonic, intuitive and affective aspects of sounds in our social lives (refer also to Duffy and Waitt 2011; Waitt and Duffy 2011; Wood, Duffy and Smith 2007). This involved two approaches. First, each participant was equipped with a small hand-held digital recorder and asked to record those performances or sounds that they considered meaningful, particularly those moments that captured their attention or gave rise to some emotional response. Second, participants were then asked to talk about the significance of what was recorded, and the importance of the festival to them and to the place in which it was held. What this project aimed to discover was how sound and music act upon bodies so that they are mobilized to respond. This material then became the basis for thinking through how the embodied affects aroused by the festival might have a capacity for social transformation, and what this could mean in terms of communal belonging.

These sound diaries were collected at the free Friday concert held prior to the main (and costly) weekend event. In contrast to the festival proper, this concert was a more relaxed affair for both performers and audience, with the latter attending in family groups or with friends and arranging themselves with picnic rugs and baskets close to the stage or with barbecues around the perimeter of the audience area. Children were given more freedom to play compared with the later ticketed festival event, and those who wanted simply to stand back from the performance, drinking and talking with friends, were able to do so. This free concert brought together friends and families from surrounding towns, and included performers from the festival program as well as the local children's choir. It was opened by a Welcome to Country performed by a representative from the Yuin Nation, the local Aboriginal community.

The 2008 festival organizers also sought to strongly connect this concert to its ocean setting, one that had originally brought European settlers into the area as farmers, loggers and fishers on the east coast of Australia (Waitt and Hartig 2000). So, following the Welcome, audience members were invited to follower recorder player Genevieve Lacey, who led them to the water's edge and shakuhachi (bamboo flute) master Riley Lee, as he emerged playing from beneath the water. A second festival welcome was performed by these artists on the foreshore, who were joined by didjeridu player William Barton. This opening concluded with all heading back to the oval accompanied by members of the percussion group TaikOz; here, the concert proper started. While offering some excerpts from the festival program, this concert was also an opportunity for the performers to work with others on the program – for example, TaikOz, Turkish musician and composer Omar Faruk Tekbilek and the Four Winds Philharmonia.

Figure 12.3 Audience of Four Winds Festival's free concert on the Bermagui foreshore, March 2008

Source: Photograph by author.

Many of those who made their sound recordings at this event also captured the immediate impact of listening to these performances, most often noting that these moments were 'spine-tingling', or else noting the ways in which particular sounds, such as those of the didjeridu, were felt to resonate in specific parts of their listening bodies. Many also talked later of the difficulty in putting their experiences into words – that these were moments 'almost beyond words'. One participant, who was also one of the festival performers, later explained why she had recorded what ended up being the muffled sounds of clapping and members of the audience calling out:

> When you come off stage, you have all this stuff in your head! And it, you're really in it still, long after you leave the stage and go behind stage, and ... that sort of the energy – I don't know if it's going to capture it, but that energy coming off in that wash, coming out the back with all those people out the back to pack your instruments and thinking what's next and getting rid of one piece of music and heading to the other. (Performer interview, March 2008)

In these comments, the ways in which 'bodies, music, affect and emotion ... are entangled in an affective assemblage of sound that then enables the possibility of communal experience are clearly depicted' (Waitt and Duffy 2011: 461). This opportunity for self-reflexive listening encouraged participants to think anew about the shared space brought about by the performances, as demonstrated by another participant who, during a later discussion, explained:

> One of the things that ... in your experiment, draws my attention to it ... like in the performance on Friday at the oval and here, getting moved by the music, and then I look around, I think this is my community, you know I look around and I, there is the women in the local corner shop and there is the people I know. And, I just think you lucky are we, how could we ... and also this community has drawn this thing [together]. (audience member interview, March 2008)

Figure 12.4   Free concert event at the Four Winds Festival, March 2008

Source: Photograph by author.

The festival is understood as providing possibilities through which place-based belongings are negotiated and (re)constituted (Thrift 2000). In this sense, the festival is not just an extraordinary event, a spectacle that lifts the event out of everyday lives and activities, but simultaneously an intensification of the everyday. Hence the ways in which those who attend the festival listen are crucial to forging subjectivity–spatial relationships. Therefore, rather than framing the music and the music festival as 'rarefied and perhaps avant-garde moments of performance, art, and counter-aesthetic', as Tim Cresswell suggests (in Merriman et al. 2008: 195), examining an engagement in music through listening is about the threading in of an everyday politics and power; it is about an emotional, aesthetically expressed and affectively shaping of people and place. As we hear in this participant's reflections on listening, belonging is defined in ways that lead her to feel 'in place' through bodily responses that are activated and moved by the music.

Further, this material demonstrates that the sonic space of the festival is always in part negotiated through an individual's embodied set of histories. The self-reflexive listening initiated by the research project's methodology brought about an increased awareness of spatial-subjective interconnections. These listening practices also triggered intense responses, as well as periods of solitary detachment, contemplation and remembering, as another audience participant suggested in her later discussion:

> I sit there with my eyes shut and I can see the type of environment, then I come back and I am looking at the environment out there – so that is very environmental that journey – [pause] [musician] Timothy leads me but you didn't know where it was going, so you followed along behind and that wasn't visual at all, it is just following along the sound and [pause] it was just that it has this peculiar aural journey where I don't know where we are going and you are taken along like the pied piper or whatever, [pause] it was very funny because, because usually I don't listen like that at all. (audience member interview, March 2008)

In each of these examples, sound and music are integral to place-making because of the ways in which affect is triggered, which then helps to facilitate making sense of one's self in the world. The affective circuits triggered by music have a fundamental part to play in understanding the dynamics of social interaction through which people make sense of their place with and in the world. It is not so much what is heard, but the affective and emotional responses to this listening, that help forge a sense of belonging and the social bonds of community (Wood and Smith 2004).

When people were asked to be attentive to festival sounds in terms of what these mean to them, these responses ostensibly focused on notions of community and place; however, other very personal sets of relationships were also uncovered that expressed values attached to both imagined and lived notions of that particular place. In the telling of what these sounds meant, festival participants in these festivals talked about their relationships and connections in terms of a particularity of community, where even in times of globalized culture, localized practices aroused strong responses in generating notions of what 'community' may mean and how it felt to be present. Through these narratives of belonging, we begin to discern how people map themselves within these spaces.

Emotional Ecologies: Sound, Listening and Affect

This final section takes up these ideas about affects, emotions and belonging generated through momentary points of individual/place and individual/

community within the music festival space. It is within these intersections that affect comes into play, and this is where affect is mobilized and translated into the various feelings of belonging that are expressed. Understanding how this works as an event unfolds is significant to understanding the constitution of community and the ongoing negotiation of belonging that surrounds it. As Nigel Thrift (2004) argues, here is located a crucial politics of affect made manifest within our everyday, and we need to critically engage with such a politics if we are to understand those new collectivities that arise (see also Back 2007). Hence affect in these instances is not simply an aesthetics of place or community, but rather instrumental in mobilizing people's affective and emotional responses. As suggested in the previous discussion of festival material, a focus on *listening* offers an opportunity to rethink these processes of belonging because of the very nature of sound. Sound has physiological and affective impacts on bodies that are immediate, that do not move through neurological pathways of cognitive thought (Levitin 2006). Moreover, sound (re)connects us to the place and people around us for, as Thibaud (2002: 2) argues,

> an ambience-oriented approach places the perceiving subject right in the middle of the world he or she perceives and puts the emphasis on its enveloping nature, rather than a face to face relation. If the ambience surrounds and submerges us, it necessarily results in perception from the inside, which throws doubt on the possibility of the subject stepping back from his or her environment.

So attention to sound means it is difficult for us to not acknowledge the ways in which we are embedded within our world. But this attention is not some passive act. Hearing and listening are understood as quite distinctive practices. Jean-Luc Nancy (2007) defines *hearing* in terms of understanding and comprehension, while *listening* (the French term *écouter*) is an experience of sound without its full translation or complete understanding. As he suggests, these are affective acts: 'to listen is *tendre l'oreille* – literally to stretch the ear … it is an intensification and a concern, a curiosity or an anxiety' (2007: 5). Moreover, Nancy associates the practices of listening with often ambiguous emotional and bodily responses, as we strive towards positioning ourselves, physically and psychologically, in relation to ourselves and other (human and non-human) selves. This tension inherent in our listening practices arises out of the very properties of sound and music, because to listen is much more than simply a sense gained through the ears; it occurs around and through our entire bodies (DeNora 2000; Duffy 2000, 2005; Nancy 2007; Smith 1994; 2000; Wood, Duffy and Smith 2007). Therefore, it is not simply that music and sound represent identity and therefore notions of belonging, as some researchers suggest. Rather, it is that subjectivities are constituted within the very *unfolding* of the sonic event (Ansdell 2004; Duffy et al. 2011; Jazeel 2005; Waitt and Duffy 2011).

These listening practices mean that auditory place-making is rendered quite differently from that created through our sense of vision, and this has implications for our experience of place and the constitution of community in three ways. First, as Douglas Kahn (1999: 27) argues, listening is crucial to recognizing the ways in which we inhabit space not as something outside of the body that is observed, but through *being in* place, 'with an all-round corporeality and spatiality' (see also Nancy 2007). In this way, we become more aware of our position in the textures of space; we make, absorb, reverberate and echo in, through and with sound. Second, as Nancy (2007: 10) suggests, sound is 'having to do with participation, sharing, or contagion'. In other words, listening impels us to attend to our world differently because we are directed to how people conceive of themselves and the world as connected and not as separate objects in space. Finally, these are affective processes in the Spinozan sense; the listening body inhabits a space in which responses to sound – or what Massumi (2002) calls 'visceral perception' – can augment or diminish a capacity to act. This has important implications for understanding the embodied affects of relations in and through festival spaces, and therefore how individuals are affected by other social bodies (see also Gilbert 2004). A focus on listening, then, brings our attention to the body as it inhabits place in ways that are intuitive, emotional and connected (Thrift 2008).

If we rethink music as part of the listening processes of place and identity formation, as more recent work has done, music becomes a medium in which social agency can be enacted. Hence the soundscapes of festivals and our everyday lives are not passive outcomes of simply hearing sounds. Rather, as Barry Truax (2001) suggests, these are an outcome of simultaneously encountering, listening, giving meaning to, responding to and interacting with the silences, and the rhythmic and tonal qualities, of music and sound. Moreover, this approach emphasizes immediacy and presence in the relationship of sound, festival, place and sociality. That is, place and social relations are constituted through sound in the very acts of people engaging with the festival event. Finally, this contributes to festivals as political mechanisms that can help constitute individual feelings of acceptance and belonging within an imagined, collective sense of 'we' (or, conversely, they can generate feelings of alienation and social exclusion).

Listening is significant to this politics. By listening closely, our attention is drawn to the ways in which our subjectivities are not separate entities situated *in* place, but rather co-constituted *through* place. This affective and emergent quality of community is illustrated in this quote from one of the Four Winds Festival participants, reflecting on what she had heard and its impact on her:

> On Friday night where a sense of belonging came through strongly for me is after the Pied Piper part of … and they were coming back in, the groups coming in from the two directions, and the drummers, and it was so strong, with the drums, and I have been to lots of events, even in my own place, where there has been lots of drumming, so it brought that deep intimacy with this world. (audience member interview, March 2008)

This approach emphasizes immediacy and presence in the relationship of music, place and sociality. That is, place and social relations are constituted through music in the very acts of people engaging with the event of the musical performance. But, as we have heard in participants' responses, this does not tell us enough about how the festival operates within its broader context. It is not simply that a study of festivals can be accomplished by examining a performance of music. Rather, it lies in examining how people are responding, reacting and performing within a sonic context, at a given time and place, and that these responses offer suggestions as to how music is conducive to certain affections or sensations that then give rise to feelings of belonging.

The discussion of these festival events and the responses generated within festival participants has sought to emphasize listening as a process that has the potential to reawaken an embodied and affective sensibility with regard to concepts of community. This emphasis requires considering the festival as part of an assemblage, and so of seeking relational rather than representational understandings (Thrift 1999) of how place and community-making processes work. The research presented here seeks to make such a contribution, through a framework of emotional ecology. As Thrift (1999: 316–17) argues, citing sociologist Avery Gordon, when we think about the ecology of place, we are engaging with a 'rich and varied spectral gathering, an articulation of presence as the entangled exchange of noisy silences and seething absences'. Music and culture are not simply aesthetic or vague, feel-good activities, but rather convey powerful and persuasive ideas – 'the noisy silences and seething absences' of which we are often unaware – that mobilize affect, and hence contribute to the sensation that we are connected (or that we may feel disconnected). The methodological approach used in this research, which draws on Thibaud's (2002) ecological approach to perception, attempts to extend our understanding of the experiences of festivals in terms of interpellating ourselves into the affective qualities of the festival, in and through which we then orient ourselves. In this way, the festival's affective qualities and the potential these have for change and transformation can be translated into feeling 'I/we belong' – or perhaps 'I/we wish to belong' – one of the overall goals of these events.

The approach taken in examining these festivals has provided a means to bring together the physiological responses with the social and cultural processes of giving meaning to particular sounds. In doing so, sonorous spatial subjectivities enable us to examine place not as a static 'stage' or 'backdrop' for social activities, but as constituted by heterogeneous and negotiated sets of relationships that enable points of dis/connection. An emotional ecology refers to this transformation; we come to feel 'in place'. Thus, new insights can be gained as to how belonging is always more than marking spaces or bodies with symbols representing various social groups. Understanding the ways in which affective processes are generated, intensified or disrupted is therefore crucial to the role of a festival in enabling a sense of belonging.

Conclusion

This chapter has sought to critically explore the impact sound has on social bodies and what such an impact means in terms of the intuitive, emotional and psycho-analytical processes of subjectivity and so community-building (Thrift 2008). Moreover – and complicating any analysis – the experiential nature of sound is a paradoxical thing; it is transient and ephemeral, yet can have such a profound effect on us as we go about our daily lives. Even so, as Susan Smith (2000: 621) argues, the significance of sonic processes is that they can 'bring spaces, peoples, places "into form"'. A focus on how sound does this directs our attention to processes of connectivity (or, in some instances, alienation). This focus demonstrates how, as Even Rudd (2004: 12) explains, the processes of sound-making 'bridge the gap between individuals and communities to create a space for common musicking and sharing of artistic and human values'. Enabling an individual to connect with a shared collective identity is a significant aspect of participating in a festival. Music is one means to provide participants with possibilities to (re)connect with each other, sustaining or generating a shared sense of belonging in and through the festival space – a belonging that then may spill out into helping individuals make sense of their everyday lives.

The affective circuits triggered by music and sound have a fundamental part to play in understanding the dynamics of social interaction through which people make sense of their place in the world. It is not so much what is heard, but our affective and emotional responses to this listening, that help forge a sense of belonging and the social bonds of community (Wood and Smith 2004). To theorize through music is to work through such moments, the 'emergence of expressive proper qualities, the formation of matters of expression that develop into motifs and counterpoints' (Deleuze and Guattari 1987: 322), to take on the lumpiness, the transitory nature and the unexpectedness of a process and experience that appear to resist the usual methods of analysis. Festivals are, then, political mechanisms that can help constitute individual feelings of acceptance and belonging within an imagined, collective sense of 'we'. But this is not simply about location. As this discussion with our participants demonstrates, belonging is also constituted beyond the immediate and physical boundaries of place – through memories, emotion and personal relations. In this way, belonging is mobile – it moves from place to place, it moves in time – and at the same time is immobile, as it is attached to particular bodies, to our actions, feelings and our experiences.

Listening in terms of an emotional ecology can play a fundamental role in understanding the dynamics of social interaction. Listening invites dialogue with self, other and place. Becoming aware of the possibilities inherent in these encounters is what an emotional economy addresses; it offers, as sociologist John Shotter (1995: 14) proposes, a means 'to discover what something is, but different possible ways in which we might relate ourselves to our surroundings – how to be different in ourselves, how to live in different worlds'. It is this circuit of encounter – of feelings, emotions, place, people – that is activated through affect and in which intimate connections to place ask us to rethink notions of community and belonging. It involves, as Thrift (2008: 12) contends, taking note of how the event will sing you as integrally embedded, embodied and sensory beings.

Acknowledgements

Appreciation is extended to all those who participated in these research projects and who gave so generously of their time and themselves. Many thanks are also given to Gordon Waitt for our collaborative projects and the many conversations we have had around these ideas.

References

The Advocate 2009. Towns comes together for Hepburn's Swiss Italian Festa. Available at: www.hepburnadvocate.com.au/news/local/news/news-features/towns-comes-together-for-hepburns-swiss-italian-festa/1648968.aspx [accessed: 30 December 2011].

Ansdell, G. 2004. Rethinking music and community: Theoretical perspectives in support of community music therapy, in *Community Music Therapy*, edited by M. Pavlicevic and G. Ansdell. London: Jessica Kingsley, 65–90.

Attali, J. 1992. *Noise: The Political Economy of Music*. Minneapolis, MN: University of Minnesota Press.

Back, L. 2003. *The Art of Listening*. Oxford: Berg.

Benzon, W. 2001. *Beethoven's Anvil: Music in Mind and Culture*. New York: Basic Books.

Browne, K. 2007. A party with politics? (Re)making LGBTQ Pride spaces in Dublin and Brighton. *Social & Cultural Geography*, 8(1), 63–87.

Browne, K. 2011. Beyond rural idylls: Imperfect lesbian utopias at michigan womyn's music festival. *Journal of Rural Studies*, 27(1), 13–23.

Clough, P. 2010. The affective turn: Political economy, biomedia and bodies, in *The Affect Theory Reader*, edited by M. Gregg and G.J. Seigworth. Durham, NC: Duke University Press, 206–25.

Connell, J. and Gibson, C. 2003. *Sound Tracks: Popular Music, Identity and Place*. London: Routledge.

Connell, J. and McManus, P. 2011. *Rural Revival? Place Marketing, Tree Change and Regional Migration in Australia*. Farnham: Ashgate.

Cohen, S. 1993. Ethnography and popular music studies. *Popular Music*, 12, 123–38.

Cremorna, V.A. 2007. Introduction: The festivalising process, in *Festivalising! Theatrical Events, Politics and Culture*, edited by T. Hauptfleisch, S. Lev-Aladgem, J. Martin, W. Sauter and H. Schoenmakers. Amsterdam: Rodopi, 5–13.

DeNora, T. 2000. *Music in Everyday Life*. Cambridge: Cambridge University Press.

Deleuze, G. and Guattari, F. 1987. *A Thousand Plateaus: Capitalism and Schizophrenia*. Minneapolis, MN: University of Minnesota Press.

Derrett, R. 2003. Festivals & regional destinations: How festivals demonstrate a sense of community & place. *Rural Society*, 13(1), 35–53.

Duffy, M. 2005. Performing identity within a multicultural framework. *Social & Cultural Geography*, 6(5), 677–92.

Duffy, M. 2009. *Music of Place: Community Identity in Contemporary Australian Music Festivals*. Germany: VDM Verlag.

Duffy, M. 2010. Sound ecologies. *Cultural Studies Review* 16(1). Available at: epress. lib.uts.edu.au/journals/index.php/csrj/index [accessed: 12 September 2011].

Duffy, M. and Waitt, G. 2011. Sound diaries: A method for listening to place. *Aether: The Journal of Media Geography*, special issue on Geographies of Music, Geographers Who Play Music, 7, 119–36.

Duffy, M., Waitt, G. and Gibson, C. 2007. Get into the groove: The role of sound in generating a sense of belonging through street parades. *Altitude*. Available at: www.altitude21c.com [accessed: 12 September 2011].

Duffy, M., Waitt, G., Gorman-Murray, A. and Gibson, C. 2011. Bodily rhythms: Corporeal capacities to engage with festival spaces. *Emotion, Space and Society*, 4(1), 17–24.

Dunphy, K. 2009. Developing and revitalizing rural communities through arts and creativity: Australia, in *Developing and Revitalizing Rural Communities Through Arts and Creativity: An International Literature Review and Inventory of Resources*, edited by N. Duxbury, H. Campbell, K. Dunphy, P. Overton and L. Varbanova. Vancouver: Creative City Network of Canada, Centre for Policy Studies on Culture and Communities, Simon Fraser University. Available at: www.culturaldevelopment.net.au/publications/revitalising-rural-communities [accessed: 9 June 2011].

Ehrenreich, B. 2007. *Dancing in the Streets: A History of Collective Joy*. London: Granta Books.

Frith, S. 1996. *Performing Rites: Evaluating Popular Music*. Oxford: Oxford University Press.

Gibson, C. and Connell, J. 2005. *Music and Tourism*. Clevedon, OH: Channel View.

Gibson, C. and Connell, J. (eds) 2011. *Festival Places: Revitalising Rural Australia*. Bristol: Channel View.

Gibson, J. 1986. *The Ecological Approach to Visual Perception*. Mahwah, NJ: Lawrence Erlbaum.

Gilbert, J. 2004. Signifying nothing: 'Culture', 'discourse' and the sociality of affect. *Culture Machine* 6. Available at: www.culturemachine.net/index.php/cm/article/view/8/7 [accessed: 4 December 2011].

Giorgi, L. and Sassatelli, M. 2011. Introduction, in *Festivals and the Cultural Public Sphere*, edited by L. Giorgi, M. Sassatelli and G. Delanty. London: Routledge, 1–11.

Hall, S. 1996. New ethnicities, in *Stuart Hall: Critical Dialogues in Cultural Studies*, edited by D. Morley and K.H. Chen. London: Routledge, 441–9.

Jansson, A. 2002. Spatial phantasmagoria: The mediatization of tourism experience. *European Journal of Communication*, 17(4), 429–43.

Jazeel, T. 2005. The world is sound? Geography, musicology and British-Asian soundscapes. *Area*, 37(3), 233–41.

Juslin, P.N. and Sloboda, J.A. 2001. *Music and Emotion: Theory and Research*. Oxford: Oxford University Press.

Kahn, D. 1999. *Noise, Water, Meat: A History of Sound in the Arts*. Cambridge, MA: MIT Press.

Keil, C. and Feld, S. 1994. *Music Grooves*. Chicago, IL: University of Chicago Press.

Keller, M.S. 2007. Transplanting multiculturalism: Swiss musical traditions reconfigured in multicultural Victoria. *Victorian Historical Journal*, 78(2), 187–205.

Kong, L. 1996. Popular music in Singapore: Exploring local cultures, global resources, and regional identities. *Environment and Planning D: Society and Space*, 14, 273–92.

Lefebvre, H. 2004. *Rhythmanalysis: Space, Time and Everyday Life*. London: Continuum.

Levitin, D. 2006. *This is Your Brain on Music*. New York: Dutton/Penguin.

Leyshon, A., Matless, D. and Revill, G. 1998. *The Place of Music*. New York: Guilford Press.

Longhurst, R., Ho, L. and Johnston, L. 2008. Using 'the body' as an 'instrument of research': Kimch'i and pavlova. *Area*, 40(2), 208–17.

Martin, P. 1995. *Sounds and Society: Themes in the Sociology of Music*. Manchester: Manchester University Press.

Massumi, B. 2002. *Parables for the Virtual: Movement, Affect, Sensation*. Durham, NC: Duke University Press.

Merriman, P., Revill, G., Cresswell, T., Lorimer, H., Matless, D., Rose, G. and Wylie, J. 2008. Landscape, mobility, practice. *Social & Cultural Geography*, 9(2), 191–212.

Nancy, J-L. 2007. *Listening*. New York: Fordham University Press.

Quinn, B. 2003. Symbols, practices and myth-making: Cultural perspectives on the Wexford Festival Opera. *Tourism Geographies*, 5(3), 329–49.

Roche, M. 2011. Festivalisation, cosmopolitanism and European culture: On the sociocultural significance of mage-events, in *Festivals and the Cultural Public Sphere*, edited by L. Giorgi, M. Sassatelli and G. Delanty. London: Routledge, 124–41.

Ruud, E. 2004. Foreword: Reclaiming music, in *Community Music Therapy*, edited by M. Pavlicevic and G. Ansdell. London: Jessica Kingsley, 11–14.

Saldanha, A. 2007. *Psychedelic White: Goa Trance and the Viscosity of Race*. Minneapolis, MN: University of Minnesota Press.

Shotter, J. 1995. *Cultural Politics of Everyday Life*. Milton Keynes: Open University Press.

Small, C. 1998. *Musicking: The Meanings of Performing and Listening*. Hanover, NH: Wesleyan University Press.

Smith, S.J. 1994. Soundscape *Area*, 26(3), 232–40.

Smith, S.J. 2000. Performing the (sound)world. *Environment and Planning D: Society and Space*, 18, 615–37.

St John, G. 2010. *The Local Scenes and Global Culture of Psytrance*. New York: Routledge.

Thibaud, J-P. 2002. *From situated perception to urban ambiences, Centre de recherche méthodlogique d'architecture (Nantes), First International Workshop on Architectural and Urban Ambient Environment, February*. Nantes: Cerma, Ecole d'architecture. Support CD.

Thrift, N. 1999. Steps to an ecology of place, in *Human Geography Today*, edited by D. Massey, J. Allen and P. Sarre. Cambridge: Polity Press, 295–322.

Thrift, N. 2000. Afterword. *Environment and Planning D: Society and Space*, 18(2), 213–55.

Thrift, N. 2008. *Non-Representational Theory: Space/politics/affect*. London: Routledge.

Truax, B. 2001. *Acoustic Communication*. Westport, CT: Ablex.

Urry, J. 1995. *Consuming Places*. London: Routledge.

Waitt, G. and Duffy, M. 2011. Listening and Tourism Studies. *Annals of Tourism Research*, 37(2), 457–77.

Waitt, G. and Hartig, K. 2000. All at sea. Rethinking fishers' identities in Australia. *Gender Place and Culture*, 12(4), 403–18.

Wood, N., Duffy, M. and Smith, S.J. 2007. The art of doing (geographies of) music. *Environment & Planning D: Society & Space*, 25(5), 867–89.

Wood, N. and Smith, S.J. 2004. Instrumental routes to emotional geographies. *Social & Cultural Geography*, 5(4), 533–48.

Yardimci, S. 2007. *Festivalising Difference: Privatisation of Culture and Symbolic Exclusion in Istanbul*. Florence: EUI Working Papers, RSCAS 2007/35, Mediterranean Programme Series, European University Institute.

Chapter 13

Festivals 2.0: Consuming, Producing and Participating in the Extended Festival Experience

Yvette Morey, Andrew Bengry-Howell, Christine Griffin,
Isabelle Szmigin and Sarah Riley

This chapter provides a series of expanding perspectives on significant transformations that have shaped music festivals in recent years. More specifically, we trace the ways in which different ways of engaging with festivals online can be seen as a reflection of wider socio-economic factors that have shaped the relationships between festivals, festival-goers and the internet. These include the commercialization, niche-ing and corporatization of the music festival industry, both online and offline over the past decade; the shift from Web 1.0 to Web 2.0 – particularly the shift to user-generated content and participatory web cultures; and the ways in which participation online is, in turn, a manifestation of the wider practices of consumption and identity-construction that characterize neoliberal and post-industrial society (Miller 1995; Walkerdine 2003). Drawing on material from a three-year study of music festivals and free parties, we explore the ways in which festival-goers engage with different platforms online. More specifically, we focus on engagements with festival web forums and the creation and sharing of festival videos on the media-sharing site YouTube. By mapping the ways in which contemporary music festivals exhort festival-goers to engage with music festivals such that they both consume and produce – or co-create – the festival experience, and exploring whether and how this takes place online, we identify the ways in which online platforms extend and multiply the meanings and identities of festivals and festival-goers alike.

Festival Nation Part I: The Social, Cultural and Economic Significance of Music Festivals

With a long history dating back to the Beaulieu Jazz Festivals of the 1950s and 1960s, and the early Glastonbury Fayres of the 1970s (McKay 2000), music festivals have become an established feature of Britain's cultural landscape. The enduring cultural significance of music festivals is due partly to a prevailing festival mythology that emerged in the aftermath of prototype events such as the

Woodstock and Monterey festivals in the late 1960s (Laing 2004). Much of this mythology is bound up with counter-cultural ideals, particularly the discourse of 'freedom' that is allied with the assumption that festivals should be free – from commerce and from the social and political structures and rules of everyday life (Anderton 2009). However, commerce has been bound up with festivals from the beginning – both Woodstock and its precedent, Monterey, were commercially funded endeavours, and Monterey paved the way for a relative surge in festivals in the United States (Laing 2004).

In keeping with these antecedents, modern music festivals remain, by and large, commercial events. However, the past decade has seen the rapid expansion of the festival industry and an unprecedented commercial boom in festivals in the United Kingdom. Despite some variance in figures cited by different sources, an estimated 600–700 events took place in 2010, reflecting a 71 per cent growth in the festival market between 2003 and 2007 (Anderton 2009; Mintel 2010). However, unlike the antecedents of festival culture mentioned above, modern music festivals are complex, differentiated events (Purdue et al. 1997), which can be characterized in a number of ways. Anderton (2011) outlines several different festival typologies according to music genre (pop, folk, metal, dance, world music), location (pastoral land, urban parkland, holiday camps and other venues) and target audience or lifestyle (eco/green, family, grassroots); however, a key distinction is between long-established mega-events such as the Glastonbury, Reading and Leeds, V and Isle of Wight festivals, and smaller boutique festivals such as the Big Chill, Latitude, Secret Garden Party and End of the Road festivals, which are aimed at particular niche markets. In this regard, the diversification of music festivals is only partly due to having to compete in a saturated marketplace (Kerr and May 2011) and largely due to the fact that music festivals have become commodities in and of themselves, with a key status in the larger tourist and leisure industries (Stone 2009).

These industries are heavily aligned with the experience economy, and consumer reports (Mintel 2008, 2010) indicate that festival attendance is part of a prevailing trend towards affordable escapism, whereby consumers are more willing to spend money on experiences than goods – although it should be noted that festivals also provide unprecedented opportunities for consumption; the side-stall aspect of festivals has grown exponentially in the last 20 years, and it is now possible to spend large sums of money on clothing, jewellery, art, books and alternative healing. In addition to their status as 'experience products', the cost of attending music festivals – the average price of a weekend festival ticket with camping in 2011 was £180 (Samuel 2011) – means that they are increasingly targeted at ABC1s – a relatively affluent, white, middle-class demographic that is highly attractive to marketers. The niche-ing and segmentation of music festivals is therefore an essential aspect of their marketing as 'experience products' congruent with the values and aspirations of this demographic.

Festival Nation Part II: The Corporatization of Music Festivals and Neoliberal Festival Consumer-producers

The niche-ing of festival brands must be considered against the backdrop of the corporatization of the festival industry over the past 15 years, particularly the monopolization of this industry by the multinational live music and events company Live Nation. Live Nation's history since its inception in 2005 is largely one of relentless mergers and acquisitions of other music promotions companies, notably Festival Republic (formerly Mean Fiddler Music Group), MCD Productions, DF Concerts and Gaiety Investments. During the period in which this research was conducted (2007–10), Live Nation achieved a position of near-dominance in the music festival industry, with outright ownership of the Global Gathering, Download, O2 Wireless and Hard Rock Calling festivals, and shares in the Glastonbury, Reading and Leeds, Latitude, Electric Picnic, The Big Chill, V, T in the Park and Oxegen festivals. Additionally, Live Nation extended its reach into the business of festivals, with deals involving the merchandizing and ticketing of festivals. Furthermore, in 2007 Carlsberg-owned Tuborg lager became the official beer of Live Nation, with exclusive pouring rights at all Live Nation festivals.

A crucial aspect of the current monopoly of the festival industry – and, we argue, what renders it distinct from the historically commercial element of festivals – is that Live Nation and other promoters remain largely invisible as companies, preferring to promote festivals as brands instead. Live Nation's monopoly has not led to the homogenization of events under a common Live Nation brand, but rather a process of segmentation in which different events have not only retained, but have enhanced, their individual brands and invested heavily in 'boundary work' that differentiates them from other festival products. What this 'boundary work' means for the identities of festival-goers can be further unpacked by discussing what Macleod (2006) refers to as the 'post-modern festival' as a reflection of late capitalism, or what Giddens (1991) and Rose (1989) respectively refer to as 'late modernity' and 'neoliberalism'. These are the terms variously used to conceptualize a series of profound shifts in the structures and institutions of advanced industrial societies over the past 50 years that have resulted in an erosion of traditional anchors for social and personal identities (Giddens 1991).

In a well-established set of arguments, theorists such as Giddens (1991), Miller (1995) and Bauman (2007) argue that in the absence of these traditional anchors, consumption is the primary basis for the construction of identities. It is theorized that we live in a consumer culture in which people increasingly constitute themselves through the consumption and display of goods and experiences (Belk 1995; Dittmar 1992; Walkerdine 2003). Choice and individuality are central to consumer culture, whereby consumption promises unlimited 'free choice' as a means of expressing individuality and identity (Slater 1997).

With regard to festivals, it is therefore possible to identify a process whereby the freedom to choose, via careful segmentation, from a range of distinct festival brands with correspondingly distinct, tailored and preferred (niche) experiences is simultaneously accompanied and enabled by drawing on an over-arching mythology of festivals that promises its own set of freedoms and opportunities, including – among other things – freedom from 'everyday structures and systems' (Laing 2004); the possibilities of hedonism and excessive consumption (Paterson 2006); authentic connections with others (Anderton 2009); and alternative expressions of identity and identity-formation (Hetherington 1998).

The experience economy requires consumers to be co-creators of their experiences, engaging in the production as well as the consumption of experiences, and as experience products encompassing multiple sites of consumption (Arvidson 2005), festivals constitute locations in which to both 'consume and display [identity and] difference' (Willems-Braun 1994). Here the experience of participation confers authenticity (Wang 1999), obscuring the corporate deployment of neoliberal imperatives around consumption and freedom, and adding further ballast to the notion of an archetypal festival experience.

The expansion and diversification of festivals, and their embedding in the wider contexts of consumer culture and neoliberalism, are not confined to festivals as physical events. In the next section, we go on to discuss the ways in which these processes are significantly mirrored and extended online.

The Mediation and Promotion of Music Festivals Online

Websites dedicated to the promotion and coverage of festivals emerged shortly after the development of the first internet browsers in the mid-1990s, and have evolved in tandem with the web, including the shift to Web 2.0, paving the way for the diversity of festival-related sites and content available today. The proliferation of festival content online can be understood in a number of ways – in part, the internet is an obvious forum for the myriad representations of the cultural significance of festivals (these will be described more fully further below); in part, it is also a significant and necessary other realm in which to market and promote festivals. In spite, or perhaps as a result of, the rapid expansion of the festival market, consumer reports indicate that nearly a quarter of festivals failed during the 2003–07 growth period, signalling that long-term success is difficult to achieve in this intensified marketplace (Kerr and May 2011). Given the timeframe of most festivals as three- or four-day events, strategies have to be devised to ensure loyalty to the festival brand throughout the year (Kerr and May 2011). Furthermore, this loyalty is even more vital in light of reports that the majority of festival-goers attend only one event annually (Mintel 2010).

According to Anderton (2009), the growth in outdoor festivals has been accompanied by further growth in the mediation of these events, pointing to the importance of television and radio in the ways in which festivals are marketed and received – and the internet is fast becoming one of the most significant sites of festival mediation. Promoters now consider the internet to be the primary channel for raising awareness of festivals (Kerr and May 2011; Kozinets 1999). The reach of the online marketing and mediation of festivals becomes apparent when we consider that the demographic for broadband internet access – 58 per cent of adults in the United Kingdom, with a bias towards the middle class and the young and middle-aged – overlaps with the primary demographic of festival audiences (Mintel 2008). According to a survey by the Association of Independent Festivals, 64.5 per cent of festival-goers find out about events online (Mintel 2010). One example is the Camp Bestival website, which was reported as the most popular festival website in 2010 with 73 per cent of attendees using the site for information about the festival (Mintel 2010). The imaginatively designed website (www.campbestival.net) is visually appealing and busy. The design draws on a range of imagery, which marries the other-worldly and carnivalesque with the reliable and everyday – albeit a taste-distinct version of the everyday including real ale and cake, tea and coffee tents – in a rural setting. Text boxes in the topmost corners declare: 'We're all going on a festi-holiday' and 'Camp Bestival – winner Best Family Festival 2008–10'. A very brief exploration of this website thus highlights the way in which online marketing works to promote and consolidate the distinctiveness of festival brands while reprising counter-cultural imagery and the associations attached to a larger festival mythology (Anderton 2009).

Alongside the general mediation of festivals online – including the whole gamut of multimedia content and coverage that is available on demand 24 hours a day – the promotion of festivals online shapes and obscures the nature of festivals as commodities. This obscuration has been aided by the shift to a more interactive participatory web in recent years. One way of realizing the objective to raise brand awareness and foster brand loyalty is through the deployment of interactive content, which enables a relationship to be forged between festivals and festival-goers online (Kozinets, in Kerr and May 2011). Moreover, the production and consumption of experience (central to neoliberal consumer identities and selves) discussed above are mirrored in the emergence of participatory web cultures online, in what has become known as the transition from Web 1.0 to Web 2.0.

Participatory Web Cultures

In its simplest form, the term Web 2.0 can be used to characterize the shift from a text-based read-only Web to an interactive, participatory and social multimedia-based Web. boyd (2009) defines the social web as a 'collection of software that [allows] individuals and communities to gather, communicate, share, and in some cases collaborate or play'. Familiar examples of Web 2.0 platforms that utilize such software are blogging and micro-blogging sites (Twitter), media-sharing sites (YouTube, Flickr), and social networking sites (Facebook, MySpace, Bebo), among many others. While the use of such platforms is not ubiquitous, several popular Web 2.0 sites account for a large percentage of all internet traffic.

The ethos of the social web is informed by two significant cultural shifts: a radical erosion of the boundaries between the public and the private, and the move to the active creation of content, or what has become known as user-generated content. A characteristic feature of many Web 2.0 platforms is that they involve the routine sharing of personal information as the basis for membership, friendship and belonging – for example, social networking and micro-blogging sites on which users update their profiles and post updates on what they are feeling, doing, thinking, reading and so on. In this regard, Snee (2008: 3) states that 'personal lives are increasingly exposed in Web 2.0 applications as part of a broader cultural shift towards openness and changing notions of privacy'. Bauman (2007) conceives the broadcasting of personal experience and information on Web 2.0 as the technologically extended and amplified practice of a 'confessional society' – a society in which identity is continuously updated and displayed in the most public of ways because to do otherwise would risk social exclusion (in Beer and Burrows 2010: 7) and, arguably, entail a negation of identity. The second significant cultural shift is towards user-generated content, and active participation and collaboration in the production, recycling and remixing of online content (Anderson 2007; Snee 2008). Anderson (2007: 14) argues that Web 2.0 entails a change in the way in which data is viewed, which is increasingly as a resource that 'can be repurposed, reformatted and reused'. This change in perception and practice, Anderson (2007) argues, can be compared with the DIY ethos associated with punk, in which young people took control of the production and promotion of their own entertainment and content by forming bands and writing fanzines. Consequently, people now see themselves as the creators of, and experts on, the online representations of their experiences and identities, and Anderson (2007: 15) argues that this poses a significant challenge to perceptions of 'who has the authority to "say" and "know"'.

The shifts outlined above are emblematic of the eroded distinction between producers and consumers (Bauman 2007; Beer 2008; Beer and Burrows, 2010). Furthermore, theorists such as Beer (2008), Fuchs (2011) and Chouliaraki (2010) argue for the radical notion that what is entailed in the public creation and consumption of personal or user-generated content is nothing short of the marketing and commoditization of the identities and selves that are constructed. Hence Bauman (in Beer 2008: 625) argues:

> the commodity they are prompted to put on the market, promote and sell are themselves ... They are, simultaneously, promoters of commodities and the commodities they promote. They are, at the same time, the merchandise and the marketing agents.

Chouliaraki (2010: 227) refers to the broadcasting of self online – 'the mediated participation of ordinary people in public culture' – as 'self-mediation', and both acknowledges and critiques the notion that this offers a new avenue for democratization. Chouliaraki conceptualizes the construction of a spectacular public space (constituted by still and moving images, sound, text, etc.) along the lines of Arendt's (in Chouliaraki 2010: 228) notion of a 'space of appearance' – a contingent space that is created by people doing things together, which involves performance and recognition, and a 'collective "mirroring back" of specific claims to identity', including claims to mundane or ordinary citizenship. However, she argues that self-mediation is a deeply ambivalent process in which the articulation and recognition of authentic citizenship, selfhood or social connection can be appropriated by 'neoliberal discourses of consumerism that increasingly marketise these spheres' (Chouliaraki 2010: 228). Drawing on Turner, Chouliaraki (2010) argues that the democratic potential of the 'space of appearance' may just as easily be appropriated by market forces in the service of private profit, whereby self-mediation is:

> at worst a corporate strategy that trivialises [insert relevant sphere] in the name of a narcissistic celebration of the 'private, the ordinary, the everyday' (Turner 2010: 22), and, at best, a form of 'unpaid labour'.

In Turner's view, there is little room for the transgressive DIY/expert possibilities posed by the new forms of authorship Anderson (2007) conceives in relation to Web 2.0. However, despite this somewhat pessimistic view, we have seen (in the citizen journalism that has documented the Arab Spring, or the 2011 UK riots) that the interactive, readily accessible and difficult-to-regulate environment of Web 2.0 also entails the possibility of broadcasting alternate and sometimes (politically) contested versions of events.

In the Field: Researching Festivals Online and Offline

The research study forming the backdrop to this chapter, *Negotiating Managed Consumption: Young People, Branding and Social Identification Processes* (ESRC RES-061-25-0129), explored how young adults negotiated different forms of marketing, branding and 'managed consumption' in two youth leisure sites – music festivals and free parties (illegal raves) – and how this impacted on their social identities and networks. The study was conducted over three years (2007–10) in two stages, with Stage 1 focusing on music festivals and Stage 2 focusing on free parties. The case studies combined an innovative range of research methods and included an online ethnographic or netnographic (Kozinets 2002) study of postings on festival-related web forums, a web-based 'mapping' of the organizational structure, corporate involvement and marketing practices associated with each festival, on-site ethnographic observation and 'market mapping' of leisure and consumption spaces documented using photographs, systematic field notes and found artefacts, on-site group discussions with festival-goers and off-site discussions with free party-goers. After embarking on the initial netnographic observation of web forum postings, we realized the full significance of online representations and constructions of festival experiences, which extended well beyond Web forums and included the use of a number of Web 2.0 platforms.

The discussion that follows is based on our initial netnographic observations focusing on two different platforms in particular – the eFestivals web forum and YouTube – to explore how the affordances of each shape the interactions of festival-goers, and what the implications might be for the identities of festivals and festival-goers. While this chapter focuses on the impact of the internet on engagement with music festivals, it is worth noting that free parties and free party networks have a significant presence online despite their non-commercial, illegal and secretive nature. The use of the internet by free party networks is divided in relation to the use of Web 1.0 and Web 2.0 platforms, and is explored elsewhere (Morey, Bengry-Howell and Griffin 2011).

The Music Festival Landscape Online: A Snapshot

The enormity of online festival content prohibits an exhaustive description; instead, we provide a snapshot of available content ahead of a more detailed examination of two platforms and the kinds of interactions enabled by each. Several years after the emergence of the first internet browsers in the mid-1990s, Neil Greenaway created The Original Glastonbury Festival Website in 1998. This was later transformed into the well-known eFestivals website (www.efestivals.co.uk), which retained the original Glastonbury content but provided coverage of a much wider range of festivals. A year later, in 1999, the rival Virtual Festivals (www.virtualfestivals.com) website was launched by Steve Jenner, with both websites featuring news, reviews, listings, photographs and interviews related to music festivals. Both eFestivals and Virtual Festivals host discussion forums that are, broadly, subdivided into general festival-related chat areas and specific forums dedicated to many of the major UK and some international festivals taking place each year.

In addition to comprehensive and long-established websites like eFestivals and Virtual Festivals, archival websites such as The Archive: UK Rock Festivals 1960–1990 (www.ukrockfestivals.com) and Fat Reg's Festies (www.fatreg.com/index2.html), both established in 2000, were other early frontrunners of festival-related content online. The former is an archive of photographs and information about a wide range of UK rock and free festivals that took place in the decades spanning 1960–90; the latter focuses solely on the Reading Festival, serving as an archive of photographs, information about lineups and a Reading Festival Timeline, among other things. Unlike the official festival websites and social media sites that exist today, the above sites are very much examples of the previous Web 1.0 incarnation of the internet – personal websites administered by individuals passionate about particular festivals or periods in festival history, featuring static (rather than interactive) published content. Existing on a continuum between websites characteristic of Web 1.0 and Web 2.0 are a large number of unofficial fan sites for particular festivals – for example, Reading Festival Fans (readingfestivalfans.co.uk), which is geared towards providing up-to-date information about each year's festival (line-up rumours and listings, information about tickets) without necessarily archiving this information. Newer and current festival-related content includes coverage provided by news and media sites such as the BBC's extensive Glastonbury website (bbc.in/1rirqBE), the Festivals Guide provided by the New Musical Express (www.nme.com/festivals) and, of course, the large number of official festival websites. Official websites serve as the main portals to many major festivals online, but many festivals also have 'official' profiles or pages across a range of Web 2.0 sites. For example, on Twitter alone, Glastonbury is represented by its official profile, GlastoFest (https://twitter.com/#!/GlastoFest), the profiles of people involved with the festival, such as Emily Eavis (https://twitter.com/#!/emilyeavis) and Worthy FM (https://twitter.com/#!/worthyfm), and the profiles of fans of the festival, such as Glasto_biz (https://twitter.com/#!/glasto_biz) and GlastoCountdown (https://twitter.com/#!/GlastoCountdown). Glastonbury also has an official channel on YouTube (https://twitter.com/#!/GlastoCountdown) and its own Facebook profile (www.facebook.com/glastonburyofficial). This is not to mention the vast amount of unofficial user-generated content shared by festival-goers across these and other Web 2.0 platforms – for example, the Glastonbury Festival group pool on Flickr, where users can upload and share their photos of the festival (www.flickr.com/groups/glastonbury_festival/pool).

Festival Forums: Learning to Be a Year-round Festival-goer

A number of festival forums exist for current and prospective festival-goers to communicate with each other by posting or commenting on a variety of threads (topics), with discussions ranging from the generic to particular aspects of festivals. The aggregated eFestivals website includes a widely used and well-known festival forum. The forum has a sizeable membership, with 112,649 members, and an archive of 1,182,773 posts at the time of writing, and is recognized as an authoritative source for festival-related information:

> eFestivals is a really useful website for anyone hunting for festival tickets, travel information and rumours on who's playing. It's also good fun, post-event, when the messageboards fill with people sharing hygiene horror stories, offering their opinions on Linkin Park's set or looking for someone they lent £20 to outside the Japanese noodle stand at 3am. (*The Guardian Guide*, 19 June 2004)

The forum is subdivided into a number of sub-sections or sub-forums. The main 'Festivals' section contains dedicated forums for particular festivals, including Glastonbury, Reading and Leeds, V, T in the Park, Download, Isle of Wight, Sonisphere, Rock Ness, Guilfest and Beautiful Days, as well as forums for 'other UK festivals' and 'international festivals'. Additionally, there are also several other sections – a dance forum, the wibble forum (for general discussions unrelated to festivals) and a general forum (for practical or administrative issues).

There is a seasonal regularity to festival forums, which tend to be dominated by certain topics at different times of the year. At the time of writing, the 2011 instalment of the Reading festival was set to take place in the very near future. A quick look at the 30 threads or topics on the first page of the Reading forum revealed that these were dominated by questions about the buying and selling of tickets (unlike Glastonbury, Reading tickets can be purchased and sold, depending on availability, right up to the event), as well as questions about whether certain items could be brought into the festival arena, requests for help and information, questions about utilities and services on and off site, questions about car parking, and questions about which of the designated camping zones is the best in which to camp. This sharing of information is one of the key functions of festival forums, whereby 'newbies' can ask regular festival-goers for advice on matters such as what to pack, or how to cope with the various demands of the festival experience (the swapping of tips and horror stories about festival toilets is a perennial favourite in this regard). Forum members are assigned a different status, displayed above their usernames, depending on the overall number of posts they've contributed to the forum. The assigned categories are ranged on a continuum that designate a member's commitment to festivals, ranging from 'addicted' (100+ posts) to 'festival freak' (1,000+ posts) to 'lives in a field' (5,000+ posts). In the period just after the festival, the threads are largely concerned with the sharing of experiences of the festival – for example, 'Well that was good then ... restored my faith in Reading'; 'Kings of Leon – discussion of their set'; and 'Pineapple! Pineapple! Never laughed so hard'. At a different point again, roughly mid-way between the last and the next festival and at the start of the festival season, forum threads contain a combination of shared reminiscences about previous festivals and anticipation of the festival to come: 'Carnage – what's been the worst year', 'Crappy things that happened to you in 2010', 'Headliner hints from Melvin Benn' and 'Weather thread'.

While festival forums are primarily text based, they often contain embedded or linked multimedia content such as photos and videos. These can be uploaded prior to an event, as part of the preparation for, and anticipation of, the festival; taken during the festival and uploaded from the site; or edited after the festival and shared with forum members (and anyone else who cares to see them). A familiar forum topic that is often revived in the run-up to festivals – particularly Glastonbury – concerns the organization of collective camping by forum members. The designated campsite is identified and located through the use of a distinctive tent flag, which is photographed and uploaded on to the forum for the benefit of other interested parties. In a similar vein, many forum members create their own tent and stage flags and upload photographs of these to the forum prior to festivals. A remarkable and unanticipated use of the forums prior to festivals was the creation and sharing of festival site maps. This practice ranged from the adaptation and editing of official maps to reflect personal preferences (for example, maps pin-pointing the position of bars selling ale on site), to the creation of entirely new types of maps (contour maps showing the best places to camp should it rain). As with the sharing of information mentioned above, the discussions and collaborations that take place on festival forums both underscore and enable a great deal of (pre-emptive) planning and organization prior to the festival itself.

On the whole, festival forums can be read by anyone with access to the internet; however, as suggested by the discussion of status categories above, active posting or commenting requires membership of the forum. Generally speaking, registration is a fairly easy and quick process, requiring the electronic furnishing of basic details and signalling agreement with the terms and conditions of the forum. Typically, forum terms and conditions contain a set of statements prohibiting the posting of offensive or explicit content – generally reflecting offline norms and etiquette around the use of discriminatory language and other causes of offence in social settings. However, while the process described above applies to membership of the eFestivals (and other) forums, this process can be different when it comes to membership of forums attached to *official* festival websites. In this regard, the Reading festival forum contains a lengthy statement concerning the forum's terms of use and code of conduct. Crucially, these terms discourage the discussion of contentious or 'unpleasant' behaviour at the festival, as well as any negative comments about the promoter, Festival Republic:

> We would appreciate it if discussion of unpleasant matters was kept at a minimum – there is no need for ****[sic], sexual assault, drink spiking or other horrible subjects to be discussed – certainly not in jest – and anyone found doing so may have action taken against them ... Please also remember that most of this forum is open to guests and is Google-indexed. While you may feel that you are amongst a group of close friends sometimes, the truth is that many unwanted eyes may be viewing your posts. We really don't know who is browsing, so try to refrain from leaving comments that could be taken out of context – if only for your own sake. The last thing many of us would like to see is a tabloid paper running a front page story about the satan worshipping, drug taking, sexual deviant and downright strange alternative lifestyles of 'heavy metal fans'. It would be all too easy for a journalist who has an axe to grind and looking for an easy scoop to do a little lazy research and take things out of context on purpose.

> Insults to Festival Republic. No one is saying you have to like the bill that has been put together, or the way the festival is organised, or the way that announcements are made. You are free to express your opinion about the organisation and so on freely. However, personal insults and threats to Live Nation staff are not acceptable. Insults and threats will simply not be tolerated. And if you think it is that bad? Then just don't go along ... There are hundreds of festivals in the UK these days. Surely one of them you might like (forums.readingfestival.com/register.aspx).

The terms set out above seem defensive and, comparatively speaking, heavy-handed in tone. They signal a much more explicit approach to the moderation and regulation of forum content, whereby the notion of a shared and co-created community space that is more or less self-regulating is undermined. This underscores the importance of, and contingency around, representations of festival brands online. As many official websites feature the names of festival sponsors (usually large alcohol or telecoms companies), there is a need to mitigate against any negative associations that might spring from talk or other content on forums. However, forums also represent an easy, accessible portal for brands wishing to promote their products inexpensively. The Gaymers cider brand pre-empted its entry into the festival marketplace by posting and initiating conversations on various festival forums in 2008. Conversely, often a loyalty to brands perceived to be part and parcel of the festival experience – such as Brother's Cider at Glastonbury – means that forum members often conduct this conversation and promotion themselves.

Broadcast Yourself: The User-Generated Festival

While festival forums are interactive, and both produced and consumed by forum members, they are relatively static in comparison with social media and media-sharing sites such as YouTube. YouTube is a public video-sharing site that allows users to watch and share videos as well as commenting on them and connecting with other users (Lange 2008). YouTube has an established policy about the kinds of content it allows and disallows; however, the sheer enormity of content uploaded to the site every day, and the existence of technology for downloading material from the site, renders the moderation and regulation of this content more difficult. In this regard, YouTube's own user statistics reveal astounding figures, with 48 hours of content uploaded nearly every minute (or eight years of content per day) and over three billion videos viewed per day. Furthermore, its status as one of the major social media sites is signalled by reports that on average more than 400 tweets containing a YouTube link take place every minute, while 150 years' worth of YouTube videos are watched on Facebook daily (Elliot 2011). While a large percentage of this material is professional or industry-created content, the platform's 'broadcast yourself' tagline underscores the central premise of uploading and sharing self-created or amateur video content. YouTube is replete with festival-related content. As mentioned earlier, most festivals have their own official channels on YouTube, while the major broadcasters that cover festivals (such as the BBC, the NME and Channel Four) broadcast festival footage on their own YouTube channels. In the midst of all the official festival footage to be found on YouTube are the large numbers of videos created and uploaded by festival-goers themselves. This footage takes a variety of forms, including short clips (usually shot with a mobile phone) of funny incidents or bands on stage, but also, significantly, short films depicting the journey or story of a festival experience. An example of the latter is Room41more's *Reading 2008 (Savage)* video (www.youtube.com/watch?v=rlz7_smEYKs), uploaded directly after the end of the festival on 29 August 2008 with 1,930 views.

Like many such videos, the footage centres on the social and playful aspects of the experience, with clips focusing on members of the friendship circle and their activities in the campsite. An amalgamation of photos and video clips edited together with an accompanying song from one of the bands on the 2008 lineup, the video portrays both a particular and authentic/generic festival experience using all the stock-in-trade devices of promotional music videos (editing, text, song). We contacted several festival-goers on YouTube to ask why they created films of their festival experiences; one festival-goer who uploaded a video of his 2008 Glastonbury experience (www.youtube.com/watch?v=D6tKcCuhGYI) gave the following account:

Re: Glastonbury video

Before I went to my first Glastonbury I had no idea what to expect from the 'wonderland' which takes place over 1000 acres. I could not comprehend the size of this festival and what to expect so turned to YouTube for other people's experiences which helped me out so much. When I returned I found I could not put into words just how great it was so thought it would be a good idea to try and show people by putting all my pics and videos together. When I'm old and in a nursing home somewhere, it's always nice to know I could show my Gran [sic] kids that even their Granddad was a young man once and had a great life. I suppose we all want to leave something behind and not be forgotten don't we? Of course I also did it to look back at the place I feel happiest, knowing I can relive the happy memories at a click of a mouse.

The video received a number of favourable comments and feedback from viewers, such as 'What a beautiful impression of the atmosphere. I bookmarked it to relive this year's festival whenever I feel like it. thank you!' However, not all videos created a favourable impression. Both Reading and Leeds have annually experienced campsite disturbances at the close of the festival on Sunday evening, with discussions of these 'riots' taking place on festival forums and in the press. In the aftermath of the 2008 festival, a number of 'riot' videos were uploaded to YouTube by festival-goers. As we were tracking these events as part of our netnography at the time, we noticed that several were taken down shortly after being uploaded to the site. We contacted the respective festival-goers to ask why their videos were no longer available and got the following response:

'Re: video unavailable?

Hey

Youtube took it off and got a warning that if i upload it again my account would be deleted. I can always send the video by email or something if needs be.

Another video, *Reading Riot 2008* (www.youtube.com/watch?v=hNDZ7jFr0EQ), featuring footage of fires, exploding gas canisters, the destruction of toilet blocks and tents and a police presence – is edited with atmospheric music ('Let The Bodies Hit The Floor by Drowning Pool') and accompanying text at the end that calls for enhanced security features and a safer Reading festival in 2009. Interestingly, this video was not removed by YouTube and has been very popular, with 37,335 views to date. However, it did receive some negative comments from other viewers and festival-goers:

> good footage but whats with the edit? song choice and slow motion, its like ur trying to make it look 'cool'.

YouTube's Community Guidelines include the right to remove inappropriate or violent content. It is unfortunately unclear whether the removal of 'riot' videos by YouTube merely reflected the enforcement of these guidelines, or whether this was at the behest of a festival promoter. Despite the aforementioned attempts, many removed videos were simply renamed and uploaded again by their creators several days later, while in the meantime many other viewers had the opportunity to download and disseminate the videos before they were removed.

Mediated Festivals/Mediated Festival-selves

A central focus of this chapter has been the exploration of how music festivals are extended online, and specifically how this is enabled by the interactive and participatory environment of Web 2.0. In order to explore this fully, it has been necessary to describe the nature of contemporary music festivals (as experience products) and the music festival industry (as a largely corporatized and monopolized entity), and to situate these against the wider socio-economic backdrop of late modernity and neoliberalism. The chapter's central premise – of festivals as experience products targeted at and chosen by festival-goers, which offer festival-goers the freedom to both consume and produce their festival identities and experiences – has been unpacked in relation to both offline and online festivals. The erosion of the traditional distinctions between producers and consumers has been noted in relation to both; however, we argue that the production and consumption of festivals online does not merely reflect but, as a result of the enabling technologies and corresponding demands of Web 2.0, extends in significant ways the creation and display of festival identities and communities. Festival forums enable an extension of outdoor festivals, as temporally and geographically bounded events, to events that can be experienced – anticipated, celebrated and re-lived – all year round. The sharing of information, provision of advice, collaboration and planning that take place on forums all speak to the co-creation and co-ownership of a shared festival experience. Membership and assigned statuses ('addicted', 'festival freak', 'lives in a field') allow for the display of an identity that is mirrored and consolidated by other members and wider readers. Furthermore, the official recognition of the number of posts contributed by members highlights the importance of the communal and social nature of the forums.

However, the mundane citizenship and social participation bestowed by the acts described above can also be seen in the light of individual self-interest and competition – the re-creation and sharing of festival maps and the exchange of information about flags and planned camping ensures that a 'good space' is secured for oneself and one's group. Furthermore, the extension of festivals on forums does not occur outside the realm of commerce or the domains of sponsors and festival organizers. Both our interviews and our monitoring of discussions on festival forums revealed that the majority of festival-goers were unconcerned about the sponsorship of festivals, with many regarding sponsorship as a necessary evil that secured the future of festivals. While not all festival organizations have the resources to host their own forums, most view forums as essential ways to monitor the preferences and practices of their target audiences – as evidenced by the participation of Gaymers cider. The unprompted promotion of brands associated with festivals – such as Brother's cider – also points to the ease with which the kinds of virtual relationships envisaged by festival promoters, sponsors and brands are enabled online. Moreover, even unallied sites such as eFestivals collect revenue from corporate advertisers and festival promoters, and it is clear that festival organizers consider these sites to be of worth in terms of predicting the consumption patterns of festival-goers.

The production and consumption of amateur festival videos represent both an individual wish to 'leave something behind', or 'not be forgotten', and the possibility of reliving a shared experience. Both speak to an extension of self beyond the temporal – beyond the duration of the festival event itself *and* beyond the present, into an imagined future – and the geographical, where the neoliberal duty to tell oneself or to be intelligible as a certain kind of self – in this instance, as a Glastonbury festival-goer – is called into being and cemented by repeated viewings. Here is evidence of Arendt's (in Chouliaraki 2010) 'space of appearance', which allows for the performance, and collective recognition and mirroring, of identity, but which nevertheless is also a contingent space. In this regard, the regulation of festival forums and removal of content from media-sharing sites such as YouTube disrupts the conceptualization of Web 2.0 as an unproblematically democratic space.

Following from the above, the reception and perception of the campsite disturbances as 'riots' at the Reading and Leeds festivals, echoed and reinforced by comments accompanying the YouTube video discussed above, point to the assimilation of this content by a wider, dominant discourse of riots that not all festival-goers – or not those taking part in these events – necessarily share. While these events are undoubtedly a source of anxiety or annoyance for some, the reactions of the festival-goers captured on the video reflect the excitement and pleasure of this part of the festival experience for them. Many of the Reading festival-goers we interviewed referred to the importance of the atmosphere, and spending time with friends in the campsites, as the primary part of their festival experience. Furthermore, some articulated a tradeoff whereby festival-goers complied with the high charges for entry, and thereafter for food and drinks on-site, in return for festival organizers turning a blind eye to the goings-on in the campsites. Given the steps taken to maintain the security of festival sites – in particular the strict policing of entry only by those with tickets – festivals and the demarcated zones within them remain fairly contained ecosystems over the duration of the festival. Consequently, the availability of 'riot' videos on YouTube radically extends the reach and duration of these events, and scuppers attempts at containment. The renaming and re-uploading of these videos evidences Anderson's (2007: 15) argument regarding users of Web 2.0 taking control of the production and promotion of their own entertainment, as well as the challenging of perceptions about 'who has the authority to "say" and "know"'.

A final and crucial point concerns the extension entailed in the mediation of festivals online to the mediation or broadcasting of festival selves and identities online. This broadcasting amounts to a display of identity that is perhaps less about broadcasting the festival and more about broadcasting the (festival) self. Stated differently, in the interactive space of Web 2.0, festival-goers are both the producers and consumers of content, but – more importantly – this content is not solely about festivals but about festival-goers themselves. This shift in perspective entails the extension of festivals and festival brands as commodities to the active identity displays of festival-goers on Web 2.0 platforms as the commodities being marketed and consumed, summoning Turner's (in Chouliaraki 2010) argument about unpaid labour and the appropriation of user-generated content by market forces.

Unlike the virtual relationship marketing entailed in the prompted and unprompted promotion of brands on festival web forums, this appropriation is not always straightforward, as the identities on display are not always congruent with festival brands and identities. This tension reveals both the commercial possibilities and the challenges inherent in young people's production and consumption of twenty-first century leisure practices and cultural identities.

References

Anderson, P. 2007. 'All that glisters is not gold' – Web 2.0 and the librarian. *Journal of Librarianship and Information Science*, 39(4), 195–8.

Anderton, C. 2009. Commercializing the carnivalesque: The V Festival and image/risk management, *Event Management*, 12, 39–51.

Anderton, C. 2011. Music festival sponsorship: Between commerce and carnival. *Arts Marketing: An International Journal*, 1(2), 145–58.

Arvidson, A. 2005. Brands: A critical perspective. *Journal of Consumer Culture*, 5, 235–58.

Bauman, Z. 2007. *Consuming Life*. Cambridge: Polity Press.

Beer, D. 2008. Researching a confessional society. *International Journal of Market Research*, 50(5), 619–29.

Beer, D. and Burrows, R. 2010. Consumption, prosumption and participatory web cultures. Special Issue of the *Journal of Consumer Culture*, 10(1), 3–149.

Belk, R. 1995. *Collecting in a Consumer Society*. London: Routledge.

boyd, d.m. 2009. Social media is here to stay ... now what? Microsoft research tech fest, Redmond, 26 February. Available at: www.danah.org/papers/talks/MSRTechFest2009.html [accessed: 20 November 2011].

Chouliaraki, L. 2010. Self-mediation: New media and citizenship. *Critical Discourse Studies*, 7(4), 227–32.

Dittmar, H. 1992. *The Social Psychology of Material Possessions: To Have is to Be*. Hertfordshire: Harvester Wheatsheaf.

Elliot, A. 2011. *10 Fascinating YouTube Facts that May Surprise You*. Available at: mashable.com/2011/02/19/youtube-facts [accessed: 20 December 2011].

Fuchs, C. 2011. Web 2.0, prosumption, and surveillance. *Surveillance & Society*, 83, 288–309.

Giddens, A. 1991. *Modernity and Self-Identity*. Cambridge: Polity Press.

Hetherington, K. 1998. *Expressions of Identity: Space, Performance and Politics*. London: Sage.

Kerr, A. and May, D. 2011. An exploratory study looking at the relationship marketing techniques used in the music festival industry. *Journal of Retail & Leisure Property*, 9, 451–64.

Kozinets, R.V. 1999. E-tribalized marketing? The strategic implications of virtual communities of consumption. *European Management Journal*, 17(3), 252–64.

Kozinets, R. 2002. The field behind the screen: Using netnography for marketing research in online communities. *Journal of Marketing Research*, 391, 61–72.

Laing, D. 2004. The three Woodstocks and the live music scene, in *Remembering Woodstock*, edited by A. Bennett. Aldershot: Ashgate.

Lange, P. 2008. Publicly private and privately public: Social networking on YouTube. *Journal of Computer-Mediated Communication*, 13, 361–80.

McKay, G. 2000. *Glastonbury: A Very English Fair*. London: Butler & Tanner.

Macleod, N. 2006. The placeless festival: Identity and place in the post-modern festival, in *Festivals, Tourism and Social Change: Remaking Worlds*, edited by D. Picard and M. Robinson. Clevedon: Channel View, 222–37.

Miller, D. (ed.) 1995. *Acknowledging Consumption: A Review of New Studies*. London: Routledge.

Mintel 2008. *Music Concerts & Festivals – UK – August 2008*. Available at: bit.ly/1BtAh5C [accessed: 20 December 2011].

Mintel 2010. *Music Concerts & Festivals – UK – August 2010*. Available at: bit.ly/1pz05rG [accessed: 20 December 2011].

Morey, Y., Bengry-Howell, A. and Griffin, C. 2011. Public profiles, private parties: Exploring the ethical dilemmas posed by digital ethnography in the context of

Web 2.0, in *Innovations in Youth Research*, edited by S. Heath and C. Walker. Basingstoke: Palgrave Macmillan.

Paterson, M. 2006. *Consumption and Everyday Life*. London: Routledge.

Purdue, D., Durrschmidt, J., Jowers, P. and O'Doherty, R. 1997. DIY culture and extended milieux: LETS, veggie boxes and festivals. *The Sociological Review*, 45(6), 647–71.

Rose, N. 1989 *Governing the Soul: The Shaping of the Private Self*. London: Routledge.

Samuel, B. 2011. Ticket prices rise dramatically since 2006. *Festival Business*, 3 June. Available at: www.festivalbusiness.co.uk/2011/06/ticket-prices-rise-dramatically-since.html [accessed: 13 December 2011].

Slater, D. 1997. *Consumer Culture and Modernity*. Oxford: Polity Press.

Snee, H. 2008. Web 2.0 as a social science research tool. ESRC Government Placement Scheme. The British Library. Available at: www.bl.uk/reshelp/bldept/socsci/socint/web2/report.html [accessed: 14 December 2011].

Stone, C. 2009. The British pop music phenomenon, in *International Perspectives of Festivals and Events: Paradigms of Analysis*, edited by J. Ali-Knight, M. Robertson, A. Fyall and A. Ladkin. Los Angeles, CA: Elsevier.

Wang, N. 1999. Rethinking authenticity in tourism experience. *Annals of Tourism Research*, 26(2), 349–70.

Walkerdine, V. 2003. Reclassifying upward mobility: Femininity and the neo-liberal subject. *Gender and Education*, 153, 237–48.

Willems-Braun, B. 1994. Situating cultural politics: Fringe festivals and the production of spaces of intersubjectivity. *Environment and Planning D: Society and Space*, 121, 75–104.

Index